AN INTRODUCTION
TO
JESUS
AND THE
GOSPELS

AN INTRODUCTION TO JESUS AND THE GOSPELS

FREDERICK J. MURPHY

Abingdon Press
Nashville

AN INTRODUCTION TO JESUS AND THE GOSPELS

Copyright © 2005 by Abingdon Press

This book is printed on acid-free paper.

Library of Congress Cataloging-in-Publication Data

Murphy, Frederick James.
    An introduction to Jesus and the Gospels / Frederick J. Murphy.
        p. cm.
    Includes index.
    ISBN 0-687-49692-6 (binding: casebound : alk. paper)
    1. Bible. N.T. Gospels—Criticism, interpretation, etc.   2. Jesus Christ—Person and offices.   I. Title.

    BS2555.52.M87 2005
    226'.061—dc22
                                                                    2005008235

05 06 07 08 09 10 11 12 13 14—10 9 8 7 6 5 4 3 2 1

MANUFACTURED IN THE UNITED STATES OF AMERICA

For my students at Holy Cross

CONTENTS

LIST OF MAPS

ACKNOWLEDGMENTS

I am grateful to the College of the Holy Cross, where I have taught since 1983, for a sabbatical leave in academic year 2003–2004, during which I wrote most of this book. During the final stages of preparation of the manuscript, I was the Joseph Visiting Professor at Boston College (2004–2005), made possible through the generosity of Dr. Eugene McCarthy and his family, who endowed the chair in memory of their son Joseph. I am very thankful to Dr. McCarthy and his family for giving me that opportunity. My department chair, Alan Avery-Peck, and my academic dean, Stephen Ainlay, kindly agreed to a year's leave so that I could be the Joseph Chair. It is one more example of the willingness of Holy Cross to support its faculty.

I am deeply appreciative of the constant support and intellectual companionship of the members of the Department of Religious Studies at Holy Cross. It is a wonderful place to live out one's academic life. During 2004–2005, the faculty of the Theology Department at Boston College welcomed me warmly and made my stay among them fruitful and intellectually stimulating. Professor Kenneth Himes, chair of the department, was particularly gracious. My year at Boston College will be a valued memory, and I will always feel a strong bond with those wonderful scholars. Special thanks go to my graduate research assistant, Peter Fritz, for helping me in all sorts of ways.

It has been a special pleasure for me to work with Abingdon Press once again. I owe profound thanks to John Kutsko for suggesting that I write this book, and to my editors, Kathy Armistead and Sarah Hasenmueller, who showed such professionalism, patience, and skill in shepherding it through its final stages. Finally, I am deeply grateful to Amy-Jill Levine of Vanderbilt University, who read the penultimate draft and made numerous corrections and suggestions that allowed me to avoid mistakes of fact, conceptualize some things more adequately, and supply more adequate explanations in many areas. Because of her this is a better book. Its remaining faults are mine alone.

I continue to enjoy the invaluable support of my wife, Leslie, and my children, Rebecca and Jeremy. I am blessed to have such a delightful, supportive, and fun family. They truly make life a joy.

INTRODUCTION

E very author must have an audience in mind, clear goals, and a way
to reach those goals. This is especially crucial for a textbook,
where readers may not have extensive background in the subject.
The author owes readers an explanation for choices made on those
matters.

AUDIENCE

This book is for undergraduates who are willing and able to engage
texts in depth, to consider historical and theological questions, and who
wish to gain knowledge and skills that will allow them to think things out
on their own. Because it avoids watering down challenging subject matter, it should also be of use to beginning graduate students in Scripture,
theology, or history, as well as to teachers and pastors.

GOALS

The Gospels are studied by many people for many reasons, using a great
variety of methods. No one book can cover the whole gamut of such study.
The present book introduces readers to methods of gospel research that
have been around for a while, have produced much insight, and are used
in one way or another by most interpreters. It also makes the reader aware
of the wider range of methods now in use, and of the expanding array of
approaches, each with its own distinctive contribution. In addition, we sit-
uate the Gospels within the context of early Christianity, both by suggesting how their content might relate to the real world of their writers and

early readers, and by considering texts not in the New Testament that are similar to the Gospels or which call themselves gospels. But our focus remains on the New Testament gospels, those accepted by the Christian churches as authoritative. (These are also called *canonical*, meaning that they belong to the canon, the list of approved books, those that appear in the Bible.) When we capitalize *Gospels*, we refer to Matthew, Mark, Luke, and John, the four biblical gospels. When the word is not capitalized, we refer to gospel as a religious message, a literary genre, or to one of the gospels outside the New Testament. The word *gospel* comes from the old English *godspel*, meaning "good news."

We also include a chapter on the historical Jesus. The New Testament gospels themselves attest to the fact that later Christian understanding of Jesus as enshrined in the Gospels goes beyond understandings of Jesus by his contemporaries, even by his disciples. Our earliest Gospel, Mark, was written around four decades after Jesus' death. By then, material about Jesus had undergone a process of selection, adaptation, and transformation. The evangelist Mark fashions this material into his own unique presentation, as do the other evangelists. (*Evangelist* means "gospel writer," from the Greek *euangelion*, meaning "gospel.") All gospels see Jesus through later Christian eyes, particularly in light of the Christian experience of Jesus' resurrection. Given all this, many scholars try to get "behind" the Gospels to learn more about how Jesus was perceived by his contemporaries, and perhaps even about how Jesus viewed himself and his mission. Our eighth chapter investigates this "quest," which is important in its own right. That chapter also sheds light on the Gospels because it raises questions about just how they relate to their subject, Jesus of Nazareth.

Ultimately, this book aims not just to convey information, but to allow readers to see things in a new light and to draw on insights of biblical experts. Most important, it intends to enable its readers themselves to interpret the Gospels in ways that do justice to the nature of those texts as historical artifacts, as sources for understanding Christian origins, as expressions of faith, and as foundations of a living religion.

METHOD

We want to equip readers to think for themselves. At the same time, we must begin somewhere, so this book argues for specific readings of each gospel. Hopefully, the argumentation is transparent enough that readers will be able to evaluate it, agree with it, or disagree with it.

For this textbook to succeed, students must become intimately familiar with the Gospels. Reading about the Gospels is no substitute for reading the texts themselves. Repeated reading of each gospel is invaluable and will generate insight available no other way. This book encourages such repeated readings through the structure of the chapters. First, we introduce each book in general terms, addressing authorship, date, and sources. Then we look at overall structure. Next we present an overview of each gospel. Then we read through the gospel, commenting on it as we go (we call this a gospel survey). Finally, we address specific issues that each gospel raises. A conclusion sums up in a few words what we have learned.

The topics chosen for special treatment include fairly routine ones, such as Christology (views on the person and work of Jesus), discipleship, and ecclesiology (teaching about church). The choice of other topics is a function of the nature of the particular gospel. For example, we look at Isaiah's influence on Luke, but not on the others. We pay special attention to Mark's view of the disciples and to Matthew's revision of it, but we do not make that a special issue in Luke or John. Mark's treatment of the disciples is rather surprising, and it makes sense to see how either Matthew or Luke, who rewrite Mark, deal with it. To save space, we deal only with Matthew, and not with Luke, thereby leaving room to discuss other issues in Luke. Such choices are inevitable, and they result in a treatment of the gospels that is not completely uniform but is tailored to the distinctive nature of each gospel as well as to the cumulative effect of our study as we proceed. Things once treated in some depth can then be assumed later.

For each of the canonical gospels, we examine how they look at women and how they treat Jews and Judaism. These questions have become so important in recent decades that no good treatment of the gospels can bypass them. Asking these questions has also led to profound insights into Christian origins, as well as into the role of women in society and church in general, and into the relationship between Jews and Christians throughout the ages. These are crucial issues, and the role the Gospels themselves have played throughout the centuries in influencing women's roles and Jewish-Christian relations cannot be ignored. In the first chapter, under the heading of "feminist criticism," we say more about what is at issue in the study of women in the Gospels. Here a few words about Jews and Judaism are in order.

The relationship between Christianity and Judaism has been a long and frequently unhappy affair. Christianity grew out of Judaism, and its efforts to define itself often resorted to contrast with and opposition to Judaism.

That is a natural process when one religion grows out of another, but that does not make it any less dangerous. In the case of Christianity and Judaism there were lamentable consequences. The language of sharp critique and even outright hostility aimed at Jews, Judaism, and Jewish leadership in the New Testament had one set of resonances, problematic as they were, when employed by a new and vulnerable religion speaking about an old, established one. As Christianity gained power in the Roman Empire and finally became its official religion in the early fourth century, such rhetoric became still more dangerous. Subsequent centuries saw the effects of such theology in Christian mistreatment of Jews that ranged from hostility and social oppression to outright murder. The Crusades and the Holocaust stand as two particularly horrific examples of what Jews have had to suffer, at least in part for having been the parent religion of Christianity. Part of the solution to Christian misrepresentations of Jews and Judaism is to confront and admit the problematic nature of some New Testament material in this regard. This book attempts to do that.

Throughout this book, we use "B.C.E." and "C.E." rather than "B.C." and "A.D.," in accord with common scholarly usage. "C.E." stands for "Common Era," meaning the era shared by Christians and Jews, and "B.C.E." stands for "Before the Common Era."

A FINAL WORD

One last word before we begin. You are about to embark on a study that is, in the last analysis, deeply enjoyable. Sure, there may be times that it becomes a bit of a struggle to absorb everything, and you will certainly appreciate some aspects of this study more than others. But there are few things more stimulating than to look at familiar things in new ways. This is particularly true in the field of religion, where we often have the impression that things are absolute, unchanging, didactic in a "boring" way, and not really open to question. Even a modicum of historical study is amazingly eye-opening. We see other possibilities for looking at things. We begin to grasp why things are the way they are—doctrine, church structure, foundational symbols, and so on. This is informative, it is liberating, and it will enrich your reading of the Gospels and your understanding of Christianity, whether you approach it as a believer or merely an interested observer. Enjoy.

ABBREVIATIONS

AB	*Anchor Bible*
ABD	Freedman, David Noel, ed. *Anchor Bible Dictionary.* 6 vols. New York: Doubleday, 1992.
BibInt	*Biblical Interpretation*
CBQ	*Catholic Biblical Quarterly*
HeyJ	*Heythrop Journal*
HTR	*Harvard Theological Review*
LCL	*Loeb Classical Library*
NJBC	Brown, Raymond E., Joseph A. Fitzmyer, and Roland E. Murphy, eds. *The New Jerome Biblical Commentary.* Englewood Cliffs, N.J.: Prentice Hall, 1990.
JBL	*Journal of Biblical Literature*
JR	*Journal of Religion*
JSNT	*Journal for the Study of the New Testament*
NovT	*Novum Testamentum*
NTS	*New Testament Studies*

STS   Schüssler Fiorenza, Elizabeth. *Searching the Scriptures: A Feminist Commentary.* 2 vols. New York: Crossroad, 1993–1994.

WCO   Kraemer, Ross Shepard, and Mary Rose D'Angelo. *Women and Christian Origins.* New York: Oxford University Press, 1999.

CHAPTER ONE

CRITICAL STUDY OF THE GOSPELS

FROM JESUS TO THE GOSPELS

Most readers of this book have at least a rough picture of Jesus of Nazareth—who he was, when he lived, what he did, and so on. Where do we get this information? Our picture comes from a variety of sources. We might have read the New Testament or parts of it, heard sermons in church, or taken classes in Sunday school or a religious school. Even if we have not grown up Christian, chances are we have formed an impression of Jesus from the culture that surrounds us. We have naturally blended and harmonized information we have received without being too conscious of just how we have put our picture together. If we engage in conversation about Jesus, we quickly learn that even among believers, people hold many pictures of him that differ in important ways. Even when we agree on some basic points, there is still much room for disagreement and interpretation. Why such variety? Do we get a single, unified view if we go back far enough in history?

If we give it a moment's thought, we realize that even if we go back to Jesus' contemporaries, we will not find a single, unanimous opinion about him. Those who encountered Jesus during his earthly life reacted to him in a range of ways. Some believed in him, followed him, and became the first members of the early church. Others opposed him, even to the point of executing him. Still others, perhaps the majority, shrugged their shoulders and continued their lives as they had before they met him. But didn't the earliest Christians all agree? We need only read the Apostle Paul's letters, our earliest extant Christian sources, to see that from the beginning there were serious disagreements among Christians on a multiplicity of things, including how to interpret Jesus and his work. But the New Testament does not include writings by Paul's opponents—so

1

doesn't the process of choosing some texts and excluding others yield a collection completely at one with itself? The answer is "no," or at least, "not entirely."

The New Testament contains twenty-seven books, composed at different times and places by different authors. The first four texts are the Gospels—Matthew, Mark, Luke, and John. That should give us pause. Four Gospels? Why four? Why not just one? Some basic facts help us answer that question. To begin with, none of the four evangelists witnessed the events of Jesus' life and death. Each depended on sources, some oral and some written. No two gospels had exactly the same sources. We must remember also that the ancient world was quite different from our own in many respects. Today we take for granted the widespread use of writing, mass production of books, recording devices such as tape recorders and video cameras, communications media such as radio, television, newspapers, magazines, and even, in recent years, the Internet, with access to a dizzying amount of information. We truly live in the information age. The ancient world was nothing like that. Few were literate. Books were copied manually, and it was next to impossible to control a book's contents once it left the author's hand and began to be copied and distributed. Travel was slow. The postal system existed only for the convenience of the ruling classes. In such a world, the production, reproduction, control of content, and dissemination of texts of any kind was not simple. Further, even if the production and control of Christian documents had been possible, who would control it? Careful study of the New Testament and early Christian literature shows that diversity characterized the churches from the outset. There was no single authority that could speak for all Christians and all churches. Conflict was common, and it involved even central matters such as Jesus' true nature and work.

Central to the Gospels is Jesus of Nazareth. All we hear about him comes from others. He himself left no writings. He was a prophet, as we shall see, and prophets often did not write down their prophecies. It was not uncommon in Israel for others who esteemed a prophet's words to write them down. That is exactly what happened in the case of Jesus. To some degree, he also fit the ancient categories of wise man and philosopher, and it was common for such figures to have their lives recorded by those who lived later and revered them. Again, the same applies to Jesus. So no matter how early our sources, we are always reading a report of what someone else says that Jesus said or did.

There was an interval between Jesus' career and the writing of the Gospels. When anything noteworthy happens in today's world, it is quickly followed by a stream of articles and books about it. Two thousand years ago, things did not automatically get reduced to writing. Excited by the amazing things that had happened among them (the ministry of Jesus, his crucifixion, and his resurrection), and convinced that God had changed the world through Jesus, the earliest Christians launched an intensive effort to convert others to their way of seeing things, to teach one another about Jesus, and to establish institutions to support their beliefs and activity. All of this involved preserving, shaping, adapting, and passing on information about Jesus. So the Jesus tradition was at first transmitted orally in the context of missionary work, liturgy, and teaching.

Some Christians, a small minority, could read and write. As years passed and it became apparent that the great eschatological events (events signaling the turn of the ages and the end of the world as we know it) that Christians expected were not going to happen immediately, they began to record what they knew about Jesus. They may have begun by collecting Jesus' teachings, and perhaps penning accounts of his powerful deeds. Eventually some perceived a need to present Jesus more fully, in a form that would relate his deeds to his words and connect both to his violent death, viewing all in light of his resurrection. The result was the Gospels. The Gospels in the New Testament were written for different local churches at different times. Mark was written first, probably around 70 C.E. Matthew and Luke soon followed, perhaps fifteen years or so later, both using Mark as a source but being unaware of each other's work. John was probably written still later, perhaps in the 90s.

The first three canonical gospels, Matthew, Mark, and Luke, are so similar that they are called the *Synoptic Gospels*. The word *synoptic* comes from the Greek meaning something like "to see together." Books called *gospel parallels* arrange these gospels in three parallel columns for easy comparison. John is quite different from the other three gospels. There is no compelling evidence that it depends literarily on the other three. It may, however, be related to them in some other way. One suggestion is that Christians in the Johannine community composed this gospel in reaction to the writing of the Synoptics, but did so on the basis of its own distinctive traditions and manner of conceiving of Jesus.

Comparison of the Gospels shows that each revises material about Jesus to apply it to new situations. The clearest examples are Matthew's and Luke's revisions of Mark. Comparing the Synoptics and John, we see that the latter dramatically transforms Jesus material. Such interpretation and adaptation also happened in earlier stages of writing and oral transmission.

To oversimplify a bit, we have three stages to keep in mind when we study material about Jesus. First, there is the historical Jesus—what he actually said and did, and what happened to him. Second, there is a period of mostly oral transmission of information about Jesus. Finally, there is the composition of the gospel accounts. The second and third stage overlapped for some time, since the writing of the Gospels did not spell an end to oral transmission. One Christian writer of the early second century, Papias, the bishop of Hierapolis in Asia Minor (modern Turkey), insisted that oral tradition was more trustworthy than written. Further, the four biblical gospels were not the only ones written. We devote a chapter to other gospels toward the end of this book. Methods that study Jesus material as it evolved over time, including the study of incorporation of preexisting traditions into the Gospels and possible stages of composition of the Gospels, are called *diachronic*, from the Greek words *dia*, meaning "through," and *chronos*, meaning "time." Methods that treat the works as literary wholes and concentrate on their present form are called *synchronic*, from the Greek *syn*, meaning "with," and *chronos*.

The collection of books eventually chosen as authoritative for the church is called the *canon*. The word comes from the Greek *kanon*, meaning a measuring rod. The canonical books are a means by which the church measures its belief and practice. The selection of Matthew, Mark, Luke, and John as the only canonical gospels was made in the course of the second century and was widely established by the middle of the third century.

WHO WROTE THE GOSPELS?

This might seem an odd question. Aren't the evangelists' names Matthew, Mark, Luke, and John? And doesn't ancient tradition tell us something about each of them? Things are not so simple.

The authors of the Gospels are called the *evangelists*. This comes from the Greek word for gospel, *euangelion*. Its literal meaning is "good news." At the beginning of the Gospels there are the headings "According to Matthew," "According to Mark," "According to Luke," and "According to John." Ancient books did not customarily begin this way, so individual authors or scribes would not have happened upon this identical formula independently. Clearly these phrases were added to the Gospels when they were gathered together, which did not happen until the second century. The formula assumes a single story of Jesus, told in four versions. We cannot be sure that the names in these formulas tell us anything about authorship. They reflect later church tradition that may or may not be based on solid information. But even if the attributions are accurate, that still does not tell us who the authors were.

The fourth-century church historian Eusebius of Caesarea (on Palestine's Mediterranean coast) quotes Papias, an early second-century bishop, as follows: "Mark became Peter's interpreter and wrote accurately all that he remembered, not, indeed, in order, of the things said or done by the Lord" (*Church History* 3.39.15). Scholars have pondered these words for years, asking whether or not Eusebius's third-hand account, written two centuries after Papias, can be trusted, and, if so, what Papias means by "interpreter" and "in order." Does "interpreter" mean that Peter's words had to be translated into Greek, or does it mean something broader? And does "in order" refer to chronology? Or is there an element of interpretation implied?

The strongest evidence against seeing Mark as having received his information directly from Peter is the Gospel itself. Its author collected small units of tradition, usually oral but perhaps sometimes written, and pieced them together into a continuous narrative. The same sorts of small units of tradition were available to Matthew, Luke, John, and any other Christian who wanted them. Mark's Gospel shows no sign that its author had access to information other than this generally available tradition.

About Matthew, Papias says that he "collected the oracles in the Hebrew language, and each interpreted them as best he could" (Achtemeier, "Mark," 542). Matthew is more than a collection of oracles (divine pronouncements), and there is no solid evidence that Matthew ever existed in anything but its present Greek. So it is difficult to know what to make of this report. Matthew is the name of the tax collector called by Jesus in Matt 9:9, and he is one of the twelve in Matt 10:3. If this is the Gospel's author, he would be an eyewitness. But Matthew does not read like an eyewitness account. In fact, Matthew bases his work on Mark's Gospel, and we know that Mark was not an eyewitness.

Luke is often thought to be the companion of the Apostle Paul, mentioned in Phlm 24; Col 4:14; and 2 Tim 4:11. The reason for the attribution may be that Acts of the Apostles is by the same author as the Gospel of Luke, and there are sections of Acts that speak in the first person plural, implying that the narrator accompanied Paul on some of his journeys. However, the use of "we" in those passages can be explained otherwise—literary convention aimed at increasing vividness, for example—and Acts's depiction of Paul contradicts what we find in Paul's letters.

The author of the Fourth Gospel is frequently equated with the unnamed beloved disciple mentioned in that gospel. But the Gospel shows signs of having been composed in stages, and it has transformed the Jesus material into something very different from what we find in the Synoptics. Most would judge the portraits in the Synoptics to be closer to the historical Jesus (see ch. 8). This argues against seeing John as an eyewitness.

The best information about the evangelists must come from the Gospels themselves. Unfortunately, that means that we cannot be sure of their names, where and under what circumstances they wrote, and their precise positions in the church. A further caveat is in order as we picture the evangelists. We are probably justified in thinking that there was a specific individual who put each gospel in its final form and who therefore is its author. Nonetheless, ideas of ancient authorship are different from our own. That is clear from the very fact that the Gospels are anonymous texts. It is also clear from the fact that Matthew and Luke took over large portions of Mark, often reproducing it word-for-word. We must also keep in mind that each evangelist makes use of traditional material that itself was chosen, transformed, and passed down by an anonymous, communal process. The Gospels are, to a large extent, community creations.

STUDY OF THE GOSPELS: PRINCIPLES AND METHODS

The Gospels have been read in many different ways over the past two millennia. Our approach to them in this book requires explanation.

The Enlightenment was an intellectual and social movement of the seventeenth and eighteenth centuries that celebrated human reason. It valued evidence and scientific method over traditional, and often religious, ideas and dogmas. One of the fruits of the Enlightenment was the launching of academic disciplines in which human reason is applied to evidence in orderly ways. We refer to the application of such methods to the Bible as "critical scholarship." The application of methodologies drawn from the fields of history, philology, literature, archaeology, anthropology, and so on has deepened our understanding of the Bible immeasurably. At various points over the past couple of centuries, many Christians have been alarmed at the application of such "secular" disciplines to their sacred texts, fearing that they would undermine faith. But over time, most "mainline" churches have come to accept critical methods as both helpful and salutary.

New Testament texts were written around two thousand years ago. For the first millennium and a half of the church's existence, it read these documents as if there were little difference between its own world and that displayed in the texts. The Renaissance brought both new attention to the ancient world and a realization that there was a gap between the world of the reader and that of the original writer and readers. This eventually led to the birth of historical criticism. Modern methods take the gap between ancient and present worlds seriously.

Critical study of the Bible has made these influential texts accessible even to non-Christians. An example is cooperation between Jewish and Christian scholars as they investigate ancient Judaism and Christianity. There are Christians who study ancient Judaism, and Jews who study ancient Christianity. The way questions are asked and answered unites such scholars. Debates about method are usually no longer conducted along confessional lines, meaning points of view determined by particular faiths. Historical questions are not resolved by resorting to religious creeds.

Critical scholars do not read the Gospels as simple transcriptions of exactly what happened in the ministry of Jesus. Christians take these texts as the products of inspiration. But inspiration need not mean word-for-word dictation of the text by God to the writer. Nonfundamentalistic churches accept the idea that the authors of the biblical texts were true authors and fully human, part of their historical situations, operating from within worldviews conditioned by their times, and having limited human understanding. Each gospel has its own conception of Jesus and his mission, depending to some degree on each evangelist's viewpoint. We might call these "portraits" to indicate that they are not simple and literal representations of historical realities. The Gospels constitute a variety of portraits of Jesus, not just one. The present book takes full account of the uniqueness of each of these portraits. Good portraits capture something essential about their subject, but they are not simply photographs. They are interpretive. Ultimately, they may contain a good deal of the artist.

Till now, we have been speaking of the "Gospels" as if we knew what a gospel is. Definition of the gospel genre has actually been a matter of discussion among scholars for some time. They have assessed the Gospels' features and sought ancient parallels to them. We devote the following section to that discussion, limiting ourselves to the canonical gospels. Other ancient texts that do not share the literary form of the canonical four claim to be gospels nonetheless. We discuss such texts in chapter 7.

GENRE

Genre is a French word that means "kind." To ask about the genre of the Gospels is to ask what *kind* of literature they are. Most discussions of genre take place in the classroom. We may imagine stodgy professors who have spent their lives exploring little-known works, splitting hairs and drawing arcane distinctions between literary works, and discussing details ordinary readers would not even notice. How many of us even use the word "genre" in everyday life? How many readers of this book, when they saw the word at the head of this section, had to stop and ask themselves what it means?

Although it might seem that literary genre is a matter just for the experts, that perception is wrong. We employ concepts of genre all the time. Every time we read something, we appeal to genre, though we may not do so consciously. There are two sorts of cases that we can imagine to show that this is true. In one, we pick up something to read thinking we know what genre it belongs to, and in the other, we pick it up not knowing what sort of literature it is. In the first case, suppose we open what we expect to be a novel, and it turns out to be written in verse—one long poem. A lot of people would quickly close the book. Or suppose we read a newspaper article and perceive strong bias on the part of the reporter. The reaction might be, "This belongs on the editorial page. It is opinion, not reporting." When we are misled in this way we react with confusion, distaste, or even anger.

Now imagine the second situation, where we pick up a book not knowing what sort of literature it is. Suppose the title is something like *True Love*. What do we expect? It could be a romantic novel, a more serious novel, a philosophical work, a theological treatise, a pious treatment of the life of Christ, or any number of things. If I am looking for a light romantic novel but find that it is a highly technical philosophical work, I will quickly return it to the shelf.

When I first look at a book, how do I find out what sort of work it is? Sometimes book jackets categorize books—fiction, nonfiction, novel, philosophy, and so on. Sometimes the jacket briefly describes the contents, explains who the author is, offers brief reviews. We might look at the table of contents (we have been trained to expect a table of contents) or perhaps read a bit of the book or even peruse the index. Our investigation need not take a lot of time. We may not even think explicitly about what we are doing.

We feel we have the right to expect certain things from certain genres. There is a sort of contract between writer and reader, and when the writer breaks that contract, the reader might be alienated, or, alternatively, the reader may be intrigued and read on. Breaking the contract might be a device the writer uses to accomplish certain aims, perhaps to get the reader to see something in an unconventional way.

A genre consists of a constellation of structure, style, and content. Some would include function. But a genre has no reality apart from the concrete works that belong to it, and such works do not always fit categories easily. So some speak of genre in terms of "family resemblances," rather than as hard-and-fast lists of necessary features. Further, genres are born, grow, and die. Genres relate to one another in various ways. Sometimes genres can include within themselves other genres—the epistolary novel, for example, that consists of letters. All of this cautions us that genre is an interpretive construct and can be fluid. When we reify our categories, that is, when we make them into "things" that are "out there" in the real world, we risk losing sight of the fact that both the literary works themselves and the categories used to classify them are social products, depending on social codes and conventions. Social products are always multidimensional and open to alternative ways of looking at them.

What is a gospel? *Gospel* has various meanings that fall into two main categories—the Christian message itself and a literary genre. Mark begins, "The beginning of the good news (gospel) of Jesus Christ ..." (1:1). Few scholars think that by "gospel" Mark means a specific literary genre. The term was not used that way before Mark, nor do Matthew, Luke, or John begin like that. Only in the second century did Christians begin calling literary works gospels, and only then did other works appear that self-consciously called themselves gospels. The use of the term *gospel* to refer to a literary form reveals consciousness of earlier works that have a certain status in Christian communities. Later works call themselves gospels to claim the authority that attaches to gospels already accepted. Ironically, those later works often are not of the same genre as the canonical gospels.

Scholars propose three possible genres for the canonical gospels: biography, history, and gospel as a new and unique genre. The English word *biography* comes from the Greek words *bios*, meaning "life," and *graphe*, meaning "writing." The ancient term for the genre is simply *bios*. Ancient biographies or "lives," like modern ones, concentrate on a single individual. They explain the character of that person. They usually treat the family, birth, childhood, and education of their subjects, and then go on to speak of their later lives. Biographies often praise their subjects and offer them as models of behavior and personal character. Such works are also called *encomiums*. Ancient biographies may show some interest in the inner life of a character, but we should not attribute to them the psychological interests characteristic of modern biographies. Ancient biographies were written well before Freud!

The ancients distinguished between biography and history. Although ancient histories may concentrate on important persons, their main interest is in the broader history involved, rather than in the exposition of the character of the persons involved in the story.

The third main option is that the Gospels represent a new genre. Since most New Testament scholars think that Mark was the first to write a gospel, Mark would be the inventor of the genre. This position has often been discredited because it has been seen to be motivated by a desire on the part of Christian scholars to see Jesus and Christianity as unique, while more "objective" scholars were more inclined to see Christianity as a specific example of Hellenistic religions generally. But it is a mistake to write off theories because of motives imputed to those who hold them. One might well hold the right opinion for the wrong reason. The question is whether or not the evidence supports this position.

Recently Yarbro Collins reviewed the arguments on all sides of this issue. She frames the question first in terms of Mark, the first of the Gospels. Unlike Matthew and Luke, Mark does not include a genealogy for Jesus, nor does it contain an infancy narrative or any information about Jesus' childhood. When it mentions his family, it does so in passing and in order to distance him from them. Mark certainly concentrates on Jesus, but its purpose is not to investigate Jesus' character but is broader. It portrays Jesus' career as central to the eschatological events (meaning end-time events) foretold and now initiated by God. In this sense, Mark resembles ancient history rather than biography, and since it is the history of eschatological events, it can be called eschatological history. Yarbro Collins demonstrates the extensive interest of ancient Jewish apocalyptic writings in historical events and how they lead to the *eschaton*, the "end" of history as we know it. She draws attention to the instances in Mark where Jewish prophecy is said to point to the end-time events taking place in the career of Jesus and of John the Baptist.

Matthew and Luke each add two chapters to the beginnings of their Gospels in which they describe Jesus' birth in miraculous terms, a feature common in ancient biographies. They also add genealogies, corresponding to ancient interest in lineage. Yarbro Collins suggests that Matthew and Luke make the story of Jesus more like conventional biography. This does not mean that they do not see Jesus within an eschatological history. Genres are not hermetically sealed categories. Just as Mark, an eschatological history, is in many respects close to ancient biography, so Matthew and Luke, who have moved closer to biography, retain Mark's interest in eschatological history.

The Gospel of John concentrates on Jesus in such a way that Jesus, his origins, his nature, his relation to God, and so on, constitute almost the entire content of the Gospel. In the Fourth Gospel, Jesus becomes a revealer figure, the one come down from heaven through whom one can escape this world below, this world of darkness, so the biographical elements John finds in the gospel genre are transposed to a new key.

There is one other aspect of the gospel genre that needs attention here. It has to do with the purpose of the writing. The Gospels are not "objective history," but an attempt to support the faith of believers or to bring unbelievers to conversion. They are religious documents, written from faith and for faith. One will not go wrong if one hears them as sermons in narrative form.

Reflections on genre help us appreciate how the Gospels would have been read in the ancient world, as well as to understand better the evangelists' purposes. Ancient readers would have perceived the Gospels as somewhat familiar, similar to other literature they knew, be it in the form of biography or history. At the same time, they would have been alert to aspects of the Gospels that distinguished them from lives and histories. The Gospels were describing events that changed the world and its relationship to its Creator. Seeing the Gospels as eschatological histories rather than as lives causes readers to focus less on Jesus as example or as great man than to see him as the agent of world-changing events being accomplished by God through Jesus.

HERMENEUTICS

In biblical studies, *hermeneutics* sometimes means ways to make the text meaningful in the present, while *exegesis* means the determination of what the text meant in its original context. Hermeneutics is also used more broadly to mean theories governing principles of interpretation. It refers less to specific methods than to the general philosophies of what we do when we interpret a text.

The study of hermeneutics is complex, and we cannot do it justice here. Excellent treatments of the subject can be found in good dictionaries of the Bible, dictionaries of philosophy, and in many other books dedicated to the topic. Philosophers who have been especially influential on biblical interpreters have been Martin Heidegger, Hans-Georg Gadamer, Paul Ricoeur, and Jacques Derrida. Since we aim at a self-conscious and self-critical examination of the Bible, we must at least look briefly at some key concepts that have proved helpful to biblical scholars as they try to understand what they themselves are doing as they analyze texts, even if we run the risk of oversimplifying a complex set of questions. As we do so, we must warn the reader that just about everything related to interpretation of texts, especially biblical texts, is being debated presently. No one way of looking at things claims universal assent.

A good place to start is to consider the importance of author, text, and reader in interpretation. Interpretation aims at grasping meaning. Is meaning located in the mind and intention of the author, is it something inherent in the text, or is it something produced by the reader? Historical criticism, described below, has traditionally thought of interpretation as discovering what the author intended. Critics of that view called it the "intentional fallacy," pointing out that we can never really get inside someone else's head, especially someone who lived long ago, and that we simply have no direct access to the author. In the mid-twentieth century, many critics located meaning in an autonomous text, finding meaning to be independent of authorial intention and waiting to be uncovered by readers. The general approach was called the New Criticism. More recent methods have emphasized the role of the reader, sometimes presenting meaning as if the reader is the source of meaning, and sometimes conceiving of the reading process as an interaction between text and reader. Such approaches are often called reader response criticism.

Another way to talk about this is to speak of the world behind the text, the world of the text, and the world in front of the text. The world behind the text is the real world of the author or authors as well as the real world to which the text refers. In the case of the Gospels, it is the world of the earthly Jesus, the scribes and Pharisees, the Romans, Jewish peasants, and early Christians. Critics use the text as a window into this world. The world of the text is the story world. It may or may not accurately reflect Jewish Palestine of the first century. It may or may not mean something to modern people. It is its own world. Critics often use literary criticism to analyze the story world. The world in front of the text is the world of readers, who read the text from their own point of view and with their own agendas and purposes. Here the text is sometimes compared to a mirror, reflecting the concerns and circumstances of the reader.

Most critical scholars of the Bible conceive of meaning as something that must include all three elements—author, text, and reader. The writing and reading of texts is an instance of communication, and communication implies that meaning is conveyed from one person or group to another. Texts are produced by an author or authors who intend to say something, and there is some correspondence between what they put on paper (or papyrus) and what they intend to convey, be that information, an attitude, an emotion, faith, an experience, and so on. At the same time, once the document is produced, it has an existence independent of its writer. The text also remains independent to some degree of its readers. Ricoeur calls this distance from writer and reader *distanciation*. As a reader reads, she or he brings a world of experience to the text that may well be quite different from what the text itself expresses. The reader enters into the world of the text, but never completely leaves his or her own world behind. Gadamer calls this a fusion of horizons, in which the horizons of text and reader both come into play, neither being obliterated, but both being transformed in some sense. Some have expressed this in terms of a sort of give-and-take, almost a conversation between text and reader in which the text retains its own existence and independence and the reader his or her own autonomy, but in which the text comes alive through the reader's interpretation and the reader is transformed by the reading.

As we read the Gospels, we are interested in what the person or persons who produced them wanted to convey. This consists not merely of information but also of attitude, worldview, and faith. We focus on the text itself, trying to understand how it does what it does through analysis of its structure, language, themes, and so on. We also pay attention to how readers encounter the text. We are interested both in ancient readers and modern ones. As we speculate about the real author of the text on the basis of what the text itself says and how it does so and as we imagine how readers of the first-century Mediterranean world would hear the text, we engage in historical study. We use the text as a window into the world in which the text was produced and we use our understanding of that world to shed light on the text. But we do not assume that the meaning of the text is simply equivalent to that historical world, nor do we equate it simply to what was in the mind of the author. We know that the text goes beyond the author's conscious intention, so that not even the author controls or fully grasps it. Modern philosophies of interpretation have taught us that there is never one, single, univocal meaning to any text. Meaning involves author, text, and an endlessly shifting set of readers. Modern theorists of reading have taught us that narratives inevitably leave much unsaid, with many gaps to be filled by a variety of readers in a multiplicity of ways. No two readings can be exactly the same. And there is always a surplus of meaning that escapes any one reading, and that even goes beyond the author's conscious intention. The history of interpretation of the Gospels, so full of variety and creativity, is evidence for this. Matthew and Luke, by taking Mark's Gospel into their own works, have interpreted it in two different ways, as well.

Analyses that concentrate on the reader fall under the heading of reader response criticism. They investigate the activity of readers as they bring a text to life in their reading. Such analysis can assume many forms. It can be a form of historical, psychological, or social-scientific criticism, for example. It can look at a sort of ideal reader that the text seems to assume, or it can posit readers that will read against the grain of the text, challenging its assumptions. It can also become quite broad, looking at the reception of the text by different readers down through history. Then it becomes what some have called *reception criticism*.

Although no metaphor can adequately encompass the nature of writing and reading, we find the image of a conversation fruitful to describe the relation of text and reader. The reader brings a good deal to the text and thus transforms it. The text says something to the reader and thus transforms her or him. Neither text nor reader is reducible to the other. Readers bring a great variety of questions to the text—historical, social, theological—some of which the text answers and others of which it does not. Ultimately, the dialogue is potentially endless.

The Gospels are meant to be revelatory. Early Christians were convinced that God had approached them in Jesus, and they wrote the Gospels as witnesses to God's revelation in Jesus. For them, an adequate reading of these texts would not stop at description of information that they convey about Jesus, or even at an accurate representation of what they believed about Jesus or how their lives had been changed by him. Rather, the texts were meant to be vehicles through which others could encounter Jesus and be transformed by the encounter. This is what Sandra Schneiders means when she entitles her treatment of Bible interpretation *The Revelatory Text*. She uses the concept of *symbol*, in which something that can be experienced on a number of levels reveals a reality beyond immediate experience. Just as those who met Jesus could experience and interpret him in terms that did not issue in his becoming God's revelation for them, so also the Bible can be analyzed in creative and insightful ways using a wide array of methods without it being revelatory to the interpreter. But if reading the Gospels does not result in an encounter with God and with personal transformation, then, from the point of view of the evangelists, their work has failed.

Another triad that casts some light on this process is explanation, interpretation, and understanding. Explanation means explicating the many aspects of the text that are not necessarily apparent to readers. This may mean supplying information about historical entities such as the Roman Empire, ancient Judaism, and early Christians. Interpretation means using the features of the text, our information about the ancient world, and concepts of Christianity and about religion in general, to arrive at plausible meanings. True understanding takes place only when we enter into a text empathetically and are transformed by it.

METHODS OF ANALYSIS

Methods determine results. Methods are sets of questions posed to a text, along with procedures to produce answers to those questions. Self-awareness and self-criticism are crucial here, lest we take our approaches as simply self-evident and as producing the only kinds of interpretations possible. For example, historical methods aim at accurate description, while theological methods might pay greater attention to the texts' truth claims, evaluating them in light of other possible ways of thinking about the world and God. Confusion about what functions can be served by what methods have led to all sorts of misunderstanding and conflict.

HISTORICAL CRITICISM

The birth of modern historical study is usually traced to the second half of the eighteenth and the beginning of the nineteenth century, although the groundwork was laid earlier, as early as the Renaissance. Critical study of Christianity and of the Bible also began around this time. By critical study of the Bible is meant the application of human reason to these texts in much the same way as other ancient texts are studied. They are treated as human artifacts produced within particular times and places. Therefore, they can be illumined through historical study. By historical study here we mean examination of sources, reconstruction of context (social, cultural, political, economic), and study of the original languages (primarily Hebrew, Aramaic, and Greek). Put simply, it is the study of what these texts meant to the people who wrote them and to their first readers and hearers, how they functioned in their original settings, and so on.

A good deal of biblical study has gone into trying to determine whether the stories these texts contain are literally true. Some of that research was spurred by a desire to show that they were not true, or that one must sep-arate the more incredible aspects of religious belief from what is more acceptable to human reason. Rationalist approaches in the nineteenth century sought to show that allegedly supernatural events could be explained "rationally" and so shown to be natural events misunderstood or purposely distorted. The task of biblical scholarship was thought to be to work back to the "real" events. The task of historical criticism in gen-eral was to reconstruct "what actually happened." Such a simple concep-tion of the historical task has been undermined in the past few decades, particularly by liberationist and postmodernist views, explained briefly below.

Historical study and study in the humanities in general has often taken science as its paradigm and has been heavily influenced by Cartesian thought. In that way of looking at things, there is a clear separation between subject and object, and the object, which is "out there" and which has a solid reality of its own, apart from the investigating subject, can be analyzed using an array of value-neutral tools made for that pur-pose. The result is objective knowledge that does not depend on the point of view of the analyst. But study in the humanities is not simply the same as in the sciences, and even the sciences have been deeply affected by such hypotheses as Einstein's theories of relativity and by the Heisenberg principle, which shows that the very act of observing something changes that thing to some degree. Historians have begun to accept that objectivity in historical study is an elusive if not unattainable goal, so that confidence that they can eventually arrive at "what actually happened" must be tempered by humility in the face of possible multiple interpretations and by recognition that everything that they think and do is profoundly influenced by their own place in the sweep of history, their culture, education, social and economic class, and so on. This has to do with the interpreter. But interpretation plays a central role in human perception, so that even witnesses to the original events have a mind-set and worldview that influence how they experience things. There never was a simple "thing" such as an event that was complete in itself and self-explanatory. As historians try to reconstruct the past, what they are in fact doing is building a construct based on evidence that has its own points of view, processed by scholars who also have their own points of view.

All that being said, some reconstructions of the past are more true to the past than others. Historians continue to strive for more adequate reconstructions through presentation of their ideas in public academic forums where they can be subject to criticism and debate. One might say that modern historical study has been chastened by criticism of a naive historical positivism but that the vast majority of historians continue to believe that they do far more than simply express their own prejudices through the pretense of historical reconstruction.

These observations are the more critical when we turn to early Christian literature, or any sort of religious literature for that matter. These texts and the traditions that went into them sprang from the faith of the earliest members of Jesus' following and from the churches that arose after his death and resurrection. They were never meant to be "objective" history in the modern sense. The gospel writers and those who shaped and passed on the tradition before them were not affected by Enlightenment ideas of scientific study, empirical proof, and objectivity. Their purpose was to proclaim what God had done in Jesus. Given what we have said about reconceptualization of the historical task in recent decades, the difference between this and the writing of history is not as great as once thought. Academic historians also have their own assumptions and agendas. At the same time, even those skeptical about the potential of modern historical study to portray the past accurately carry on their studies as if they believe otherwise. One may no longer accept without qualification the "scientific" model of investigation, but one still believes that reasoning based on evidence is a necessary antidote to simple faith affirmations in historical study, and that the two are not simply identical.

Historical scholars are still interested in critical reconstructions of the past and think that they can achieve these through critical study, even though they may have a more sophisticated notion of what that might mean. But it would be a mistake to characterize historical-critical study as restricted to just this task, especially if it is thought of as deciding whether Jesus' story as told by the evangelists is accurate. Scholars pursue a broader agenda. For example, the Gospels are written in ancient Greek, in which most modern readers are not versed. The most basic task of translating them into modern languages depends on a detailed knowledge not only of ancient Greek vocabulary and grammar, but also of a nuanced historical appreciation of how words, symbols, concepts, and so on were used in the historical situations in which the Gospels came to be. Further, we have already noted the importance of genre in interpretation. Understanding of ancient genres is crucial, and that means detailed acquaintance with a large body of ancient literature and understanding of the historical context of that literature.

Since the Gospels are full of references to historical persons, events, places, and institutions, it is important that historical study shed light on these. The Pharisees are an historical Jewish group prominent in the gospel narratives, for example. Comprehending the gospel narrative assumes at least minimal knowledge of who they were. Further, the gospel portrayal of them is problematic, something that becomes apparent only when all historical sources are utilized to reconstruct a more adequate picture. This sort of insight can shed light on the story world of the gospel as illumined by literary criticism. But study of the Gospels' historical milieu also enables us to hazard some educated guesses about why the Gospels were written, the roles they played in their own churches, what light they shed on their churches' situations, what they say about Christianity's origins, and so on. The Gospels are also witnesses to early Christian thought, attitudes, and practices. The texts themselves are historical artifacts.

New materials have come to light in the past couple of centuries that have aided in historical study of the Gospels. The Dead Sea Scrolls, discovered in the Judean desert in 1947 and onward, are the library of a priestly, apocalyptic sect that existed from the second century B.C.E. to the first century C.E. We discuss it in the next chapter. Other Jewish texts have been discovered over the centuries, designated by the umbrella term *Pseudepigrapha* since they often employ pseudepigraphy—the fictional attribution of works to important figures in Israel's history. Until relatively recently they have not been fully exploited for what they reveal about the Jewish worlds in which Christianity was born. The Nag Hammadi library, found in Egypt in 1945, contains a wealth of Christian and non-Christian gnostic texts. Other finds, along with the ongoing efforts of archaeologists, have given scholars more materials with which to work.

TEXTUAL CRITICISM

We do not possess the original manuscripts of the Gospels. Instead, we have a large number of later manuscripts of varying dates and provenances that disagree with each other in many details and sometimes on larger matters. Textual critics study these manuscripts to determine the text's history of transmission and to reconstruct the most likely original readings. This work is crucial, for it determines the very substance of the documents we study.

Besides its goal of providing the best critical text possible for the New Testament, text criticism also studies the tendencies of particular manuscripts and families of manuscripts (meaning groups of manuscripts that demonstrate a relationship to each other and therefore to a particular strand of translation and transmission). The differences between manuscripts can be due to simple scribal mistakes, but they can also be intentional, due to theological, social, or literary reasons.

SOURCE CRITICISM

The gospel writers obviously had sources. They did not make up their material out of whole cloth. They were heirs to several decades of transmission of material about Jesus. The general term for this material is *tradition*, from the Latin word for "to hand on." Specific stories, sayings, and so on, handed down over time, are referred to as traditions, too. These traditions could be oral or, perhaps less commonly, written.

Source criticism has been most fruitful when applied to the Synoptic Gospels, which clearly have some sort of literary interdependence. Most of Mark appears in Matthew, and a good deal of it appears in Luke. The traditions shared by all three gospels are called the *triple tradition*. In addition, Matthew and Luke share much material that is not in Mark, called the *double tradition*. Further, both Matthew and Luke have a lot of material that is unique to themselves. So the Synoptic Gospels resemble each other markedly, but they also disagree in many respects. The verbal agreement between many passages shared by all three gospels, as well as the closeness of language in material shared only by Matthew and Luke, make a strong case for some sort of literary dependence between the three. The question of the relation between the Synoptic Gospels is called the *Synoptic Problem*. A good deal of effort in the nineteenth century went into trying to solve this problem. The ultimate goal was often to discover which gospel was the earliest and therefore supposedly most useful for historical purposes, a preoccupation of that century. Determining the relationship of the gospels is perhaps more important as a clue to how they were composed and as an aid in determining their theological tendencies, as we shall see.

At the end of the eighteenth century, a German scholar named J. J. Griesbach proposed that Matthew was the earliest gospel, that Luke used it in writing his Gospel, and that Mark then used both Matthew and Luke, abbreviating them dramatically. The Griesbach hypothesis still has its defenders, but they are few. It is difficult to see why Mark would have abbreviated Matthew and Luke so drastically. Scholars also note that where Matthew, Mark, and Luke share material (called the *triple tradition*), they often agree with Mark's order. When Matthew and Luke diverge from Mark's order, they do not do so in quite the same way, as one would expect if Luke depended on Matthew. In the nineteenth century, the theory of Markan priority became dominant and remains so to this day. That is, Mark was the first gospel, while Matthew and Luke used Mark as a source. This was a major step in solving the Synoptic Problem.

Scholars had still to solve the riddle of material shared by Matthew and Luke, often involving close to word-for-word correspondence, that they did not get from Mark. This constitutes a substantial amount of material in the two gospels. Possible solutions to this problem are three: Matthew depended on Luke, Luke depended on Matthew, or each depended on another source, no longer extant. The first solutions create more problems than they solve. If one asks how and why Matthew rewrote Luke or the converse, one does not get convincing answers. Why did they omit so much good material? And why does their rewriting not show more consistency and purpose? Scholars in the nineteenth century posited the existence of another source, now lost. They named it Q, the first letter of the German word for "source," *Quelle*. One can tentatively reconstruct Q by collecting all instances of shared material not in the triple tradition. Of course, one will then have two versions of every part of Q, one from Matthew and one from Luke, and will have to choose which, if either, is closer to the original, or whether one can, on the basis of these two gospels, suggest a likely original. Scholars have done just that. The International Q Project has collaborated on reconstructing Q (see Robinson). All reconstructions of Q result in a document composed primarily of sayings of Jesus, usually without context. Since Luke seems to preserve the order of Q more faithfully than Matthew, it is now a convention to refer to passages from Q using the chapter and verses of Luke. For example, Q 3:7-9 is the same as Luke 3:7-9, with the qualification that one does not thereby assume that Luke has preserved the actual content without alteration.

The solution of the Synoptic Problem that posits two sources for Matthew and Luke—Mark and Q—is called the *two-source solution*. But that is not the whole story, for Matthew has a good deal of material that he did not get from either Mark or Q, and the same can be said for Luke. For convenience, Matthew's special material as a whole is called M, and Luke's is called L. Neither M and L are literary sources, as is Q. They are simply umbrella designations indicating material, written or oral, unique to one of these two gospels.

A strong argument for the validity of the two-source theory is that it "works." That is, it explains a lot of things. When we look at redaction criticism below we shall see that when we assume that Matthew used Mark and then ask why he makes changes—omissions, revisions, additions—those changes fall into patterns and make sense. The same can be said for Luke. As they say, the proof of the pudding is in the eating.

The following chart illustrates the two-source solution to the Synoptic Problem.

Two-Source Solution to the Synoptic Problem

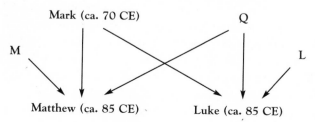

21

Did Mark also use written sources? That is disputed, but Mark may have used a miracles collection (see Achtemeier, "Isolation"). The parables in chapter 4 may also come from a written source. It is less clear whether other parts of the Gospel—the apocalyptic discourse in chapter 13, for example, or the passion narrative—are originally Mark's compositions or are at least partly based on preexistent sources (see Donahue).

A final question concerns the relation between John and the Synoptics. John is thought by most to be later than the Synoptics. Did he depend on them? There are intriguing similarities between John and the Synoptics, but direct dependence has not been conclusively demonstrated. This question remains unsolved.

FORM CRITICISM

The narratives of Matthew, Mark, or Luke are "bumpy." The story moves from episode to episode quickly, sometimes with little in the way of transition. The reason that the Synoptic Gospels are so uneven is that they are constructed from smaller units of tradition, smaller forms. Through these forms, early Christians passed down traditions about Jesus orally. Mark incorporated small units and perhaps a few written sources into his larger narrative, supplying the narrative thread tying the units together. Matthew and Luke accepted Mark's basic narrative structure, supplementing it with Q, along with some other traditional material, and recasting the whole according to their own lights. By "dissolving" the narrative frameworks of the Gospels and examining the forms on their own, comparing them to other forms in the Gospels and from other ancient texts, and so on, we can to some degree work our way back behind the Gospels, thereby learning something about how the early church chose, reshaped, and passed down tradition, reflecting the circumstances and concerns of each church. The pioneers of New Testament form criticism were Rudolf Bultmann, whose major work in the field was published in 1921, and Martin Dibelius, whose book appeared in 1919.

The process of transmission of Jesus traditions orally reminds us of the game "telephone." In that game, one person whispers a "message" to another, then that person whispers it to another, and so on down the line. By the time the message reaches the end of a line of people, it can change substantially, sometimes comically. But this analogy limps badly. First, the early Christians were not whispering to each other. These stories and traditions were passed down within the Christian community, probably at meetings for liturgies, teaching, and so on. They probably also appeared in missionary speeches. There was ample opportunity for asking questions, getting clarifications, and challenging facts. Second, even though our texts show that the early church reshaped tradition with some freedom, a desire to preserve tradition is also evident. This does not mean that Christians acted as video cameras or recording machines, nor does it deny the church's remarkable creativity, but it warns us against ruling out substantial continuity between Jesus and the church's view of him. This becomes an important issue when trying to get back to the historical Jesus, a topic we take up later in this book. It also has implications for understanding how the evangelists use traditional material.

The evangelists picked and chose the material they wished in order to enhance the picture of Jesus they wished to convey, and they altered the traditions they used. At the same time, they did not always rewrite traditions so thoroughly that everything fit perfectly together. The result is occasional unevenness and narratives that are not always consistent according to modern standards. Apparently, many ancients had a higher degree of toleration for some forms of inconsistency than we. Today, an author might review his or her work numerous times to remove inconsistencies (something made a lot easier by computers). That is not always the case with ancient writers.

The Gospels were constructed using small units of traditional material often without transitions. In fact, the early manuscripts do not have punctuation, ways of designating proper nouns, paragraphs, or section titles. Therefore, we must notice how the constituent parts are placed—for example, what comes before what, what is "framed" by what, and so on. We must also be aware that seemingly small changes in the way an evangelist treats the text provide important clues about his point of view.

Parables

We turn now to specific forms. We look first at parables. The word *parable* had a broader range of meanings in the ancient world than today. Then it could be used to denote any figurative language. We tend to use it now to designate a fictional short story meant to convey a lesson or point of view. Dodd presents a classic definition of a gospel parable: "A metaphor or simile drawn from nature or common life, arresting the hearer by its vividness or strangeness, and leaving the mind in sufficient doubt about its precise application to tease it into active thought" (Dodd, 16). Note the elements of "strangeness" and "doubt" in Dodd's definition.

Aren't parables meant to illuminate something? Why then do they contain elements that seem to undermine that? Dodd's observations are confirmed by the struggle, beginning with the Gospels themselves, or even before they were written, to determine what many of the parables really mean.

Research in recent decades has concentrated on the elements of strangeness and doubt. Rather than inculcating a simple lesson, the parables change how we think about the world. For example, they can make us question our view of what justice truly is, or how we categorize people as good or bad. Because this use of parables is radical, meaning that it challenges basic assumptions, the church has often attempted to "tame" the parables, to make them simply into short stories to convey a lesson. An excellent example is the Good Samaritan (Luke 10:30-37). A Jew traveling from Jerusalem to Jericho is ambushed, robbed, and left for dead. A priest passes him by, as does a Levite. But then a Samaritan rescues the man, binding his wounds and taking him to an inn where he promises to pay the man's bills.

Luke turns this parable into an *example story*, an illustration of how one ought to live. He does so by framing the parable with a confrontation between Jesus and a lawyer who is trying to trip him up (10:25-29, 36-37). The lawyer asks what he must do to gain eternal life. Jesus asks him what is in the Torah, and the lawyer says one must love God and one's neighbor. Torah, most simply, is Jewish sacred tradition and instruction, particularly as preserved in the first five books of the Bible, but see the next chapter for a fuller explanation. The lawyer asks Jesus who is his neighbor. Jesus tells the parable of the Good Samaritan, and then asks the lawyer who proved neighbor to the man by the roadside. The lawyer admits that it was the Samaritan, and Jesus says, "Go and do likewise." There is a discontinuity here. First, we are told that one must love one's neighbor. Then, at the end of the parable, we are told that our neighbor is the one who helps us. So should we love just those who help us? Or is the neighbor the man in the ditch who needs help, so that love means helping those in need? The confusion arises because Luke's interpretation is secondary to the parable itself. So what was the parable's original import? If we see the parable apart from its Lukan context, another reading is possible, one that is startling. We can do this on formal grounds, by focusing our attention on the short narrative that comprises the parable.

There is little question that Jesus would have applauded the actions of the story's protagonist. But some years ago, John Dominic Crossan suggested a different way of reading this parable. Jesus is a Jew telling this story to other Jews in Jewish territory. It is striking that the main character is not Jewish, but a Samaritan. Relations between Jews and Samaritans were tense in Jesus' time. It would have been difficult for Jews to accept a story in which a Jewish priest and Levite turn their backs on a Jew in need, while a Samaritan proves himself a true neighbor. The real point of the story is the "impossible" juxtaposition of the terms "good" and "Samaritan." If one experiences this story as narratives are meant to be experienced—by entering into the story world and accepting its premises—then one's assumptions will be upended.

Another way to "tame" parables is to allegorize them. The best example is the parable of the Sower (Mark 4:3-8). A sower sows seed on various types of soil—a path, rocky soil, among thorns, and finally, on good soil. The seed sown on good soil yields "thirty and sixty and a hundredfold," while the seed sown on the other soils fails. The point is the unbelievable yield of the seed sown on good soil. Could seeds yield so much? Farmers would find such a harvest unrealistic. That is the parable's thrust. Jesus claims that his ministry will have "unrealistic" results. Christians had already allegorized this parable before Mark incorporated it into his gospel. Nowhere else does Jesus explain his parables except in Matt 13:36-43. He usually simply lets his audience figure out what he means. The allegorical exposition of the Sower is inconsistent. It begins by identifying hearers of the message with the soil and the message with the seed ("the sower sows the word," 4:14), and then it shifts to identifying the seed with the types of hearers and the different types of soil with their situations. In other words, we go from soil = hearers and seed = message to soil = situation and seed = hearers. Verse 15 confuses the two interpretations: "These are the ones sown along the path where the word is sown."

Mark may be responsible for an increased emphasis on persecution in both the parable and its interpretation. Mark 4:5-6 is awkward and does not really match the other parts of the story. The following table shows this clearly.

The Parable of the Sower in Mark

Sections	Parable	Allegorical Interpretation
A	4:3 A sower went out to sow.	4:14 The sower sows the word.
B	4:4 And as he sowed, some seed fell on the path, and the birds came and ate it up.	4:15 These are the ones on the path where the word is sown: when they hear, Satan immediately comes and takes away the word that is sown in them.
C	4:5 Other seed fell on rocky ground, where it did not have much soil, and it sprang up quickly, since it had no depth of soil. 4:6 And when the sun rose, it was scorched; and since it had no root, it withered away.	4:16 And these are the ones sown on rocky ground: when they hear the word, they immediately receive it with joy. 4:17 But they have no root, and endure only for a while; then, when trouble or persecution arises on account of the word, immediately they fall away.
D	4:7 Other seed fell among thorns, and the thorns grew up and choked it, and it yielded no grain.	4:18 And others are those sown among the thorns: these are the ones who hear the word, 4:19 but the cares of the world, and the lure of wealth, and the desire for other things come in and choke the word, and it yields nothing.

| E | 4:8 Other seed fell into good soil and brought forth grain, growing up and increasing and yielding thirty and sixty and a hundred-fold. | 4:20 And these are the ones sown on the good soil: they hear the word and accept it and bear fruit, thirty and sixty and a hundredfold. |

Section C of the parable is repetitive and wordy. Compare it to the simplicity of the parable's section B. The interpretation of section C is also embellished, as is clear when compared to its interpretation. Persecution is an important issue for Mark, so we propose that he enhances sections of the parable and its interpretation to address it. Alternatively, Mark already found the parable and its interpretation in this form, so that someone before Mark embellished the part taken to refer to persecution.

Sayings

This is one of the most important forms of Jesus tradition. *Sayings*, also called *logia* (*logion* in Greek means "little word," and *logia* is its plural), are brief sayings, sometimes one-liners, sometimes longer. Wisdom books (such as the books of Proverbs, Sirach, and Wisdom) are full of such sayings, usually in the form of proverbs. A *proverb* is a short saying encapsulating an insight about life, for example, or an instruction on behavior. Modern proverbs include such sayings as, "A stitch in time saves nine," "An apple a day keeps the doctor away," and "The early bird gets the worm." Proverbs are anonymous and capture conventional wisdom. We utter them in everyday conversation as an argument from "common sense." Jesus sometimes uses proverbs. An example is "No one can serve two masters" (Matt 6:24). Sometimes proverbs take the form of questions, as does this one from Jesus: "Can any of you by worrying add a single hour to your span of life?" (Matt 6:27). They can also be commands: "Do not worry about tomorrow, for tomorrow will bring worries of its own" (Matt 6:34), and "Do not throw your pearls before swine" (Matt 7:6).

Jesus also speaks prophetic and apocalyptic sayings in the Gospels. For example, he says, "Not everyone who says to me, 'Lord, Lord,' will enter the kingdom of heaven, but only the one who does the will of my

Father in heaven" (Matt 7:21), and "There are some standing here who will not taste death until they see that the kingdom of God has come with power" (Mark 9:1). Apocalyptic sayings include, "For in those days there will be suffering, such as has not been from the beginning of the creation that God created until now, no, and never will be" (Mark 13:19).

There are also legal sayings, which are sometimes radical: "Anyone who divorces his wife, except on the ground of unchastity, causes her to commit adultery; and whoever marries a divorced woman commits adultery" (Matt 5:32).

Collections of Sayings

Q is a collection comprised mostly of Jesus' sayings. The *Gospel of Thomas*, discussed in chapter 7, is also a sayings collection. There may well have been other collections of Jesus' sayings. Sayings could be arranged on the basis of topic, of words in common, or randomly. Luke's parable of the Unjust Steward has attracted to itself a set of sayings having to do with money (16:1-13). They do not all make the same point. In fact, some are mutually contradictory.

Parable of the Unjust Steward and Appended Sayings (Luke 16:1-13)

16:1 "There was a rich man who had a manager, and charges were brought to him that this man was squandering his property. 16:2 So he summoned him and said to him, 'What is this that I hear about you? Give me an accounting of your management, because you cannot be my manager any longer.' 16:3 Then the manager said to himself, 'What will I do, now that my master is taking the position away from me? I am not strong enough to dig, and I am ashamed to beg. 16:4 I have decided what to do so that, when I am dismissed as manager, people may welcome me into their homes.' 16:5 So, summoning his master's debtors one by one, he asked the first, 'How much do you owe my master?' 16:6 He answered, 'A hundred jugs of olive oil.' He said to him, 'Take your bill, sit down quickly, and make it fifty.' 16:7 Then he asked another, 'And how much do you owe?' He replied, 'A hundred containers of wheat.' He said to him, 'Take your bill and make it eighty.'

16:8 And his master commended the dishonest manager because he had acted shrewdly; for the children of this age are more shrewd in dealing with their own generation than are the children of light.

16:9 And I tell you, make friends for yourselves by means of dishonest wealth so that when it is gone, they may welcome you into the eternal homes.

16:10 Whoever is faithful in a very little is faithful also in much; and whoever is dishonest in a very little is dishonest also in much.

16:11 If then you have not been faithful with the dishonest wealth, who will entrust to you the true riches?

16:12 And if you have not been faithful with what belongs to another, who will give you what is your own?

16:13 No slave can serve two masters; for a slave will either hate the one and love the other, or be devoted to the one and despise the other. You cannot serve God and wealth."

In 16:8, the words translated "his master" could as well be translated simply, "the lord." In that case, this would be Jesus' first comment on the story he has just told. The lesson drawn in 16:8 may well be the closest to Jesus' original meaning. Those who pursue material goals work harder than those who dedicate themselves to spiritual things. Verse 9 advocates the use of money to earn eternal life. Verse 10 rejects dishonesty altogether and may be a proverb. The same applies to 16:12. Verse 11 applies this lesson to spiritual riches. Finally, 16:13 asserts the incompatibility of pursuit of wealth and service of God.

Pronouncement Stories

Sayings were often preserved by placing them in a narrative context. Such stories are called *pronouncement stories* because their purpose is preservation of a particular saying. These stories have parallels called *chreia* in the Hellenistic world. Chreia are short narratives containing brief words or deeds of a particular character. They demonstrate something important about the character, such as wisdom. In the Gospels, pronouncement stories sometimes attract to themselves a number of sayings that bear on a given topic.

In Mark 2:23-28, Jesus passes through grainfields with his disciples on the Sabbath. His disciples begin to pluck heads of grain. Suddenly, the Pharisees appear and ask him why his disciples do what is not lawful on the Sabbath. The artificiality of the setting is apparent. It is unlikely that the Pharisees are taking a Sabbath stroll with Jesus. It is equally improbable that they are tarrying in the grain, waiting to catch him. Rather, the narrative presents sayings of Jesus as retorts to his opponents, and the Pharisees are stereotypical opponents. This is typical of the *chreia*. Since Jesus conflicts with the Pharisees here, the story belongs to a subset of pronouncement story—the controversy story.

Jesus answers the Pharisees, reminding them that Scripture says that when David and his men were hungry, they ate sacred bread that only the priests were supposed to eat (1 Sam 21:1-6). So there is biblical precedent for the principle that human need overcomes ritual prohibition. The story does not end here, although it could. A new beginning introduces another saying of Jesus: "Then he said to them, 'The sabbath was made for humankind, and not humankind for the sabbath.'" This states a general principle in accord with the legal precedent Jesus has just stated. Finally, the story ends with the statement, "So the Son of Man is lord even of the sabbath." In its present form, this means Jesus has authority over the Sabbath. This is a different point from that made by the preceding two.

Healings and Exorcisms

These are common in the Gospels. They illustrate Jesus' power. They generally consist of three parts. Someone comes to Jesus looking for a cure, Jesus cures him or her, and those present react with amazement, fear, praise, and so on. Such stories can be developed to address an issue beyond Jesus' healing abilities. For example, in Mark 2:1-12, a healing becomes the setting of a clash between Jesus and some scribes about Jesus' authority to forgive sins. Thus the miracle story becomes a controversy story.

Form Criticism: Miracle Story Turned into a Controversy (Mark 2:1-12)

Mark's Text as It Stands

2:1 When he returned to Capernaum after some days, it was reported that he was at home. 2:2 So many gathered around that there was no longer room for them, not even in front of the door; and he was speaking the word to them. 2:3 Then some people came, bringing to him a paralyzed man, carried by four of them. 2:4 And when they could not bring him to Jesus because of the crowd, they removed the roof above him; and after having dug through it, they let down the mat on which the paralytic lay. 2:5 When Jesus saw their faith,

Simple Healing Story

2:1 When he returned to Capernaum after some days, it was reported that he was at home. 2:2 So many gathered around that there was no longer room for them, not even in front of the door; and he was speaking the word to them. 2:3 Then some people came, bringing to him a paralyzed man, carried by four of them. 2:4 And when they could not bring him to Jesus because of the crowd, they removed the roof above him; and after having dug through it, they let down the mat on which the paralytic lay. 2:5 When Jesus saw their faith,

he said to the paralytic, "Son, your sins are forgiven." 2:6 Now some of the scribes were sitting there, questioning in their hearts, 2:7 "Why does this fellow speak in this way? It is blasphemy! Who can forgive sins but God alone?" 2:8 At once Jesus perceived in his spirit that they were discussing these questions among themselves; and he said to them, "Why do you raise such questions in your hearts? 2:9 Which is easier, to say to the paralytic, 'Your sins are forgiven,' or to say, 'Stand up

and take your mat and walk'?
2:10 But so that you may know
that the Son of Man has authority on earth to forgive sins"—

he said to the paralytic—2:11 "I
say to you, stand up, take your
mat and go to your home." 2:12
And he stood up, and immediately
took the mat and went out
before all of them; so that they
were all amazed and glorified
God, saying, "We have never
seen anything like this!"

he said to the paralytic—2:11
"I say to you, stand up, take
your mat and go to your home."
2:12 And he stood up, and immediately took the mat and went
out before all of them; so that
they were all amazed and
glorified God, saying, "We have
never seen anything like this!"

Nature Miracles

These are works of power that are not simply healings or exorcisms. They include raising the dead, walking on water, calming the sea, and multiplying loaves. We find the same basic threefold structure of the other miracles—preparation for the miracle by description of circum- stances, the miracle itself, reaction of witnesses.

Summaries

This is a different sort of form. It is not a unit of tradition passed down orally. Rather, it is a composition of the evangelist. Summaries are brief descriptions of Jesus' activity. As such, they are not, for example, miracle stories—that is, accounts of a specific miracle—but generalizations, such as, "He had cured many, so that all who had diseases pressed upon him to touch him" (Mark 3:10). Because they are generalizations, summaries reveal the authors' characteristic emphases.

The Importance of Form Criticism

Toward the beginning of the twentieth century, form critics thought that they could describe with great accuracy the development of the Jesus tradition in the period between Jesus and the writing of the Gospels. Most scholars are now more modest in their claims. However, form criticism retains its importance. First, it reminds us that there was a period of transmission of Jesus material before the writing of the Gospels. During this time, the church shaped the tradition in light of its own needs and views. This tells us a lot about the church, and it also makes it more difficult to reconstruct the historical Jesus. Second, it helps us to see how tradition is a living thing. It is dynamic and is transformed repeatedly over time. There is both continuity and discontinuity in the transmission process.

Form criticism also furnishes specific ways to read the tradition. The evangelists contextualize units of tradition by incorporating them into narratives that encourage certain interpretations. When we reverse this process, we see other possibilities. Luke wants us to read the parable of the Good Samaritan as an example story. Separated from Luke's context, the parable regains some of its earlier shock value and can fulfill its parabolic role of challenging human categories of the "other."

REDACTION CRITICISM

The 1950s saw the emergence of redaction criticism (see Bornkamm, Marxsen, Conzelmann). Redaction criticism is the detailed study of how writers use sources. The most fruitful use of the method is possible when the researcher possesses a document's sources. In the New Testament, this applies primarily to the Synoptic Gospels. Redaction critics observe how Matthew and Luke changed Mark and then make educated guesses about why they did so. The method assumes that Matthew and Luke adapted Mark to their own situations. Thus there is a good deal of emphasis on historical and social circumstances. For example, Matthew changed Mark to increase respect for Torah and to encourage observance of it. From that we deduce that Matthew may be a Jewish Christian, writing for a church in which Torah observance is a concern.

Redaction critics often use small alterations in the text as evidence of a point of view of the redactor. It is most powerful when the critic can demonstrate that a particular sort of change is systematic throughout a gospel. For example, in one study it was shown that Matthew methodically rewrites the miracle stories in Mark so the miraculous elements are abbreviated in favor of augmenting the interaction between Jesus and the petitioner (see Held). Further, Matthew is much more apt than Mark to have people call Jesus "Lord" and worship him and to have Jesus call God his Father. When a change is not an isolated instance but is part of a systematic rewriting apparent throughout the gospel, that becomes a powerful argument that the evangelist has deliberately rewritten tradition to convey a point.

Redaction criticism concentrates on how Matthew and Luke rewrite the parts of Mark that they incorporate into their Gospels, but other factors, such as whether the Markan material is juxtaposed with material not found in Mark, or whether Matthew or Luke rearrange the material in specific ways, are also relevant. At that point, redaction criticism shades into composition criticism.

Redaction criticism is best shown in action. We now look at the story of the calming of the storm as told in Mark and Matthew.

Matthew Redacts the Calming of the Storm

Mark 4:35-41	Matt 8:18-27
4:35 On that day, when evening had come, he said to them, "Let us go across to the other side."	8:18 Now when Jesus saw great crowds around him, he gave orders to go over to the other side.
	8:19 A scribe then approached and said, "Teacher, I will follow you wherever you go." 8:20 And Jesus said to him, "Foxes have holes, and birds of the air have nests; but the Son of Man has nowhere to lay his head." 8:21 Another of his disciples said to him, "Lord, first let me go and bury my father." 8:22 But Jesus said to him, "Follow me, and let the dead bury their own dead."
4:36 And leaving the crowd behind, they took him with them in the boat, just as he was.	8:23 And when he got into the boat, his disciples followed him.
Other boats were with him.	
4:37 A great windstorm arose, and the waves beat into the boat, so that the boat was already being swamped.	8:24 A windstorm arose on the sea, so great that the boat was being swamped by the waves;

4:38 But he was in the stern, asleep on the cushion; and they woke him up and said to him, "Teacher, do you not care that we are perishing?"	but he was asleep. 8:25 And they went and woke him up, saying, "Lord, save us! We are perishing!"
4:39 He woke up and rebuked the wind, and said to the sea, "Peace! Be still!" Then the wind ceased, and there was a dead calm. 4:40 He said to them, "Why are you afraid? Have you still no faith?"	8:26 And he said to them, "Why are you afraid, you of little faith?" Then he got up and rebuked the winds and the sea; and there was a dead calm.
4:41 And they were filled with great awe and said to one another, "Who then is this, that even the wind and the sea obey him?"	8:27 They were amazed, saying, "What sort of man is this, that even the winds and the sea obey him?"

In Mark, this is a story about Jesus' power. It is a nature miracle. It remains so in Matthew, but subtle changes transform it into a guide to discipleship as well. In Mark, Jesus says, "Let us go over to the other side." Matthew says "he gave orders" to that effect. Then Matthew inserts two sayings from Q concerning discipleship. When Jesus gets into the boat, Matthew says, "the disciples followed him," while in Mark they simply embark together. "To follow" is a common verb used throughout each of the Gospels to indicate discipleship. Matthew omits Mark's notice that there were other boats with them, for they play no role in the story and their presence is puzzling. When the disciples panic, Mark's Jesus concludes that they have "no faith," while Matthew's says that they have "little faith." Matthew thus retains Jesus' criticism of them without going as far as Mark does. In Mark the disciples call Jesus "teacher," and they suggest that he does not care about them. In Matthew the disciples call him "Lord" and utter a prayer: "Lord, save us!" In Mark Jesus calms the storm and then talks to them. In Matthew the order is reversed. The lesson is that one can pray to Jesus for deliverance in the midst of trouble.

Matthew also rewrites Mark's second boat scene, where Jesus walks on water, in similar fashion, making it too a guide to discipleship (Matt 14:22-33; Mark 6:45-52). There Matthew inserts the account of Peter walking on the water, not present in Mark. He does so to illustrate true discipleship. The sea is whipped up by a strong wind that scares Peter. He begins to sink and shouts, "Lord, save me!" Jesus does so but then criticizes him for his "little faith." The similarities in the way that Matthew rewrites Mark's versions of the sea miracles reveals that he does so deliberately, with the aim of reinforcing lessons about discipleship. In both stories the disciples are in trouble because of a storm at sea, in both they utter a prayer to Jesus, in both they have "little faith," and in both Jesus exercises awesome power to save them.

Lessons about discipleship are always appropriate. Matthew is concerned to help his fellow Christians weather troubles that they are encountering, troubles that many in the church find alarming. It is difficult, on the basis of these two stories alone, to be more specific about what situation such revisions might reflect. Analysis of the Gospel as a whole might suggest a possible scenario, such as that conflicts with local synagogue authorities are causing distress in the church.

Redaction criticism was a major step forward in gospel studies. Form critics concentrated on individual units of tradition, dissolving the gospel framework to salvage these units. Redaction criticism refocused attention on the Gospels as integral works and credited their authors with points of view expressed through their redactional activity. The evangelists did not just collect bits of tradition. They interpreted small units by bringing them into a larger construct and by rewriting them so as to fit the concerns and themes of that larger view.

COMPOSITION CRITICISM

Composition criticism is more broadly conceived than redaction criticism, although it assumes it. Composition criticism looks not only at how Matthew and Luke rewrite Mark, it also explores how each gospel was composed—what the broader structures are, how the materials are arranged, how sources are used in the gospel (kept as blocks or dispersed, for example), or what is the significance of sequences of stories.

LITERARY CRITICISM

In the past, literary criticism meant mainly form and redaction criticism. Now it is a broad category that includes all sorts of approaches. The most common form of literary criticism applied to the Gospels is narrative criticism. This includes analysis of such things as plot, characters, tone, point of view, devices such as flashbacks and foreshadowing, and dramatic irony. Most students will be familiar with this sort of criticism through analyses they have done of short stories and novels.

SOCIAL-SCIENTIFIC CRITICISM

The social sciences study societies. They look at individuals as members of groups and at groups as parts of larger societies. Both sociological and anthropological approaches shed light on the Gospels and other ancient literature. Cultural anthropology has been especially helpful in understanding ancient societies because anthropologists usually study societies other than their own. Similarly, the ancient society depicted within the Gospels' stories and the real societies within which the Gospels were written were very different from our own. Recent research in this area has stressed that our society is individualistic, whereas theirs defined people more in terms of groups, our society is largely urban while theirs was mostly rural, we tend to picture a large middle class, whereas most people in the ancient world were what we would consider rather poor, and so on.

THEOLOGICAL CRITICISM

Our discussion of hermeneutics above stresses the importance of author, text, and reader in interpretation. Theological criticism (sometimes called by the German name *Sachkritik*) assumes a variety of forms, but generally it attempts to discover what each text and the Bible as a whole has to say about God, Jesus, humanity, and the world. It does not take a fundamentalistic stance, but rather it distinguishes between the gospel as God's self-revelation, what Martin Luther called the "living voice of the gospel," and the concrete biblical texts, a distinction held by Martin Luther. We can again conceive of a conversation in which believers read in the light of their own faith, experience of the Spirit, and engagement in their own societies and historical circumstances. Such criticism resists taking the text as self-explanatory and absolute, but it also tries to avoid the trap of foisting one's own theology on Scripture and refusing to listen to the text. It understands that the text is a product of historically conditioned persons and circumstances, but it recognizes its ability to transcend those circumstances to speak to readers through the centuries.

LIBERATIONIST APPROACHES

The 1960s saw the birth of liberation theology in Latin America. In 1972, Gustavo Gutiérrez published his influential book *Teología de la*

Liberación. Liberation theology has since become a worldwide movement influential in First World countries as well. Liberation theology bases itself on a particular reading of the Bible. It is convinced that the biblical God in both testaments is a champion of the poor and oppressed. This theology advocates activism to change oppressive structures and so transform the world in concrete ways. Liberationist biblical scholarship unmasks the sinful structures inscribed in the Bible itself, and it also finds in the Bible's pages resources for human liberation. God's freeing of the Israelites from bondage in Egypt, portrayed in Exodus, is paradigmatic for God's action throughout the Bible. Jesus brings liberation from all that oppresses humans (physical illness, poverty, political oppression) and preaches a coming kingdom characterized by social justice.

AFRICAN AMERICAN CRITICISM

The term *liberationist* can apply to any readings of the Bible whose aim is to marshal religious resources in the service of human liberation. The civil rights movement sees the biblical God as an ally in the struggle for justice for African Americans. African American readings of the Bible spring from a combination of black experience in America, the role of the church in the life of the community, and attention to the Bible as a sacred text that gives meaning to the struggle for freedom and dignity.

FEMINIST CRITICISM

Feminist biblical criticism began at the end of the nineteenth century with Elizabeth Cady Stanton. She reasoned that since the Bible is the foundation of Western law, feminist interpretation of the Bible was necessary to reform legal systems that deprived women of full citizenship. Feminist scholarship is not one thing but many. What joins together various approaches are the basic insights that sprang originally from examining views of women in both the biblical texts themselves and in biblical interpretation within the churches and the academy. Generally, feminist scholars seek to disclose structures of oppression contained within the biblical texts and in the societies and churches that produced these texts, to recover aspects of women's history and women's contributions to the early Christian churches, and to reread biblical texts in the interest of justice for women.

Feminist readings have unmasked structures of patriarchy (domination and control of males over females) and androcentricity (a male-biased way of looking at things in which the male is the "ideal" human). But the focus of feminists has not been narrow. Rather, most feminist scholars have broadened their concerns to attend to all instances of the use of power—political, social, and economic—to privilege one group in society over others. They have also done justice to the fact that women are not a monolithic group. Women are rich and poor, belong to all ethnic groups, live in rich and poor countries, form part of all socio-politico-economic classes, and subscribe to the full range of possible worldviews. Feminist criticism is not a finished project but an ongoing process.

POSTCOLONIAL CRITICISM

Not long ago, much of the world lived under the control of European colonial powers. Those powers were Christian, and so they found in the Bible justification for their domination of the world. Although it is no longer fashionable to use the Bible to rationalize one country's control over another, practitioners of this mode of criticism pay special attention to the effects of colonialism on both the colonized and the colonizer. They question Western assumptions about history, the biblical text, Western ways of interpreting the Bible, and the identification of the core of Christianity with theologies and philosophies that originate in the cultures of the colonizers. Such interpreters do not necessarily demand that other biblical scholars abandon more traditional approaches to the text, but they call for them to do so in a global context, one that takes into account the experience of previously colonized parts of the world. The way a peasant in South America might read the Gospels could be quite different from how an affluent citizen of the United States who has graduated from an elite institution might. Professional interpreters of the Bible, who in the United States are more apt to belong to the latter category, would profit from investigating how Jesus' words might be read as a critique of their own privilege, for example.

POSTMODERN CRITICISMS

The term *postmodern* indicates that this sort of criticism defines itself in contrast to "modern" biblical criticism, particularly criticism that sees itself as objective, scientific, and as able to disclose the one, true meaning of a text. Postmodern criticism sees traditional criticism as standing between reader and text in a way that preserves power for the professional interpreter. Scholars construct systems that seem "scientific" in a modernistic sense, meaning that the development and refinement of proper tools will allow interpreters to attain accurate and final knowledge of the text. Postmodern interpreters do not necessary condemn established criticisms as illegitimate in themselves, but they question claims of exclusive expertise in saying what texts mean. These critics pride themselves on being open to a plurality of approaches to the text, unfettered by rules of the academy. They turn reason back on itself and show that assumptions of objectivity and "scientific" reasoning, especially in the humanities and social sciences, are often naive and overly optimistic with respect to their abilities to arrive at truth. Postmodern critics emphasize the self-reflexive and socially constructed nature of all human knowledge. In other words, no matter how hard we try to arrive at objective truth through solid evidence and scientific methods, we are always limited by many factors—particular worldviews, social convictions, historical circumstances. Postmodernist criticism is a constant reminder of the limits of human reason and of critical methods.

THIS BOOK'S METHODOLOGIES

This book's approach can best be termed eclectic. Indeed, most interpretations of the Bible are to some degree eclectic, drawing on a variety of approaches and methods. Few adhere to one method to the exclusion of all others. Our treatment of the texts is generally historical-critical, relying mainly on insights drawn from source, form, redaction, and literary criticism, but it will also be informed to some degree by social-scientific and feminist criticism.

It is perhaps inevitable that my reading of the Gospels will be influenced by my being a twenty-first-century American male, Catholic, trained originally in what this chapter has described as traditional methods of source, form, redaction, and literary criticism, whose basic paradigm in approaching these texts is an historical one. I often use the pronouns *us* and *we* because I picture readers accompanying me on the investigative journey presented in these pages. There are times I assume a certain commonality of circumstance between myself and my readers, for example, when I describe differences between today's world and that of the gospel writers. That approach has its limits, of course. To the extent that readers find themselves approaching the text from a different social location, I can only hope that the resulting tension between this book and its readers contributes to a better understanding of the Gospels and of how they might be read.

BIBLIOGRAPHY

Achtemeier, Paul J. "Toward the Isolation of Pre-Markan Miracle Catenae." *JBL* 89 (1970): 265-91.

———. "Mark, Gospel of." *ABD* 4:541-57.

Adam, A. K. M. *What Is Postmodern Biblical Criticism?* Minneapolis: Fortress, 1985.

Bornkamm, Günther, Gerhard Barth, and Heinz Joachim Held. *Tradition and Interpretation in Matthew*. Philadelphia: Westminster, 1963.

Brenner, Athalya, and Carole Fontaine, eds. *A Feminist Companion to Reading the Bible: Approaches, Methods and Strategies*. Sheffield: Sheffield Academic Press, 1997.

Bultmann, Rudolf. *History of the Synoptic Tradition*. New York: Harper & Row, 1963. First published in German in 1921.

Burridge, Richard A. *What Are the Gospels? A Comparison with Graeco-Roman Biography*. New York: Cambridge University Press, 1992.

Coggins, R. J., and J. L. Houlden, eds. *A Dictionary of Biblical Interpretation*. Philadelphia: Trinity, 1990.

Conzelmann, Hans. *The Theology of St. Luke*. Philadelphia: Fortress, 1961.

Crossan, John Dominic. "The Good Samaritan: Towards a Generic Definition of Parable." *Semeia* 2 (1974): 82-112.

Dibelius, Martin. *From Tradition to Gospel*. New York: Scribner, 1965. First published in German in 1919.

Dodd, C. H. *The Parables of the Kingdom*. New York: Scribner, 1961.

Donahue, John. *Are You the Christ?: The Trial Narrative in the Gospel of Mark*. Missoula, Mont.: Society of Biblical Literature for the Seminar on Mark, 1973.

Elliott, John H. *What Is Social-Scientific Criticism?* Minneapolis: Fortress, 1993.

Fowler, A. *Kinds of Literature: An Introduction to the Theory of Genres and Modes*. Cambridge, Mass.: Harvard University Press, 1982.

Gadamer, Hans-Georg. *Truth and Method*, 2d ed. New York: Continuum, 1994.

Gamble, Harry Y. *Books and Readers in the Early Church: A History of Early Christian Texts*. New Haven: Yale University Press, 1995.

Harrington, Daniel J. *Interpreting the New Testament: A Practical Guide*. Collegeville, Minn.: Liturgical, 1979.

Hayes, John H., ed. *Dictionary of Biblical Interpretation*. Nashville: Abingdon, 1999.

Heidegger, Martin. *Being and Time*. New York: Harper, 1962.

Held, Heinz Joachim. "Matthew as Interpreter of the Miracle Stories." Pages 165-299 in Bornkamm, Günther, Gerhard Barth, and Heinz Joachim Held. *Tradition and Interpretation in Matthew*. Philadelphia: Westminster, 1963.

Iser, Wolfgang. *The Act of Reading: A Theory of Aesthetic Response*. Baltimore: Johns Hopkins University Press, 1980.

Koester, Helmut. *Ancient Christian Gospels: Their History and Development.* Philiadelphia: Trinity, 1990.

Marxsen, Willi. *Mark the Evangelist.* Nashville: Abingdon, 1969.

McKnight, Edgar V. *What Is Form Criticism?* Philadelphia: Fortress, 1969.

Perrin, Norman. *What Is Redaction Criticism?* Philadelphia: Fortress, 1969.

Ricoeur, Paul. *Essays on Biblical Interpretation.* Ed. Lewis S. Mudge. Philadelphia: Fortress, 1980.

Robinson, James M., John S. Kloppenborg, and Paul Hoffmann, eds. *The Critical Edition of Q.* Minneapolis: Fortress, 2000.

Schneiders, Sandra M. *The Revelatory Text: Interpreting the New Testament as Sacred Scripture.* San Francisco: HarperSanFrancisco, 1991.

Schottroff, Luise. *Let the Oppressed Go Free: Feminist Perspectives on the New Testament.* Louisville: Westminster John Knox, 1993.

Schüssler Fiorenza, Elisabeth. *In Memory of Her: A Feminist Theological Reconstruction of Christian Origins.* New York: Crossroad, 1983.

———. "Feminist Hermeneutics." *ABD* 2:783-91.ßß

———. *Searching the Scriptures: A Feminist Introduction.* 2 vols. New York: Crossroad Publishing Company, 1993–1994.

Scott, Bernard Brandon. *Hear Then the Parable: A Commentary on the Parables of Jesus.* Minneapolis: Fortress, 1989.

Segovia, Fernando, and Mary Ann Tolbert, eds. *Reading from This Place: Social Location and Biblical Interpretation.* 2 vols. Minneapolis: Fortress, 1995.

Sugirtharajah, R. S. *Postcolonial Criticism and Biblical Interpretation.* New York: Oxford University Press, 2002.

Talbert, Charles. *What Is a Gospel? The Genre of the Canonical Gospels.* Philadephia: Fortress, 1977.

Wills, Lawrence. *The Quest of the Historical Gospel: Mark, John, and the Origins of the Gospel Genre.* New York: Routledge, 1997.

Wimbush, Vincent L., ed. *African Americans and the Bible: Sacred Texts and Social Textures.* New York: Continuum, 2000.

——— *The Bible and African Americans: A Brief History.* Minneapolis: Fortress, 2003.

Yarbro Collins, Adela. "Is Mark's Gospel a Life of Jesus? The Question of Genre." Pages 1-38 in *The Beginning of the Gospel: Probings of Mark in Context.* Minneapolis: Fortress, 1992.

CHAPTER TWO

RECONSTRUCTING ANCIENT WORLDS: GOSPEL CONTEXTS

The Gospels were written almost two thousand years ago in the Eastern Mediterranean region, an area including territory today the site of the countries of Israel, Syria, Lebanon, Turkey, Greece, and Egypt. It is possible that Mark's Gospel was written in Rome, which had extended its hegemony to the east. The Gospels come from a world very different from our own. They tell of people, places, and institutions we have never directly encountered. And yet many of us feel quite at home with the Gospels. When we hear or read them, we do not experience them as foreign. We have grown so used to them that they have become part of our own world. We have assimilated them. In a sense, we have tamed them. They seem fully at home in the twenty-first century and completely harmonious with our way of looking at life, at religion, and at Jesus.

Our comfort with the Gospels is due not just to our familiarity with them but also with their nature as "classics," as literature that reaches across the ages and addresses concerns common to ancient and modern people in ways that survive vast differences in culture, worldview, and historical circumstances. It is also due to their nature as "revelatory texts," writings that have proved their ability to mediate God's presence and serve as a foundation for individual and communal faith.

Given all this, why subject the Gospels to analysis? Doesn't this just detract from their religious value? Ultimately, historical study need not undermine such realizations of the texts in our present. The mainstream churches have found that it actually enriches such realizations. Use of Scripture for religious purposes today gains, not loses, from a deeper understanding of the texts in their original environments. Application of Scripture can then come from a true dialogue between ancient and modern meanings, even to some extent between ancient and modern believers.

Historical study aims to illuminate meanings of the texts in their original contexts. To do that, we study the original languages in their original contexts. We ask what the words, symbols, ideas, and stories meant to their original writers and readers. And to begin to get at that, we need also to have some appreciation of history. When the Gospels speak of Pharisees, how much do we know about that group? When they talk of Jesus going to the temple, just what do we think the temple is and what does it represent? When Jesus and his contemporaries argue over Torah, do we fully comprehend what Torah is, by what principles they make their arguments, and why they might disagree? So we begin our study with a brief sketch of some things we need to begin to understand if we are to pursue our study.

We must consider at least two levels of history. One has to do with the story world of the text—the Jewish world of Judea, Samaria, and Galilee around the year 30 C.E. The other is the context in which the Gospels themselves were written. These two levels have things in common—in both cases we are speaking of the Hellenistic world, for example, and in both Rome is the absolute political power. However, the cosmopolitan, Greek-speaking cities in places like Syria, Asia Minor, and the Italian peninsula that have been suggested as the venues for the evangelists were quite different in many ways from the rural Galilean countryside and the small villages and towns that provide the setting for much of the gospel stories.

THE BIBLICAL STORY

Almost every verse of the New Testament assumes knowledge of the persons, events, institutions, and symbols in Israel's history and religion. Jesus was Jewish, as were his disciples and the earliest Christians. Early Christians believed Jesus to be the Jewish Messiah (see below for the meaning of *messiah*). They regarded Jewish Scripture as their Bible. They considered Israel's history to be Christianity's prehistory and the preparation for Jesus' advent. Israel's prophets foretold Jesus, according to them. The story of Jesus and the church was the continuation of the great narrative of salvation history begun with Abraham and continued through Moses and David. Wherever one looks in early Christianity, one encounters Judaism.

We begin our study with a whirlwind tour of Israel's story. Almost two thousand years of history in a couple of pages! Obviously, we must abbreviate a bit. In fact, quite a lot. We also pass over inconsistencies and problems in the text. We aim simply to outline the main storyline of Israel. Whether or not the narrative corresponds fully to what actually happened is not our concern here. Jews and Christians of the first century would not question the texts concerning their historical accuracy. For them, there is no distinction between sacred story and actual history. In what follows, we touch on only those points necessary for understanding the Gospels.

The first book of the Bible, Genesis, begins with creation (Gen 1–2). God's Spirit hovers over formless waters. God brings order to this formlessness. God restricts the primeval waters and creates dry land for earth creatures and space above the earth for flying creatures. God creates living creatures for each of the resultant realms—earth, sea, and sky. God separates light and darkness to create day and night, places the sun, moon, and stars in the firmament, and finally forms the first human beings, Adam and Eve. God puts the humans in the Garden of Eden, an idyllic place where all is as it should be, as God intended it to be. But human sin mars the picture. Adam and Eve disobey God's command not to eat of the tree of the knowledge of good and evil (Gen 3). God banishes them from the garden, sentencing them to suffering and death. This is called humanity's fall.

Genesis tells of humanity's growing wickedness leading to its destruction through the flood sent by God (Gen 6–9). Noah survives because he is righteous. God tells him to build an ark (a large boat) to save himself, his family, and animals to repopulate the earth later. After the flood recedes, they emerge from the ark to begin history anew. But the wickedness of humans reappears when they build a tower in Babel to try to reach the sky and challenge God's sovereignty (Gen 11). God divides the single human language into many languages and disperses humans over the face of the earth to prevent another such attempt.

Against the background of human disobedience, God chooses Abraham and Sarah as progenitors of a new nation to be God's own (Gen 12). God promises Abraham land, numerous progeny, and that the nations will bless themselves through him. God overcomes Sarah's age and infertility to give them a son, Isaac, and Isaac's wife Rebekah gives birth to Jacob. The relationship between God and Abraham and Abraham's offspring is later called a *covenant*, an agreement (Gen 15:18).

In Gen 17, God requires circumcision as a symbol of the covenant. Jacob (whose name is eventually changed to Israel) begets twelve sons and a daughter. God overcomes infertility in the case of Rebekah, Jacob's wife Rachel, and perhaps Jacob's wife Leah. The descendants of the twelve sons become Israel's twelve tribes. Benjamin is the youngest, and Joseph the next youngest. The ten oldest brothers sell Joseph into slavery because they are jealous of Jacob's love for him (Gen 37–50). Joseph is brought to Egypt and distinguishes himself there, becoming the Pharaoh's right-hand man. (The Pharaoh is the Egyptian king.) Joseph eventually brings his entire family to live in Egypt.

Hundreds of years later, another Pharaoh enslaves Israel, subjecting them to hard labor (Exod 1–2). When the Israelite population grows, the Pharaoh commands that their male newborns be killed because he fears their increasing strength. The newborn Moses escapes when his mother places him in a basket on the Nile, and he is found by Pharaoh's daughter, who raises him as her own. But Moses does not forget his roots. He defends an Israelite from an Egyptian overseer and then flees to the desert near Mount Sinai (Exod 2). There God appears to him and commands him to return to Egypt and lead his people to freedom (Exod 3). Pharaoh is reluctant to lose his free labor, but God, through Moses, coerces him by sending ten plagues, the last of which is the killing of all the firstborn of Egypt, human and animal alike (Exod 7–12). God saves Israel from the last plague by having them daub their doorways with the blood of a lamb, thereby warding off the angel of death. Pharaoh changes his mind and pursues Israel. When they are trapped between the desert and the Red Sea, God parts the sea, allowing Israel to escape. The Egyptians follow, but God brings the sea back and drowns them (Exod 14–15). This episode is called the *exodus*, from the Greek word meaning a "going out." God commands a yearly feast, Passover, to commemorate the event.

Israel travels to Mount Sinai in the desert. There a covenant (formal agreement) is formed between God and Israel (Exod 19–Num 10). God promises to be Israel's God, protecting them and bringing them success and prosperity, if they will obey his Law (in Hebrew, *torah*). The people agree, and God gives them the Torah through Moses, who ascends Mount Sinai to receive it. The covenant is sealed in a ceremony in which Moses sprinkles sacrificial blood on the people and on the altar, creating a bond between Israel and God (Exod 24). God commands Moses to construct an ark, a traveling shrine consisting mainly of a box to contain the tablets of the Law. God designates the tribe of Levi to be the priestly tribe, to serve God at the altar where animals are sacrificed to God. Aaron becomes the first priest and the first head priest. Later priests will sometimes be called the sons of Aaron.

As head priest, Aaron is anointed, meaning that oil is put on his head. The word *messiah* is from Hebrew and Aramaic and means "anointed one." In ancient Israel, anointing with oil meant being set apart for a specific task, and being empowered to perform that task. Most commonly, kings and high priests were anointed. The prophet Isaiah says that he was anointed by God's Spirit (61:1).

Israel leaves Sinai and God leads them through the desert to the land of Canaan, located between the Mediterranean Sea and the Jordan River (Num 10–14). God intends to lead the people into the land, displacing its inhabitants before them. When Israel shows lack of confidence in God, God condemns them to forty years of wandering in the desert. There they undergo many trials and experience God's support and forgiveness repeatedly (Num 15–36). Most memorable are God's gift of water and food. The food comes in the form of manna, a miraculous food.

Moses dies within sight of Canaan without entering it himself. Before he dies he delivers a long sermon reminding Israel of all God has done for them and urging them to obey God's Law. The long sermon constitutes the book of Deuteronomy. We have just recapitulated the story line of "the Torah" defined as the first five books of the Bible—Genesis, Exodus, Leviticus, Numbers, and Deuteronomy. These books encompass the essential elements of the relationship between God and Israel—history, election, Law, worship. Later rabbinic thought considers the rest of the Bible a commentary on this Torah. (The rabbis were Jewish teachers who flourished after the destruction of the Jerusalem temple by the Romans in 70 C.E. and who gradually transformed Judaism.) Over the centuries, Torah as a symbol expands, taking in the rest of the Bible, oral tradition that eventually assumes written form in the rabbinic texts beginning in about 200 C.E., and ultimately Jewish life as a whole insofar as it embodies God's will for Israel.

Israel enters the land under Moses' successor, Joshua, and comes to control most of it (book of Joshua). They consider it a gift from God. Texts such as Deuteronomy insist that possession of the land depends on obedience to God's Law. After a couple of centuries of loose tribal federation under leaders called *judges* (book of Judges), God establishes the monarchy (1 Sam 8–10). Samuel, a transitional figure between the judges and the kings and the one who anoints Israel's first kings, is born when

God overcomes his mother Hannah's infertility (1 Sam 1–2). Saul is the first king, but his son does not succeed him. Instead, David becomes king and following him, his son Solomon (1 Sam 16). God calls Solomon "son of God" (2 Sam 7:14). Only under David and Solomon are all twelve tribes united, and David's reign is later remembered as a golden age. David conquers Jerusalem, makes it his capital, and brings the ark of the covenant there to symbolize God's presence (2 Sam 6). Solomon builds a temple for the ark on Mount Zion in Jerusalem (1 Kgs 5–8). Solomon's chief priest is Zadok. Throughout the history of the monarchy, God raises up prophets whose message is often critical of the kings. Except for several decades during the sixth century B.C.E., the temple stands in Jerusalem for around a thousand years. It is the religious and political center not just for inhabitants of the surrounding Jewish area but for all Jews wherever they might be in the world.

At Solomon's death, the kingdom splits into two kingdoms, Israel to the north and Judah to the south (1 Kgs 12). The Davidic dynasty rules the south. Nine (or ten, depending on the source) of the twelve tribes belong to the northern kingdom. In the eighth century B.C.E. the expanding Assyrian Empire gobbles up the north and exiles its people. The way the southern sources, preserved in the Bible, tell the story, those tribes are lost, to be restored only in some future, idyllic age (2 Kgs 17). The Bible contains prophetic predictions that ultimately God will restore and unite all twelve tribes. The Assyrians, again according to the southern version, resettle the northern kingdom with foreigners who adopted the Torah. Their center is in the former royal city of Samaria, therefore we know them as Samaritans. The Samaritans themselves (some still exist) see themselves as the legitimate descendants of the citizens of the northern kingdom. They build a temple on Mount Gerizim.

In the sixth century B.C.E., Jerusalem and its temple are destroyed by the Babylonians, and its most prominent citizens are exiled to Babylonia (2 Kgs 24–25). Within a couple of generations, the Persians conquer the Babylonians and allow the Judahites to return and rebuild Jerusalem and the temple. Returning exiles build the temple between 520 and 515 B.C.E. Persian authorities do not allow them to reinstitute the monarchy (Ezra 1–6). This is the beginning of the Second Temple period. It ends in 70 C.E., when the Romans destroy the Jerusalem temple. Scholars usually reserve the term *Israelite* to apply to all of Israel during the period before the Babylonian exile, especially the time before the fall of the northern kingdom, and *Jew* and *Jewish*, which

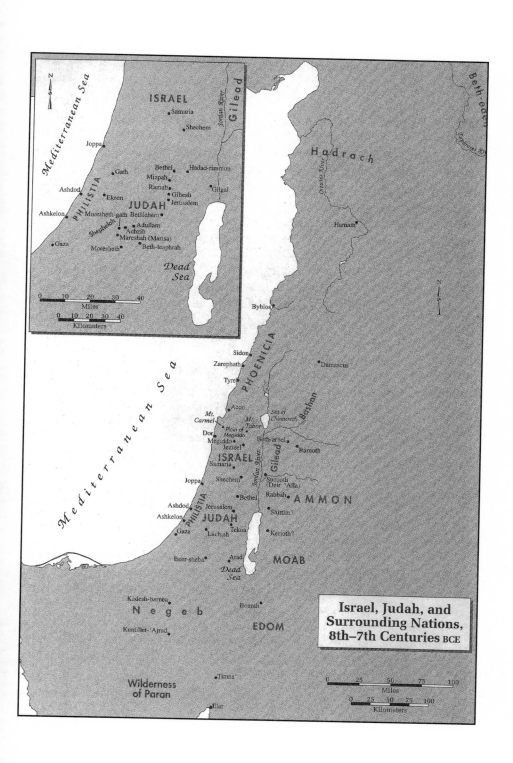

ISRAEL

Samaria
Shechem

Gilead

Jordan River

Mediterranean Sea

Joppa

Bethel   Hadad-rimmon
Mizpah
Ramah   Gigal
Gath
Ashdod   Ekron   Gibeah
Jerusalem
PHILISTIA   JUDAH
Ashkelon   Moresheth-gath Bethlehem
Moresheth-gath
Shephelah   Adullam
Achzib
Gaza   Mareshah (Marisa)
Moresheth   Beth-leaphrah

Dead
Sea

N

0 10   20   30   40
Miles
0 10 20 30 40
Kilometers

Beth-eden

Hadrach

Orontes River

Euphrates Ri

Hamath

Byblos

Mediterranean Sea

Sidon
Zarephath   Damascus
Tyre
PHOENICIA

Acco
Mt.   Mt.
Carmel   Tabor   Sea of
Chinnereth
Dor   Plain of   Bashan
Megiddo
Megiddo   Beth-arbel
Jezreel   Gilead   Ramoth
ISRAEL
Samaria
Joppa   Shechem   Succoth
(Deir 'Alla)
Bethel   Rabbah   AMMON
Ashdod   Jerusalem
Ashkelon   PHILISTIA   Shittim?
Gaza   JUDAH
Lachish   Tekoa
Kerioth?
Beer-sheba   Arad
MOAB
Dead
Sea

Kadesh-barnea
Bozrah
N e g e b
Kuntillet-'Ajrud   EDOM

N

Israel, Judah, and
Surrounding Nations,
8th–7th Centuries BCE

Mediterranean Sea

Wilderness
of Paran
Timna

0   25   50   75   100
Miles
0   25   50   75   100
Kilometers

Elat

derive from "Judah," for the period after the exile. *Judahite* is a term appropriate for the southern kingdom after the split between the northern and southern kingdoms and for the province of Judah during the Persian period.

During the Persian period, the Jews who remain in Babylonia wield influence in Judahite affairs. Priests and scribes in Babylonia collect Israel's sacred stories, epics, and laws and construct literary works that become the core of the Hebrew Bible (the Jewish Scriptures). Ezra the scribe brings to Judah part of the results of that work, probably the first five books of the Hebrew Bible (Ezra 7; Neh 8). Those five books are the Torah. The Hebrew word *torah* means "instruction," or sometimes "law." Greek sources, including the ancient Greek translation of the Bible, called the Septuagint, translate it as *nomos*, Greek for "law." The Torah, however, contains more than laws. It contextualizes the laws that God gives Moses on Sinai in a narrative beginning with creation, stretching through the flood and Noah, to the election of Abraham, the story of his descendants, their sojourn in Egypt and escape at the exodus, their covenant with God at Sinai, their wanderings in the desert, and their approach to the land of Canaan.

Between 333 and 323 B.C.E., Alexander the Great conquers the Persian Empire, including Jewish lands. This initiates the Hellenistic period. Alexander's conquest entails not just military and political changes for the eastern Mediterranean, it also causes cultural changes. Greek becomes the lingua franca of the eastern Mediterranean, and Greek philosophy, religion, architecture, and institutions exert great influence over the peoples of a vast area. New cultural mixes arise throughout the Mediterranean region and the Middle East, resulting from the interaction of Greek culture with local cultures. This process is called *Hellenization*. This is especially prominent in the cities.

Judah falls under the rule first of Alexander and then of his successors. At Alexander's death, his realm is divided between several of his generals. Two found dynasties of particular importance to Israel, one in Syria with its capital in Antioch, called the Seleucid dynasty, and another in Egypt with its capital in Alexandria, called the Ptolemaic dynasty. Judah falls first under the Ptolemies, and then around 200 B.C.E. it comes under the sway of the Seleucids. Many in the Jewish community see Hellenistic culture and politics as a threat, though some embrace them.

In 175 B.C.E., some Jewish priests in Jerusalem try to turn Jerusalem into a Greek city, enhancing the status of Jews and of themselves in the Hellenistic world (1–2 Maccabees found in the Catholic Old Testament and in the Apocrypha of many Protestant Bibles). Because many oppose this engagement with Greek culture, this results in struggles within the Jewish community, with the eventual outcome that the Seleucid emperor, Antiochus IV, outlaws and persecutes Judaism. The persecution sparks a successful Jewish revolt in 167 B.C.E. resulting in Jewish independence lasting about a century. The priestly family leading the revolt is known by the nickname of its most famous warrior, Judah, called Maccabee, which means "hammer." The family becomes a dynasty called the Hasmoneans. Judah recaptures the temple and rededicates it. To commemorate the event, the feast of Hanukkah (Hebrew for "dedication") is instituted.

Three important Jewish groups came into being during this period—Sadducees, Pharisees, and Essenes. Most think that it was the Essenes who collected the library known as the Dead Sea Scrolls, discovered in caves along the shore of the Dead Sea beginning in 1947.

In 63 B.C.E., two Jewish pretenders to the throne appeal to the Roman general Pompey to settle their dispute. Pompey's intervention leads to the incorporation of Judah into the Roman Empire. Its Latin name is Judea. The word *Jew* comes from "Judah" and "Judea." Not long afterward, Jesus of Nazareth is born. We discuss the Roman Empire in the next section.

The following is but a partial list of ways in which this history plays into our study of the Gospels.

Jewish Scripture and History and Early Christianity

- Jewish Scripture was the word of God for early Christians. They therefore legitimated Christianity by appeal to Torah, the prophets, the psalms, and other sacred literature.
- Jesus was pictured in conflict with the religious groups and authorities of his day—Pharisees, Sadducees, priests, scribes, and elders.
- Many of Jesus' conflicts with the authorities assumed the form of arguments over Torah.
- Jesus was interpreted in terms of Jewish hopes and expectations. Titles such as "Son of David," "Messiah," "Son of God," and "Son of Man" all have their roots in such hope.

- Jesus lived his life under Roman rule. Ultimately, the Roman prefect Pontius Pilate executed him for crimes against Rome.
- Early Christians had to take up some position vis-à-vis Judaism. Some did not consider Christianity a new religion, some thought that Christianity had surpassed Judaism, and some took up positions in between.
- Apocalypticism, so important in many Jewish texts of the late Second Temple period, permeates New Testament texts. Apocalyptic scenarios of the end-time sometimes anticipate the restoration of idyllic conditions on earth, like those that existed before the fall.
- Basic Jewish symbols, traditions, and institutions were taken over and transformed by Christians—for example, exodus, Passover, prophecy, Torah, descent from Abraham, hopes for restoration of the twelve tribes, hopes for restoration of the Davidic monarchy, and so on.
- Jerusalem, as center of Judaism, played a crucial role in Jesus' life. He is executed when he clashes with its priestly elite. After his death, the Jerusalem church is very important in the early church's life.
- Mary's virginity and her kinswoman Elizabeth's infertility are foreshadowed by the infertility of mothers of key figures in the Hebrew Bible.
- The fact that Jesus had twelve apostles derives from the hope that all twelve Israelite tribes will one day be restored.
- Loss of the monarchy led to hopes for a future royal messiah that were used to interpret Jesus.
- The Samaritans, who appear in the Gospels, derive ultimately from the split of the Israelite kingdom into north and south and the subsequent exile of the northern kingdom.
- The Gospels are in Greek, lingua franca of the eastern Mediterranean since the conquests of Alexander the Great.
- The Gospels were influenced by Greek oral and literary forms, since Judaism and then Christianity were part of the Hellenistic world.
- Jewish categories for understanding Jesus had already been influenced by Greek models and thought.
- The spread of Christianity was deeply affected by the cultural effects of Hellenism and political and social arrangements arising from Roman rule.

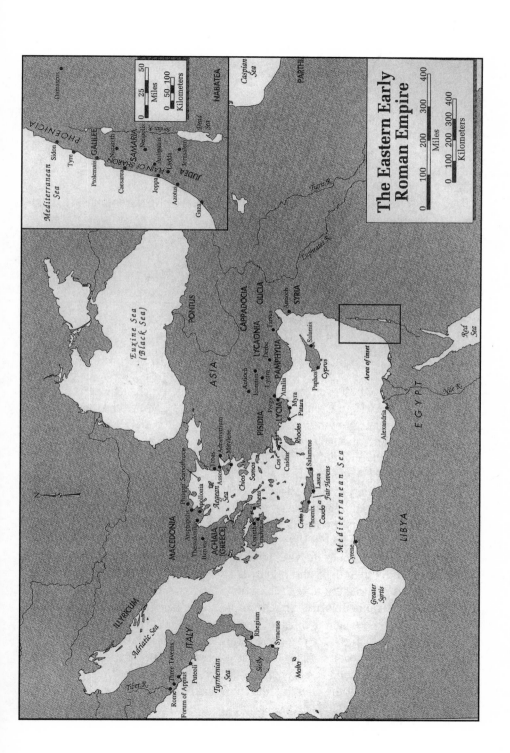

THE ROMAN EMPIRE

Our sources for the first century C.E. are not plentiful. Most important are the extensive writings of Josephus, a Jerusalem priest born in 37 C.E. who participates in some of the events he narrates and who becomes a client of the Roman imperial family, the Flavians (Vespasian, Titus, and Domitian). Thus we use the Latinized form of his name and often call him Flavius Josephus. The New Testament yields historical information when used critically. Rabbinic documents, although they are easily misused since they come from a later period and assume far different conditions from those that held in the Second Temple period, are sometimes helpful. Finally, we have noncanonical Jewish documents that are referred to collectively as the Pseudepigrapha ("false writings" in the sense that they are fictitiously attributed to earlier Jewish heroes).

By the time the Romans annexed it, Jewish Palestine had been under foreign rule for centuries. It was a colonized area. The Romans ruled through local elites when possible. After around twenty years of trying to administer Judea and surrounding areas through the Hasmoneans, the Romans turned to a non-Hasmonean, Herod the Great. Herod hailed from Idumea, an area south of Judea that the Maccabees forcibly converted to Judaism in the second century B.C.E. Herod's father, Antipater, had been a general for a Hasmonean high priest and was for a time Roman administrator of Jewish Palestine. Herod proved capable when his father gave him authority over Galilee. The Roman Senate appointed him king in 40 B.C.E. He died in 4 B.C.E., after a long and politically repressive reign. Jesus was born toward the end of his rule.

When Herod died, repressed resentment erupted in uprisings around the country. Varus, Roman governor of Syria, mercilessly crushed them, crucifying thousands of rebels. Following military victory, the Romans divided Herod's territory among his three sons. They denied them the title of king, instead calling them *tetrarchs* (literally, "ruler of a fourth"). Philip took land north of Galilee, Archelaus received Judea, and Herod Antipas acquired Galilee, Trachonitis, and an area east of the Jordan River called Perea, site of John the Baptist's baptizing. John was a Jewish prophetic figure of the first century C.E. Herod Antipas arrested and beheaded the Baptist. Antipas administered the area until deposed by the Romans in 39 B.C.E. Since Jesus was born and raised in Galilee and carried on most of his public work there, he fell under the jurisdiction of

Herod Antipas. Luke mentions a trial of Jesus before Herod Antipas (23:6-12).

Archelaus's rule in Judea was unsuccessful. The Romans removed him in 6 C.E. and began to rule the area directly through prefects. Prefects were Roman citizens who administered local areas that did not qualify as full provinces. The prefects enlisted the help of the local aristocracy— Jerusalem's priestly establishment—following usual Roman governing practice. The prefect lived in Caesarea, a city on the coast rebuilt in Hellenistic fashion by Herod the Great and named after Caesar. They went to Jerusalem when necessary, such as during the volatile feast of Passover. When the Romans began direct rule, one of their first acts was to conduct a census for purposes of taxation. It is probably this census that Luke mistakenly has in mind when he speaks of Jesus' birth. The census provoked further opposition, which was soon quashed.

The infamous Pontius Pilate, who condemned Jesus to death, administered Judea from 26 to 36 C.E. Pilate was ruthless. Eventually his brutality motivated the emperor Tiberius to remove and exile him. The high priest at the time was Caiaphas, who held that position from 18 to 36 C.E. The coincidence of Caiaphas's and Pilate's terms of office indicates that they worked well together. This is not necessarily a criticism of Caiaphas. Roman rule was oppressive, but it was worse when local leaders did not cooperate with imperial administrators.

These basic political and geographical facts have an impact on the gospel story. When Jesus passed from Galilee to Judea, he moved from one political jurisdiction to another. His activities in Galilee apparently did not incur the ire of Herod Antipas (but see Luke 13:31). When he went to Jerusalem and confronted the Jerusalem establishment, he placed himself in jeopardy. Since the priests were part of the ruling mechanism of the Romans, and since the Roman prefect was in Jerusalem for Passover, he made himself vulnerable. That explains why he died on a cross, a Roman form of execution, at Pilate's order.

Resistance to Roman rule in Jewish Palestine took various forms (see Horsley). The Jews resorted to armed rebellion when Herod died (4 B.C.E.), and again in 66 C.E. when they initiated a war that resulted in the destruction of Jerusalem and its temple in 70 C.E. and the capture of the fortress of Masada in 74 C.E. Between those two uprisings, there were other sorts of protests. A tax rebellion took place in 6 C.E., when Archelaus was deposed and the Romans began to administer Judea directly. The rebellion consisted of refusal by some to pay taxes and does not seem to have been an armed uprising. In 36 C.E., a Samaritan prophet led a group onto their sacred mountain, Gerizim, promising that God would restore the Samaritan temple. Pilate had them slaughtered. Roman authorities thought he had been too brutal and removed him from office. When in 40 C.E. the emperor Caligula attempted to set up a statue of himself in the Jerusalem temple, an almost unthinkable sacrilege, Jewish peasants left their fields and came to Petronius, governor of Syria, in non-violent protest.

Prophets arose who convinced some that God was about to intervene on Israel's behalf. Later in the decade (ca. 45 C.E.), Theudas predicted the sign that God would split the Jordan River, allowing his followers to pass over it, as Joshua had done when he led Israel into the promised land, in imitation of the splitting of the Red Sea under Moses earlier. In the following decade (ca. 56 C.E.), a Jewish prophet from Egypt came to Jerusalem and promised that its walls would fall, allowing his followers to enter it and presumably take possession. The expectation is modeled on the fall of Jericho's walls when Joshua and Israel captured it. The examples of the Samaritan prophet, Theudas, and the Jewish prophet from Egypt show the sort of eschatological prophecy of the first century C.E. that expected God to intervene in history to liberate Israel or at least those within it judged faithful. John the Baptist is yet another prophet who expected something similar, and Jesus himself has characteristics of an eschatological prophet.

Bandits, a label of contempt fixed on outlaw groups who threatened established authority with a mixture of political, social, and religious motives, emerged in the 30s, 40s, and 60s. Some were crucified. This sheds light on the two "bandits" crucified with Jesus, as well perhaps on the enigmatic figure of Barabbas, supposedly released by Pilate at Jesus' trial, who is said to have "committed murder during the insurrection" (Mark 15:7). We know nothing of this insurrection, but Barabbas is clearly a political rebel. Some of those who resisted may have claimed messianic status, including the three rebel leaders of 4 B.C.E. and two leaders of the rebellion of 66–74 C.E. A clear instance of a political messianic leader who led a revolution against Rome is Bar Kokhba, who fought the Romans during the years 132–135 C.E.

Overall, the first century C.E. was an unsettled period, characterized by resentment of Roman rule, opposition to the Jewish leadership that cooperated with that rule, hope for God's intervention, eschatological prophecy, disagreements and splits between Jewish groups and individual

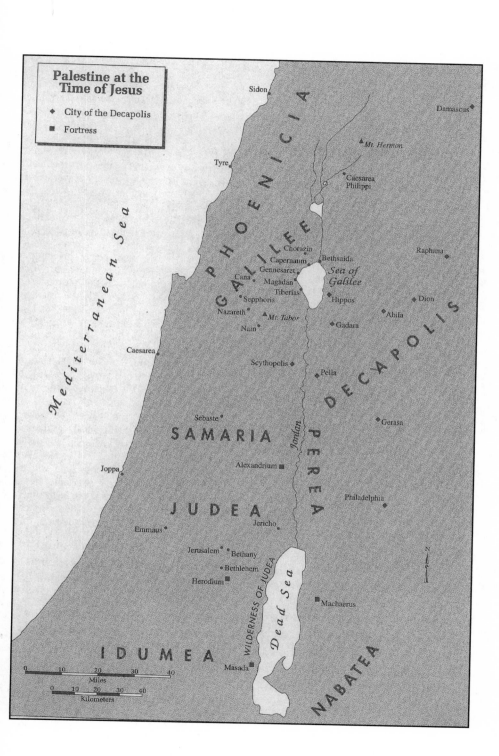

Palestine at the Time of Jesus

◆ City of the Decapolis
■ Fortress

Mediterranean Sea

PHOENICIA

GALILEE

DECAPOLIS

SAMARIA

PEREA

JUDEA

IDUMEA

NABATEA

Sidon

Damascus

▲ *Mt. Hermon*

Tyre

Caesarea Philippi

Chorazin

Bethsaida

Raphana

Capernaum

Gennesaret

Sea of Galilee

Cana

Magadan

Tiberias

Hippos

Dion

Sepphoris

Abila

Nazareth

▲ *Mt. Tabor*

Gadara

Nain

Scythopolis

Pella

Caesarea

Sebaste

Gerasa

Joppa

Alexandrium ■

Philadelphia

Emmaus

Jericho

Jerusalem ● Bethany

● Bethlehem

Herodium ■

WILDERNESS OF JUDEA

Dead Sea

Machaerus ■

Masada ■

Jordan

N

0   10   20   30   40
Miles

0   10   20   30   40
Kilometers

leaders, and occasional violence. This is the historical context of Jesus' career.

Looking at our other level of history, the situations in which the Gospels were composed, we note that one trend in recent research is to read the Gospels as to some degree responses to the political, economic, and religious structures of the Roman Empire. The last book in the New Testament, the book of Revelation, makes an attack on the empire its main focus. Critiques of the empire are more subtle in the gospel narratives, but scholars are making the case that they are there nonetheless. Examples of such research are that of Richard Horsley on Mark and Warren Carter on Matthew. Such considerations are central in work on the historical Jesus by scholars such as John Dominic Crossan.

VARIETY IN JUDAISM

The Gospels look like history. We read them sympathetically, so we tend to assume that they are historically accurate. As we read, we form a picture of ancient Jewish society in Palestine. Then we assume that this is an accurate picture. This is a seductive but dangerous process, because these are texts that have influenced relations between Jews and Christians over the centuries and continue to do so. Their purpose is to support Christians in their belief that Jesus is the Jewish Messiah, whom the majority of Jews did not accept. The Gospels tend to blame Jewish unbelief on their leadership. One cannot expect a balanced, fair view of Jesus' fellow Jews from these writings.

In biblical studies, any sentence that contains "the Jews" is apt to be at best only partially true. Judaism at this period was diverse. The first-century Jewish historian Josephus tells us that there were four main groups in Palestinian Judaism at this time—Sadducees, Pharisees, Essenes, and a fourth group similar to the Pharisees but who held a revolutionary ideology. In fact, there were even more groups, but we know little about them.

Most Jews in the ancient world lived outside the homeland. This is called the *Diaspora*, a Greek word meaning "dispersion." For the most part Diaspora Jews spoke Greek, and although they had a strong Jewish identity, they lived it out as a minority, most often in the great cities of the empire—Rome, Alexandria, Antioch, and the cities of western Asia Minor, for example. They stood out from the general population for a number of reasons, prominent among which were circumcision, Sabbath observance, and dietary restrictions. Over time, they translated the

Hebrew Bible into Greek. The term *Septuagint* is a general way of referring to a diverse collection of material, much of it a translation of books originally in Hebrew, some of it additions to those books, and some books actually composed in Greek.

Since it is the Jews of Judea and Galilee that we encounter within the Gospels, we concentrate on them in what follows. These Jews were inhabitants of the Hellenistic world, too. There were Greek cities along the Mediterranean coast and in Galilee, and Jerusalem itself was to some degree exposed to the main currents of the age. However, most Jews in the area spoke Aramaic and in many cases they were less hellenized than their compatriots in the Diaspora. This would be particularly true in the countryside, such as the small village of Nazareth from which Jesus came.

WHAT ALL JEWS SHARED

Generalizations are always to some degree oversimplifications, but since we do often speak of "the ancient Jews" or "ancient Judaism," we start with an attempt to sketch what this broad term signifies. What holds together this vast group of people scattered throughout the Mediterranean?

Jews were monotheistic. Although they believed in powerful, superhuman beings such as angels and demons, there was but one all-powerful God, Creator of all, who deserved to be worshiped. In their monotheism, the Jews as a group were unique in the ancient world until the advent of Christianity. A few philosophers and some others believed in some form of monotheism, but the vast majority of the world into which Christianity was born was polytheistic. It was the one God who was also God of the Jews whom Christians were to worship as well.

Jews saw themselves as Abraham's descendants, so they were all related, all of the same extended family. They also shared the common history outlined above. God chose the Jews to be God's own, special people. This is called *election*. Torah, temple, and land were especially important for most Jews. God gave the Torah to Israel when it entered into a covenantal relationship with God on Mount Sinai. Clearly, this made the Jews a special people within God's creation. Torah was the perfect expression of God's will, and the Jews felt themselves blessed by God who entrusted it to them. Jews could and did disagree over how to interpret Torah and how to live it, but few denied that Torah was the foundation

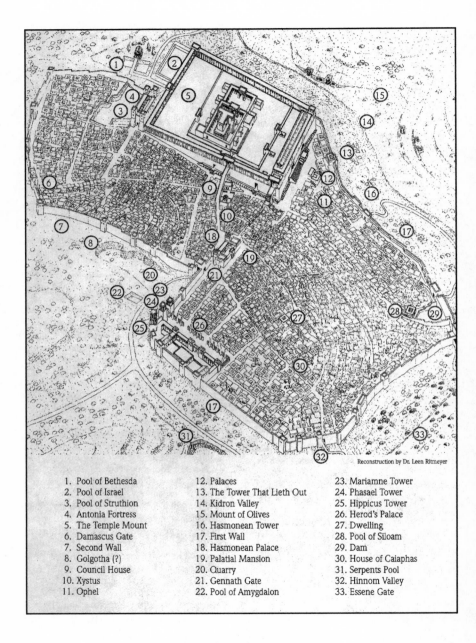

1. Pool of Bethesda
2. Pool of Israel
3. Pool of Struthion
4. Antonia Fortress
5. The Temple Mount
6. Damascus Gate
7. Second Wall
8. Golgotha (?)
9. Council House
10. Xystus
11. Ophel

12. Palaces
13. The Tower That Lieth Out
14. Kidron Valley
15. Mount of Olives
16. Hasmonean Tower
17. First Wall
18. Hasmonean Palace
19. Palatial Mansion
20. Quarry
21. Gennath Gate
22. Pool of Amygdalon

23. Mariamne Tower
24. Phasael Tower
25. Hippicus Tower
26. Herod's Palace
27. Dwelling
28. Pool of Siloam
29. Dam
30. House of Caiaphas
31. Serpents Pool
32. Hinnom Valley
33. Essene Gate

Reconstruction by Dr. Leen Ritmeyer

Jerusalem at the Time of Jesus

of Jewish life. Everything that follows in this chapter relates in one way or the other to Torah.

The temple was God's house, God's presence within the land of Israel. By Jesus' time a temple had stood in Jerusalem for almost a thousand years, except for a brief interlude during the Babylonian exile in the sixth century B.C.E. The temple in Jesus' time was an impressively large and beautiful place, admired even by foreigners, and it dominated Jerusalem. It served as a focal point for Jews the world over. It was the only place in the entire world that sacrifice could be offered to the Jewish God. Jews from everywhere paid an annual tax for its upkeep. Since images were forbidden by God in the Ten Commandments, there were no human images in the temple, something that was very unusual in the ancient world. Scholars use the word *aniconic*, meaning having no images, to describe ancient Jewish worship. Nonetheless, there is archaeological evidence that not all Jews everywhere observed this restriction strictly.

Caligula

The land belonged to God and was the most fitting place for God's people to dwell. Exile from the land was understood by many as punishment for sin. Dominance of foreigners over the land was seen as improper, to be remedied by God at some future time. An important strand of Jewish eschatological expectation hoped for reunion of the twelve tribes, restoration of the Davidic monarchy, and establishment of a purified cult. That is not to say that Jews everywhere agreed on one, well-defined eschatological scenario. Rather, it is to insist that when God set things right, the world would be in accord with key elements of the past that had been lost.

JEWISH INSTITUTIONS AND PRACTICES

CULT

Cult means something quite different in current discourse than it does in the study of religion. Here we use the term to indicate the system of worship centered in the temple. Used in this way, *cult* carries none of the denigrating overtones that the word carries in modern usage. The cultic system was prescribed by Torah, so it was divinely dictated. In postexilic Israel, God allowed sacrifice only in the Jerusalem temple, the place God had designated as the divine dwelling on earth. The temple consisted of three sections. An innermost chamber called the *holy of holies* was where the ark of the covenant was kept in the first temple. The ark was lost when the temple was destroyed by the Babylonians, so the room was

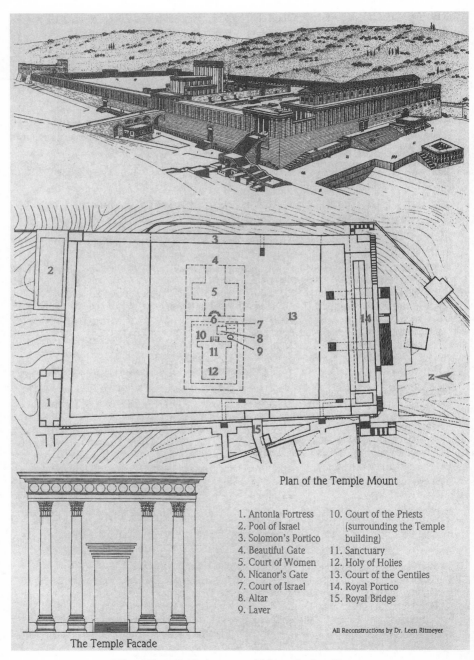

Plan of the Temple Mount

1. Antonia Fortress
2. Pool of Israel
3. Solomon's Portico
4. Beautiful Gate
5. Court of Women
6. Nicanor's Gate
7. Court of Israel
8. Altar
9. Laver
10. Court of the Priests (surrounding the Temple building)
11. Sanctuary
12. Holy of Holies
13. Court of the Gentiles
14. Royal Portico
15. Royal Bridge

All Reconstructions by Dr. Leen Ritmeyer

The Temple Facade

The Temple Mount of Herod the Great

empty in the second temple. It was thought of as the place of God's presence. The temple's main room saw much priestly activity—lighting lamps, offering incense and bread, and so on. The temple had a porch in front with two large pillars in front of it. Just outside the temple building was a large altar for burning sacrifices. Blood not used for purification was poured out at the foot of the altar, thus giving the animal's life, contained in the blood, back to God.

The temple of Jesus' day, expanded and beautified by Herod the Great, was located on a massive platform, the essential lines of which can still be seen today on what is called the Temple Mount. The courts created a series of concentric areas of decreasing holiness. The holy of holies was at the center. Beyond that was the rest of the temple itself, then the court of the priests where sacrifices were offered, then the court of male members of Israel, then females, then a court for Gentiles. The image can be carried further, for Jerusalem itself was a holy city, and the land of Israel was a holy land. Such an elaborate system served various purposes. It symbolized God's presence in the land and among the people, and at the same time it portrayed in stone and wood the structure of society itself, with the high priest at the center as the only one who could enter the holy of holies, the priests at the head of the people, the males over the females, and Israel as a whole being that segment of humanity closest to God.

Priests and Levites were the main temple personnel. Priests were empowered to bring sacrifices to the altar. Levites constituted a lower clergy who performed other functions in the temple. Both groups interpreted Torah. Since they also possessed political power, they were able to enforce their rulings within Judea. The high priest was drawn from one of several prominent families. He was not just a religious, but also a political leader. Only he could enter the holy of holies, and he did so but once a year, on the Day of Atonement.

Torah commands animal sacrifices of many kinds, clearly specifying the type of animal for each sacrifice. Categorizing them and understanding the precise function of each type continues to occupy scholars. Only unblemished animals were acceptable. Among the major sacrifices were sin offerings, which used animal blood as a sort of ritual detergent to purify impurities caused by sin. Sin offerings presented once a year on the Day of Atonement were particularly important in keeping the temple pure and fit for God's presence. Others were peace offerings. These were of various sorts. Some were celebratory. Some were to petition God or to thank God. Holocausts (a word from the Greek meaning "entirely burned") were completely burned and so given in their entirety to God. They constituted a small percentage of the total offerings. Most sacrifices were eaten by the priests or people.

Tithing was the practice of donating a tenth of major agricultural produce to the temple. In addition, the land's first fruits as well as the firstborn of animals were owed to God. In place of giving firstborn humans to the temple, a substitution was made, tailored to some degree to the economic position of the family.

It is generally thought that the biblical book of Psalms is a collection of songs sung in the temple during the Second Temple period. It is rich treasurehouse of ancient Jewish symbols, expressions of piety, and hopes. It became popular among early Christians is often quoted or alluded to in the New Testament.

A certain level of purity was required to participate in the cult (see below). This is called ritual purity. It means freedom from anything that would exclude one from the degree of proximity to God appropriate to one's status in the cultic community.

FEASTS

Sabbath (Saturday) was a day of abstinence from work. This observance was strange to others in the ancient world, who sometimes accused Jews of laziness as a result. Special offerings took place on that day. Observance of the Sabbath in the synagogues probably consisted of prayers and hymns as well as Torah reading and interpretation (see Luke 4). The word *synagogue* can be used to refer both to the place where Jews gathered for prayer and study and to the gathering of people itself.

The Day of Atonement (Yom Kippur) occurred once a year, in the fall. On that day the temple was purified from defilements caused by Israel's sins and transgressions of the previous year. Leviticus 16 describes the day's complex rituals. Central to them are the use of animal blood to purify the holy of holies in the temple.

Torah ordains three pilgrimage feasts, feasts which Israel was to celebrate in the Jerusalem temple if possible. The combined feast of Passover (Pesach) and Unleavened Bread was observed in the spring. It marked the barley harvest and commemorated the exodus. A lamb was killed and eaten, in Jerusalem if possible. Pentecost, or Weeks (Shavuot), took place fifty days after Passover and marked the wheat harvest. It celebrated God's gift of the Torah to Israel. Tabernacles, or booths (Sukkoth), marked the fall harvest. In addition to thanking God for the harvest, Israel prayed for sufficient rain for the following year.

PURITY

Purity played an important role in ancient Judaism. Generally, purity meant freedom from defilement, be it moral, physical, or ritual. The description and interpretation of purity rules in ancient Judaism is complex and is an ongoing topic in modern scholarship. Purity rules formed a system (or systems, since some forms of purity stand side by side with others without being fully integrated with them) determining what and who was pure, how impurity is incurred and how remedied, what degree of purity was demanded by certain statuses or functions, and so on. The impurity that prevented one from participating in the cult was ritual impurity. It is important to distinguish this from moral impurity. Ritual impurity was not sinful. It could result from such things as touching a dead body or having an involuntary emission of bodily fluids, such as menstruation. Ritual purification was necessary before participating in the cult, but to be impure was not equivalent to being in a sinful state. Indeed, many forms of ritual impurity would not impact a person's daily life at all, unless that person needed to enter the temple.

Some forms of impurity, for example, skin disease called leprosy but not identical with what we now know as Hansen's disease, could restrict one's social contacts. Smaller groups within such societies could use purity rules, such as those centered on the consumption of food, to distinguish themselves from others. Thus social arrangements received religious sanction.

Deliberate transgression of ritual purity rules related to the temple could endanger the entire community. If one violated the rules of a smaller group, one was asserting that one did not belong to that group and that one did not share that group's view of society and judgment of members within it.

DIETARY RULES

Some foods were clean and fit for human consumption and some not (see Lev 11). People today are perhaps most familiar with the Jewish prohibition on pork and shellfish. It was never permissible to eat blood, so meat had to be killed in such a way that the blood ran out of the animal. Such dietary rules are called *kosher laws*. Unusual food restrictions were one of the things that made the Jews stand out in the wider world.

CIRCUMCISION

In Gen 17, God demands circumcision (cutting off the male foreskin) as a sign of the covenant.

SYNAGOGUE

Jesus regularly frequents synagogues in the Gospels. The impression is that they were plentiful in his environment. The Jewish historian Josephus gives the same impression. There is much about the origin of the institution of the synagogue that we do not understand. Some hypothesize that it began among the exiles in Babylonia. The synagogue was the site for meetings, discussion of and teaching of Torah, prayer services, and Sabbath observances. Its leadership may have varied from place to place.

SANHEDRIN

The Greek word *synedrion* means "council." There were local councils, but the Sanhedrin or Council in the Gospels is the aristocratic council of Jerusalem. It was advisory to the high priest. It consisted of the leading priests and scribes and the heads of prominent families. It could serve a judicial function.

APOCALYPTICISM

Apocalypticism is a worldview prominent in Jewish Palestine in the latter centuries before the Common Era and in the first couple of centuries of the Common Era. Many scholars believe that Jesus thought in apocalyptic terms, although many others contest this. Apocalypticism heavily influences the Gospels and early Christianity in general.

Apocalypticism is a worldview found in apocalypses but not limited to them. *Apocalypses* are revelatory literature in which a superhuman figure, often an angel, imparts a vision or spoken revelation to a human, often referred to as a *seer*, since he or she often sees visions. The revelation has to do with the unseen world that influences or even determines what happens in the seen world, and eschatology, that is, what is to happen at the end of the world as we know it. This does not necessarily involve a total end to the world. It may simply mean its transformation. In some apocalypses, the minority, the eschatology is personal—it involves the fate of the individual after death, not a cosmic transformation. There are two apocalypses in the Bible—Daniel in the Hebrew Bible and Revelation in the New Testament.

There is great variety in apocalypses and apocalyptic scenarios. We sketch here a general picture that illuminates what we find in the canonical gospels, especially the Synoptics. Apocalypses speak of an unseen world populated by God, God's superhuman agents (angels), superhuman figures inimical to God (demons, devils), and a leader of the superhuman forces hostile to God (usually Satan, but also known by other names—Beelzebul, for example). Central to this form of apocalypticism is the conviction that the world is not as it should be. Cosmic forces hostile to God control part or all of creation. This may be because of human or angelic sin. God is about to intervene in history and take creation back, resulting in the conquest of those forces that oppose God and either a transformation of heaven and earth or its annihilation (usually the former). The transformation often involves a reversal of the problems caused to creation by humans or superhuman beings, so that the end becomes like the beginning—images such as the tree of life from the garden of Eden and an earth that is preternaturally fertile are not uncommon. Apocalypticism involves determinism—history is determined and will take a preordained course, and dualism—humans and superhumans are lined up on one side or the other of the cosmic struggle. It is often thought that history falls into stages, and the seer learns what these are. Persuasive "predictions" of history are fictitiously put into the mouths of ancient seers. They are really predictions written after the event. Pseudonymity (a "false name," that is, the apocalypse is attributed to an ancient hero who did not really write it) occurs in most apocalypses, but not in the book of Revelation in the New Testament.

Apocalypticism takes the power of God's enemies seriously. The divine intervention does not come without a struggle between God's forces and those that oppose God. These struggles often entail suffering for humans on God's side. God's intervention does not always include the appearance of a messiah, but it can do so. The transition of creation from a state of alienation from God and control by demonic powers to a situation of reconciliation with God and full conformity to God's will is a cosmic event. It is not simply individual, or social, or moral. Since it is cosmic, it is often accompanied by cosmic catastrophes, such as earthquakes, famines, the sun darkening, the moon turning the color of blood, and the stars falling to the earth.

GNOSTICISM

Gnosticism is a much-disputed topic. Until the middle of the twentieth century, we knew of it primarily through the arguments against it found in writers of the mainstream Christian church of the second century and beyond who considered it heretical. Gnosticism was a broad movement, originating in the second century or perhaps the first. In 1945, a rich cache of gnostic documents was found at Nag Hammadi in Egypt, now referred to as the Nag Hammadi library. We furnish a quick sketch of the movement's beliefs, with the caveat that the picture is in fact more complex than we have space to show. Karen King provides a recent discussion of the movement's complexity. Although the elements we are about to enumerate occur in many gnostic texts, she demonstrates that exceptions can be found for every one of them. Indeed, some now question the usefuless of the broad term *Gnosticism*.

Gnostic thought sometimes involved a complicated mythology in which the divine world consisted of multiple divine figures. The physical world was created by one of the lower-ranking ones. In that physical world were imprisoned sparks of divinity. Certain humans embody those sparks, although they do not know it. They are said to be drunk or asleep. A revealer comes down into the physical world and awakens these people, giving them knowledge (Greek *gnosis*) of where they come from and how to get back to the spiritual world. In Christian systems, this revealer is Christ. If this sounds a bit like the Jesus of the Gospel of John, then it will not surprise us to find that John was the gnostics' favorite gospel. Although the points of contacts between John and Gnosticism are striking, the Gospel is not in the end gnostic, as we shall see.

JEWISH GROUPS

PRIESTS

Jewish priesthood was hereditary. The tribe of Levi was the priestly tribe. The book of Leviticus, the third book of the Torah, takes its name from that tribe and is full of detailed prescriptions for rituals, sacrifices, and even some aspects of daily life. The most characteristically priestly function was to carry on the rituals in the temple, especially animal sacrifice. But ancient Jews did not distinguish between religion and politics clearly as we do. Torah covers all aspects of life—religious, political, economic, and civil. So priests were not just "religious" figures, but played important roles in most aspects of ancient Israelite and Jewish society.

Before the Babylonian exile, priests shared power with kings, who outranked them. Afterwards, in the absence of kings, priests were even more powerful. The main priestly families in Jerusalem were an important segment of the elite. They were wealthy and influential. Legal interpretation and ruling had always been a priestly function. After the Babyonian exile, the introduction of written Torah initiated a new set of dynamics. Groups could come up with their own interpretation of the written text, and there could be increased variety of interpretation within the priesthood itself. The Qumran community was founded by priests who disagreed with the Jerusalem priestly elite on matters of law. In effect, written Torah opened up a new source of power and influence. Groups formed their identity and criticized others during the Second Temple period through interpretation of sacred texts and use of sacred traditions. We observe this in Jesus' career and in the desire of early Christians to legitimate themselves through appeal to the Jewish Scriptures.

Over the years the number of priests grew naturally. Political and religious factors caused some priestly families to become more prominent than others. The Zadokites, descendants of Solomon's chief priest, Zadok, were one of the most prominent priestly groups in the Second Temple period. There were four main families from which the high priests were drawn. High priests were supposed to serve for life, but in the Roman period first Herod and then the Roman administrators appointed and deposed high priests as they saw fit, which increased Herodian and then Roman control over religious, social, and political affairs in Judea. For a while, the Romans retained possession of the high priestly vestments, necessary for the rituals. This also increased their control.

SADDUCEES

Sadducees were a small group of powerful priests and their allies in Jerusalem. Josephus presents them as one of the main groups in first-century Palestinian Judaism. We have no writings we can confidently trace back to the Sadducees. Their name may derive from Zadok. If so, their very name reveals a claim to authority. The Sadducees are first mentioned in connection with a Hasmonean king of the second century B.C.E., where they are opponents of the Pharisees, who had a different interpretation of Torah. Josephus says that the Sadducees were influential among the wealthy, in contrast with the Pharisees, who he says were favored by the people.

The New Testament tells us that the Sadducees did not believe in resurrection of the body, in angels, or in demons. Josephus says that they did not believe in the afterlife. This may be due to a conservative view of Scripture and tradition. We find the first clear Jewish reference to resurrection in the book of Daniel, written around 165 B.C.E. The belief may have entered the Jewish world through Persian influence. Such belief is not represented in the Torah itself.

The Gospels tend to lump all Jewish leaders together and paint them as hostile to Jesus. They show little interest in differences between groups. Mark, the earliest of the Gospels, mentions the Sadducees only once. It is not surprising that he does so at the end of Jesus' career, when he is in Jerusalem, for the Sadducees were close to the high priest. They challenge Jesus on resurrection, for they "say that there is no resurrection" (12:18). Matthew inserts the Sadducees into several more passages. He strengthens the indictment of the Jewish leaders generally. His additions do not show more detailed knowledge of this group or greater interest in distinguishing them from others. Indeed, he associates them with the Pharisees, their rivals, even in terms of their teaching, a main point of divergence between the two groups.

Acts of the Apostles provides the best New Testament information about the Sadducees. Acts 4:1 associates them with temple priests and the "captain of the temple." In 5:17, in response to the apostles' preaching in the temple, "the high priest took action; he and all who were with him (that is, the sect of the Sadducees)." When Paul is on trial in Jerusalem before the Sanhedrin, he

> noticed that some were Sadducees and others were Pharisees, he called out in the council, "Brothers, I am a Pharisee, a son of Pharisees. I am on trial concerning the hope of the resurrection of the dead." When he said this, a dissension began between the Pharisees and the Sadducees, and the assembly was divided. (The Sadducees say that there is no resurrection, or angel, or spirit; but the Pharisees acknowledge all three.) (Acts 23:6-8)

Things get rowdy between the factions, and Pharisaic scribes stand up and defend Paul.

PHARISEES

The Pharisees have perhaps been the most maligned Jewish group among Christians. Even today, few would consider it a compliment if one were to say, "You are a real Pharisee." In the popular mind, that means hypocritical, self-righteous, manipulating religion for self-promotion, and, worst of all, opposing Jesus and Christianity. This portrayal of Pharisees is unfair and ultimately anti-Jewish.

When Judaism underwent dramatic changes after the war against the Romans in 66–74 C.E., Pharisees were crucial to the process. Older scholarship asserts simply that the Pharisees evolved into the rabbis. Jacob Neusner and his students have refined such simplistic conceptions, but they have confirmed that the Pharisees were important in the transformation of Judaism, ultimately into what we now know as rabbinic Judaism. When Christians denigrate the Pharisees, they cast aspersions on the origins of rabbinic Judaism. It is as if a non-Christian were to say to a modern Christian, "I think Christians today are fine people, but the apostles were all hypocrites."

We have no texts that we can confidently attribute to the Pharisees. Our knowledge of them comes from three sources—Josephus, the New Testament, and the rabbinic writings. Each of these has its own agenda and so must be used with caution for historical reconstruction.

Historical research cannot decide whether the Pharisees were hypocritical or not. It can observe, however, that the earliest Christians had a vested interest in presenting the Pharisees in a bad light. If Jesus allegedly fulfilled Jewish expectations, yet a prominent group, known for its expertise in Torah, did not accept him, this challenges Christian claims and helps to explain the negative view of Pharisees in the Gospels. It strains the imagination to believe that thousands of people (Josephus sets their number at six thousand) who pursued a stringent interpretation of Torah and a demanding lifestyle were one and all hypocrites. Undoubtedly there were hypocrites among the Pharisees, as there are among any group, religious or otherwise, but to label the entire group that way is highly problematic. Then to use them routinely as illustrations of hypocrisy and self-righteousness is irresponsible.

Jesus and the Pharisees clash on Torah interpretation in each of the four canonical gospels. Disagreement over Torah was a hallmark of the period. It is not likely that it was this sort of disagreement that led to the later split between Christianity and Judaism. The historical Jesus had some who followed him and many who did not, like most Jewish prophetic figures of the time. The later split between synagogue and church became inevitable when Christians did not observe Torah and when they began to make claims about Jesus, that he was divine or that he had authority to override Torah, that the vast majority Jews could not accept. James Dunn offers a helpful treatment of the gradual split between Christianity and Judaism.

Jesus and the Pharisees are not always at odds. They agree, against the Sadducees, on resurrection. Luke says that they warn Jesus against Herod's plot to kill him (13:31). The same author shows Jesus dining with Pharisees, and Acts of the Apostles says that Pharisees were among the earliest Christians in Jerusalem (15:5). Paul tells us that he himself was a Pharisee (Phil 3:5; Acts 23:6).

Christians have other misconceptions about the Pharisees. Although they are prominent as Jesus' opponents in the Gospels, they were not the political leaders of the time. That is not to say, of course, that they had no political interests. Religion and politics went hand in hand at this time, and Torah's purview included all aspects of Jewish life. Some evidence points to tension between them and both the Herodian administration in Galilee and, at times, Judea's priestly administration. Individual Pharisees were influential because they were wealthy or had influential contacts, but apparently not because of their identity as Pharisees. There were certainly disagreements between some Pharisees and Jesus (as there were between individual Pharisees), but there were also agreements. In any case, they had no part in his death. The Synoptic Gospels give them no such role, nor do the issues argued between Jesus and the Pharisees lead to his death. He is killed for other reasons.

The Pharisees existed during the same time period as the Sadducees—from the second century B.C.E. until the war against the Romans in 66–74 C.E. and its immediate aftermath. Josephus and rabbinic texts portray them as the Sadducees' rivals, both in terms of their teaching and politics. Josephus says that the common people admired them for their knowledge of Torah and for their strict observance. Both the New Testament and rabbinic documents attribute to them an interest in Sabbath observance, tithing, and ritual purity. Their rulings and practices regarding such concerns set the Pharisees apart. Indeed, a possible etymology of their name is the Aramaic *perushim*, meaning "those separated."

Pharisaic rules dealing with tithing agricultural produce and ritual purity center around food—its harvesting, presentation in the temple, and eating. Neusner suggests that they applied to themselves purity rules meant for temple priests. The Jewish table becomes analogous to the sacred altar. In this interpretation, Pharisaic purity rules were constant reminders of God's presence and kept attention focused on God's will.

ESSENES

In 1947, a young nomad searching for his sheep near caves overlooking the Dead Sea made an astounding discovery—earthen pots containing ancient documents. Subsequent events are full of intrigue, suspense, politics, and deception. Slowly, over time, searches by different people and groups unearthed a large library of ancient texts distributed through eleven caves. The texts, in various stages of disintegration, were part of a cache of about eight hundred manuscripts hidden almost two thousand years ago. Subsequent research convinced most that they belonged to a group that lived in a nearby settlement whose ruins still exist and whose name in Arabic is Qumran. The texts are of three main types—manuscripts of biblical books, texts written by members of the people of Qumran and others from the same movement, and nonbiblical texts not written by group members.

Most scholars believe that the people of Qumran are the same as the Essenes, mentioned by Josephus, Philo (a Jewish philosopher from Alexandria in Egypt and a contemporary of Jesus), and Pliny the Elder (a Roman writer of the first century C.E.). Josephus calls them one of the main groups of Jews. The scrolls attest to diversity within the group, but certain main lines emerge.

Some time in the second century B.C.E., a small group of Jewish priests and others allied with them left Jewish society to form a community on the shores of the Dead Sea. They judged that the leadership in Jerusalem, including the Hasmoneans and others—perhaps the Pharisees and the Sadducees—were untrue to God's will. They opposed them on legal matters. They may have resisted Hasmonean claims to kingship and to the high priesthood, since the Hasmoneans were neither heirs of David nor were they Zadokites.

As the group grew, some lived at Qumran, while others dwelled in the villages and towns of Jewish Palestine. Community structure was hierarchical, Zadokite priests occupying top positions. The movement interpreted Torah strictly and considered those outside the movement to be in violation of God's Law. The most prominent early leader of the movement, called the Teacher of Righteousness, claimed divine inspiration for his interpretation of Scripture, both legal and prophetic. He interpreted sacred texts, the prophets and the psalms in particular, as containing predictions of his own career and of the community's history.

Those who wrote the Dead Sea Scrolls had an apocalyptic worldview. They thought they were living in the final age and expected God and the angels to intervene soon to overthrow Belial (another name for the prince of demons) and humans in league with him. They divided humanity into the righteous and the wicked, a division corresponding to the community and those outside of it. They prepared for the end-time by perfect obedience to Torah, possible for them alone because only they had the true interpretation of Torah. They had stringent purity rules, because they wanted to be ready for holy war when it came and because they believed that God's angels were already present among them. Admission to the community was not easy. There were long periods of probation and close examination by the community. The Qumran community perished in 68 C.E. during the war against the Romans.

The apocalyptic worldview to which the scrolls attest informs early Christianity as well. Both movements thought that they lived at the end of times. Both thought a war between satanic and divine forces was in progress or was imminent. Both expected a resolution of the conflict soon, with God's forces victorious. Both claimed true interpretation of the Jewish Scriptures, eschatological interpretation of the prophets and the psalms figuring largely in that interpretation. Christians thought that the words from Isa 40 concerning the voice crying in the desert to prepare the way of the Lord referred to John the Baptist as the forerunner of Jesus, and the Qumran community applied it to themselves, obeying the Torah in the desert in preparation for God's arrival. In both groups, obedience to Torah was an issue. Sabbath observance and the role of ritual purity were addressed by both groups. None of this indicates direct connection between the people of Qumran and Jesus or his movement. Rather, it shows that they inhabited the same world.

SCRIBES

Scribes read and wrote for a living. They were found in all groups in ancient Israel, and in most social strata. Saldarini suggests the analogy of "secretary" in today's world. Secretaries range from the secretary of a third-grade classroom to the American Secretary of State. Similarly, in first-century Jewish Palestine, there were scribes who knew about enough to write basic contracts for villagers, and there were scribes who belonged to the ruling class. Some priests were scribes. Most scribes were retainers—those who served the upper classes (see Lenski). They did so in a number of capacities such as scribes, stewards (economic overseers), military officers, and administrators. Many would be what we consider middle class economically, but that can be misleading, given their complete dependence on the upper classes.

Since being a scribe was an occupation and does not indicate whether one belonged to a group, such as the Pharisees, or one's precise economic status, it makes little sense to attribute to them a single point of view. There were scribes in the Jerusalem bureaucracy and scribes at Qumran who condemned that very establishment. The Gospels obscure this reality. For the most part, scribes in the Gospels are negative figures. The reason for this is that they were thought to be hostile to Jesus. In the Gospels, *scribes* most commonly refers to those who serve the Jerusalem establishment.

ELDERS

Elders were leaders of the Jewish community. They were called elders because they were generally the eldest males. Like scribe, elder is a fairly general term. Village elders commanded much respect in their hometowns but did not have status in Jerusalem. Jerusalem elders were among the leaders of the nation. It is the latter group who are usually meant in the Gospels. Like the other Jewish groups, they are thought to be inimical to Jesus, and they, along with the chief priests and scribes, plot Jesus' death during his last days.

MESSIANIC HOPES

CHRISTIAN MISCONCEPTIONS

Christians today still have deeply ingrained misconceptions about messiahship in ancient Judaism. They have often wondered why Jesus' Jewish contemporaries did not recognize him as the Messiah. After all, did not Scripture clearly point to him as God's anointed? Were not Israel's prophetic predictions obviously fulfilled in him? We too frequently miss the implications of such questioning. If Jesus clearly was the Messiah, then a reasonable explanation that past and present Jews would refuse to believe in him would be that they oppose God and God's plans for the world and for themselves. And that is precisely what many Christians down through the ages have concluded, beginning with the New Testament writers themselves.

Inaccurate history leads to inadequate theology and dire social results. Christians often assume that the Jews as a whole had a single concept of messiah, which Jesus fit, and that despite the obviousness of his messiahship, the Jews deliberately opted to reject him. Where does this Christian concept of the Messiah for whom all Jews were waiting originate? It comes from Christian faith, which constructs a picture of what Messiah means based on Christian conceptions of Jesus, then assumes that this constructed figure is in fact what Jews expected. Where Jewish elements can be enlisted to support this construction, they are used. Where they contradict it, they are considered Jewish misconceptions that God, through Jesus, corrected. Clearly this is a circular and self-legitimating process.

MESSIAH

Second Temple Jewish society (520 B.C.E. to 70 C.E.) was one in which things were not quite right. Even during the relatively peaceful and prosperous periods, Jews could see that their sacred traditions envisaged the world in a way that did not correspond to their contemporary reality. At times this discrepancy gave birth to what we refer to as messianic hopes.

Messianic implies that the new state of affairs will involve a messiah. A thorough examination of what are often called messianic hopes in Second Temple Judaism requires going beyond just those passages where a messiah is mentioned to looking at other scenarios where eschatological salvation is depicted even without a messianic figure, or with a figure who is like a messiah in that he plays a prominent role in eschatological events, although he is not explicitly identified as a messiah. The book of Daniel is the only apocalypse in the Hebrew Bible. Its eschatological scenario does not include a messiah in our sense. The only messiahs mentioned are two high priests of the past, who were not eschatological figures.

There was a good deal of variety in Jewish eschatological hope in the Second Temple period. Some Jews expected a messiah; some did not. Of those who did, some expected a Davidic king, some a priest, and some both. Still others expected a heavenly figure (4 Ezra and the *Similitudes of Enoch*, for example). There is evidence in the Dead Sea Scrolls that the community that wrote them expected three eschatological figures—a messianic king, a messianic priest, and a prophet. And, of course, it is possible that there were some who did not harbor eschatological expectations. The Sadducees, for example, being associated with the priestly establishment in Jerusalem, may have disapproved of hopes that God would intervene to change the present order. After all, such hopes expressed dissatisfaction with the present, and the Jerusalem priests were the guardians of the status quo. Even that is an oversimplification, however, for the case has been convincingly made that some priests fostered apocalyptic hopes (see Cook, for example), and there were certainly priests unhappy with Roman rule or with contemporary arrangements, political and religious. Zadokite priests were the leaders of the Qumran community. But not all would have the same interest in change or would want the same sort of change. When the Galilean and Judean Jews revolted against the Romans in 66 C.E., internal strife was a feature of the rebellion. The Roman general Vespasian delayed his advance on Jerusalem because the Jews were fighting among themselves and weakening their own cause.

SON OF GOD

In addition to the term *messiah*, we should look briefly at two other titles commonly applied to Jesus in the Gospels—*Son of God* and *Son of Man*. To the modern ear, it sounds like Son of God indicates the divinity of Jesus, while Son of Man designates his humanity. But that is misleading. Son of God means a variety of things in ancient Judaism. In Gen 6, it indicates heavenly beings, later considered angels (see also Job 38:7). But the phrase more often refers to humans. The prophet Hosea calls Israel God's son, as does Isaiah. The Wisdom of Solomon calls the righteous person God's son (Wis 2:13, 16, 18).

Several passages refer to Israel's king as God's son. Of special interest are two texts that caught early Christian attention. The first is in 2 Sam 7 (see also Ps 89:26, and Ps 2:7 below). In that chapter, David expresses to the prophet Nathan his desire to build a temple for God. God gives Nathan a message for David of which the following is an excerpt:

> The LORD declares to you that the LORD will make you a house. When your days are fulfilled and you lie down with your ancestors, I will raise up your offspring after you, who shall come forth from your body, and I will establish his kingdom. He shall build a house for my name, and I will establish the throne of his kingdom forever. I will be a father to him, and he shall be a son to me.... Your house and your kingdom shall be made sure forever before me; your throne shall be established forever. (1 Sam 7:11b-14a, 16)

"House" is used in two senses. When God says that God will build David a house, "house" means "dynasty." When God says that David's son, Solomon, will build God a house, God means a temple. The promise to David of an unending kingdom became a source of messianic hope after the Judean monarchy ceased to rule at the beginning of the Babylonian exile in 586 B.C.E. Second Samuel 7 brings together the titles of *messiah* (implicit in Solomon's kingship) and *Son of God* and applies them to Solomon, who is also son of David.

Psalm 2 was probably recited or sung at the king's coronations. It dates from when Israel ruled an empire. It was common for subject kingdoms to attempt to throw off foreign rule when one king died and the next had not yet solidified his power. This is the situation the psalm assumes, where the kings of the earth plot "against the LORD and his anointed [Messiah, Christ]" and plan to throw off Israel's rule. God derides them and says God has already set his king on Mount Zion, the holy hill in Jerusalem where the temple and royal palace sit. The next words were probably recited by the king himself: "I will tell of the decree of the LORD: / He said to me, 'You are my son; today I have begotten you'" (Ps 2:7). So again son of God means king of Israel, a messiah.

SON OF MAN

This was not used as a title at the time of Jesus, but it is a phrase applied to a messianic figure in two Jewish texts from the first century B.C.E.—*4 Ezra* and *The Parables of Enoch* (chs. 37–71 of *1 Enoch*). It appears frequently in the Gospels. The image of the Son of Man in these texts comes originally from Daniel. As do all apocalypses, Daniel has an interest in eschatology. In Dan 7, the seer sees four strange and fearsome beasts rising from the sea (7:3-8). In the mythologies of the ancient Near East and the ancient Mediterranean, the sea represents forces of destruction and chaos inimical to God's creation. Some creation myths tell of a god who conquers the sea and thereby brings peace and order to the world. The beasts in Daniel therefore originate in a place known for its opposition to God. We find out later in the chapter that they represent four kingdoms that have oppressed Israel (7:15-27).

The scene shifts to God's heavenly throne and court. God, the "Ancient One," sits on a throne, surrounded by thousands upon thousands of attendants. A judgment scene begins, and books of judgment are opened. The scene suddenly swings back to earth, and Daniel watches the fourth beast destroyed and power taken from the other beasts. The next part of the vision captured the imaginations of later Jews and Christians, perhaps of Jesus himself.

> I saw one like a human being [literally, "Son of Man"]
> coming with the clouds of heaven.

> And he came to the Ancient One
> > and was presented before him.
> To him was given dominion and glory and kingship,
> > that all peoples, nations, and languages
> > > should serve him.
> His dominion is an everlasting dominion
> > that shall not pass away,
> and his kingship is one
> > that shall never be destroyed. (7:13-14)

The one like a Son of Man here is likely an angel, probably Michael. Angels in the Hebrew Bible and in other Jewish and Christian literature are frequently spoken of as resembling humans, hence the phrase "like a son of man." Angels are also often called the "holy ones" (the same word can be translated "saints"). Michael was Israel's angel (see Dan 10:21; 12:1). The idea of Dan 7 is that as Israel's angel assumes royal power in heaven, so Israel rules the earth. This is the probable meaning of verse 27 later in the chapter: "The kingship and dominion / and the greatness of the kingdoms under the whole heaven / shall be given to the people of the holy ones of the Most High." The people of the holy ones, meaning the people of the angels, is Israel.

A CULTURE DIFFERENT FROM OURS

A DIFFERENT WORLD
Suppose you find yourself suddenly transported to another place and culture, very different from your own—to Iran, perhaps, or to a Pacific island, or to Thailand or China, or to Kenya, or to Poland. You would soon find that many things you took for granted are now misinterpreted and can get you into trouble. Can you look someone in the eye? Is that a sign of honesty, or is it a sign of arrogance? If you are a male, can you speak to females in public? When meeting someone, do you shake hands? Or bow? Can you laugh out loud at something funny? Or is that considered vulgar and ill-bred? Are there places you are not allowed to go? How do you know? Are there signs telling you that, or are you just supposed to know? Imagine that all this is complicated by your not speaking the language.

Modern biblical criticism insists that the Gospels are documents from a time and place very different from our own in countless ways, written in a language few of us can read (Greek), about a people who spoke yet a different language (Aramaic). Before the rise of historical criticism, this distance was not felt in the same way. Often Christians have interpreted the Gospels as if there were no distance between the world of the interpreters and that of the Gospels.

What must we understand about the ancient Mediterranean world in order to grasp something of the Gospels' original import? The more we know, the better, but most of us do not have time to make this a full-time study. Even those who dedicate their lives to it admit that their understanding is limited by many factors. One is the lack of evidence. Another is the sheer size and scope of biblical research. Still more basic is the fact that we can never reenter fully the ancient world, no matter how much knowledge we have. But over the years scholars have achieved some basic insights that can aid us to come closer to it. In this section we address just a few common misconceptions that hinder us from understanding the Gospels more deeply. Misconceptions about specific aspects of Jewish society of the first century are addressed in other sections in this chapter. This section deals with more general matters.

RELIGION, POLITICS, ECONOMICS, KINSHIP

Modern Western societies draw a line between politics and religion, between economics and religion, and between kinship and religion. Separation of church and state is a mantra in American politics. Precisely what that means is hotly debated, and the courts are often called upon to adjudicate between different positions on the issue, but it is clear that the American system of government, the First Amendment in particular, forbids the establishment of any one religion.

Such distinctions would make little sense to the ancients. Jews, Greeks, and Romans all found a place for the divine in public life. Divine beings took an active interest in politics. Israel's God was concerned not just about temple worship, but also about whether there was a Davidic king on the throne of Israel. God also cared about the distribution of goods within society. Poverty and abundance were not neutral situations but raised moral questions concerning which God had definite thoughts. One quick lesson we can take from this is that when we see "religious" figures such as priests and scribes involved in politics or economics, we should not immediately condemn them for it. Also, the denigration of Jewish "nationalism" (itself an anachronism since true nationalism is a modern phenomenon) as being this-worldly while Christian spirituality is something higher misunderstands the ancient world. This becomes important when comparing Jewish and Christian ideas of messianism, for example.

INDIVIDUALISM

Another major difference between the ancients and ourselves has to do with individualism. Modern Westerners tend to think in individualistic terms, while the ancients and many societies in other parts of the world today think in terms of groups. This is of course a broad generalization, and distinctions are in order based on particular ethnic groups, cultural systems, and particular religions and philosophies. But it is a generalization that points us in the right direction. The Gospels often paint groups with a broad brush—be they smaller groups such as scribes, Pharisees, and Sadducees, or larger groups such as Jews and Romans. It is ill-advised and even dangerous to base historical judgments on such generalizations without examining them closely. Further, feminist scholarship has alerted us to issues of gender in the ancient world (and in our own). We now see that understanding ancient gender roles and their effect on the presentation of individuals as male or female influences our analysis of ancient narratives.

ECONOMICS

Another source of misconception is economics. We assume much about how the economy works, and we tend to transfer those assumptions to the ancient world. To reorient our thinking, we can begin with the fact that ancient society consisted of three strata, broadly speaking: (1) a very small ruling class, perhaps only a few percent or less of the population; (2) a class that existed to serve the ruling class in positions such as business managers (stewards), soldiers, and priests (some of whom themselves could be in the ruling class), some artisans, most of whom we might consider the working poor; and (3) those who worked the land (peasants), comprising as much as 85 to 90 percent of the population. There was little social or economic mobility. One tended to stay in the geographical place and socioeconomic class of one's parents. There were exceptions, but this was the general rule.

LITERACY

Most of the ancient world was illiterate. The very fact that the evangelists could write and write fairly well says something about their social status. Their prose does not equal that of great writers, and it may have appeared rustic to more sophisticated readers, but it was respectable and is comparable to that of other popular literature. Prose quality varies a bit between the Gospels. Mark is less polished, while Luke is quite good. In any case, the great majority of those exposed to the Gospels would hear them, not read them.

THE BIBLE

When the Gospels were written, the Christian Bible was the Jewish Scriptures. There was, of course, no New Testament. The Bible was not in the form of physical books, but in scrolls. This was well before the printing press, so uniformity of text was hard to come by. We know from the biblical manuscripts at Qumran and from the Greek translation of the Hebrew Scriptures, called the Septuagint, that there were different versions of biblical books available. Further, ancient interpreters, both Jewish and Christian, took more liberties with the text than we might expect. The limits of the canon itself were also not fully fixed at this time. Some books were considered sacred and authoritative by some and not by others. Attempts to understand all of this is still very much in process.

THEOLOGY

We often speak of the theology of the Bible and of the Gospels in particular. This is appropriate, given their interest in God and God's relation with the world. However, we stand at the end of two thousand years of development of Christian doctrine and theology, and we tend to think in terms of carefully worked out systems of thought with a long history. In dealing with the Gospels, we must remember that Christians had had only a few decades to process what had happened in the life, death, and resurrection of Christ. Many significant developments in theology and Christology lay in the future and are not to be found in the Gospels, at least not in fully developed form. Further, the Gospels are narratives, not theological treatises. Systematic presentations of the thought that they assume are possible, but such presentations are scholarly and theological constructs subject to critique. The Synoptic Gospels are more interested in functional Christology, that is, they do not really explore metaphysical questions about Christ characteristic of Christian thinkers of the second through the fifth centuries. The Gospel of John is far more interested than the Synoptics in the person of Christ in that sense, but it still is not the sort of philosophically informed and worked-out theology common in subsequent centuries.

THE WORLDS OF THE EVANGELISTS

To this point, this chapter has concentrated on Jewish Palestine of the first century C.E. This is the real-world counterpart to the Gospels' story world. The gospel narratives transpire in the world of temple and purity, Pharisee and Sadducee, Torah and scribe. Most, however, think that the Gospels themselves were written after the Romans destroyed the temple in 70 C.E. and Jewish life in Judea was disrupted. Guesses about their places of composition are just that, guesses, and are vigorously debated, but most agree that they were composed in the broader Greco-Roman world, perhaps in cities like Antioch in Syria and Rome in Italy. The influence of these venues on the Gospels is less obvious than is the milieu of Jewish Palestine, but it can be important for interpretation nonetheless. For lack of space, we can say only a little about this.

Jews of the Diaspora, that is, of the communities living outside the land of Israel, lived in constant and close contact with their non-Jewish neighbors. They went to synagogue, obeyed aspects of Torah that did not depend on presence in the land of Israel itself (circumcision, dietary rules, and a host of commands regulating everyday life). Sometimes their differences from their neighbors caused tension, but just as frequently they lived as accepted inhabitants of cities that were filled with a variety of ethnic groups, practicing many religions. It is perhaps among Diaspora Jews that Christianity found its first opening into the wider Hellenistic world.

The non-Jewish, Hellenistic world was polytheistic. Its inhabitants saw no problem with combining worship of many gods. Religion consisted of relating to the gods in such a way that one was protected and successful in this life. There was less belief in the afterlife than one finds in Judaism and Christianity. There was a great variety of gods to choose from, from the great and most powerful, like Jupiter and Zeus, to civic gods that protected cities, like Athena, to household gods. Mystery religions, still shrouded in secrecy as we try to penetrate their closely guarded beliefs and rituals, concentrated on the individual and created a bond between believer and god or goddess designed to protect the believer in this life and perhaps gain him or her happiness in the next. Many divine beings were portrayed as saviors, able to rescue their adherents from the many dangers inherent in the ancient world—disease, early death (life expectancy may have been as short as forty years), attack by robbers and thieves, shipwreck, ruin at the hands of public officials, warfare, and so on. Belief as such was far less important to religion than was proper service to the gods so that they would benefit humans.

The unseen world was also populated by demons and beings less than gods but greater than humans. Religion and magic helped to control these beings and ensure their positive attitude toward humans. In the face of a world that was often hostile, astrology afforded a way to know one's fate.

There was no firm boundary between religion on the one hand and politics and kinship on the other. Each citizen had to attend to local duties, including being loyal to his or her own city or village, as well as broader duties, such as loyalty to the empire and rendering both financial and religious support to the emperor and his household and "friends," political allies. Worship of the emperor, called the *emperor cult* or *imperial cult*, was an important way that provincials could show loyalty to the supreme political authorities. Emperors claimed to bring peace, prosperity, and justice to the world. Good emperors were thought to join the pantheon at death, so that their sons on the thrones were considered sons of gods.

The line between divinity and humanity was far less clearly drawn in this world than it was in the Jewish world (although even in Judaism left room for many figures who although they were not equal to God nonetheless were divine in some sense), and mythology told of half-human, half-divine figures such as Heracles and Dionysus, and miraculous and semi-divine status was attributed to some humans. Apollonius of Tyana was a contemporary of Jesus who was depicted as a teacher and miracle worker in ways similar to the ways in which the Gospels depict Jesus, although the source for this is late and may be influenced by Christian stories.

Philosophy was of interest not just to the elite. Its influence was felt more widely in society. Three main streams of thought—Platonism, Aristotelianism, and Stoicism—affected the way just about everyone thought about the world. Philosophy was interested in doctrine but also in behavior. It was slanted toward encouraging lifestyles that would let one live in accord with nature and with one's own place in the universe, thus engendering happiness and success.

These few comments show how complex a task it is fully to appreciate the multiple contexts that gave rise to the Gospels. At the least, it raises awareness in us as readers that the world behind the Gospels is quite different from our own and that it requires effort on our part to understand it.

CONCLUSION

The Gospels were written about two thousand years ago in the eastern Roman Empire. They were composed in Greek and were influenced by Hellenistic literary genres and culture. They describe a world of Galilean and Jewish peasants and artisans who speak Aramaic and whose symbolic universe is formed largely by Judaism's sacred texts. They root the Jesus movement deeply in the traditions and institutions of Israel and yet they manifest serious discontinuities with that realm. They participate in an apocalyptic worldview in which the events of Jesus' life, death, and resurrection have cosmic significance and change forever the relationship of God with humanity and with the world.

It is hardly surprising that countless scholars have found more than a lifetime's work in trying to master just a fragment of the knowledge helpful to understand the Gospels as products of their time and place. This chapter, brief as it is, supplies enough information to correct some common misperceptions, contextualize some issues, and allow our historical imaginations to begin to fill in gaps in the texts more effectively. We now plunge into the Gospels themselves, realizing that we are entering a world quite different from our own.

BIBLIOGRAPHY

Barclay, John. *Jews in the Mediterranean Diaspora: From Alexander to Trajan* (323 B.C.E.–117 B.C.E). Berkeley: University of California Press, 1996.

Beard, Mary, John North, and Simon Price. *Religions of Rome*. Cambridge: Cambridge University Press, 1998.

Boring, M. Eugene, Klaus Berger, and Carsten Colpe. *Hellenistic Commentary to the New Testament*. Nashville: Abingdon, 1995.

Cohen, Shaye J. D. *The Beginnings of Jewishness: Boundaries, Varieties, Uncertainties*. Berkeley: University of California Press, 1999.

———. *From the Maccabees to the Mishnah*. Philadelphia: Westminster, 1987.

Collins, John J. *The Apocalyptic Imagination: An Introduction to the Jewish Matrix of Christianity*. New York: Crossroad, 1984.

———. *Apocalypticism in the Dead Sea Scrolls*. New York: Routledge, 1997.

———. *Between Athens and Jerusalem: Jewish Identity in the Hellenistic Diaspora*. 2nd ed. Grand Rapids: William B. Eerdmans Pub., 2000.

———. *The Scepter and the Star: The Messiahs of the Dead Sea Scrolls and Other Ancient Literature*. New York: Doubleday, 1995.

Cook, Stephen L. *Prophecy and Apocalypticism: The Postexilic Social Setting*. Minneapolis: Fortress, 1995.

Daube, David. *The New Testament and Rabbinic Judaism*. Peabody, Mass.: Hendrickson, 1956.

Dunn, James D. G. *The Partings of the Ways: Between Christianity and Judaism and Their Significance for the Character of Christianity*. Phildelphia: Trinity, 1991.

Goodman, Martin. *The Roman World, 44 B.C.–A.D. 180*. New York: Routledge, 1997.

———. *The Ruling Class of Judea: The Origins of the Jewish Revolt against Rome, A.D. 66–70*. Cambridge: Cambridge University Press, 1987.

Hanson, K. C., and Douglas Oakman. *Palestine in the Time of Jesus: Social Structures and Social Conflicts*. Minneapolis: Fortress, 1998.

Hengel, Martin. *The "Hellenization" of Judea in the First Century after Christ*. London: SCM Press, 1989.

———. *Judaism and Hellenism: Studies in Their Encounter in Palestine during the Early Hellenistic Period*. Philadelphia: Fortress, 1979.

Horsley, Richard A., and John S. Hanson. *Bandits, Prophets and Messiahs: Popular Movements in the Time of Jesus*. Harrisburg, Penn.: Trinity, 1999.

Jaffee, Martin. *Early Judaism*. Upper Saddle River, N.J.: Prentice-Hall, 1997.

Jeremias, Joachim. *Jerusalem in the Time of Jesus*. Philadelphia: Fortress, 1969.

Klawans, Jonathan. *Impurity and Sin in Ancient Judaism*. New York: Oxford University Press, 2000.

Lenski, Gerhard E. *Power and Privilege: A Theory of Social Stratification*. New York: McGraw-Hill, 1966.

Malina, Bruce. *Christian Origins and Cultural Anthropology: Practical Models for Biblical Interpretation*. Atlanta: John Knox, 1986.

———. *The New Testament World: Insights from Cultural Anthropology*. Atlanta: John Knox, 1981.

Murphy, Frederick J. *Early Judaism: The Exile to the Time of Jesus*. Peabody, Mass.: Hendrickson, 2002.

Neusner, Jacob. *From Politics to Piety: The Emergence of Pharisaic Judaism*, 2d ed. New York: Ktav, 1979.

Overman, J. Andrew, and William Scott Green. "Judaism (Greco-Roman Period)." *ABD* 3:1037-1054.

Peters, Melvin K. "Septuagint." *ABD* 5:1093-1104.

Price, S. R. F. *Rituals and Power: The Roman Imperial Cult in Asia Minor*. Cambridge: Cambridge University Press, 1984.

Rhoads, David. *Israel in Revolution, 6–74 C.E.: A Political History Based on the Writings of Josephus*. Philadelphia: Fortress, 1976.

Safrai, S., and M. Stern, eds. *The Jewish People in the First Century*. 2 vols. Assen, Netherlands: Van Gorcum, 1974–1976.

Saldarini, Anthony J. *Pharisees, Scribes and Sadduces in Palestinian Society*. Wilmington: Michael Glazier, 1988.

Sanders, E. P. *Judaism: Practice and Belief, 63* B.C.E.–66 C.E. Philadelphia: Trinity, 1992.

Schiffman, Lawrence H. *From Text to Tradition: A History of Second Temple and Rabbinic Judaism*. Hoboken, N.J.: Ktav, 1991.

Schürer, Emil. *The History of the Jewish People in the Age of Jesus Christ (175* B.C.–A.D. 135). Revised and edited by Geza Vermes, Fergus Millar, and Matthew Black. 3 vols. Edinburgh: T & T Clark, 1973–1987.

Schwartz, Seth. *Imperialism and Jewish Society, 200* B.C.E. *to 640* C.E. Princeton: Princeton University Press, 2001.

Segal, Alan F. *Rebecca's Children: Judaism and Christianity in the Roman World*. Cambridge: Harvard University Press, 1986.

Sherwin-White, A. N. *Roman Society and Roman Law in the New Testament*. Oxford: Clarendon Press, 1963.

Stambaugh, John E., and David L. Balch. *The New Testament in Its Social Environment*. Philadelphia: Westminster, 1986.

Stegemann, Ekkehard W., and Wolfgang Stegemann. *The Jesus Movement: A Social History of Its First Century*. Minneapolis: Fortress, 1999.

Tcherikover, Victor. *Hellenistic Civilization and the Jews*. Peabody, Mass.: Hendrickson, 1999.

Turcan, Robert. *The Cults of the Roman Empire*. Oxford, U.K.: Blackwell, 1996.

VanderKam, James. *The Dead Sea Scrolls Today*. Grand Rapids: Eerdmans, 1994.

———. *An Introduction to Early Judaism*. Grand Rapids: Eerdmans, 2001.

Vermes, Geza. *The Dead Sea Scrolls in English*, 3d ed. Baltimore: Penguin, 1987.

CHAPTER THREE

THE GOSPEL OF MARK

INTRODUCTION

Mark is our oldest gospel and our shortest one. It has just over fifteen chapters. The name *Mark* was added to the beginning of the Gospel only in the second century, when the four canonical gospels were collected, so we cannot be sure of the author's name. Early Christian tradition about gospel authorship is not necessarily reliable. By convention, we continue to call the author Mark and also to refer to the Gospel itself as Mark.

All we can know about the author we learn from the Gospel itself. He was reasonably well educated. Few in the ancient world could read and write, and Mark was an exception. His writing exhibits sophistication and subtlety, even if his Greek is a bit rough. He was probably from somewhere outside Palestine, considering misconceptions he has about Palestinian geography. He probably writes for Gentiles, since he needs to explain Jewish customs (7:3-4).

Most scholars date the Gospel to around 70 C.E., when the Romans destroyed the temple in Jerusalem. The event looms large in Mark 13. The Gospel is partly a response to this catastrophe. Mark emphasizes the world's hostility to Jesus and warns Christians to expect the same treatment. Mark wrote not long after Nero's persecution of Christians in 64 C.E. Later tradition connects the Gospel with Rome or Alexandria. We have no firm evidence that Mark used sources other than oral tradition about Jesus, but some have suggested that a written source lies behind the parables collection in chapter 4, a miracles collection behind some of the miracles, an apocalyptic discourse behind chapter 13, and a basic passion narrative behind Mark's account of Jesus' death and resurrection.

STRUCTURE

THE BEGINNING

Matthew and Luke begin with birth narratives, and each has a genealogy of Jesus. Luke includes a short story about Jesus' childhood. All this accords with conventions of ancient biography. Mark has none of this. His Gospel opens with a brief descriptive title and then immediately tells of John the Baptist's mission. John comes in fulfillment of ancient prophecy to prepare the way for Jesus. Jesus appears, is baptized, goes to the desert to struggle with Satan, and comes back to begin his ministry. All this transpires within fifteen verses.

THE END

Modern translations provide three endings for the Gospel, based on different manuscripts. In the best manuscripts, the Gospel ends at 16:8. There are no resurrection appearances recounted. Women visit Jesus' tomb, find it empty, and an angel tells them to report Jesus' resurrection to the apostles, but "they said nothing to anyone, for they were afraid" (16:8). This is an odd ending, requiring explanation. There are no resurrection appearances.

THREE MAIN PARTS

The Gospel is in three main parts. The first extends to 8:26. In this section, Jesus publicly exorcises demons, does miracles, and teaches. He calls disciples to follow him. The second part is 8:27–10:45, framed by healings of blind men in 8:22-26 and 10:46-52. Here he privately teaches his disciples that he must suffer, die, and rise. The third part consists of Jesus' activity in Jerusalem, his suffering and death, and the scene of the empty tomb (11:1–16:8).

TURNING POINT

The first scene of section 2 transpires at Caesarea Philippi, north of Galilee (8:27–9:1). Jesus asks Peter, "Who do you say that I am?" Peter answers, "You are the Messiah." Jesus describes his impending suffering, and Peter refuses to accept it. Jesus rebukes Peter and teaches his disciples about the necessity of his (and their) suffering. The scene introduces the Gospel's second part, where this threefold pattern occurs two more times: prediction of the passion, misunderstanding by the disciples, and Jesus' teaching. The entire section is in the context of a journey to Jerusalem for the Passover. It is to be a fateful trip.

THE PASSION NARRATIVE

Passion means Jesus' suffering and death. Mark has been called a passion narrative with an introduction because it emphasizes Jesus' passion. This characterization does not do justice to other elements of the Gospel. It is true, however, that all other elements—be they miracles, teaching, or travels—are all colored by the passion.

No outline of any gospel can be fully satisfactory. There are almost as many outlines as there are interpreters. But outlines are useful as aids to getting a picture of entire gospels and of their basic shapes. The outline below takes the summaries as the key to the structure of Mark's first part. Each section of the first part ends with a summary, except for the last.

Part I: Jesus' Public Ministry (1:1-8:21)
  Introduction (1:1-15)
  First Section: First Day of Ministry (1:16-34)
  Second Section: Jesus Defines His Ministry (1:35-39)
  Third Section: Conflicts with Authorities (1:40–3:12)
  Fourth Section: Further Ministry in Galilee and across the Sea of Galilee (3:13–6:6)
  Fifth Section: Further Ministry in Galilee and across the Sea of Galilee (6:7-56)
  Sixth Section: Further Ministry in Galilee and Surrounding Areas (7:1–8:21)
Part II: Teaching the Disciples on the Way to Jerusalem (8:22–10:52)
  Opening Frame: Healing of Blind Man in Stages (8:22-26)
  First Teaching Cycle (8:27–9:29)
  Second Teaching Cycle (9:30–10:31)
  Third Teaching Cycle (10:32-45)
  Closing Frame: Healing of Blind Man (10:46-52)
Part III: Jesus in Jerusalem (11:1–16:8)
  Confrontation with Authorities (11:1–12:44)
  Apocalyptic Discourse (13:1-37)
  Passion and Death (14:1–15:47)
  Empty Tomb (16:1-8)
  Added Endings: The Shorter Ending and the Longer Ending

OVERVIEW

Mark sees the world in apocalyptic terms. The world is subject to Satan. History is predetermined, and God plans to reassert sovereignty over the world. Jesus appears announcing that the time is fulfilled and God's kingdom has drawn near (1:15). Humans should repent and believe this good news (gospel). Jesus, designated "Son of God" at his baptism, is God's eschatological agent, but no one grasps Jesus' true identity. Peter comes closest when he declares Jesus to be Messiah, but even he does not fully understand Jesus' mission.

Jesus' first acts are to confront Satan and his demons and to begin the final battle against them. In this battle, there are only two sides. The religious leaders prove themselves to be against God's agent. Jesus argues with them about God's will, particularly as expressed in Torah. He travels to Jerusalem, home to God's temple. He confronts the religious authorities, especially the priests, to whom God has entrusted Israel and the temple. He disrupts commercial activity in the temple, a prophetic action that leads to his death. He predicts the temple's destruction.

In the battle with Satan, those on God's side suffer. John the Baptist and then Jesus are handed over to those who kill them. Peter refuses to accept suffering as part of messiahship, so Jesus calls him Satan. Peter is on the wrong side of the eschatological struggle. Jesus insists that not only must he suffer in this struggle, but disciples must also be handed over to persecution and death. In the face of this opposition, first Jesus and then the disciples must oppose Satan through exorcisms and proclamation of God's kingdom. Ultimately, Jesus will return as the Son of Man to rescue his elect and to effect the consummation of all history. Ultimate victory is assured.

Things to Look For

- There is no infancy narrative at the beginning and no appearances of the risen Jesus at the end.
- Mark's story moves quickly. Note the frequent use of the adverb "immediately." An eschatological urgency pervades the Gospel. It has many apocalyptic elements.
- Mark forges small traditional units into a narrative structure.
- Jesus' identity is a recurrent issue. The most common reactions to him are misunderstanding, fear, amazement, and puzzlement.

- Jesus hides his identity. The demons understand who he is, for they belong to the superhuman world.
- The generally fast pace of the narrative slows down during the passion narrative. Many elements of the Gospel point forward to Jesus' death and resurrection.
- Jesus comes from Galilee and much of his ministry is carried out there. His trip to Jerusalem brings about his death.
- Exorcisms are prominent and are part of Jesus' end-time battle against Satan and the coming of God's kingdom.
- Jesus tries to keep the miracles quiet.
- The title *Son of God* is kept secret from the characters. Those who know it are God, Jesus, and the demons, and, in the end, the centurion at the crucifixion.
- The common people come to Jesus for healing.
- The leaders are almost all hostile to Jesus and plot against him.
- The disciples generally fail to fully understand Jesus. In the end, they abandon him to his fate.
- Mark frequently uses ring structure. It can be a simple ABA or can be more complicated. Mark often uses this to frame one event with another, or to structure sections. The events cast light on one another.
- Jesus is presented in human terms. He gets angry, is sad, has limited knowledge, and is not always able to do miracles.
- Irony pervades the Gospel. Readers know more than characters (dramatic irony). Characters say things whose implications they do not grasp, although the readers do.

GOSPEL SURVEY

Part I: Jesus' Public Ministry (1:1–8:21)

Introduction (1:1-15)

1:1: Descriptive Title. Readers learn right away that Jesus is Messiah and Son of God. Defining these terms is central to the Gospel. As we follow the plot, we pay attention to what degree the characters understand what the readers find out at the beginning. We also ask whether readers, who have been told Jesus' identity, truly understand it. Mark intends to change his readers' understanding of what it means to be Messiah and Son of God.

1:2-13: Beginning of the Eschatological Drama; Jesus' Commissioning. Mark begins his narrative with John the Baptist, who prepares Jesus' way. These verses are like a trumpet flourish, signaling the gravity of the eschatological events about to unfold. John appears "as it is written in the prophet Isaiah." Mark quotes from ancient prophecy to the effect that God foretold John's mission. He combines a verse from Malachi with one from Isaiah and brings in some material from Exodus, mistakenly ascribing all of this to Isaiah. Malachi predicts a messenger from God, sent to prepare for one to follow (Mal 3:1). In Exod 23:20, God tells Israel that God will send an angel before it in the desert. Isaiah speaks of a voice in the desert telling his hearers to "prepare the way of the Lord." Mark applies these prophecies to John the Baptist. Later in his book, Malachi predicts that before God comes in judgment, the ancient Israelite prophet Elijah will come to warn the people (4:5-6). Mark implicitly identifies John with Elijah. John is in the desert, preaching a baptism for the forgiveness of sins, and great crowds flock to him. John looks like Elijah (Mark 1:6; see 2 Kgs 1:8) and is himself a prophet, foretelling Jesus' coming: "The one who is more powerful than I is coming after me; I am not worthy to stoop down and untie the thong of his sandals. I have baptized you with water; but he will baptize you with the Holy Spirit" (1:7-8). Fulfillment of John's words comes immediately, for Jesus appears and is baptized.

The desert has many possible connotations among ancient Jews. It can be the place of danger and of evil spirits. It can be a refuge from oppressive leaders, foreign and domestic. It can recall Israel's escape from Egypt and God's protection in the wilderness and forming of a covenant with Israel at Sinai.

After Jesus' baptism, the heavens open and the spirit descends on him in the form of a dove, and a voice comes from heaven saying, "You are my Son, the Beloved; with you I am well pleased" (1:11). The voice is God's, so the reader receives confirmation from God of what the Gospel's first line reveals—Jesus is Son of God. This makes Jesus a reliable character in whom readers have a dependable guide to God's purposes. God commissions Jesus as Son of God to accomplish a specific job. The nature of that job becomes clear in the ensuing narrative. Note that none of the characters in the narrative except Jesus are said to see the heavens opened, the Spirit descend, or to hear God's voice.

After his baptism, Jesus "is driven" out into the desert by God's Spirit to be tested by Satan (1:12). Conflict between Jesus and Satan pervades the Gospel, paralleling Jesus' struggle with human opponents. John is arrested—literally, "handed over" (1:14). The same verb (*paradidomi*) is later applied to Jesus (when the NRSV says that Judas "betrays" Jesus in ch. 14, the Greek has *paradidomi*) and to Christians (ch. 13), so John's arrest and death (6:14-29) foreshadow that of Jesus and of Christians.

David Aune argues that this beginning to the Gospel substitutes for the usual information about a person's origins at the opening of biographies. In Jesus' case, one need not know about his genealogy, education, or childhood to grasp his true origin. Jesus is God's chosen representative whose way God has prepared through Israel's prophets and John's prophetic mission. Those who accept this find in Jesus the key to under-standing God's action in the world. Jesus' career is eschatologically charged, and Mark's narrative exhibits the urgency of the last days. Jesus' deeds and words are the way that God's eschatological power becomes present to the world.

Summary (1:14-15). After John's arrest, Jesus enters Galilee, "pro-claiming the good news (gospel) of God, and saying, 'The time is fulfilled, and the kingdom of God has come near; repent, and believe in the good news.' " This describes not a single act but is a generalization, a summary. Jesus utters an eschatological proclamation. The fulfillment of the time assumes the determination of history common in apocalypticism. All of history leads up to this point. Jesus announces the impending arrival of God's kingdom, implying that until now God has not been in full control of creation.

The reader now knows the following: Jesus is Son of God and Messiah, his coming concerns "good news," Jesus' career forms part of God's end-time action which is near, Jesus is commissioned by God as Son of God, this designates an eschatological role, and this role entails conflict with Satan.

First Section: First Day of Ministry (1:16-34)

1:16-20: First Disciples Called. At the beginning of the first day of his public ministry, Jesus calls four fishermen to follow him. They do so instantly and without any explicit motivation. The Gospel is moving fast, and Jesus' mission sweeps up the disciples. The power of Jesus' presence may overwhelm them. They leave behind their families and jobs. Since they are present from the beginning of Jesus' career, they witness all of it.

1:21-28: Exorcism. Jesus' first public act is to exorcise an "unclean spirit" in a synagogue. For Mark, an unclean spirit is a demon in Satan's service. *Unclean* means what should not come into God's presence. Mark uses the term eleven times for evil spirits. *Unclean* or *impure* does not necessarily imply sinful, as we noted in the previous chapter, but here it has the meaning of moral impurity. By presenting exorcism as Jesus' first act, Mark highlights his conflict with Satan, prince of demons. The demon recognizes Jesus' eschatological task—he comes to battle demonic forces. Exorcisms and demonic recognition of Jesus continue throughout part I. Jesus silences the demon to keep his identity unknown. This aspect of the Gospel is called the *messianic secret*.

The crowds marvel at Jesus' accomplishment but do not know who he is. They know only that this is a "new teaching" and that Jesus' authority exceeds that of the scribes. The crowds comment on Jesus' teaching, but the reader hears no specific teachings. For Mark, the exorcism itself is authoritative teaching. It shows God's power present in Jesus to defeat Satan. The contrast between Jesus and the scribes foreshadows Jesus' conflict with religious authorities.

1:29-31: Peter's Mother-in-Law. We will address Jesus' cure of Peter's mother-in-law in our section on women. It is important to note here, however, that Jesus' first cure, aside from the exorcism, is done for a woman. We must keep in mind as we proceed that many other cures referred to in the summaries throughout the Gospel would have been of women.

Summary (1:32-34). A summary stresses Jesus' growing fame, his healings and exorcisms, and the fact that the demons know his identity and he silences them. Jesus hides his identity but cannot keep his healings quiet. The crowds know only that he possesses tremendous power to heal and exorcise.

Second Section: Jesus Defines His Ministry (1:35-39)

1:35-38: Other Villages. Early in the morning Jesus rises to pray (1:35-38). Peter looks for him, for the crowds seek him. Jesus informs Peter that he must go to other villages to preach. He is itinerant, always on the move. He must spread his message as widely and as quickly as possible. It is why he has come.

Summary (1:39). A short summary speaks of Jesus preaching the message in "their" synagogues and exorcising (1:39). The use of the word "their" distances Mark's readers (and Jesus) from Jewish synagogues.

Third Section: Conflicts with Authorities (1:40–3:12)

1:40-45: Curing a Leper, Confronting the Priests. Jesus touches a leper. Lepers were impure, and Lev 13:45-46 says that lepers had to live "outside the camp" and warn people of their presence by shouting "unclean." Thus, they lived outside of proper society. Jesus' touch cures, and so purifies, the man. As we have said before in our discussion of purity (see ch. 2), most people would be ritually unclean most of the time, and this would mean only that they could not participate in the cult. Before doing so, they would have to undergo a purification ritual. But in the case of leprosy, the underlying cause of uncleanness, leprosy, must be cured before any purification can be effected. Leprosy isolates the person (see Lev 13). Jacob Milgrom notes that leprosy was associated with death (see, for example, Num 12:12). Purification will allow the person to rejoin society fully, to be able to enter the temple, and so on.

Jesus should have become unclean by touching the leper. From one point of view, this is hardly a major problem for him, since it would become an issue only if he were to enter the temple. If he wished to do that, he could undergo a purification ritual. At the same time, it is symbolically important that in a situation where the leper has a disease that renders him unfit to participate in the cult, and where Jesus himself can be excluded from the cult, even if only temporarily, Jesus' touch instead spreads purity, a state that enables one to participate in the cult. The point is not a criticism of the purity system. Rather it is that Jesus is the one through whom God's power becomes present.

Jesus tells the cured man to complete his reintegration into society by following Torah in showing himself to the priests and making the proper offering. On one level, Jesus merely tells the man to follow the procedures laid out by Torah for a cured leper. On another, Jesus sends a signal to the priests, announcing his power and forcing them to validate it. The episode introduces five conflicts and foreshadows Jesus' showdown with the priests at the end of the Gospel. Jesus also tells the man to keep the miracle quiet. The man disobeys and spreads the word everywhere.

2:1-12: Authority to Forgive Sins. People bring a paralytic to Jesus, circumventing the crowd by letting the man down through the roof. Jesus forgives the man's sins. The scribes accuse him of blasphemy, since he arrogates to himself authority proper to God. The charge reappears when Jesus appears before the Sanhedrin, and that body agrees that he deserves to die, the appropriate punishment for blasphemy (14:61-64). There he is accused of blasphemy because he admits that he is the Son of God. Most critical scholars agree that this reflects later Christian belief, and so the trial scene is not historical in that respect (see our discussion of Jesus' death in ch. 8). There is a debate among scholars about just what blasphemy consisted of at this time. The *Mishnah*, a rabbinic collection of mainly legal rulings and beliefs, dating to around the early third century, says that the divine name must be pronounced aloud for there to be blasphemy (*m. Sanh.* 7a). In the New Testament, making oneself equal to God or claiming divine authority is considered blasphemy, as here. The term *blasphemy* can also be applied to humans and designate disrespectful or abusive speech, and applied to God, it can mean such speech directed against God, even if the divine name is not mentioned. Darrell Bock argues that Jesus' claim to authority would have been considered an affront to God and so blasphemous. This is indeed how Mark and other New Testament texts see it, although we side with those who see this as an early church development.

To prove that "the Son of Man" (Jesus himself) has such authority, Jesus cures the man. This is the only incident in Mark's Gospel where Jesus performs a miracle to prove something. As the proclaimer of God's kingdom, Jesus can free humans from all that oppresses them, be it physical infirmity or their own sin that distances them from God's healing power. The crowd is amazed and praises God, saying, "We have never seen anything like this!" The crowd regards Jesus as unique, but they still do not quite understand him.

Clearly, this is not a straight miracle story. Most miracle stories would consist of the coming of the petitioner and description of the illness, the cure, and the reaction of witnesses. This one is more complicated. It becomes a controversy between Jesus and the scribes. A controversy story would consist most simply of some sort of objection raised by Jesus' opponents and his response. One can extract from this passage a simple healing story, and then compare it to Mark's text to see how it has been turned into a controversy story. There is some narrative awkwardness in 2:10, which might indicate that Mark or his source actually did take an existing healing and transform it.

2:13-17: Eating with the Wrong People. Jesus calls Levi the tax collector and then dines with a disreputable crowd, including sinners and tax collectors. The precise meaning of "sinners" here is debated. We take up this question in chapter 8, when we discuss the historical Jesus. Tax collectors are not popular figures in any culture, but here they may be seen as allied with the Romans or with Herod. The scribes and Pharisees criticize him. He responds, "I have come to call not the righteous but sinners." God's action in Jesus does not confirm the religious and social status quo; it challenges it. As Jesus touching the leper does not make him impure but purifies the leper, so Jesus eating with tax collectors and sinners does not put him outside the people of God—it redefines God's people. If Jesus has not come for the "righteous," then the righteous are so only in name. Those who experience God's eschatological sanctifying and salvific action are those who gather around Jesus.

2:18-22: Fasting. Jesus defends his and his disciple's refusal to fast on the grounds that his ministry is comparable to a joyful wedding celebration. Jesus predicts that when he is gone, the church will again fast. His metaphor that one does not put new wine into old wineskins implies that what Jesus does is incompatible with the "old" religious ways, an implicit affirmation that Judaism is being surpassed.

2:23-28: Working on the Sabbath. The Pharisees consider the disciples' plucking of grain a Torah violation, for the Ten Commandments require refraining from work on the Sabbath. Jesus frames a legal argument, pointing out that religious prohibitions were suspended in the case of King David (a precedent), enunciating the general principle that humans come before religious institutions, and claiming for himself, as Son of Man, the right to rule on Sabbath observance.

3:1-5: Curing on the Sabbath. Jesus dramatically teaches that human need overrides Sabbath regulations by curing on the Sabbath. He is angered at his opponents' objections and at their refusal to stretch their notions of religious propriety to make room for God's healing action. Torah prohibits work on the Sabbath, but precisely what sorts of activity that excluded was debated in first-century Judaism. Later rabbinic evidence allows medical treatment when a life is in danger, but there is also evidence that some rabbis had a still more lenient interpretation. So it is not at all clear that this story is a question of Jesus opposing contemporary Jewish law in general. Rather, we ought to see it as Jesus engaging in a controversy in which many of his fellow Jews were also engaged.

3:6: Plot against Jesus. "The Pharisees went out and immediately conspired with the Herodians against him, how to destroy him." This foreshadows Jesus' passion and death. Mark thereby connects the preceding controversies with Jesus' death.

Summary (3:7-12). A summary forms a transition between the initial section and the next part of Jesus' ministry. It stresses Jesus' growing fame, his healings and exorcisms, and his silencing of the demons since they recognize him as "the Son of God."

Fourth Section: Further Ministry in Galilee and across the Sea of Galilee (3:13–6:6)

3:13-19a: Appointment of the Twelve. Jesus appoints the twelve apostles. He does so on a mountain, a conventional scene of religious events. Jesus calls "whom he wanted," emphasizing his authority. He chooses Judas, said to be the one "who betrayed him," so he in some sense is party to his own demise. Jesus' death is part of God's plan. Jesus commissions the disciples to "proclaim the message (preach), and to have authority to cast out demons." They do what Jesus does. Discipleship follows Christology. As Jesus carries on the eschatological battle against Satan, so do they.

3:19b-21: Charge of Insanity. Jesus' family tries to seize him because people say he is insane (3:19b-21). This, together with the episode involving the family in 3:31-35, creates a frame around Jesus' conflict with Jerusalem scribes over his exorcisms. The effect is to associate his family with those who think Jesus is insane and with the scribes who accuse him of collaboration with Satan.

3:22-30: Scribes Accuse Jesus. The Jerusalem scribes do not deny that Jesus does exorcisms; they accuse him of doing so by Satan's power. This is ironic. He explains his exorcisms as plundering Satan's house (the world) and ending his kingdom. He condemns the scribes for attributing to Satan the work of the Holy Spirit. The entire episode has an apocalyptic flavor.

3:31-35: Jesus' Family. As Jesus teaches, his mother and brothers stand "outside." When he is told they are asking for him, he asks, "Who are my mother and my brothers?" Looking at those around him he says, "Here are my mother and my brothers! Whoever does the will of God is my brother and sister and mother." Jesus apparently does not go outside to see his family, who appear to be outsiders. He redefines his family as those who obey God, which means, in effect, following him. Tension between family and mission is echoed further on, when Jesus teaches about discipleship.

4:1-34: Parables. Here we finally get a sizable chunk of Jesus' teaching. It turns out to be puzzling teaching, for it is not fully open to all. For Mark, Jesus uses parables not to teach some lesson but to preserve "the secret of the kingdom of God." He begins with the parable of the Sower, which tells of a variety of ways in which people might react to God's word, most of which are negative. Those who accept the word become a part of something that seems small but has huge results. The allusion to Jesus and his movement is obvious.

When asked by his disciples what the parable means, he does explain it to them privately (4:14-20). To them has been given the "secret of the kingdom of God" (4:11). They are the chosen. He uses parables so that people on the outside "may indeed look, but not perceive, and may indeed listen, but not understand; so that they may not turn again and be forgiven" (4:12). Apocalypticism often interprets the world's refusal to heed its message by saying that it is open only to the few elect. This is what Mark's Jesus does here. But the message does not stay hidden forever. Eventually all will know the truth. In the parabolic saying about not hiding one's light under a basket, Jesus discloses that the veil of secrecy will be lifted in the future (4:21-22). That will be a time of judgment (4:23-25). We learn elsewhere that this happens after Jesus' resurrection (9:9). Meanwhile, Jesus explains everything to his disciples, the insiders. They receive the secret of the kingdom (4:11), and he elucidates the parables for them (4:33-34).

The parable of the Growing Seed makes the point that once the word is planted, the growth of the kingdom is mysterious. The harvest, often used as a figure for the judgment, will be obvious. The parable of the Mustard Seed claims that small beginnings have large outcomes, a pattern that applies to Jesus and his followers.

4:35-41: First Boat Scene. Three boat scenes punctuate part I (4:35-41; 6:45-52; 8:14-21). They describe intimate interaction between Jesus and his followers. Mark uses these opportunities to portray the disciples' lack of understanding of Jesus and his mission. The first of the scenes follows the parable collection. It is night, and Jesus and the disciples are in the middle of the Sea of Galilee. A storm arises, and Jesus is asleep. In a panic, the disciples awaken him and say, "Teacher, do you not care that we are perishing?" He awakens, calms the sea, and says, "Why are you afraid? Have you still no faith?" The disciples are "filled with great awe" and say to one another, "Who then is this, that even the wind and the sea obey him?"

Resonances of the Hebrew Bible are perceptible here. God's power over the sea signifies divine sovereignty over all creation. The psalmist sings to God: "You rule the raging of the sea; / when its waves rise, you still them" (Ps 89:9). This psalm is messianic—it is about the Davidic king. Speaking of the king, God says, "I will set his hand on the sea / and his right hand on the rivers" (89:25). The psalm originally means that Israel's king will rule over the area between the Mediterranean and the rivers (the Euphrates and its tributaries). The psalm's language can be taken mythologically, as in Mark. As Messiah, Jesus shares God's power over the waters. What is surprising is that the disciples do not understand this. After all, they know the secret of the kingdom (4:11).

5:1-20: The Gerasene Demoniac. Jesus enters Gentile territory and encounters a man with an unclean spirit. The spirit exclaims, "What have you do to with me, Jesus, Son of the Most High God? I adjure you by God, do not torment me" (5:7). The spirit knows Jesus comes to overthrow Satan's dominion. Jesus demands to know the demon's name. It is "Legion," an allusion to the Roman army. A legion is a Roman division. So the demon turns out to be many demons. Jesus orders them into nearby swine, who rush into the lake and drown. Jewish readers would enjoy demonic representation of Roman soldiers and their confinement to pigs, an unclean animal. Mark, however, seems to be writing mainly for Gentile Christians. They too would be pleased with this condemnation of Roman power, particularly in light of Nero's persecution of Christians in 64 C.E. and possible further Roman hostility.

5:21-43: Curing a Woman and a Girl. Jairus, a synagogue leader, asks Jesus to cure his daughter. As he goes to Jairus's house, a woman suffering from a hemorrhage touches his garment, hoping to obtain a cure. Her hopes are fulfilled. Jesus praises her faith. He then arrives at Jairus's house to find his daughter dead. He raises her and commands that the event be kept private. The family is amazed. Both stories illustrate Jesus' possession of God's eschatological power to heal, even to defeat death.

6:1-6a: Rejection at the Nazareth Synagogue. Jesus teaches in his hometown synagogue. They are astounded at his wisdom and power. How can one whom they know have such wisdom and power? They take offense. Jesus explains, "Prophets are not without honor, except in their hometown, and among their own kin, and in their own house." The episode reinforces the impression from chapter 3 that Jesus' family, his "kin," objects to his ministry. Misunderstanding and rejection continue. It is noteworthy that their lack of faith results in a disabling of Jesus' healing ministry: "He could do no deed of power there." Mark quickly adds, "Except that he laid hands on a few sick people and cured them." This reads like a correction to the notice that lack of faith limits what Jesus can do. Perhaps Mark added it to a traditional story.

Summary (6:6b). Despite rejection at the Nazareth synagogue, Jesus continues teaching in the villages.

Fifth Section: Further Ministry in Galilee and across the Sea of Galilee (6:7-56)

6:7-13: Mission of the Twelve. Jesus sends out the twelve, two by two, granting them authority over unclean spirits. They are itinerant and live off the support of others. They take no bread, or bag, or money. Those who do not listen to them are in turn rejected by the disciples. They proclaim repentance, exorcise, and heal, a ministry that extends that of Jesus.

6:14-29: Death of John the Baptist. Herod hears of Jesus and thinks that he is John the Baptist, raised from the dead. He decides this after hearing what others think—that Jesus is John the Baptist raised from the dead, or Elijah, or a prophet like the ancient prophets. Herod is wrong about Jesus, as is everyone else in the Gospel, but his connection of Jesus with John is correct, not just because the two did have a relationship, but also because, for Mark, both play key roles in the eschatological drama. John's fate foreshadows that of Jesus and the church.

6:30-44: Feeding Five Thousand. The crowds follow Jesus to a deserted place and Jesus miraculously feeds them with bread and fish. Two such feeding miracles occur in Mark, differing mainly in numbers fed and baskets left over (see 8:1-10). The miracle recalls a very similar incident in the career of the prophet Elisha, protégé of Elijah (2 Kgs 4:42-44). The same God at work in Elijah and Elisha now acts in Jesus. There is also an allusion to God feeding the people with manna in the desert when Moses was leading them. The feedings foreshadow the institution of the Eucharist at the Last Supper. In all three places, Jesus blesses, breaks, and gives the bread (6:41; 8:6; 14:22).

6:45-52: Second Boat Scene. The disciples set out across the sea without Jesus, who retreats to the hills to pray. In the middle of the night, the wind rises and they have difficulty making headway. Jesus comes to them walking on the water. They are terrified. He identifies himself and tells them not to fear. Jesus gets into the boat, the winds die down, and they immediately make landfall. "They were utterly astounded, for they did not understand about the loaves, but their hearts were hardened."

There are allusions to the Hebrew Bible in this episode, just as in the first boat scene. It is common in the Bible for people to react with fear when God or some other figure appears from the unseen world (for example, Exod 3:1-6; 19:16-25; Ezek 1; Dan 7; 8:15-17; 10). The figure sometimes says something like "Fear not." Such appearances are called *theophanies* (appearances of God) or *angelophanies* (appearances of angels). Jesus walking on the sea recalls God walking on the sea in Job 9:8 and 38:16, signifying the Creator's power. References to the exodus sometimes speak of God walking on or through the sea (Ps 77:19). The disciples miss all this; their hearts "were hardened." The passive voice may mean that God hardens their hearts. This usage is common in Jewish and some Christian literature. But, as in the case of God's hardening Pharaoh's heart at the exodus, that does not absolve them of guilt. By this time the disciples should understand.

Mark attributes the disciples' lack of understanding of the sea miracle to their inability to understand the multiplication of loaves. That miracle recalls God's action through Elijah and Elisha, as well as God's gift of manna to Israel, and it points forward to the Last Supper, where Jesus speaks of his suffering and death and its importance for the new covenant.

Summary (6:53-56). A summary stresses Jesus' fame and healings. He is mobbed by people begging him for healings. Everyone even touching the fringe of his cloak is healed. Jesus is a pious Jew, who wears fringes on his garment in obedience to God's command (Num 15:37-41). Jesus' healing power is undeniable, and the sick are drawn to it, but no one really grasps its full significance.

Sixth Section: Further Ministry in Galilee and Surrounding Areas (7:1–8:21)

7:1-23: Controversy over Purity. Jesus challenges Pharisaic views of purity. Pharisees and scribes from Jerusalem ask why his disciples eat with unwashed hands, transgressing the rules of purity. Jesus condemns Pharisaic purity rules as human regulations and charges that their human-made rules undermine Torah. For example, they use regulations to avoid giving financial support to parents. He quotes Isaiah, who condemns honoring God with the lips but not the heart. They are hypocrites and opposed to God's Law.

Jesus claims that nothing entering a person from outside can cause uncleanness. This seems to negate dietary regulations, which are so important to Judaism. Mark draws that conclusion explicitly: "Thus he declared all foods clean" (7:19b). So for Mark, Jesus annuls a fundamental practice of Judaism.

There are historical problems with Mark's contention that all Jews followed the purification rituals he enumerates. These are practices of a smaller group within Judaism, those who followed Pharisaic injunctions. Mark's association of the Pharisees and the Jerusalem scribes is also problematic. The two groups did not themselves entirely agree on rules of purity. But this is typical of the Gospels. They lump the leaders together in opposition to Jesus and draw minimal distinctions. Further, Jesus probably did not annul dietary rules. We address this in our chapter on the historical Jesus. Note that Mark does not present these as words of Jesus. They are an editorial comment by Mark himself. Many translations even place parentheses around them.

7:24-30: Exorcism of a Syrophoenician Woman's Daughter. This is the only occasion in Mark where Jesus has extended interaction with a Gentile. She begs him to exorcise her daughter. Jesus at first refuses, since his mission is to Israel: "It is not fair to take the children's food and throw it to the dogs." She replies, "Even the dogs under the table eat the children's crumbs." Jesus says, "For saying that, you may go—the demon has left your daughter." She returns home and finds the demon gone. Remarkable are the woman's persistence in the face of Jesus' initial reluctance to help her, the importance of exorcism, Jesus' attitude to Gentiles and his insistence that he is here for Israel, her persuading Jesus, and Jesus curing from a distance.

7:31-37: Cure of a Deaf Man. This happens in the Decapolis, Gentile territory for the most part, so the man may be a Gentile, although Mark does not say so. Jesus employs techniques typical of the day to cure him—spitting, touching in certain ways—that he does not use elsewhere. Perhaps for this reason, Matthew and Luke omit the story. As usual, Jesus commands the witnesses to silence, but they spread the word. All are "astounded beyond measure."

8:1-10: Feeding Four Thousand. The second feeding differs from the first only in details. Some think that the first feeding—five thousand people with twelve baskets left over—represents feeding Israel (twelve tribes), and the second feeding—four thousand people with seven baskets left over—symbolizes feeding Gentiles, since in some texts the world has four corners and consists of seventy nations. The second feeding takes place in Gentile territory while the first is in a Jewish area.

8:11-13: Request for a Sign. The Pharisees demand a sign from Jesus. Mark says, "He sighed deeply in his spirit and said, 'Why does this generation ask for a sign? Truly I tell you, no sign will be given to this generation.' " Whenever Jesus speaks of "this generation," it is in negative terms because of unbelief. Jesus' refusal to give a sign fits the messianic secret and accords with Mark's disapproval of miracles as signs.

8:14-21: Third Boat Scene. In a third and climactic boat scene, tension between Jesus and the disciples comes to a head. The scene is again closely tied to the preceding multiplication of loaves. The disciples have forgotten to bring bread with them and have only one loaf. Jesus warns the disciples about the yeast of the Pharisees and Herod. He means "yeast" figuratively, probably referring to his opponents' teaching (see Matt 16:12). In Jewish culture, yeast could be seen as negative. The house must be cleared of yeast before the feast of the Passover and Unleavened Bread. Small amounts of yeast can have a large result. All of this plays into how Jesus uses the term. But the disciples are, as usual, slow on the uptake, and so they discuss why Jesus speaks about yeast when they have no bread.

Jesus' frustration erupts. He castigates them, saying, "Why are you talking about having no bread? Do you still not perceive or understand? Are your hearts hardened? Do you have eyes, and fail to see? Do you have ears, and fail to hear? And do you not remember?" Jesus gives them a "spot quiz" on the two feedings. They pass easily. They remember the precise number of baskets of leftovers. Jesus says, "Do you not yet understand?" They do not. Close attention to the details of the miracles has not issued in true perception.

PART II: TEACHING THE DISCIPLES ON THE WAY TO JERUSALEM (8:22–10:52)

Part I ends with the disciples' failure to comprehend, so in part II Jesus teaches them about his messiahship. As he instructs them, they travel from Galilee to Jerusalem for Passover. The journey setting lends added urgency to his teaching, for he prepares them for what is to happen at journey's end. As there are three boat scenes, so Jesus' teaching unfolds in three cycles. Each has three parts: Jesus tells of his passion, they misunderstand, and he teaches about his mission and their discipleship.

Opening Frame: Healing of Blind Man in Stages (8:22-26)

Mark frames part II with two healings of blind men. The first is odd in that it takes Jesus two tries to cure the man (8:22-26). At first, the man regains only some sight. He sees "people, but they look like trees, walking." Jesus' second attempt succeeds. In the story that closes the frame, Jesus cures the man on the first attempt (10:46-52).

Neither Matthew nor Luke reproduces the two-step healing, because they do not accept that Jesus was initially unsuccessful. For Mark, the first healing symbolizes Peter's progress toward understanding. Peter's confession, immediately following, shows insight into Jesus, but it is inadequate. The second healing story raises hope that Peter and the others will eventually comprehend and accept the mission of Jesus. Full comprehension does not come to the disciples within part II, or even within the confines of the Gospel as a whole.

First Teaching Cycle (8:27–9:29)

8:27–9:1: Peter's Confession and Misunderstanding; Jesus' Teaching. In a scene that marks the Gospel's turning point, Jesus asks Peter who people say that he is. Peter answers that they think that he is John the Baptist, Elijah, or one of the prophets. Their answers make some sense. John and Jesus belong in the same eschatological set of events. Jesus does do the sorts of things Elijah and Elisha did. Finally, Jesus is a prophet, as he himself indicates in 6:4. But none of these answers really grasps his identity.

Then Jesus asks who Peter thinks Jesus is. Peter says, "You are the Messiah." Peter's answer is better than that of the others. As readers, we already know that Jesus is Messiah (1:1). Peter does not say, however, that Jesus is Son of God, the other title Mark applies to Jesus right at the beginning of his Gospel (1:1, 11). Peter's understanding is deficient. Jesus responds to Peter's confession by predicting his suffering, death, and resurrection, stressing suffering and death (8:31). The narrator says, "He said all this quite openly." We have observed repeatedly that Jesus keeps his identity secret and even attempts to hide news of his miracles. But things have now changed. The Galilean public ministry has drawn to a close, and the Gospel enters a new phase in which Jesus privately teaches his followers about the key to his mission—suffering and death. Although the disciples have received the secret of the kingdom already (4:11), this is the first explicit indication that they learn about the passion.

Peter reproaches Jesus, apparently for his teaching about his suffering and death, and Jesus in turn condemns Peter, even calling him Satan. Peter sees things as humans do rather than as God does and therefore aligns himself with Satan in the apocalyptic struggle (8:33). Jesus goes on to describe true Christian discipleship. As he suffers, so must they. They must follow Jesus to the cross, losing their lives in order to find them. The section concludes, "Those who are ashamed of me and of my words in this adulterous and sinful generation, of them the Son of Man will also be ashamed when he comes in the glory of his Father with the holy angels" (8:38). The implication is that Peter is ashamed of Jesus' words.

9:2-8: Transfiguration. The transfiguration follows immediately. Jesus and three of his closest disciples—Peter, James, and John—ascend a mountain, where Jesus is transformed before them (9:2-8). He appears as a heavenly figure, reminiscent of angelic figures and even of God in the Hebrew Bible and elsewhere in Jewish literature (for example, Dan 7, 10). A cloud overshadows them—an allusion to cloud theophanies in the Hebrew Bible—and from the cloud comes "a voice" (God's) that says, "This is my Son, the Beloved; listen to him!" (9:7). The words recall God's pronouncement at Jesus' baptism (1:11). Here God adds "Listen to him" because in the previous scene Peter has *not* done so. He has not heeded Jesus concerning the central point of the Gospel, that the cross is central to Jesus' messiahship, a point first made fully clear in the preceding scene.

9:9-13: Elijah. On the descent from the mountain, Jesus orders them to keep silent about what they have seen "until after the Son of Man had risen from the dead." The injunction to silence is typical of Mark, but it applies only until after Jesus' resurrection. Then Jesus' prediction in 4:22 will come to pass that "there is nothing hidden, except to be disclosed; nor is anything secret, except to come to light." The disciples do not know what resurrection means. They then ask about the ancient prophecy that Elijah must come first (Mal 4:5-6). Jesus says that Elijah has come and "they did to him whatever they pleased." He refers to John the Baptist.

9:14-29: Exorcism. Mark completes the section with a story in which Jesus' disciples cannot exorcise a demon from a boy. Jesus expresses frustration: "You faithless generation, . . . how much longer must I put up with you?" The world is not a friendly place for God's agent. Here he faces not outright hostility, but lack of faith. He explains, "All things can be done for the one who believes." The boy's father cries out, "I believe; help my unbelief!" Jesus exorcises the demon because he sees a crowd gathering and he does not want to attract attention. At the end of the unit, he explains to the disciples that they can cast out this type of demon only through prayer. In 3:15 and 6:7, Jesus commissions them to cast out demons. Here they have failed to do that.

Second Teaching Cycle (9:30–10:31)

9:30-31: Second Prediction of the Passion. In 9:30-31, Jesus predicts his passion a second time. The narrator reminds the reader that Jesus is passing through Galilee, presumably on the way to Jerusalem. He wants to keep his movements unknown, because he is teaching his disciples privately.

9:32-34, 38: Misunderstanding. His disciples do not understand and are afraid to ask for an explanation. Then he confronts them on why they were arguing on the journey. They are too embarrassed to admit that they were quarreling about which of them is the greatest. They fail to comprehend Jesus' messiahship, their own discipleship, and the relation between the two.

9:35-37; 9:39–10:31: Teaching. Jesus teaches that whoever welcomes a child welcomes him. By insisting that his disciples receive a child as they would him, Jesus is saying that their concern must be for the lowly rather than for those of high status. Another point is that Jesus' disciples themselves are like lowly children who must be accepted by those to whom they are sent.

In the next unit, the disciples report that someone not of their group is exorcising, implying that Jesus should stop it. Jesus declines, saying, "Whoever is not against us is for us" (9:40). His disciples are concerned with control and status, while Jesus is interested in liberating people from Satan's power.

The rest of the section also concerns discipleship (9:42–10:31). Disciples must not scandalize any of God's "little ones," they must take extreme steps to avoid sin, and they must remain at peace with one another (9:42-49). They must accept Jesus' radical teaching against divorce, and they must receive God's kingdom as children (10:1-16). The rich young man is told that to follow Jesus he must sell everything and give it to the poor, a demand he cannot fulfill (10:17-22). Jesus laments that it is almost impossible for the rich to enter the kingdom of heaven. To do so, they must be willing to enter a new society with different rules, one in which they must surrender their status (10:23-27).

Peter asks what the disciples, who have given up everything including family and property, will receive in return. Peter is interested in what they will get out of following Jesus. Jesus replies that they will get a new family (other Christians) and new property (the common property of Christians), but that these will be accompanied by persecution (10:28-31).

Third Teaching Cycle (10:32-45)

10:32-34: Third Prediction of the Passion. In Jesus' third prediction of the passion and resurrection, the emphasis on the passion is clear. In the NRSV, the prediction of suffering and death takes up about forty-five words, while the prediction of the resurrection uses only seven.

10:35-39: Misunderstanding. Again lack of understanding meets Jesus' prediction. James and John request seats at Jesus' right and left hand in his glory. They anticipate a kingdom in which Jesus will distribute the spoils of victory among his faithful lieutenants.

10:40-45: Teaching. Jesus responds by saying that among the Gentiles, rulers "lord it over" them, but that in the church, this should not be the case. Rather, in the church the great must serve the rest, and those of the first ranks must be slaves of all. Jesus' teaching ends with words encapsulating his ministry: "The Son of Man came not to be served but to serve, and to give his life a ransom for many" (10:45).

Closing the Frame: Cure of Blind Man (10:46-52)

The section closes with the healing of a blind man. This time Jesus succeeds immediately. Mark leaves open whether he ever manages to open his disciples' eyes. As usual, Jesus praises the faith of the healed man.

PART III: JESUS IN JERUSALEM (11:1–16:8)

This section consists of Jesus' time in Jerusalem, his passion and death, and the scene of the empty tomb. There are no resurrection appearances.

Confrontation with Authorities (11:1–12:44)

11:1-11: Entry into Jerusalem. Jesus, displaying miraculous knowledge, sends his disciples to fetch a colt from a village. He rides it into Jerusalem, to the adulation of the people, who carry palm branches and lay their cloaks on the road before him. The crowd shouts, "Hosanna! / Blessed is the one who comes in the name of the Lord! / Blessed is the coming kingdom of our ancestor David!" This is a blessing recited over pilgrims entering Jerusalem (Ps 118:25-26). For Mark it has added significance, for Jesus comes as God's eschatological agent.

11:12-25: Cleansing the Temple. Mark frames the cleansing of the temple (11:15-19) with the cursing of the fig tree (11:12-14, 20-25). The cleansing brings to a head Jesus' confrontation with the religious leadership headquartered in Jerusalem. The cursing of the fig tree symbolically expresses God's condemnation of the Jerusalem establishment. In this context, Jesus teaches the disciples about the power of faith, a faith that Jerusalem's elite lack. Ultimately, the fault of the Jerusalem leadership is that it does not accept Jesus, as we learn when they confront him a few verses further on.

Jesus enters the temple and drives out those engaged in commercial enterprises there. He condemns the keepers of the temple, the priests, with having turned the house of prayer into a den of robbers. His condemnation quotes Scripture, combining Isa 56:7 and Jer 7:11. The context of the prophetic quotes discloses that religious faith in itself means little if accompanied by self-serving uses of religion and a lack of dedication to social justice.

11:27-33: The Leaders Question Jesus' Authority. The chief priests, scribes, and elders react swiftly. They confront Jesus in the temple and demand to know what authority he has for his action. Jesus parries their question with one of his own—do the leaders accept the message of John the Baptist? The leaders are stymied, for if they say yes, they have no excuse for not changing their ways, and if they say no, they will anger the crowd, which has believed in John. Jesus cleverly evades their challenge, but Jesus is clearly in danger. The plot against Jesus hatched by the Pharisees and Herodians in 3:6 will bear fruit through the actions of the Jerusalem elite.

12:1-12: Parable of the Wicked Tenants. Jesus' attack on the religious leaders continues. Isaiah 5 portrays Israel as God's vineyard. Jesus' parable draws on that image and portrays Israel's leaders as tenant farmers who refuse to give to the Lord of the vineyard his due. They reject the master's emissaries, including his son. This is an allegory for God's sending the prophets and then the Son of God to the leaders. The parable ends with a quotation of Ps 118:22-23, predicting that the rejected one (Jesus) will become the cornerstone of God's new edifice. The narrator informs us that the leaders know that Jesus is attacking them, but they are afraid to move against him because he has popular support.

12:13-34: Jesus Answers Challenges. This section consists of three questions to Jesus from different leaders. The first two questions are hostile, while the last is not. First, the Pharisees and Herodians try to trap him by asking him whether Roman taxes should be paid (12:13-17). This pairing of groups reminds us that they have been plotting against Jesus for some time (3:6). Jesus answers cleverly, saying that what is God's should be given to God, and what is Caesar's to Caesar. The onus is on his questioners to decide what belongs to each. This passage has been explained in a number of ways. Given the context in Mark, it is likely that Jesus is exposing their entanglement with Rome's oppressive power and their failure to give God what belongs to God. Torah forbids images but they carry Caesar's image. The Sadducees pose the second question; they do not believe in resurrection. Jesus defends belief in resurrection. The third question comes from a scribe sympathetic to Jesus. It concerns the most important commandment in Torah. Jesus and the scribe agree that it is love of God and neighbor. The scribe himself declares this more important than sacrifice. Remarkably, Jesus says, "You are not far from the kingdom of God" (12:34).

12:35-37: Jesus' Question about David's Son. Teaching in the temple, Jesus asks how the scribes can teach that the Messiah is Son of David when Ps 110:1, taken messianically and assumed to have been written by David, calls the Messiah "Lord." It is not that Mark denies that Jesus is Son of David. The blind man acclaims him as such in 10:46-52, apparently with Mark's approval. It is simply a title that can mislead. Mark rejects Christology that does not place Jesus' suffering, death, and resurrection at its center, and he mistrusts miracles as indicators to Jesus' identity because of their potential to shift attention away from the passion. When Peter confesses him as Messiah in 8:29, Jesus turns Peter to his impending passion. Perhaps for these reasons, Mark is reticent about using the title "Son of David," maybe seeing in it resonances of a military conqueror and powerful ruler. The crowds do not explicitly declare him Son of David when he enters Jerusalem (11:9-10) as in Matt 21:9 or king as in Luke 19:38.

12:38-44: Criticism of the Scribes. We should read the criticism of the scribes in 12:38-40 with story that follows it, that of the widow's offering to the temple (12:41-44). Preachers often see the widow as exemplifying self-sacrificing generosity. The rich take great pride in contributing ostentatious sums to the temple, but they can well afford to do so. Their gifts are not really sacrifices. The widow, on the other hand, puts in everything she has. Mark says she puts in her *bios*, her "life."

When we read 12:38-40 and 12:41-44 together, we get a different picture. The scribes find in religion an opportunity for self-aggrandizement. To that end, they "devour widows' houses" (12:40). Although rich, they greedily accept the widow's donation, small as it is. Jesus' words are a devastating condemnation of the temple establishment. It fits everything Mark has already said about the religious leaders and leads into the apocalyptic discourse in chapter 13, which predicts the temple's destruction. This follows perfectly on the allusions to Jeremiah's critique of the temple that Jesus alludes to during the cleansing of the temple (11:17). Jeremiah also criticized those in charge of the temple for social injustice, and he also threatened the temple's destruction as punishment. We ought not read this as a simple description of the temple establishment, however, for it also engaged in support of the poor. We must always remember that we are reading one side of an argument, and the evangelists are not supplying us with a fully balanced picture.

Apocalyptic Discourse (13:1-37)

We treat this discourse in detail below. Here we simply note that it continues Jesus' condemnation of the religious establishment and assumes an apocalyptic worldview. The end of the world as presently constituted is coming, and one can be saved only by adherence to Jesus, the Son of Man, who at the end will come to "gather his elect from the four winds" (13:27). Jesus says that even he does not know when the end will come (13:32).

Passion and Death (14:1–15:47)

14:1-11: Leaders' Plot, Woman's Anointing, Judas's Betrayal. The passion narrative opens by stating that the chief priests and scribes are searching for a way to eliminate Jesus (14:1-2). To avoid arousing the crowds, they must proceed cautiously.

An unnamed woman anoints Jesus (14:3-9). Some protest the waste of costly ointment, but Jesus defends the woman, declaring that she has anointed him for burial. Judas arranges to betray Jesus for money (14:10-11) and carries out the betrayal in Gethsemane (14:43-50) after the Last Supper.

14:12-31: The Last Supper. Jesus eats a final meal with his disciples, a Passover meal (14:12-31). At the meal he shows foreknowledge that one of them will betray him. He institutes the Eucharist (a ritual meal memorializing his death) and indicates that his death is "for many." He calls his blood "my blood of the covenant," recalling the blood ritual performed by Moses in Exod 24:6-8, discussed below. Jesus looks forward to drinking wine in the coming kingdom (14:25). He foretells Peter's betrayal, which transpires shortly afterward in the high priest's courtyard. Throughout the Gospel, Jesus has prophetic powers. His predictions always come to pass. As the climax of the Gospel approaches, the disciples look worse.

14:32-52: Gethsemane. Mark depicts Jesus' dread of his fate (14:32-42). Although he knows that it must happen, he prays that it might pass. His disciples fall asleep, failing to support or comfort him.

14:53-65: Trial before the Sanhedrin. Jesus is brought before the Sanhedrin, the supreme council in Jerusalem that advises the high priest, consisting of the chief priests, the elders, and the scribes. They seek testimony to condemn him but find no credible witnesses. Their accusation that Jesus said he would destroy the temple may be rooted in Jesus' prediction in chapter 13 of the temple's destruction. The high priest finally asks him whether he is the Messiah, the Son of God (14:61). Jesus says that he is and that the high priest will see the Son of Man coming on the clouds to judge the earth (a reference to Dan 7:13-14), implying that to reject Jesus is to invite divine judgment. For the first time, Jesus unambiguously accepts these titles, and he does so only in the context of the passion, the only setting in which they can be correctly understood. The high priest convicts him of blasphemy and sends him off to Pilate, but not before the guards beat him and ridicule him as a false prophet. As Jesus predicted, Peter betrays him by denying that he knows him.

15:1-20: Jesus and Pilate. Pilate asks Jesus the question that would concern a Roman administrator: "Are you the King of the Jews?" (15:2). An affirmative answer would be seditious. Only the Romans may appoint kings in their empire. Jesus gives an ambiguous answer: "You say so." Jesus is king, but not in the usual sense. He is Messiah, but not as most would conceive of that.

Pilate attempts to reason with the leaders on Jesus' behalf. They in turn stir up the crowd. Pilate realizes that they act out of jealousy and that there is no reasoning with them. He offers to release a prisoner to them, and they choose Barabbas, an insurrectionist, and insist that he crucify Jesus. Pilate finally agrees. The overall impression of the scene is that Pilate is far less to blame for Jesus' death than are the Jewish leaders, a dubious proposition, historically speaking. Mark increases their guilt by having them urge the crowd to demand that Pilate release Jesus rather than Barabbas. The soldiers abuse and mock Jesus as a ridiculously phony royal pretender.

15:21-39: Crucifixion and Death. Jesus is led to Golgotha, a hill just outside the city, to be crucified. The official charge written above his head is "The King of the Jews," a warning against rebellion. He is crucified between two "bandits," a noun that may well mean political rebel. The first-century Jewish historian Josephus sometimes uses it to denigrate revolutionaries. These details show that Rome had a vested interest in his elimination. Passersby mock him as one who threatened the temple. The chief priests and scribes deride his messianic pretensions.

Mark's portrayal of Jesus' death is starkest of any of the Gospels. The reader cannot escape its horror. People often think that Jesus said "seven last words" during his passion, but that is so only if we combine all the Gospels. In Mark, Jesus says but one thing: "My God, my God, why have you forsaken me?" (15:34). Then he "gave a loud cry and breathed his last" (15:37). Between these two verses we read that the people misunderstood him to be calling Elijah when he called on God (15:35-36), and that the temple's curtain is torn in two as he dies (15:38). Bracketing out these elements for a moment, one can sketch Jesus' actions simply: he cries out asking God why God has forsaken him, he screams, and he dies. It is not a comforting picture. Then Mark makes the astonishing statement, "Now when the centurion, who stood facing him, saw that in this way he breathed his last, he said, 'Truly this man was God's Son!' " (15:39). The centurion realizes that Jesus is God's son precisely because of the *way* he dies. There is no indication that the centurion has heard any of Jesus' teachings, nor any hint that he has seen or heard about Jesus' miracles. The centurion comes to his realization because he observes the manner of Jesus' death. Mark is absolutely clear that for him the meaning of Jesus can be found only in the cross. This is not to deny the significance of Jesus' mighty acts or his teaching, nor does it deny the importance of the resurrection. But neither Jesus' acts nor his teaching result in understanding his mission for anyone in the Gospel, and even the women who hear of the resurrection react with terror and amazement. Only the centurion truly understands Jesus, and he does so only through the death, presented in the starkest terms.

When Jesus dies, the temple veil is torn in two. Exactly what this means has been the source of much speculation. It is not at all clear. It is not even clear which curtain is meant, for there was one separating the holiest, innermost part of the temple from the rest, and another between the temple proper and the forecourt. Some take the tearing of the veil to refer to the destruction of the temple, predicted by Jesus in chapter 13, and something that became an issue in his trial before the Sanhedrin (14:58). Another possibility, not necessarily incompatible with the first, is that the tearing indicates a condemnation of the priests who had charge of the temple and had a hand in Jesus' death. Josephus tells us that there were zodiacal signs woven into the veil at the main entrance of the temple, so it is possible that its rending symbolizes a splitting of the heavens. Some interpretations see the tearing of the veil as a sign that God has departed, and others see it as a sign that Jesus' death brings about more direct access to God. It has also been suggested that the tearing of the veil is a sign of mourning for Jesus' death, for tearing of clothes was a common sign of mourning. If so, this may be an ironic allusion to the high priest's tearing his veil at Jesus' supposed blasphemy (14:63). The difficulty of arriving at a decision of what this symbol means, as important as it clearly is since it occurs at the death of Jesus, is a valuable reminder of the multiple meanings possible in a narrative text (and other sorts of texts as well), a point we made in chapter 1.

Empty Tomb (16:1-8)

Three women—Mary Magdalene, another Mary, and Salome—go to the tomb after the Sabbath to anoint Jesus' body. They find a "young man," an angel, who announces that Jesus has been raised and instructs them to tell the disciples that Jesus will meet them in Galilee, as previously arranged. The best manuscripts end with the following words: "So they went out and fled from the tomb, for terror and amazement had seized them; and they said nothing to anyone, for they were afraid" (16:8). Mark recounts no resurrection appearances. This seems an odd ending. What happens next? Why would Mark end his Gospel in this way?

The best solution to the Gospel's ending is the following. It is not that Mark denies the resurrection. Jesus predicts his resurrection repeatedly, and the tomb is empty precisely because Jesus has risen. The angel orders the women to tell the disciples that Jesus has risen. Mark chooses this ending to emphasize Jesus' death, and to challenge his readers to continue the narrative in their own lives, to succeed where the disciples have failed.

Added Endings: The Shorter Ending and the Longer Ending

The Shorter Ending. Some early Christians were unhappy with this odd ending and so composed two others that survive in some manuscripts. The shorter of the two directly contradicts the statement in 16:8 that the women told no one what they had seen at the tomb: "And all that had been commanded them they told briefly to those around Peter."

The second part of the ending claims that Jesus sent out the disciples to preach "the sacred and imperishable proclamation of eternal salvation." This is clearly not Markan language. In one short sentence, there are six words not used elsewhere in Mark. Jesus sending out the disciples to preach throughout the world sounds like the end of Matthew. *Salvation* as a noun is characteristic of Luke. Whoever added this ending wanted to bring more satisfactory closure to Mark's Gospel, and in so doing, drew on material not found in Mark.

The Longer Ending. The same is true of the longer ending. Unhappy with the lack of resurrection appearances, this author added some. The first is to Mary Magdalene (16:9-11). This echoes Matthew and John; Jesus appears to Mary and others in Matt 28:9-10, and to Mary alone in John 20:11-18. The longer ending says that Jesus cast seven demons out of Mary, a detail from Luke 8:2. Mary tells others of the resurrection, but they do not believe her (see Luke 24:11). Jesus then appears to two disciples walking in the country, which sounds like the Emmaus episode in Luke 24:13-35. The disciples do not believe these two either.

Now Jesus appears to the eleven while they are at table (see Luke 24:36-43; Acts 10:41). He rebukes them for not believing the others and sends them out to proclaim the gospel throughout creation (see Matt 28:19: Luke 24:47; John 20:21; Acts 1:8). Those who believe are saved, and those who do not are condemned (see John 3:18). Many signs accompany them—exorcisms, the gift of tongues, and healings (as in many places in the New Testament). They are guaranteed safety from deadly snakes and poisons (see Luke 10:19; Acts 28:3-6). Jesus ascends into heaven and sits at the right hand of God (only in Luke–Acts does Jesus ascend this way, but in several New Testament passages he is at the right hand of God).

It is clear that the author of the longer ending drew on each of the other three canonical gospels and perhaps on other early Christian traditions. In so doing, he or she has brought closure to Mark's Gospel and described the early missionary church.

APOCALYPTIC DISCOURSE: KEY TO MARK'S SITUATION

Chapter 13 is an apocalyptic discourse. It speaks of the end of the world as we know it and of God's intervention in history that changes things forever. This is the one place where Jesus speaks explicitly and at length about what is to happen to the church after his death and resurrection. For that reason, it is particularly valuable as evidence for Mark's own historical situation.

Central to this chapter is Jesus' prediction that the Jerusalem temple will be destroyed. This is why most interpreters think that Mark was written around the time of the temple's destruction by the Romans in 70 C.E. The chapter begins as Jesus and his disciples emerge from the temple and the disciples express awe over its size. In response, Jesus predicts the temple's destruction. The disciples inquire when this will happen and what will be the sign of its imminence. This leads into Jesus' long discourse.

Jesus admonishes the disciples to "beware," because many will attempt to lead them astray. They will come in Jesus' name and say, "I am he!" (13:6). Later in the chapter he warns that many will come saying, "Look! Here is the Messiah!" (13:21). We do not know for sure what all this refers to. We do know that during the first century C.E. prior to the war with the Romans (66–70 C.E.), there arose eschatological prophets proclaiming that God was about to liberate Israel from its oppressors, and that these prophets attracted followers. We also know that during the war prophets arose to foretell the Romans' defeat and that some leaders in the conflict seem to have had messianic (royal) pretensions. It is perhaps to prophets and leaders like these that Mark's Jesus refers. A different suggestion is that Jesus refers to some who claimed to be he, come a second time. This builds on expectations that Jesus was to come back, an event called the *second coming*.

Jesus predicts a time of confusion caused by eschatological fervor and the sorts of enthusiastic and misleading claims and rumors inevitable in such a climate. This plausibly describes the experience of Mark's own church. Despite such events, Jesus insists that one must not think that the end is right around the corner. Wars and rumors of wars must take place, but that "the end is still to come." Since Jesus has just predicted the temple's destruction, we think immediately of the war with the Romans. It "must take place," for it is part of God's plan for the end. But "the end is still to come. For nation will rise against nation, and kingdom against kingdom; there will be earthquakes in various places; there will be famines. This is but the beginning of the birthpangs" (13:7-8). Such feverish expectation distracts Mark's fellow Christians from preaching the gospel to all nations, and from facing the persecution and death such preaching entails (13:9-10). The Holy Spirit will give them the words to say, but even family members will oppose and betray them. Everyone will hate them because of their attachment to Jesus, "But the one who endures to the end will be saved" (13:13).

There were no widespread persecutions of Christians as such in the first century, but in 64 C.E. Nero brutally butchered Christians in Rome on the pretext that they ignited the great fire that devastated large portions of the city, a fire that some suspected Nero himself set. When a few years later the Romans ravaged the land of Israel and destroyed the temple, many Christians feared general persecution. Mark notifies his readers to expect sufferings as part of the eschatological events. Again, this does not mean that the end will come immediately. They should just do their job—preach the gospel.

Jesus says that when the "desolating sacrilege" is set up where it ought not to be, those in Judea should flee to the mountains—"Let the reader understand." The sacrilege alludes to Dan 11:31, where it refers to an idolatrous statue of the Greek god Zeus in the Jerusalem temple. This happened in the second century B.C.E. under the Hellenistic dynasty of Syria, the Seleucids, who ruled the area. In Mark 13, its reference shifts to the desecration of the temple in 70 C.E. People should flee "for in those days there will be suffering, such as had not been from the beginning of the creation that God created until now, no, and never will be" (13:19). This is typical apocalyptic language. Even in the midst of all this suffering, Christians ought not to expect speedy release, even though God has shortened the time on their behalf (13:20).

The next section of the discourse is crucial for understanding the logic of the chapter.

"But in those days, after that suffering,
   the sun will be darkened,
     and the moon will not give its light,
   and the stars will be falling from heaven,
     and the powers in the heavens will be shaken.

Then they will see 'the Son of Man coming in clouds' with great power and glory. Then he will send out the angels, and gather his elect from the four winds, from the ends of the earth to the ends of heaven." (13:24-27)

Note the words, "In those days, after that suffering." It is only *after* all that has been described—wars and rumors of wars, earthquakes, famines, persecution, betrayal by family, and unimaginable suffering, that the end will come. And it will come with unmistakable signs. Christians need not worry that they will miss the end. Using language from the prophets about God's judgment and its effect on the cosmos, common in apocalyptic literature, Jesus describes cosmic calamity involving sun, moon, and stars (Isa 13:10; 34:4; 50:2-3; Ezek 32:7-8; Joel 2:10, 31; Amos 8:9; 4 Ezra 5:4-5; Rev 6:12-14). The cosmos comes apart. Its order disintegrates. Only then will the Son of Man come to rescue the elect. So they must both resign themselves to terrible suffering and take comfort in the fact the Son of Man will ultimately save them.

Finally, Jesus says that no one knows when the end will come, not even the angels or "the Son," that is, he himself (13:32). His command is, "Keep awake." This is not an invitation to calculate the time of the end. The chapter argues against that. It is an order to continue the work of Jesus himself, to preach the gospel.

MARK AS APOCALYPTIC DRAMA

In discussing the gospel genre, we noted it is most like ancient biography or life *(bios)*, but it differs from other biography because of its eschatological orientation. Jesus appears as the one sent by God at the preordained time to initiate the end-time events. Thus it is appropriate to look at Mark as eschatological drama.

The drama has three stages. The first is the Baptist's ministry. John, predicted by the ancient prophet Isaiah, comes preaching repentance and preparing the way for one mightier than he. The reader soon learns that the one for whom John prepares is Jesus, Messiah and Son of God. After John completes his task and just before Jesus begins his ministry, John is "handed over" (1:14). The Greek verb here *(paradidomi)* is often translated "arrested," but this obscures the parallel between what happens to John and what Jesus and then the disciples endure, for they too are "handed over." Herod arrests and beheads John, foreshadowing what is to happen to Jesus and the disciples (6:14-29).

The drama's second stage is the ministry, suffering, death, and resurrection of Jesus. As John preached, so does Jesus. John preached repentance to prepare for Jesus, and Jesus preaches the kingdom of God. John's preaching results in his being handed over to the authorities to be executed, and this is precisely the result of Jesus' preaching. He too is handed over, betrayed by one of his own disciples (3:19; 9:31; 10:33; 14:10-11, 18, 21, 41-42, 44).

After trial before the high priest, Jesus is "handed over" to Pilate, the Roman prefect (15:10, 15). Then Pilate "hands over" Jesus to be crucified (15:15).

The third part of Mark's apocalyptic drama happens outside the boundaries of the narrative. Jesus commands his disciples to preach the gospel to all nations and predicts that they will suffer as a result. They will be "handed over" to suffer and die (13:9-13).

CHRISTOLOGY

Mark pays special attention to three titles for Jesus—Messiah, Son of God, and Son of Man. In the past, scholars have examined the titles of Jesus in the Gospels as keys to the evangelists' meaning. They began to appreciate the limits of this approach because of two factors. First, research revealed the titles to be capable of different meanings in first-century Judaism and in the early church. Second, within a specific gospel, the titles assume connotations peculiar to each evangelist. But when we combine these approaches—careful study of various usages of the titles in Jesus' and the Gospels' environments and analysis of how the evangelists interpret them—they can illuminate the Gospels' Christologies.

SON OF GOD AND MESSIAH

In chapter 2, we note that in ancient Jewish literature, *Son of God* can mean a heavenly being, usually an angel (Gen 6:1-5; Job 38:7). More often it refers to humans. The title is at times associated with *Messiah*, meaning king of Israel. In 2 Sam 7, Solomon, son of David, is called "God's son," and in Ps 2 the Messiah is called "God's son" as well. It can also mean Israel as a whole (Hos 11:1), or righteous members of Israel (Wis 2:13, 16, 18).

Mark introduces *Son of God* at strategic points in his Gospel. Significantly, it appears at the beginning and end. The Gospel begins, "The beginning of the good news [gospel] of Jesus Christ, the Son of God" (1:1). Some early manuscripts do not have the words "the Son of God," but at Jesus' baptism several verses later, Jesus sees the heavens torn open and the Spirit descend on him, and God's voice says, "You are my Son, the Beloved; with you I am well pleased" (1:11; combining allusions to Ps 2:7, Gen 22:2, and Isa 42:1).

There is also a reference to Jesus as God's son at the Gospel's end, at Jesus' death. Jesus feels forsaken by God, and he screams and dies. When the centurion sees this, he declares Jesus to be the Son of God. This is the only time in the Gospel that any human acknowledges this. For Mark, this ignominious death is essential to what it means for Jesus to be Son of God and Messiah.

We have identified the Gospel's turning point as Peter's confession (8:27-33). Not surprisingly, we find reference to Jesus' divine sonship associated with that episode, too. Peter recognizes Jesus as the Messiah, but he refuses to accept suffering, death, and resurrection as part of Jesus' mission. The next scene is the transfiguration, where God reveals to Peter, James, and John that Jesus is God's Son and insists that they listen to him (9:2-8). Since the transfiguration follows on Peter's confession, Mark means in particular that Peter must listen to Jesus concerning the nature of divine sonship and messiahship.

This leaves only three more occurrences of Son of God, two in part I and one in part III. In both instances in part I, demons declare Jesus to be Son of God (3:11 and 5:7). They recognize Jesus as God's agent to defeat them, and in that capacity they declare him Son of God. So this is also part of what it means to be Son of God. It means that God has appointed Jesus to carry on the eschatological struggle against Satan and his demons. In keeping with the messianic secret, only the demons and Jesus make this connection.

The remaining reference occurs during Jesus' trial before the high priest. The high priest demands, "Are you the Messiah, the Son of the Blessed One?" (14:61). Jesus answers, "I am." Throughout the Gospel, Jesus keeps his identity secret. He now reveals it because he is embarking upon his passion. We see the terms *Messiah* and *Son of God* linked in Ps 2:7, Ps 89:26, and 2 Sam 7:14. They are also connected in the Dead Sea Scrolls (4Q Florilegium 10-14). But nowhere in Jewish literature of the time is either title used for a suffering messiah. That is new in Mark. And he insists on it. To him, it is of the essence.

SON OF MAN

Son of Man was not a title among Jews of Jesus' time, but the Gospels use it as such and always apply it to Jesus. The Synoptic Gospels have three categories of "Son of Man" usage: a figure of authority during his earthly ministry, one who suffers and dies, and a figure who comes at the end of history. The three categories may have originated with Mark himself, for Matthew and Luke depend on Mark. Each evangelist, including John, uses this flexible title in his own way. In Mark's case, the suffering Son of Man receives most attention.

The phrase *Son of Man* occurs twice in part I. In both cases it is associated with Jesus' authority. In 2:10, it has to do with Jesus' authority to forgive sins. In 2:28, Jesus has authority over the Sabbath. These occurrences are what we mean by the earthly Son of Man. They stress his divine power over central functions and institutions of religion.

Mark uses the threefold image of the Son of Man to shed light on what he means by *Son of God* and *Messiah*. Mark fears that the latter titles will be taken to designate Jesus as a powerful figure who conquers enemies. Mark's correction of such a view is clearest at the Gospel's turning point, where Peter confesses Jesus as Messiah (8:27–9:1). Rather than accepting this designation, as in Matt 16:17, Jesus orders Peter to keep silent and then teaches that the Son of Man must suffer, die, and rise. Suffering receives the most attention. Peter refuses to accept this, so Jesus calls him Satan, since he arrays himself on the wrong side in the eschatological battle. Jesus proclaims that when the eschatological Son of Man comes in glory to judge, people will be judged on the basis of whether they have accepted Jesus as Messiah in the specific terms that Jesus lays out in this passage. Suffering and eschatological "Son of Man" figures are associated in this passage in a symmetry of cause and effect. Acceptance of the suffering Son of Man determines one's status before the end-time Son of Man.

Jesus is both Son of Man and Son of God. *Son of Man* designates the "whole package" in three aspects. It is the same person who pursues a public ministry, who suffers and dies, and who returns to judge. This Son of Man is identical to the Son of God and the Messiah. Titles are not ends in themselves, but elucidate aspects of Jesus and his mission. Mark redefines divine sonship. He is saying, "Yes, Jesus is Son of God, but not in the sense that you think. Only if you include in divine sonship what Son of Man designates—earthly authority, suffering and death, return in glory as judge—do you understand 'Son of God.' And if you do not accept this, then the Son of Man will reject you."

TRANSFORMATION OF MEANINGS

We now return to the earlier observation that Mark reveals Jesus' divine sonship at the beginning and at the end of his Gospel. Read from start to finish, Mark's narrative guides us through the story of Jesus' ministry, suffering, and death. We perhaps begin this trip with one idea of what it means for Jesus to be Son of God and end it with a very different idea. Mark's narrative has transformed our view of Jesus and therefore of the world.

ATONEMENT

The concept of atonement has deeply influenced Christian theology. Atonement means setting right the relationship between God and humanity. The New Testament has varied ideas of atonement. Later Christian doctrines of atonement frequently posit sin as what separates God and humanity and see Jesus' death as the means by which the separation is overcome. This can be thought of as substitution (humans deserve to die but Jesus does so in their stead) or representation (Jesus is the representative human, so all die in him). It is debatable whether ideas of substitution or representation are present in the Jewish ideas of sacrifice that form the background of atonement in the New Testament. The idea may be more of dealing with the effects of sin. For example, Milgrom's theory holds that sin defiles God's sanctuary which must then be purified by blood as a sort of ritual detergent. If the separation between God and humanity is imagined more as a cosmic force separating God and humanity, as in Paul, then atonement signifies victory over that force. Jesus' death is part of a battle against Satan.

Sacrificial atonement is found in Rom 3 and in Hebrews. It is not, however, prominent in the Gospels. In Mark, some suggest its presence in 10:45, where Jesus says that he gives his life as a "ransom for many." However, the image there is not atonement, but of purchasing a slave or a prisoner of war. The price paid for human freedom is Jesus' life, but it is not clear in what sense. To whom is the price paid? God? Satan? Mark probably does not intend the image in an overly literal way. The other relevant verse in Mark is 14:24: "This is my blood of the covenant, which is poured out for many." This recalls the covenant ceremony on Sinai related in Exod 24:3-8. There Moses splashes the blood of sacrificed oxen on an altar and on the people as a sign of the bond between the people and God and of the obligations the covenant places on both. The sacrifice in question is not a sin-offering, nor does it entail the substitution of the sacrificial victim for the people, who themselves deserve to be punished because of sin. Rather, it is a ratification ceremony (see also Zech 9:11). The text designates it a sacrifice of "well-being." It has nothing to do with atonement, but rather is celebratory. Jesus' words imply that his death initiates a new covenant, a new "agreement" between God and humanity.

THE MESSIANIC SECRET

Throughout Mark people try to understand Jesus and fail. In chapter 1, those who witness his exorcism in the synagogue know that he teaches with authority and commands the unclean spirits, but they miss its full significance (1:27). When Jesus forgives the paralytic's sins, the scribes wonder who he is (2:1-12). At the end of that episode, the narrator says of everyone present, "They were all amazed and glorified God, saying, 'We have never seen anything like this!'" In chapter 3, scribes from Jerusalem accuse him of casting out demons by Satan's power and even charge him with being possessed by Satan (3:22). Jesus' own family tries to seize him when others say that he is insane, and Jesus refers to them as "outside" (3:21, 31-35). The disciples obtain inside information about Jesus but fall short of understanding him (for example, 4:11, 34, 41). In chapter 6, Jesus' home villagers take offense at him. The very fact that he comes from their village seems to blind them (6:1-6). Shortly afterward, Herod hears about Jesus and learns that some think he is John the Baptist raised from the dead, others that he is Elijah, and others that he is one of the ancient prophets (6:14-16). Herod believes that he is John. Throughout the Gospel, the prevalent reactions to Jesus are astonishment, puzzlement, and fear.

It is an odd feature of Mark's Gospel that Jesus takes pains to keep his messianic identity secret. At the beginning of the twentieth century, Wrede convincingly argued that this was part of Mark's theology. Mark devised the messianic secret, not Jesus. Wrede saw this as Mark's way of reconciling the early church's belief that Jesus was the Messiah with the fact that Jesus' own Jewish contemporaries did not accept him as such. Our take on the messianic secret is different. Mark has Jesus hide his identity because for Mark, Jesus' messiahship cannot be understood properly until his death and resurrection. Humans associate messiahship with power, victory, and glory. God associates it with Christ's death. This is what Jesus means when he says that Peter thinks as humans do, and not as God does (8:33).

We must distinguish between Jesus keeping his identity secret and trying to keep his miracles quiet. Jesus succeeds in preventing people from recognizing him as Son of God but fails to keep his miracles quiet. No matter how hard he tries, word gets out. Jesus wants to keep the miracles quiet because they lead to misunderstanding, but word spreads, and, sure enough, they mislead. The miracles can potentially help one identify Jesus as Messiah, as undoubtedly they inform Peter, and Mark knows that the miracles are part of Jesus' work as Son of God and Messiah. It is not wrong to associate them with Jesus' messianic function. But they mislead. For a correct understanding, one must make suffering and death central, then one can put the miracles into perspective. If one begins with the miracles, then it is all too likely that, like Peter, one will not accept Jesus' passion.

With the Gospel's very first verse, readers are privy to Jesus' identity. So Mark employs dramatic irony. No one within Mark's story world understands who Jesus is except Jesus himself, God, demons, and, finally, the centurion at the foot of the cross at the Gospel's end. But even the readers need to reevaluate how they see Jesus. Jesus' divine sonship is grasped only by one who accepts his terrible death.

Mark portrays the Baptist as Jesus' precursor but never says that John recognizes Jesus as Son of God, Messiah. When Jesus emerges from the water at his baptism, the text says that *Jesus* sees the heavens opened and the Spirit descend on him. It does not say anyone else saw that. God speaks directly to Jesus saying, "You are my Son, the Beloved; with you I am well pleased" (1:11). There is no indication that anyone else hears.

Superhuman figures, the demons and Satan, know who Jesus is. They belong to the unseen world that determines the visible world, in the apocalyptic worldview. They know that the eschatological battle between God and God's opponents has commenced and is ongoing in Jesus' ministry. The demons understand the title *Son of God* in this sense (1:24, 34; 3:11-12; 5:7). Jesus prohibits them from revealing his identity. The crowds know that Jesus can exorcise and heal, but they lack the demon's insight.

Jesus' parables have puzzled ancient and modern commentators alike. This made it easier for Mark to bring them into the service of the messianic secret. For him, Jesus tells parables to *hide* his message. When the disciples request an explanation for the parable of the Sower, Jesus responds, "To you has been given the secret of the kingdom of God, but for those outside, everything comes in parables; in order that / 'they may indeed look, but not perceive, / and may indeed listen, but not understand; / so that they may not turn again and be forgiven'" (4:11-12). This is a quotation of Isa 6:9-10. To know the secret of the kingdom is to understand Jesus. Mark closes the parable collection with the words, "With many such parables he spoke the word to them, as they were able to hear it; he did not speak to them except in parables, but he explained everything to his disciples" (4:33-34).

There are insiders and outsiders. Outsiders cannot understand Jesus. The truth is hidden from them. That will not always be the case: "There is nothing hidden, except to be disclosed; nor is anything secret, except to come to light" (4:22). After the passion and resurrection, the church will preach the truth publicly. During Jesus' ministry, he imparts the secret to his disciples alone. They too miss the point (see below). In the transfiguration God identifies Jesus, and on the way down the mountain Jesus orders the disciples "to tell no one about what they had seen, until after the Son of Man had risen from the dead" (9:9). This confirms that the period of secrecy is limited (see 4:22). Once the passion and resurrection occur, there will no longer be any reason to keep things secret.

EXORCISMS AND MIRACLES

For many today, exorcisms are not part of their world, so it is puzzling to discover that Jesus spent a lot of time doing them. The prominence of exorcisms in Mark accords with Mark's apocalyptic viewpoint.

Belief in evil spirits was widespread in the ancient world. Demons took the blame for a wide range of ills, including sickness, mental illness, bad luck, and even everyday occurrences like the wearing out of clothes! In late Second Temple Judaism we also find the notion of an army of evil spirits or fallen angels under the command of a leading figure, often called *Satan*. In apocalypticism the world is usually seen as alienated from God, while Satan and his minions have great power. They sometimes even rule the world. This is what Jesus means in the Gospel of John when Jesus speaks of the "ruler of this world" (12:31; 14:30; 16:11). The book of Revelation describes Satan cast out of heaven with his angelic followers and descending to earth to battle God's faithful (Rev 12). The epistle to the Ephesians says, "Our struggle is not against enemies of blood and flesh, but against the rulers, against the authorities, against the cosmic powers of this present darkness, against the spiritual forces of evil in the heavenly places" (6:12).

In Mark, Jesus' first action after receiving his commission in the baptism is to go to the desert to be tempted by Satan. The Greek word translated "tempt" can also be translated "test," recalling how God tests Israel, particularly during their wilderness wanderings. Testing is associated with the end time in apocalypticism—those times, near the close of history, when divine and demonic forces are locked in battle and Satan besieges those loyal to God. Early Christians felt themselves to be living in this time. The petition in the Lord's Prayer "Lead us not into temptation" has this eschatological coloring. Jesus' temptation is the beginning of a career-long struggle. He is the "point man" in God's onslaught on Satan's dominion.

Returning from the desert, Jesus proclaims that the kingdom of God has drawn near (1:15). He preaches about the kingdom and initiates it through his deeds. Jesus then calls four disciples (1:16-20). Next he enters a synagogue and casts out an "unclean spirit," who realizes that Jesus is from God (1:21-28). The role of divine Son becomes active in the exorcism. These events, recounted early in the Gospel, set the tone for the Gospel as a whole. Jesus encounters demons repeatedly in the Gospel, and each time they recognize him as their adversary (1:24, 34; 3:11-12; 5:7).

A summary emphasizes Jesus' healings and says that the demons declare him to be God's Son (3:7-12). Jesus appoints the Twelve and commissions them to preach and cast out demons (3:13-19). In 3:22, scribes come from Jerusalem and accuse Jesus of being possessed by Satan, thereby having power to cast out demons. Jesus points out the absurdity of Satan opposing himself and offers the following explanation of his exorcisms: "No one can enter a strong man's house and plunder his property without first tying up the strong man; then indeed the house can be plundered" (3:27). The strong man is Satan, his house is this world, and the plunder represents Satan's human subjects. Jesus comes to break Satan's power, and the exorcisms are one of the means by which he does so. He exorcises through the power of the Holy Spirit. The scribes are guilty of an unforgivable sin because they attribute the Spirit's work to Satan.

The campaign against Satan does not terminate with Jesus' death. He commissions the disciples in 3:15 to cast out demons, and their exorcisms are closely related to their mission to preach the kingdom. Preaching and exorcising go together. In 6:7-13, the disciples pursue the mission. Mark's community continued to practice exorcism and found its motivation in Mark 3.

THE DISCIPLES

The disciples' story helps unify Mark's narrative. The disciples are fairly dense in the first two parts of the Gospel, and in the third they leave Jesus to his fate. That is not the last word, for the angel informs the women at the tomb that the risen Jesus will meet the disciples in Galilee, as planned (16:7). But the meeting takes place outside the confines of the gospel narrative. It is in the future. Within the Gospel's borders, the disciples do not look good.

Discipleship is modeled on messiahship. As Jesus preaches the kingdom and casts out demons, he commissions the disciples to do the same. As Jesus suffers in his struggle with Satan and his human allies, so the disciples will suffer in the same battle. If the disciples do not appreciate these aspects of Jesus' ministry, neither do they grasp their own role.

The disciples' portrait in Mark is not unrelievedly bad. There are bright spots. At the beginning of the Gospel there are two "call stories." In the first, Jesus calls the brothers Peter and Andrew (1:16-18), and in the second, James and John, sons of Zebedee (1:19-20). He commands them to follow him and they obey without hesitation. There is no indication that they know anything about Jesus. We might "fill in the gaps" by assuming that they had heard of Jesus or were already acquainted with him, but the Gospel does not say that. It is more likely that Mark intended for this to be puzzling. It is a tribute to Jesus' powerful presence that they abandon their lives and follow him unquestioningly. Their readiness to follow may speak well of them, but Mark may be more interested in showing Jesus' mysterious power.

In chapter 4, the disciples are insiders. Jesus tells them the secret of the kingdom and explains all (4:11, 34). In 3:13-19, he calls the Twelve to "be with him" and "to proclaim the message, and to have authority to cast out demons." In 6:7, he sends them out to preach and exorcise.

Despite these positive points, the overall picture of the disciples in Mark is unflattering. In part I, they follow Jesus and see his exorcisms, experience his miracles, and hear his words. They even carry on a ministry themselves, preaching and casting out demons. But they do not quite get it. They fail to penetrate the secret of Jesus' role. In part II, Jesus instructs the disciples about messiahship and discipleship, and they consistently fail to apprehend his teaching. Finally, in part III, the disciples desert Jesus during his passion. We analyze these elements in our survey, so we review them only briefly here.

PART I

In the first three chapters, the disciples accompany Jesus in his ministry, are commissioned to be with him, and do the sorts of things that he did, including going out on missions in which they preach and exorcise. In those opening chapters, Jesus' ministry quickly engenders misunderstanding by some and outright hostility by the leaders. Chapter 4 brings much of these positive and negative elements to a head by portraying the kingdom of God as a secret shared only with the disciples (4:11). At that crucial point they begin to fail. They ask for an explanation of the parable of the Sower (4:10), and Jesus, after pointing out that they have been given the secret, says, "Do you not understand this parable? Then how will you understand all the parables?" (4:13). One senses Jesus' incipient frustration with the disciples. After further parables, some of which refer to the mysterious nature of the kingdom, Mark says that Jesus speaks to outsiders only through parables, "but he explained everything in private to his disciples" (4:34).

The parables lead directly into the first of three boat scenes. Each features Jesus alone with his disciples. In the first, Jesus calms the raging sea (4:35-41). The disciples ought to understand, but instead they ask who Jesus is. They know the secret of the kingdom and therefore (presumably) of Jesus' identity and have seen his miracles and exorcisms. Their fear suggests that they have no faith. Jesus' frustration with them is growing. The other two boat scenes, analyzed in our survey, tell much the same story— revelation by Jesus of what is essential to his mission, and failure to understand by the disciples. They form part of larger literary complexes in which Jesus multiplies loaves and feeds the crowds, followed by the boat scenes. In the second boat scene (6:45-52), the disciples encounter Jesus walking on the water and are utterly astounded, for they did not understand the significance of the multiplication of the loaves, a key to Jesus' identity. In the third boat scene, Jesus quizzes the disciples about the two feedings (8:14-21). They are keen observers of the miraculous details, but they miss their meaning.

PART II

This section begins with Peter's confession. Peter knows that Jesus is the Messiah, but he "rebukes" Jesus when he speaks of his suffering. Jesus calls Peter "Satan" for standing in the way of Jesus' mission. This is the first of three predictions of the passion, each of which is followed by misunderstanding by the disciples, and then Jesus' teaching of them. This pattern structures part II.

PART III

Judas betrays Jesus (14:43-45). Peter denies him (14:66-72). The rest of the disciples flee after Jesus' arrest (14:50). At the end of the scene, the narrator says, "A certain young man was following him, wearing nothing but a linen cloth. They caught hold of him, but he left the linen cloth and ran off naked" (14:51-52). This stresses the haste with which the disciples escape.

On Easter morning, the two Marys and Salome come to anoint Jesus' body (16:1-8). They find the tomb empty and a "young man," doubtlessly an angel, tells them to inform the disciples, and Peter, that Jesus has risen and will meet them in Galilee as planned. This means that Jesus forgives the disciples' failure and that the movement will continue in spite of it. The explicit mention of Peter is significant, because Peter has actually denied Jesus. The reader can look forward to a time outside the Gospel's narrative limits when the disciples can continue following Jesus. Still, Mark does not award the reader a comfortable ending. He ends on a note of unresolved tension in his picture of the disciples, for even the women "went out and fled from the tomb, for terror and amazement had seized them; and they said nothing to anyone, for they were afraid" (16:8).

WOMEN

Mark is enmeshed in the patriarchalism and the androcentrism of his time and of his church. He does not directly address the issue of women in the church. For the most part, women play predictable roles. But there are some aspects of the depiction of women that merit closer attention. Dewey argues that Mark is ultimately a gospel of liberation. When we correct for its historically bound myopia concerning women, it can be a liberating text.

Women are implicitly present in many of Mark's stories. They would have been among those cured (as in the case of Peter's mother-in-law in 1:29-31), among the witnesses to Jesus' miracles and exorcisms, and among those whom Jesus taught. In Greek, the masculine plural form is used for groups consisting of both males and females, and words such as *anthropos*, often translated "man" but really meaning more generally human being, are inclusive. The word *disciples* need not be exclusively male, either. Mark contains indications that Jesus had women disciples.

A brief review of the Gospel with an eye toward its attitudes on women will be useful. Jesus cures Peter's mother-in-law in chapter 1. This happens within a private home, the "proper" place for a woman, and when cured, she rises and serves Jesus and his disciples, the "proper" role for a woman. But Jesus will insist, especially in chapter 10, service is central to discipleship. And we must remember that women play key public roles in the Gospel (the Gentile woman who bests Jesus in argument in chapter

7, for example, or the woman who anoints him in chapter 14). Of course, although women served in the home, they also went to temple, to synagogue, to market, and so on. So a categorization of male and female social roles purely in terms of public and private activities is simplistic. In chapter 3, when Jesus redefines his family as those who do the will of God, he explicitly identifies females as part of his following (3:21, 31-35).

In chapter 5, Jesus heals a woman and raises a girl from the dead. Interpretations of these events often refer to purity issues, although Mark does not raise them explicitly. In two stories that are tightly woven together through Mark's favorite technique of concentric structure (5:21-43), a woman who has suffered from hemorrhages for twelve years approaches Jesus, seeking a cure. She hopes to do so without being noticed, perhaps because it might seem forward to touch a man in public, especially a stranger, perhaps because she is unclean because of her flow of blood, so her touching Jesus may render him unclean, or perhaps simply because she is approaching a man of power who is in some ways intimidating. She is cured by the power that flows from Jesus. He praises her initiative. In the other part of this complex, Jesus raises a twelve-year-old girl to life by taking her by the hand. Again, Jesus incurs ritual impurity by touching a dead body, but he brings the girl back from the dead.

Recent interpreters have rightly questioned the role purity concerns play in these episodes. After all, it is more than likely that most people were in a state of ritual impurity most of the time. And ritual impurity was neither sinful, nor did it become important unless one needed to enter the temple. For these sorts of reasons, many now argue that commentators have misunderstood issues of purity in ancient Judaism, particularly as they influence Jesus' career.

In chapter 6, we read about the execution of John the Baptist. Herod, ruler of Galilee and Perea, imprisons John for denouncing Herod's marriage to his brother's former wife, Herodias. Herodias resents John and plots his death. At a banquet, Herod and his guests watch Herodias's daughter dance, and Herod promises her whatever she wishes. Her mother prompts her to ask for John's head on a platter. Herod reluctantly complies. So Mark blames the woman for John's death. She exercises power indirectly, through the leverage over Herod she gains through her daughter's dance, which has sexual undertones. In the ancient world, men often saw women as dangerous, entrapping men with their sexuality and manipulating them to get their way. But in many instances, women, if they were to influence events and their own fate, had to use indirect means. They were denied equality and then criticized when they used the resources left to them. Josephus also speaks of the death of John but has nothing of this scene. He blames Herod for John's death and says that Herod kills John because he fears his influence over the people.

In chapter 7, a Gentile woman approaches Jesus and begs him to exorcise her daughter. He refuses. He has come to serve Israel, not Gentiles. She persists and is successful. The scene is remarkable in that not only does Jesus debate with a woman, she bests him. And she bests him on an important issue. Mark's church was composed primarily of Gentiles. Here he credits a woman with persuading Jesus that his mission must embrace Gentiles.

In chapter 10, Jesus forbids divorce. Some interpret this as an enlightened move by Jesus, since in divorces women usually suffered more than men. By forbidding divorce, Jesus was protecting women. Others see this as unlikely (see Levine). Mark also forbids wives divorcing their husbands, and that would hardly be to protect them. Further, there were safeguards for women in divorce proceedings.

At the beginning of the passion narrative, a woman anoints Jesus with costly ointment, incurring the disapproval of the others (14:3-9). Jesus defends her, declaring that she has anointed his body for burial. This occurs at the beginning of the passion narrative, and she seems to have greater insight into what is to happen than anyone else. Jesus says, "What she has done will be told in remembrance of her" (14:9). Ironically, her name has been lost. The story inspired the title of a key work of feminist criticism, *In Memory of Her*, by Elisabeth Schüssler Fiorenza.

Women witness the crucifixion from a distance (the males all flee) and are the first witnesses to the resurrection, or at least to the empty tomb. They also follow Jesus during his Galilean ministry, but readers do not find that out until 15:40-41, after Jesus dies. He says that these women "provided for him." Mark may want to limit their role to material support, which, though important, is a supportive role and one appropriate, in his view, to women. Mark's failure to inform the reader earlier about women who followed him in Galilee suggests that what counts most for Mark is Jesus' preparation of male followers for leadership in the new movement.

The women at the tomb play a conventional role—anointing the body for death (16:1-8). But they are the only disciples with the courage to show up at the tomb. The women are privileged to hear the news of Jesus' resurrection from the angelic figure, a detail that accords with indications in the other gospels that women were the first witnesses to the resurrection, but their mission is to tell the men, Peter in particular, about the resurrection and the future meeting in Galilee.

Despite indications that Jesus had women disciples, Mark features mostly male disciples. The four whom Jesus calls at the beginning of his ministry are all male (1:16-20), and when he appoints his inner circle of Twelve, there are no women among them. Those closest to Jesus of the Twelve, Peter, James, and John, are all male. The all-male nature of the inner core of disciples remains constant throughout the Gospel, as far as the reader can tell (see, for example, the mission of the Twelve in 6:7-13). We return to Dewey's point that although Mark's Jesus is not explicitly a champion of women's equality, the Gospel as a whole contains a liberating vision for society. Jesus portrays his own mission as one of service, and he defines discipleship in the same terms. His followers are to be as little children (i.e., the lowliest in society; 10:15), give up their possessions and follow Jesus, become members of a new community, and be persecuted (10:17-31). Among Jesus' followers and in the coming kingdom, "many who are first will be last, and the last will be first" (10:31). Leaders must be as slaves, in imitation of the Son of Man who came not to be served but to serve. In Jesus' community, social relations are to be transformed, and in this transformation, present systems of hierarchy are overturned.

JEWS AND JUDAISM

Mark was a Gentile and wrote for a church that was primarily Gentile. He assumes some knowledge about Judaism and the Bible, but any Christian community would have basic information about those things. At times, Mark finds it necessary to explain Jewish customs and laws (for example, 7:3-4).

Jesus was Jewish as were his followers. No gospel pictures him pursuing a ministry to Gentiles. So most of the Gospel's characters are Jewish. That means that the reactions to Jesus, be they positive or negative, are mostly by Jews. Jews oppose him, but Jews also accept and follow him. The common people are for the most part favorably disposed to Jesus. They recognize his power and approach him for healing and exorcisms. They do not, however, understand who he really is. Rulers and their retainers are hostile to Jesus, for the most part. An exception is the scribe in chapter 12, who agrees with Jesus that the greatest commandment is love of God and neighbor and to whom Jesus says, "You are not far from the kingdom of God" (12:34), and Jairus, a leader in the synagogue (5:22).

Within the opposition to Jesus, different groups play somewhat different roles. The Pharisees, for example, oppose Jesus mainly during his mission in Galilee. They argue with him on matters of Torah. They challenge his eating with tax collectors and sinners (2:16), the failure of his disciples to fast (2:18), and his disciples' working on the Sabbath (2:24). Jesus always has the better of the arguments. When he eats with sinners, Jesus fulfills God's will for him to go to those who need him and to save the lost. The Pharisees' fasting proves their blindness to the presence of God's agent, Jesus, at whose presence they ought to rejoice. Their strict observance of Sabbath overrides human need. In all three cases, Pharisees separate themselves from God's will.

These three conflicts take place within the five-episode section on Jesus' conflict with religious authorities (2:1–3:6), a section that culminates with the statement, "The Pharisees went out and immediately conspired with the Herodians against him, how to destroy him" (3:6). Mark thereby implicates the Pharisees in Jesus' death, yet when we read the passion narrative, they do not appear. Mark has no specific traditions linking the Pharisees to Jesus' death but wants to include all segments of Jewish leadership in that event.

In chapter 7, Jesus castigates the Pharisees and scribes for undermining God's word with their own religious traditions. Mark thinks that Jesus abrogates Jewish food laws, although he states this as an editorial comment, not as a direct pronouncement by Jesus (7:19b). He apparently has no statement of Jesus about this.

In 8:11, the Pharisees demand a sign from Jesus to prove his divine authority. Jesus sees this as their refusal to accept him as God's agent. At the end of part I, Jesus warns the disciples to avoid the "yeast" of the Pharisees and of Herod. By this he means not to belong to their camp, not to follow their teaching. Again Mark associates the Pharisees and the Herodians, recalling 3:6, thereby including most of part I under the heading of opposition of Jewish leaders to Jesus.

The only time the Pharisees appear in part II is when they question Jesus on the lawfulness of divorce. The only time they appear in part III is when they and some Herodians challenge Jesus about the appropriateness of paying taxes to the Romans (12:13-17). This is a trick question, since they know that many Jews will disapprove if he says to pay taxes and that he will be in trouble with Rome if he says not to do so. Jesus avoids the trap by requesting to see an imperial coin, observing Caesar's image, and saying that what belongs to Caesar should be given to Caesar. It is ironic that the Pharisees carry such coins around, since the coins violate Torah's injunction against images (Exod 20:4). Jesus thereby demonstrates their subservience to Rome. Later, other leaders will use Rome to dispose of Jesus.

When Jesus arrives in Jerusalem, home of the temple and its politico-religious establishment, he begins his activities there by performing a symbolic action in the temple, the tipping over of the tables of the money changers (11:15-19). The changing of money was necessary for the operation of the temple. Money with human and animal images had to be changed for money without them. Mark's Jesus sees such commerce as defiling the temple, which was meant for prayer. At the end of chapter 12, Jesus condemns the temple establishment for social injustice ("devouring" widows' houses; 12:40) in the name of religion. To them, piety is a path to status. In chapter 13, Jesus foretells the destruction of the temple, corresponding to his symbolic action in chapter 11. Jesus is acting in the tradition of several of the prophets, who also protested a disjunction between what the temple ought to be and what it had become through the shortcomings of people or leaders (Isa 58; Jer 7; Zech 14). But it is important to remember that the reason this mattered to Jesus was that he saw the temple as God's house. He taught and worshiped there, and he celebrated Passover in its shadow.

Jesus' action and words against the temple leadership provoke a reaction. The chief priests, scribes, and elders send armed men to Gethsemane to arrest him (14:43-46). There follows a trial before the Jerusalem authorities, presided over by the high priest (14:53-65). The trial concludes with the high priest accusing Jesus of blasphemy for claiming to be Messiah and Son of God (see our discussion of 2:1-12). They hand Jesus over to the Roman authorities in the person of the prefect Pontius Pilate for execution. Mark narrates the trial before Pilate in such a way that Jesus' death is primarily the responsibility of the Jewish leaders, not Pilate.

When Jesus dies, the curtain of the temple is torn in two (15:38). As we saw above, it is not obvious how this is to be read. One major strand of interpretation sees it as corresponding to Jesus' condemnation of the temple authorities, and as a result of their refusal to accept him as the one sent by God. Jesus' death brings to a climax God's eschatological plans. Most think that Mark's community had already broken with Judaism, and Mark may well have composed his Gospel soon after the destruction of the temple. Mark thought apocalyptically. God, first through Jesus and now through the church, was struggling against Satan and was bringing Satan's kingdom to an end. The kingdom of God was near. Those who followed Jesus, either personally or by joining the church, belonged to the community formed by Jesus' death. They were "ransomed" (10:45), plundered from Satan's treasure (3:27). Others were on the side of Satan. This included the temple leaders, who, as Mark saw it, refused to accept the Son of God.

CONCLUSION

Mark was the first to write a gospel, as far as we know. Before that time, Jesus traditions were passed on orally or in collections of smaller units—perhaps miracles, a passion narrative, sayings. Through his connected narrative, Mark combines various elements of the Jesus tradition into a coherent whole. His Gospel guides the reader into a proper understanding of key aspects of Jesus' ministry. The passion and death of Jesus are central, so that messiahship, miracles, discipleship, and resurrection are seen in light of it. The power of Mark's presentation lies in this focus, but, as we shall see, the evangelists who followed him found that he did not do full justice to other aspects of Jesus' career. Matthew and Luke wrote their gospels at least in part to present what is for them a more adequate presentation.

BIBLIOGRAPHY

Achtemeier, Paul J. "Mark, Gospel of." *ABD* 4:541-57.

———. "Toward the Isolation of Pre-Markan Miracle Catenae." *JBL* 89 (1970): 265-91.

Anderson, Gary A. "Sacrifice and Sacrificial Offerings (OT)." *ABD* 5:870-86.

Anderson, Janice Capel, and Stephen Moore, eds. *Mark and Method: New Approaches in Biblical Studies*. Minneapolis: Fortress, 1992.

Bock, Darrell L. *Blasphemy and Exaltation in Judaism and the Final Examination of Jesus*. Tübingen: Mohr Siebeck, 1998.

Boomershine, T. E., and G. L. Bartholomew. "The Narrative Technique of Mark 16:8." *JBL* 100 (1981): 213-23.

D'Angelo, Mary Rose. "(Re)Presentations of Women in the Gospels: John and Mark." *WCO*, 129-49.

Dewey, Joanna. "The Gospel of Mark." Pages 470-509 in *Searching the Scriptures: A Feminist Commentary*, edited by Elisabeth Schüssler Fiorenza. New York: Crossroad, 1994.

Donahue, John R., and Daniel J. Harrington. *The Gospel of Mark*. Sacra Pagina, vol. 2. Collegeville, Minn: Liturgical, 2002.

———. *The Theology and Setting of Discipleship in the Gospel of Mark*. Milwaukee: Marquette University Press, 1983.

Fowler, Robert M. *Let the Reader Understand: Reader-Response Criticism and the Gospel of Mark*. Minneapolis: Fortress, 1991.

Juel, Donald. *A Master of Surprise: Mark Interpreted*. Minneapolis: Fortress Press, 1994.

Kelber, Werner. *Mark's Story of Jesus*. Philadelphia: Fortress, 1979.

Kermode, Frank. *The Genesis of Secrecy: On the Interpretation of Narrative*. Cambridge: Harvard University Press, 1979.

Kingsbury, Jack Dean. *The Christology of Mark*. Philadelphia: Fortress, 1984.

———. *Conflict in Mark: Jesus, Authorities, Disciples*. Minneapolis: Fortress, 1989.

Klauck, Hans-Josef. "Sacrifice and Sacrificial Offerings (NT)." *ABD* 5:886-91.

Levine, Amy-Jill. "Jesus, Divorce, and Sexuality: A Jewish Critique." Pages 113-29 in *The Historical Jesus through Catholic and Jewish Eyes*. Edited by Bryan F. LeBeau, Leonard Greenspoon, and Dennis Hamm. Harrisburg, Penn.: Trinity, 2000.

Marxsen, Willi. *Mark the Evangelist: Studies on the Redaction History of the Gospel*. Translated by James Boyce et al. Nashville: Abingdon, 1969.

Matera, Frank J. *What Are They Saying about Mark?* New York: Paulist, 1987.

Milgrom, Jacob. *Leviticus*. 3 vols. New York: Doubleday, 1991–2001.

Perrin, Norman, and Dennis Duling. *The New Testament: Proclamation and Parenesis, Myth and History*. 3d ed. Forth Worth: Harcourt Brace College Publishers, 1994.

Räisänen, Heikki. *The "Messianic Secret" in Mark*. Translated by Christopher M. Tuckett. Edinburgh: T. & T. Clark, 1990.

Tannehill, Robert. "The Disciples in Mark: The Function of a Narrative Role." *JR* 57 (1977): 386-405.

———. "The Gospel of Mark as Narrative Christology." *Semeia* 16 (1979): 57-92.

Tuckett, Christopher M. "Atonement in the New Testament." *ABD* 1:518-22.

———, ed. *The Messianic Secret*. Philadelphia: Fortress, 1983.

Yarbro Collins, Adela. *The Beginning of the Gospel: Probings of Mark in Context*. Minneapolis: Fortress, 1992.

———. "The Charge of Blasphemy in Mark 14:64." *JSNT* 26 (2004): 379-401.

———. "The Origins of the Designation of Jesus as 'Son of Man'." *HTR* 80 (1987): 391-407.

Rhoads, David, and Donald Michie. *Mark as Story: An Introduction to the Narrative of a Gospel*. Philadelphia: Fortress, 1982.

Weeden, Theodore. *Mark: Traditions in Conflict*. Philadelphia: Fortress, 1971.

Wrede, William. *The Messianic Secret*. Translated by J. C. G. Greig. Cambridge: J. Clarke, 1971.

CHAPTER FOUR

THE GOSPEL OF MATTHEW

INTRODUCTION

Questions about this Gospel's author center around whether he was Jewish or Gentile. Those who think he was Jewish point to the Jewish nature of the Gospel, the insistence on observance of Torah, the interest in literal fulfillment of the Hebrew Bible, the genealogy, and other features. Those who do not think that he was Jewish rely on apparent confusion about Sadducean teaching, hostility not only to Jewish leaders but perhaps to the Jewish people as a whole, and lack of understanding of some biblical passages. The debate continues. The most important aspect of the discussion is Matthew's attitude to Torah, something we discuss below.

Second-century attribution of the Gospel to Matthew is of uncertain historical value, but we can inquire what those who made this attribution had in mind. The First Gospel rewrites Mark's account of the call of Levi the tax collector (Matt 9:9-13; Mark 2:13-17), changing his name from Levi to Matthew. Matthew's Gospel includes "Matthew the tax collector" as one of the Twelve (10:3). Matthew is among the Twelve in Mark, but Mark does not call him a tax collector. Could it be that the Gospel's author was Matthew the tax collector, one of the Twelve? This is unlikely. Matthew depends heavily on Mark and uses Q for much of his sayings material. Early Christian tradition does not consider Mark an eyewitness. It is implausible that the Apostle Matthew, eyewitness to Jesus' ministry, would depend on someone else's gospel, not an eyewitness, for his basic story. It is especially unlikely that he would depend on someone else's account of his own call.

From the Gospel itself, we can tell that Matthew was educated, intelligent, and fluent in Greek. He knew the Jewish Scriptures well. He was especially interested in the relationship between the Christian movement and the Judaism of his day. Since he uses Mark as a source, we know that he wrote after Mark, perhaps fifteen years or so. He also uses Q, and he had at his disposal other material, too. His special material we designate M. The term M is an umbrella term covering anything that Matthew does not get from Mark or Q. It was not a single written source, as was Q.

Several features of the Gospel hint at the circumstances of its composition. The first is the Pharisees' enhanced role. They are prominent in Mark, but Matthew increases their presence substantially and always depicts them negatively. Another is Matthew's attitude toward Torah. There are signs in Mark's Gospel that his community has definitively broken with the synagogue and that it does not observe Torah. There is evidence that Matthew considered his church to be Torah-observant. These features make it likely that Matthew took shape within a largely Jewish-Christian community in tension with local synagogue leadership. At the time, Judaism was redefining itself in the wake of the loss of the temple and its cult. It was eventually to become rabbinic Judaism. Pharisees were an important part of this process. Matthew saw his community home to the true observers of Torah, and he saw non-Christian Jewish leadership as a rival, leading Jews astray.

We subscribe to the two-source solution to the Synoptic Problem. That means that we think that Mark was the first of the Synoptics to be written, and that Matthew and Luke used Mark as a source. They also used a source no longer extant that we call Q. Since Matthew relies on Mark as a source, we can observe how Matthew adds to, subtracts from, and rewrites Mark. Redaction criticism describes these changes, assesses their significance, and evaluates how they correspond to Matthew's historical situation.

MATERIAL ONLY IN MATTHEW

Noting what is unique to Matthew is a first step in getting a feel for the Gospel. The following list is not exhaustive, but illustrative.

Infancy Narrative (1:1–2:23)
- Virgin birth related to Isa 7:14
- Magi from the east
- Herod tries to kill the infant Jesus
- Flight of Jesus, Mary, and Joseph to Egypt

- Family unable to settle in hometown of Bethlehem, so they resettle in Nazareth

Formula Quotations throughout the Gospel (for example, virgin birth fulfulls Isa 7:14 in Matt 1:22-23; see also 2:5-6, 17-18, and so on)

> John resists baptizing Jesus (3:14-15)
>
> Sermon on the Mount (chs. 5–7) shows a special interest in Torah, in acts of piety, and in ethics
>
> Jesus' teaching insisting on importance of the Torah (5:17-20)
>
> Six antitheses radicalizing or changing the Torah (5:27-48)
>
> Teaching on almsgiving, prayer, and fasting (6:1-8, 16-18).
>
> Pearls before swine (7:6)

Inclusion of eschatological material in Discourse on the Disciples' Mission (10:17-25)

Temple tax (17:24-27)

Parables

- Weeds and Its interpretation (13:24-30, 36-43)
- Hidden Treasure and Pearl (13:44-46)
- Net (13:47-50)
- New and Old Treasure (13:52)
- Unmerciful Servant (18:23-35)
- Laborers in the Vineyard (20:1-16)
- Two Sons (21:28-32)
- Ten Bridesmaids (25:1-13)

Last judgment scene (25:31-46)

Death of Judas (27:3-10)

Cry of the crowd, "His blood be on us and on our children!" (27:25)

Guard at the tomb (27:62-66)

Bribing of the soldiers and rumor that Jesus' body was stolen (28:11-15)

The risen Jesus commissions the eleven disciples to teach the whole world (28:16-20)

STRUCTURE

Matthew's basic structure depends on Mark's, but there are important differences. Mark contains nothing of Jesus' birth or childhood, while Matthew begins his Gospel with an infancy narrative (chs. 1–2). Mark narrates no resurrection appearances. Matthew adds two.

Even a casual reader of this Gospel will notice the prominence of Jesus' discourses. Mark has two major discourses of Jesus—the parables (ch. 4) and the apocalyptic discourse (ch. 13). Matthew has five. He includes a parable chapter, modeled on Mark's but with more parables (ch. 13). Like Mark, he has an apocalyptic discourse (ch. 24), which he prefaces with a lengthy diatribe against the scribes and Pharisees (ch. 23) and follows with three eschatological parables (ch. 25). Jesus' first discourse in Matthew, the Sermon on the Mount (chs. 5–7), has no counterpart in Mark. Comparison with Luke shows that Matthew constructed this sermon on the basis of a sermonlike collection within Q, but Luke's sermon occupies only 6:20-49, thirty verses, while Matthew's is three whole chapters, one hundred eleven verses.

In addition to these three discourses, Matthew has a missionary discourse in chapter 10, similar to the one in Luke 10, and a discourse on the church in chapter 18, unique to Matthew. Matthew closes each of the five discourses in a formulaic way. Each ends with something like "When Jesus had finished saying these things . . ." (7:28). Counting chapters 23 and 25, the discourses occupy nine of twenty-eight chapters in Matthew. Close analysis reveals a relationship between the narrative preceding each discourse and the discourse itself.

The following outline takes its lead from the position of the discourses in the Gospel. We follow Meier's structural analysis. As we said when providing a structural outline of Mark's Gospel, there are many ways to view a gospel's structure. It is helpful to have in mind a basic idea of a gospel's shape as we read it, for that helps to orient us to where material is and how it is arranged. This also gives us one way of getting at an author's meaning. In the case of Matthew, for example, this structural outline emphasizes the importance of Jesus' discourses (speeches) and shows how other material is arranged around them.

Prologue: Infancy Narrative (1:1–2:23)

Book I
Narrative (3:1–4:25)
First Discourse: Sermon on the Mount (5:1–7:29)
Book II
Narrative (8:1–9:34)
Second Discourse: (10:1–11:1)

Book III
  Narrative (11:2–12:50)
  Third Discourse: Parables (13:1-52)
Book IV
  Narrative (13:53–17:27)
  Fourth Discourse: The Church (18:1-35)
Book V
  Narrative (19:1–23:39)
  Fifth Discourse: Apocalypticism (24:1–25:46)
Climax: Passion, Death, and Resurrection (26:1–28:20)

OVERVIEW

Matthew applies the prophecy of Isa 7:14 to Jesus. He is *Emmanuel*, "God with us." We make the case below that this does not mean full divinity as in later christological formulations, but it does mean that in Jesus we have God's definitive revelation, revelation that does not negate Torah but rather interprets it in full accord with God's will. Jesus is the supreme Torah teacher. His teaching takes up a substantial portion of the Gospel. He is the Son of God who takes away humanity's sins and reveals to them what his Father wants. At the end of the Gospel, the risen Jesus commissions his disciples to go to all nations to teach them what Jesus commands. He does so as the one to whom God has given all authority in heaven and on earth, and he promises to remain with the church till the end of the age.

Things to Look For

- There is an infancy narrative (chs. 1–2) and resurrection appearances (28:9-10, 16-20).
- There is more of Jesus' teaching, arranged in five major discourses.
- There are many formula quotations, where an event or aspect of Jesus' ministry is said to fulfill a prophetic prediction.
- Miracle stories are rewritten to emphasize interaction between Jesus and the petitioner and to highlight the petitioner's faith.
- There is less emphasis on exorcisms, but they are still present.
- The messianic secret is downplayed.
- The figure of Jesus is exalted. He frequently calls God his Father. Followers of Jesus call him "Lord."

- The title *Son of David* is prominent and is associated especially with healing.
- Torah receives special attention. Jesus clashes with Jewish leaders on issues of Torah and claims to be the true interpreter of it. For Jesus, love and mercy are at Torah's center.
- Jesus is often said to teach. The disciples teach only after Jesus' resurrection.
- The Pharisees are portrayed particularly negatively. Sadducees play a somewhat larger role than in Mark.
- There is more interest in church discipline and behavior. Only Matthew uses the word *church*, and he stresses the importance of deeds.
- The eschaton seems further away, but he emphasizes the last judgment.
- The disciples understand more.

GOSPEL SURVEY

PROLOGUE: INFANCY NARRATIVE (1:1–2:23)

1:1-17: Genealogy. Only Matthew and Luke contain a genealogy of Jesus, and only Matthew begins his Gospel with it. Genealogy was of great importance to ancient Judaism. Israel was not just a religion but a people, an extended family that claimed descent from Abraham (although one could join Judaism by conversion). Within Israel, important subgroups were defined by biological descent. Priesthood was hereditary, as was Davidic kingship. Matthew's genealogy of Jesus stresses his descent from Abraham and from David.

The genealogy is in three parts, each containing fourteen generations. (Or at least that is what Matthew claims in 1:17. In fact, there are only thirteen in the third section of the genealogy.) This indicates that history proceeds according to God's plan. The number fourteen may allude to David. Ancient Hebrew did not have numerals but used letters instead (as did Latin, for example). The numerical value of the letters in the name *David* is fourteen.

1:18–2:23: Birth and Infancy. The author structures the rest of the infancy narrative around five "formula quotations" (1:22-23; 2:5-6, 15, 17-18, 23). These are citations of Scripture introduced by a formula to the effect that the biblical verse has been fulfilled. For Matthew, the prophets foretold every aspect of Jesus' infancy and childhood—virgin birth, birth in Bethlehem, Herod's attempt on his life, being called out of Egypt, and growing up in Nazareth. Other formula quotations punctuate the rest of the Gospel. God controls the action by communicating with Joseph through dreams and angels.

Only in Matthew does Jesus flee to Egypt and then return to the land of Israel. Jesus thereby recapitulates the history of his people and embodies the culminating act of God's care for Israel. There is also a parallel with Moses, both because Moses led Israel out of Egypt, and because when Moses was born, the king of Egypt commanded the death of all male Israelite babies. Moses escaped by God's providence and the actions of his mother. When Jesus is born, King Herod seeks his life. Seeking to kill Jesus, he commands the death of all male Jewish babies. Jesus escapes through God's providence and his father's (Joseph's) action.

Matthew says that the virgin birth fulfills Isa 7:14: "Look, the virgin shall conceive and bear a son, / and they shall name him Emmanuel" (Matt 1:23). Matthew explains that this Hebrew name means "God is with us." Ancient names were often symbolic. Isaiah gave his children names that conveyed prophetic messages (7:3; 8:3-4). Emmanuel from Isa 7:14 may originally have been one of Isaiah's sons. Matthew applies Isaiah's prophecy to Jesus, indicating God's presence among the people through Jesus. This forms a frame with the end of the Gospel, where Jesus says that all authority in heaven and on earth has been given to him, so he exercises God's authority: "Remember, I am with you always, to the end of the age" (28:20). The same notion of Jesus' presence appears in the church discourse: "For where two or three are gathered in my name, I am there among them" (18:20).

Reference to a virgin is found only in the Greek version of Isa 7. In the Hebrew, the prophet says only that a "young woman" will conceive and give birth. Therefore, Matthew's fulfillment motif works only with the Greek text, not the Hebrew.

As noted above, ancient names, including names in the Bible, are often symbolic. Only in Matthew do we get an interpretation of the name *Jesus*. Matthew tells us that Jesus receives his name because "he will save his people from their sins" (1:21). *Jesus* is the Greek form of the Hebrew name "Yeshua" or "Yeshu," themselves shortened forms of "Joshua." *Joshua* can be seen as deriving from the Hebrew root ysh῾, "to save." Matthew interprets Jesus' name as meaning "He will save." Jesus has come to save "his people," Israel, from their sins (see 10:5; 15:24).

The infancy narrative foreshadows Jesus' passion. "Wise men from the East" appear, inquiring about the one born king of the Jews. They know of him because they have observed his star in the sky. The word translated "wise man" is *magos*, from which the English word "magician" comes, as does the traditional designation "the magi." *Magos* often means an astrologer from the East, from Mesopotamia, so it makes sense that the wise men follow an unusual star. Herod tries to deceive the wise men into locating the child so that he can eliminate this rival. After they visit Jesus and give him royal gifts, a dream warns them to avoid Herod, so they return home by a different route. The episode presages the Gospel's final chapters, where Jesus again faces hostility from a Jerusalem establishment that seeks the aid of Gentiles to eliminate him. The Gentile wise men also foreshadow Gentiles who enter the church later (28:19).

BOOK I

Narrative (3:1–4:25)

3:1-17: Jesus and John the Baptist. Chapter 3 recounts the interaction between John the Baptist and Jesus. Only in Matthew does John preach the kingdom of God (3:2). This makes the connection between John's mission and that of Jesus clearer, because John's proclamation is precisely the same as that of Jesus in 4:17. Matthew adds John's preaching from Q that reinforces his image as an eschatological, even apocalyptic, prophet (3:7-10).

Matthew's treatment of this scene shows his concern about the relationship between John and Jesus. Mark's version might leave the impression that John is superior to Jesus. Matthew obviates any such conclusions by adding 3:14-15. John says that he is unworthy to baptize Jesus; rather, Jesus should baptize him. Jesus says that they must "fulfill all righteousness." For Matthew this always means to fulfill God's will. So John baptizes Jesus because it is part of God's plan.

When Jesus emerges from the water, the spirit descends on him and God's voice declares him God's son. God speaks not to Jesus, as in Mark, but to the crowd. Instead of Mark's "You are my Son" Matthew has "This is my son." Matthew's Jesus does not hide his messiahship.

4:1-11: The Temptation. Jesus goes to the desert to be tempted by Satan, as in Mark. Matthew draws on Q to elaborate. Temptation in the desert echoes Israel's temptations between leaving Egypt and entering Canaan. Matthew finds three temptations in Q. Satan first tempts Jesus to turn stone into bread, because Jesus is hungry. This recalls Israel's need for bread in the desert. Jesus answers by quoting from Deuteronomy, where Moses tells Israel why God at first let them hunger and then bestowed manna on them. It was to teach them that humans live not just on physical bread but on God's word (Deut 8:3). In the second temptation, Satan suggests that Jesus throw himself from temple's pinnacle to prove that God will protect him. In the third, Satan offers Jesus power over all earthly kingdoms. In the second and third temptations, Jesus quotes Deuteronomy again. These are more words of Moses to the people concerning their desert experiences. Deuteronomy 6:16 says that one should not test God, and Deut 6:13 insists on worship of God alone. The overtones of Israel's desert experience accord with Matthew's theme of Jesus retracing Israel's history. Israel succumbed to temptation in the wilderness; Jesus resists it.

4:12-25: Beginning of Jesus' Ministry. After John's arrest, Jesus moves to Galilee in fulfillment of scripture (4:14-16) and begins to preach the kingdom. He calls the first disciples, and then Matthew gives a summary of his ministry, based on Mark 1:39 and 3:7, 8, 10. Mark says that Jesus "went throughout Galilee, proclaiming the message in their synagogues and casting out demons" (1:39), while Matthew has,

> Jesus went throughout Galilee, teaching in their synagogues and proclaiming the good news of the kingdom and curing every disease and every sickness among the people. So his fame spread throughout all Syria, and they brought to him all the sick, those who were afflicted with various diseases and pains, demoniacs, epileptics, and paralytics, and he cured them. (4:23-24)

Matthew emphasizes healing more than exorcism, although exorcism is present. Matthew highlights Jesus' teaching. Matthew omits Mark's notice that the demons knew Jesus and that he silenced them. He has little interest in Mark's messianic secret.

First Discourse: Sermon on the Mount (5:1–7:29)

We discuss this discourse in detail under the heading of "Jews and Judaism." Here we characterize it briefly. The Sermon on the Mount is Matthew's first discourse, and it lays out Jesus' message. As Moses ascended the mountain to obtain the Law and bring it to Israel, Jesus ascends the mountain to deliver his definitive interpretation of the Law.

Some interpreters term this a "new" Torah, but Matthew considers it the same Torah as Moses received (5:17-19).

The sermon begins with Matthew's version of the Beatitudes (5:3-12), which he found in Q. Luke's Beatitudes are probably closer to their form in Q, so Matthew or his church has developed them. Matthew has nine, while Luke has only four. Matthew spiritualizes them. While Luke says that the poor and hungry are blessed, Matthew speaks of the poor in spirit and those who hunger for righteousness (5:3, 6). True to his interest in Torah, Matthew adds the term "righteousness" twice to the Beatitudes (5:6, 10). True to his insistence that mercy is at the center of Torah, Matthew's Jesus blesses the merciful (5:7).

Throughout the sermon, Jesus emphasizes deeds. Righteousness is not an abstract virtue. It is something one does. Jesus' ethic here has been called radical because of its extreme demands. Do not get angry, do not have lustful thoughts, do not divorce, do not take oaths, do not retaliate, and love enemies. Piety is never for the purpose of gaining status—it should be private. Do not pursue financial security—God will provide. Do not judge; pray; know that it is hard to enter life, that is, to establish and maintain a good relationship with God and thereby to inherit the kingdom, to go to heaven. Doing miracles in Jesus' name counts for nothing, unless one keeps Jesus' demands. The golden rule, treat others as you would be treated, is the essence of the Torah and prophets. Those who obey Jesus' commands will be saved; those who do not will suffer eternal, fiery damnation. The sermon ends with a formula: "When Jesus had finished saying these things. . . ."

The crowds are "astounded" at Jesus' teaching, "for he taught them as one having authority, and not as their scribes" (7:29). This comes from Mark 1:22. There we noted that although Mark mentions Jesus' teaching activity, he relates little of Jesus' teaching. Matthew rectifies that.

BOOK II

Narrative (8:1–9:34)

8:1–9:34: Ten Miracles. The narrative portion of book II consists of ten miracles taken mostly from Mark, interspersed with material on discipleship. As Jesus shows himself mighty in word in the Sermon on the Mount, he now reveals himself mighty in deed as well. The number of miracles may be another parallel with Moses, who was instrumental in the ten plagues in Egypt.

Matthew systematically rewrites the healing stories he inherits. He enhances interaction between Jesus and petitioners, emphasizing the petitioners' faith and prayerful approach to Jesus, and stressing Jesus' power and control. Matthew arranges the miracles in three groups consisting of three, three, and four miracles respectively.

8:1-4: Cure of a Leper. Jesus cures a leper by touch. As in Mark, this should make Jesus unclean, but instead it cleanses the leper. (See our discussion of the passage on which Matthew depends here, Mark 1:40-45). Jesus orders the cured man to show himself to the priests, as Torah requires. Matthew omits that the man disobeys Jesus' command to keep his cure quiet (Mark 1:45). He does not want to portray disobedience to Jesus.

8:5-13: Cure of the Centurion's Servant. There follows a miracle from Q where Jesus cures a Roman centurion's servant. Jesus praises the centurion's faith (8:5-13). In both Luke and Matthew, and also in Q, the Gentile centurion's faith contrasts with Israel's lack of faith. Matthew underscores the point by inserting a saying from Q about people from east and west dining with Abraham, Isaac, and Jacob, while the "heirs of the kingdom" are excluded. He takes "heirs of the kingdom" to be Israel and those from east and west to be Gentiles. Luke has those words in a different place, where there is no contrast with Gentiles (Luke 13:28-30).

8:14-15: Cure of Peter's Mother-in-Law. When Peter's mother-in-law is cured in Mark, she serves "them," but in Matthew she serves "him," Jesus.

8:16-17: Summary. Jesus performs exorcisms and healings "with a word," a phrase added by Matthew to underscore Jesus' power. A formula quotation asserts that Jesus' cures fulfill prophecy (8:17; Isa 53:4).

8:18-22: Sayings on Discipleship. Between the first and second groups of cures, Matthew inserts sayings from Q on discipleship. They emphasize the necessity of leaving everything behind to follow Jesus, including home and family.

8:23-27: Calming the Sea. The first miracle in the next group of three is the calming of the sea. Matthew heavily redacts it to make it an allegory of the church, one of his recurrent concerns. We analyze this in chapter 1, under the heading "Redaction Criticism." Jesus is the Lord of the church, to whom Christians pray in the storms that threaten the church.

8:28-34: Exorcism of the Gadarenes. The second miracle is the exorcism of the Gadarenes from Mark 5:1-20, where Jesus casts the demons into swine, who rush into the sea. Matthew abbreviates the story, which he often does, and he omits that the demons are named "Legion," an allusion to Roman oppression.

9:2-8: Forgiveness of Sins; Cure of a Paralytic. In the third story Jesus cures a paralytic, first forgiving his sins. The scribes accuse him of blasphemy, insisting that only God can forgive sins (see our discussion of Mark 2:1-12). Matthew and Mark use the term *Son of Man* when asserting Jesus' power to forgive sins. Different from Mark is that the story ends with the people giving thanks that God has "given such authority to human beings." This foreshadows Jesus giving the ability to "bind and loose" to Peter in chapter 16 (see our discussion there) and to all the disciples in 18:18, and in turn demonstrates Matthew's interest in church matters. Forgiveness of sins now occurs within the church.

9:9-17: Teaching on Discipleship. Between the second and third group of miracle stories Matthew inserts a second block of material on discipleship. Jesus calls Matthew the tax collector to follow him (called "Levi" in Mark), and he then enjoys a meal with tax collectors and sinners. The Pharisees ask Jesus' disciples why he eats with sinners. Jesus hears their question and explains that it is the sick that need a physician. Matthew adds, "Go and learn what this means, 'I desire mercy, not sacrifice,'" a quote from Hos 6:6. Matthew uses Hos 6:6 again in 12:27, where the conflict between Jesus and religious authorities intensifies. For Matthew, mercy is central to Torah.

Matthew agrees with Mark that fasting is inappropriate while Jesus, the bridegroom, is present, but that after he is gone the disciples will fast (9:14-15). He also follows Mark in saying that new wine cannot be put into old wineskins, or a new patch sewn on old cloth, meaning that something new has happened in Jesus and that some of the old ways no longer apply (9:16-17). Matthew diverges from Mark when Jesus closes the section by saying, "Both are preserved." The old and the new must both be kept. This accords with Matthew's theme that Jesus, although he represents the new and definitive action of God in history, does not abrogate what has gone before. Jesus does not bring the end of Torah. Judaism has not been superseded.

9:18-26: Cure of Woman with a Hemorrhage and Raising of Jairus's Daughter. The first two of the final four miracles in this section are the interwoven stories of the woman with the hemorrhage and the girl who is dead, from Mark 5:21-43. In Mark the woman approaches Jesus unnoticed, touches his garment, and power flows from him to cure her, so he asks who touched him. For Matthew, Jesus is more clearly in control. When the woman touches the fringe of his garment, she is not cured. Rather, Jesus knows that he has been touched and by whom, and he says, "Take heart, daughter; your faith has made you well." The narrator says, "Instantly the woman was made well," stressing the efficacy of Jesus' word. We remember from our discussion of Mark 6:56 that Jesus' wearing fringe is a sign of his being a pious Jew. It is noteworthy that where Mark has simply "garment" in the story of the woman here, Matthew introduces the detail that she touched the fringe of his garment. Matthew may be emphasizing Jesus' Jewishness.

9:27-31: Cure of Two Blind Men. The third miracle is Matthew's creation, fashioned on the basis of Mark 10:46-52. He also reproduces Mark's version where Mark has it (Matt 20:29-34), so it becomes a doublet (a unit that occurs twice in the Gospel). We look first at how he rewrites Mark 10:46-52 in Matt 20:29-34. In Mark 10, Jesus cures one blind man, while Matt 20 has him cure two, enhancing his power. In Mark, the blind man calls out, "Jesus, Son of David, have mercy on me" (10:47). In Matthew, they cry, "Lord, have mercy on us, Son of David" (20:30). In Matthew, Jesus is frequently addressed as "Lord," more often than in Mark. Not only do the blind men address Jesus as "Lord," they do so twice. As we return to Matt 9, we see that here also Jesus cures not one but two blind men, and they address Jesus as "Lord." Further, the dialogue between petitioners and Jesus is increased. When they ask them to heal them, Jesus says, "Do you believe that I am able to do this?" They answer, "Yes, Lord." He touches their eyes and says, "According to your faith let it be done to you." This story illustrates Matthew's enhancement of Jesus' power, his depiction of Jesus as Son of David, his association of that title with healing, his increase of dialogue between the petitioner and Jesus, and his attention to faith.

9:32-34: Cure of a Mute Demoniac. Matthew rounds out these two chapters with a tenth miracle. It is unique to him. He constructs it on the basis of Mark 3:22, where Jesus is accused of being allied to Satan. Matthew rewrites that section of Mark in Matt 12:22-24, resulting in another doublet. Here in Matt 9:32-34, Jesus casts out a demon that causes inability to speak. The crowds exclaim, "Never has anything like this been seen in Israel." Again Matthew's concern with how Jesus relates to Israel is at the forefront. The Pharisees charge, "By the ruler of the demons he casts out the demons." Scribes from Jerusalem, not Pharisees, make this accusation in Mark 3:22. When Matthew reproduces the story where Mark has it (Mark 3:22; Matt 12:22-24), he again changes the accusers from scribes to Pharisees. The doubling of the Pharisees' accusation intensifies the conflict between Jesus and the Pharisees.

9:35: Transitional Summary. Matthew makes the transition between chapters 8–9 and the missionary discourse by means of a summary stressing Jesus' teaching and healing, built on Mark 6:6b, 34. Jesus has compassion on the crowds because they are "like sheep without a shepherd," a criticism of their leadership reminiscent of Ezek 34. Matthew adds a saying from Q to the effect that there are few laborers to send into the harvest. The human race is ripe to be "harvested" for God, but there are not enough missionaries for the job. This is an apt transition into the missionary discourse.

Second Discourse: The Disciples' Mission (10:1–11:1)

In Mark 6:6b-13, Jesus sends the apostles out with brief instructions. Both Matthew and Luke construct a missionary discourse using Mark's missionary instructions, supplemented by material from Q. Matthew also incorporates material from Mark's apocalyptic discourse into his own missionary discourse, thus blurring the distinction between the disciples' mission and end-time events. For Matthew, Jesus' death sets off cosmic disturbances (27:51-53), signaling the beginning of the end of the present age. Jesus' missionary instructions in chapter 10 apply to the church, following Jesus' death and resurrection. So the mission does take place in the last times. But would that apply to a mission of the disciples before Jesus' death as well? In this connection, it is perhaps significant that whereas Mark and Luke both follow the missionary instructions with the notice that the disciples actually carried out a mission (Mark 6:12-13; Luke 9:6), Matthew does not. So the missionary instructions, although given to the apostles during Jesus' life, may really apply to the period after his death as an eschatological turning point.

Matthew introduces the missionary discourse with Jesus' appointment of the twelve apostles (10:1-4), thus bringing together their call, from Mark 3, with their mission, from Mark 6. He thereby ties the office of apostle more securely to the church's mission. The Twelve are given authority to do what Jesus does—cast out demons, cure diseases, and preach the good news. They are not said to teach, however. That commission is given only after the resurrection (28:20). During his ministry, only Jesus himself teaches.

Matthew's Jesus instructs the disciples, "Go nowhere among the Gentiles, and enter no town of the Samaritans, but go rather to the lost sheep of the house of Israel" (10:5-6). Later Jesus insists that his own mission is only to Israel (15:24). In contrast, the risen Jesus orders his disciples to go to all nations (28:19), so the restriction to Israel holds only for the time of Jesus' earthly life. Jesus' mission is to the Jews. They must be told the good news first. This creates a certain discontinuity in the discourse if, as suggested above, it really applies to the postresurrection church. But such a discontinuity is not surprising if the evangelist is addressing his own church's concerns and circumstances within a narrative that deals with the earthly career of Jesus.

Jesus predicts that many will reject the missionaries (10:14-23). The disciples must even be willing to break with their families for the sake of the kingdom (10:21, 34-37). When Christians are persecuted, they retrace the steps of Jesus. As he was rejected and persecuted, so will they be (10:24-25). Their rejection is part of the end-time sufferings (10:23). Matthew exhorts his readers to remember the final judgment. The persecution is nothing compared to the punishment that can be meted out by God (10:26-33). Those who endure persecution, and those who welcome the missionaries, will receive their reward (10:32, 40-42).

BOOK III

Narrative (11:2–12:50)

11:2-19: Jesus and John the Baptist. The section begins with a block of Q material about John the Baptist. John sends to Jesus from prison and asks, "Are you the one who is to come, or are we to wait for another?" (11:3). He asks this because he has heard "what the Messiah was doing" (literally, "the deeds of the Messiah"). Jesus asserts that what he is doing—healings, raising from the dead, and preaching the good news to the poor—ought to convince John. Jesus praises John, saying he is "Elijah who is to come" (11:14). Mark only implies that John is Elijah; Matthew makes it explicit. Jesus explains that John is a prophet and more than a prophet. As Elijah, he prepares Jesus' way as Messiah. As forerunner, he is less than the one who comes afterward. In fact, anyone in the kingdom is greater than John, who only prepares for it (11:11). Matthew has John preach the kingdom (3:2), but the kingdom is present in Jesus and his ministry. Jesus recognizes that his own career, marked by healings and forgiveness, contrasts with that of John. He complains of those who accept

153

neither him nor John. John's ascetic lifestyle earns him the accusation that he is possessed, and Jesus' nonascetic lifestyle incurs the charge that he is a "glutton and a drunkard" (11:18-19; see Deut 21:20). Jesus expresses frustration with "this generation," and says, "Wisdom is vindicated by her deeds" (11:19; see below). Some see Jesus as identified with personified wisdom here, since the "deeds" in question are his own.

11:20-24: Woes to Unrepentant Villages. Jesus prophesies doom to those who have not accepted him, the Galilean cities of Chorazin and Bethsaida in particular. Matthew draws on a passage from Q that considers Jesus' miracles motivations for people to believe in him and heed his call to repentance. Matthew does not share Mark's disapproval of using miracles as signs.

11:25-30: Jesus and Wisdom. Not all reject Jesus. He has the power to reveal the Father to those who accept him: "All things have been handed over to me by my Father; and no one knows the Son except the Father, and no one knows the Father except the Son and anyone to whom the Son chooses to reveal him" (11:27). Jesus issues a warm invitation to the weary and burdened: "My yoke is easy, and my burden is light." Later rabbinic literature speaks of the yoke of the Torah (*m. Abot* 3:5; *m. Ber.* 2:2; see Jer 5:5), and personified Wisdom, herself equated with Torah in some literature, uses similar invitations (Prov 8), and "yoke" is associated with wisdom in several texts (Sir 6:30; 51:26). This is wisdom Christology—Jewish speculation about God's wisdom, particularly the personification of wisdom, used to elucidate Jesus' person and work.

12:1-14: Working on the Sabbath. Chapter 12 begins with two episodes from Mark where Jesus works on the Sabbath. In the first, Jesus and his disciples walk through grain fields on the Sabbath and the disciples pick grains to eat (12:1-8). The Pharisees accuse them of violating the Torah. Matthew makes notable changes to Mark's version. Mark makes the case that Jesus does not violate Torah; Matthew argues the point more strongly. He first refers to the same precedent in the Bible as does Mark—that David and his men ate holy food when in need. Human need trumps religious law. Matthew adds another precedent. Priests work on the Sabbath, because sacrifices must continue to be offered in the temple on that day. "Something greater than the temple is here," so those who follow him may override certain precepts. The "something greater" is either Jesus himself or his mission.

Then Matthew quotes Hos 6:6, as he did in chapter 9. God requires mercy rather than sacrifice. This reinforces Matthew's view that mercy is at the center of Torah. Matthew omits Mark's saying, "The sabbath was made for humankind, and not humankind for the sabbath" (Mark 2:27). Matthew makes the same point in his account, but perhaps he feels that putting it so starkly invites the attitude that one can override Torah easily.

12:9-13: Healing on the Sabbath. In the next story, Jesus questions rhetorically whether it is lawful to do good on the Sabbath. Matthew replaces this with Jesus' definitive legal pronouncement, "It is lawful (i.e., in accord with Torah) to do good on the sabbath" (12:12).

12:14-16: Pharisees Plot to Destroy Jesus. Matthew concludes these conflicts with the statement that the Pharisees conspire to destroy Jesus. He omits Mark's information that the Pharisees collude with the Herodians (Mark 3:6), either because he realizes that Herodians and Pharisees are an unlikely combination, or because he focuses on the Pharisees. Jesus departs the area. Crowds follow and he cures "all of them," a typical Matthean enhancement of Jesus' activity, and he orders them "not to make him known." This is not equivalent to Mark's messianic secret, nor is it a general desire to keep the miracles quiet. Rather, Jesus is avoiding the Pharisees' snares.

12:17-21: Jesus and the Gentiles. Through a formula quotation of Isa 42:1-4 we learn that Jesus is God's chosen servant, on whom God has placed the divine Spirit, and that he will "proclaim justice to the Gentiles." The word *justice* is the same as "righteousness" in Greek, so Matthew chooses a passage containing a word related to Torah. The servant preaches to the Gentiles and they hope in him.

12:22-32: Accusation of Collusion with Satan. Matthew omits the charge that Jesus is insane and that his family tries to seize him (Mark 3:21), perhaps because it offends him. He substitutes the Pharisees for the Jerusalem scribes as the ones who accuse Jesus of collusion with Satan (as in 9:34). Following Q, Matthew prefaces the controversy with a short exorcism. In Luke (and probably Q), the demon causes muteness, while in Matthew, ever enhancing Jesus' powers, it causes both muteness and blindness. Only in Matthew does the exorcism, also a healing, cause the crowd to ask, "Can this be the Son of David?" (12:23), reinforcing Matthew's emphasis on that title and his association of it with healing. Jesus knows what his adversaries are thinking, a detail from Q. As in Mark, Jesus says that the meaning of his exorcisms is that Satan's dominion is being attacked and overthrown, freeing humanity. Jesus accuses his detractors of an unforgivable sin. He acts through the power of God's Spirit, yet they accuse him of acting through Satan.

12:33-37: Jesus Attacks His Opponents. Jesus calls his opponents a "brood of vipers." They "speak good things," but they are evil. This reflects Matthew's ambivalence about Jewish teachers. In chapter 23, Jesus will tell his hearers to listen to and heed what the scribes and Pharisees say, but not do what they do. They do have insight into Torah, but their deeds do not match their words. This passage condemns their words as evil, too (12:36-37). Since this passage follows on their condemnation of Jesus and attribution of his actions to Satan, their evil words may mean their accusation that Jesus works through Satan.

12:38-42: The Sign of Jonah. In Mark when the Pharisees ask for a sign, Jesus simply says that no sign will be given to them (8:12). Q has Jesus say that Jesus' opponents will receive no sign except for the sign of Jonah (Q 11:29-32). In Q, this means that Jonah preached and his hearers repented, so Jesus' hearers should also heed his preaching and repent. Matthew uses Q's version of the episode in 16:4. Here in chapter 12 he adds another interpretation of the sign of Jonah, not found in Q. As Jonah was three days and nights in the belly of the sea monster, Jesus will spend three days in the earth between his death and resurrection. There is a clear progression through these documents in the direction of trying to prove Jesus' authority through signs. Mark says no sign will be given. Q says the sign of Jonah will be given, which means Jesus' preaching. Matthew says that the sign of Jonah is both Jesus' preaching and his resurrection. In any case, the scribes and Pharisees are "an evil and adulterous generation" for demanding a sign.

12:43-45: Return of the Evil Spirit. Jesus says that when a demon is cast out of a person, unless that person becomes "filled" with something else, the demon will return with seven worse spirits. Jesus' opponents are not filled with God's Spirit and have themselves been taken over by evil demons, evidence of which is their evil deeds and words.

12:46-50: Jesus' True Family. Chapter 12 closes when Jesus' mother and brothers come to ask for him. As in Mark, Jesus does not go out to them but defines his true mother and brothers are those who do "the will of my Father in heaven" (12:50). The point is the same as the one made in Mark. Matthew's editorial work is evident in his characteristic language about God's will and in Jesus calling God his Father.

Third Discourse: Parables (13:1-52)

Matthew's parable chapter differs from Mark's in several ways. Mark proposes that Jesus' parables hide the secret of the kingdom of God from outsiders. Quoting Isaiah, Jesus says, "For those outside, everything comes in parables; in order that / 'they may indeed look, but not perceive, / and may indeed listen, but not understand; / so that they may not turn again and be forgiven' " (Mark 4:11-12). Matthew changes this in a subtle way: "The reason I speak to them in parables is that 'seeing they do not perceive, and hearing they do not listen, nor do they understand' " (13:13). Matthew's Jesus does not tell parables to hide his message. He does so because, since they do not understand, they need the device of parables to make the message clearer to them.

At the end of Mark's parable collection, the narrator explains that he speaks to the crowds in parables but explains everything to his disciples (4:33-34). Jesus seems to tell all of the parables in the chapter to everyone. Matthew moves the verse about Jesus speaking to outsiders in parables to a position partway though the discourse (13:34), and he follows it with a formula quotation—Jesus' use of parables fulfills a prophecy found in Ps 78:2. Then the narrator says, "Then he left the crowds and went into the house" (13:36). From that point on, Jesus instructs his disciples privately. The impression is that Jesus tries to illuminate people by the parables but is unsuccessful, so that he turns his attention to the disciples.

A number of Matthew's parables elucidate his view of the church. The parable of the Weeds (13:24-30), unique to Matthew and one of the few parables for which Jesus supplies an interpretation (13:36-43), shows that the church is a mixture of good and bad people. It will stay that way until the end of the age, when the good and bad will be separated. Satan, the evil one, is responsible for the presence of bad people in the church. The parable of the Net again stresses that the church is a mixture of good and bad, to be separated only at the end of time (13:47-49). The interest in final judgment throughout this chapter is typical of Matthew.

The parables of the Mustard Seed and the Yeast claim that the small beginnings of the church will have a large result in the end (13:31-33). The parables of the Pearl and the Treasure teach that one must be willing to sacrifice everything to accept Jesus' message of the kingdom (13:44-46). The parables of the Weeds, the Pearl, the Treasure, and the Net are all unique to Matthew among the canonical gospels, although the parables of the Pearl and the Treasure are in the *Gospel of Thomas* (sayings 76 and 109). Matthew omits Mark's parable of the Seed Growing

Secretly (Mark 4:26-29), perhaps because of his emphasis on deeds, whereas the parable seems to indicate that the kingdom grows on its own, without human action. The chapter ends with a parabolic saying comparing Christian scribes to a master who "brings out of his treasure what is new and what is old," indicating Torah and the new interpretation Jesus brings to it (13:52).

In Mark, there is no indication that the disciples understand the parables, despite Jesus' special instruction. Matthew has Jesus ask them whether they understand. They respond, quite simply, "Yes" (13:51). Mark follows the parables discourse with the scene of the calming of the storm at sea, which causes the disciples to ask, "Who then is this?" (4:41). Matthew moves that scene to another spot (8:24-27). It makes no sense to place a story illustrating the disciples' ignorance immediately after a statement that they understand Jesus.

The potential of the parables to challenge worlds and assumptions is as evident here as in Mark. The entire chapter is permeated with the motifs of the newness, surprising nature, and power of the kingdom preached by Jesus.

BOOK IV

Narrative (13:53–17:27)

These chapters contain a mixture of conflict with authorities and teaching about the new community.

13:54–14:12: Opposition. Book IV begins with Jesus being rejected in his hometown synagogue (13:54-58). This is followed by John's arrest and execution by Herod (14:1-12), foreshadowing Jesus' passion.

14:13-21: First Feeding Scene. Matthew preserves both Markan scenes of the multiplication of loaves. The scenes have obvious overtones of the Eucharist and are rooted in images of God's care for Israel in the desert. Matthew enhances the role of the disciples as go-betweens between Jesus and the people.

14:22-33: Second Boat Scene. Matthew rewrites Mark's first boat scene to make it an allegory for the church (Matt 8:23-27; see our treatment of this in chapter 2). He also substantially rewrites the second boat scene, also with a lesson to the church in mind (14:22-33). Matthew makes few changes in Mark's account until the disciples see Jesus walking on the water, think it is a ghost, and he calms their fears. At that point, Matthew adds a whole section (14:28-32). Peter asks Jesus to tell him to come to him. Jesus does so, and Peter begins to walk on the water. Seeing the storm, he begins to lose heart. When that happens, he begins to sink and cries out, "Lord, save me!" Jesus grabs him and says, "You of little faith, why did you doubt?" They get into the boat, the wind ceases, and the disciples say, "Truly you are the Son of God."

As he turned the first boat story into an allegory of the church, Matthew turns the second into an allegory of discipleship. In the earlier story the boat is threatened with a storm; here an individual disciple is in danger. In the first story the disciples cry out, "Lord, save us!" and here Peter does the same thing. Peter begins to sink when he loses faith. Nonetheless, he prays to Jesus for help, and Jesus comes through, as in the first boat scene. Both stories provide a lesson for what church members should do as they feel their faith failing. Matthew frequently calls his disciples "people of little faith." Matthew sees his own church the same way.

At the story's end, the disciples recognize Jesus as the Son of God. This is remarkable when we compare it to Matthew's source, where they are "utterly astounded, for they did not understand about the loaves" (Mark 6:51-52). Mark is careful with the title *Son of God*, allowing no humans to use it until the high priest does contemptuously during the trial and the centurion does at Jesus' death. Matthew is freer with the title. While Matthew's disciples acclaim Jesus as Son of God here, Mark's disciples still do not get it.

14:34-36: Summary. Jesus incurs the leaders' enmity, but the people still flock to him for healing. Even touching the fringe on his cloak cures them, a strong statement of Jesus' power (and another reminder that Jesus wears the fringes decreed by Num 15:37-41).

15:1-20: Controversy over Unwashed Hands. The conflict between Jesus and the religious authorities, especially the Pharisees, continues. Matthew rewrites the dispute with the Pharisees and Jerusalem scribes over a purity issue—eating with hands unwashed (Matt 15:1-20; Mark 7:1-23). In both versions, Jesus accuses them of making human laws that override God's laws, since the Pharisees' practices meant to implement and supplement Torah in fact nullify it. Jesus says that this accords with Isaiah's words, which condemn those who teach human precepts as divine.

Matthew's addition to this passage is significant. When the disciples tell Jesus that the Pharisees have taken offense, Jesus answers, "Every plant that my heavenly Father has not planted will be uprooted. Let them alone; they are blind guides of the blind. And if one blind person guides another, both will fall into a pit" (15:13-14).

Jesus says that it is not what enters a person from the outside that makes him or her unclean but what comes out of a person, and Mark takes that to mean that Jesus annuls Jewish food laws (Mark 7:19b). Matthew omits Mark's assertion, because he believes no such thing. Rather, he concludes the section by bringing the focus back to hand washing. Enumerating the sins that originate from within a person, he concludes, "These are what defile a person, but to eat with unwashed hands does not defile" (15:20).

Matthew omits Mark's explanation of hand washing, in which Mark claims that "all the Jews" follow this practice (7:3). Matthew may omit the explanation because he can assume his Jewish-Christian audience already knows of the practice. He may also disagree with Mark that "all the Jews" do this. He may picture this as an intra-Jewish debate in which the Pharisees have a custom to which not all Jews subscribe.

15:21-28: The Canaanite Woman. Matthew changes Mark's "Syrophoenician" woman to a "Canaanite," an ancient appellation with biblical overtones. The Canaanites were the inhabitants of Canaan, the region that became the land of Israel. He may do this to emphasize the fact that she is a Gentile, even a member of a group that had been a rival to Israel in the land. Matthew increases the amount of direct address between Jesus and the woman. At the same time, he increases Jesus' initial reluctance to deal with her. She begins by shouting what sounds like a prayer: "Have mercy on me, Lord, Son of David; my daughter is tormented by a demon." Again, Matthew associates the title *Son of David* with healing. Jesus ignores her. When his disciples request that he do something about her, he says, "I was sent only to the lost sheep of the house of Israel" (cf. 10:5-6). She responds with another prayer, "Lord, help me." Jesus replies that it is not right to give the children's bread to the dogs, and she answers that even the dogs eat the crumbs that fall on the floor. In Mark, Jesus cures her "for saying that," while Matthew highlights her great faith. In Mark, the woman goes home to find her daughter cured, while in Matthew, "her daughter was healed instantly."

15:29-31: Summary. Matthew follows this exorcism with another summary, although the summary does not mention exorcism. Jesus ascends the mountain, but he does not teach. His public teaching is now drawing to a close, at least until he arrives in Jerusalem. Jesus merely heals. When the crowds see it, "They praised the God of Israel." The specification that the God "of Israel" heals through Jesus is typical of Matthew.

15:32-39: Feeding the Four Thousand. This story is essentially the same as Mark's second feeding miracle.

16:1-4: Demand for a Sign. This episode reproduces the one found in Mark 8:11-13, where the Pharisees demand a sign and Jesus refuses. Matthew adds Sadducees to the scene. He includes the Sadducees in three stories, while Mark and Luke have them in only one. This serves Matthew's intensification of Jesus' conflict with religious authorities. Following Q, he says that the only sign they will be granted is the sign of Jonah. Matthew has already developed this scene further in 12:38-42.

16:5-12: The Yeast of the Pharisees and Sadducees. Mark's third boat scene is transferred to the land in Matthew. Jesus orders his disciples to beware of the yeast of the Pharisees and Sadducees, while Mark has the yeast of the Pharisees and Herod. Either pairing is historically questionable, since the Pharisees were rivals of both the Herodians and the Sadducees. The pairing of Pharisees and Sadducees happens only in Matthew. Mark leaves "yeast" undefined, while Matthew's Jesus explains that it means teaching, a typical concern of Matthew. Mark leaves the disciples in the dark about Jesus' meaning, while Matthew says they understand. Although Matthew softens the picture of the disciples, Jesus still reprimands them for being slow to understand.

Omission of Blind Man. The story of the cure of the blind man that opens the frame of part II of Mark's Gospel (8:22-26) is absent in Matthew. He may have left it out because Jesus makes two attempts to cure the man. That has rich symbolism in Mark, but Matthew may have seen it as diminishing Jesus' stature.

16:13-28: Peter's Confession. Matthew rewrites Peter's confession to develop his theme of church. He retains the idea that Peter refused to accept Jesus' suffering but softens it. Mark says simply that Peter rebukes Jesus. Matthew adds Peter's words: "God forbid it, Lord! This must never happen to you" (16:22). The effect is to have Peter concerned primarily for Jesus' welfare. Nonetheless, as in Mark, Jesus calls Peter Satan and accuses him of reasoning not as God does, but as humans do.

So much for the negative. When Matthew's Peter confesses his belief in Jesus, he says not merely that Jesus is Messiah, but that he is "Son of the living God." In Mark, no human pronounces this title until the Gospel's end. In Matthew, the disciples already declare Jesus to be the Son of God in the second boat scene (14:33).

In Mark, the narrative moves directly from Peter's confession to Jesus' demand that he keep quiet and then to the conflict between Jesus and Peter. But in Matthew, as soon as Peter says that Jesus is the Messiah and Son of God, Jesus' blesses Peter, attributing his insight to the Father. Jesus then declares Peter the rock on which he will build his church and gives him the power to bind and loose. The terms *bind* and *loose* appear in rabbinic documents to designate religious authority. The precise meaning in Matthew is not fully clear. Suggestions have been that the phrase indicates authority over legal matters, church discipline, excommunication, forgiveness of sin, or exorcisms. In the church discourse, Jesus conveys this authority to the disciples in general (18:18). The occurrence of the word *church* in 16:18, 18:15, 17, and 21 is significant. Matthew is the only evangelist of the canonical four to use this term, and he does so twice in the Fourth Book. After teaching that he must suffer, Jesus says that the church must suffer, too.

17:1-13: Transfiguration. Matthew's account of the transfiguration follows Mark in the main. Matthew adds the typical features of a theophany, where the witnesses are terrified and the supernatural figure tells them not to fear. As they descend from the mountain, Jesus warns them to say nothing of what they have seen until after his resurrection. In Mark, they wonder what resurrection from the dead could mean. Matthew omits this expression of ignorance. Matthew explicitly identifies John the Baptist with Elijah, an identification that Mark only implies.

17:14-21: Exorcism. Matthew's version reinforces the motif of the disciples' smallness of faith in a story where the disciples cannot cast out a demon. Jesus says they cannot do so because of their little faith, while in Mark, Jesus says simply that they can cast it out only through prayer.

17:22-23: Second Passion Prediction. In this second prediction, Matthew says that the disciples are "greatly distressed" by what Jesus says, while Mark says, "They did not understand what he was saying and were afraid to ask him" (9:32). Again Matthew softens Mark's portrait of the disciples.

17:24-27: Temple Tax. The collectors of the temple tax ask Peter why Jesus does not pay it (17:24-27). Peter reports this to Jesus, who declares that he and his followers are free of the tax because they are "children," presumably children of God whose house the temple is, but he then has Peter pay the tax for both of them, having Peter find the money miraculously in a fish's mouth. The story is unique to Matthew, and it is another instance of Jesus' clash with religious leaders, in this case with the temple establishment. It asserts Jesus' and the church's special relation with God, and it recalls Jesus' earlier statement that he is greater than the temple (12:6).

Fourth Discourse: The Church (18:1-35)

The first part of this discourse uses terms such as *child* and *little one* to teach that Christians should be humble like children and that they should never scandalize the least in the church (18:1-9). Jesus uses the parable of the shepherd who leaves ninety-nine sheep to search for the lost sheep to show God's care for the little ones (18:10-14).

The second part of the discourse concerns church discipline (18:15-35). When there is a recalcitrant sinner in the community, church members should speak to the offender privately. If that is not successful, one or two witnesses should confront the offender. If that does not work, the entire church should be brought into the matter. If there is still no successful resolution, the person should be ejected from the community. It is remarkable that Jesus says that this person should be treated "as a Gentile and a tax collector" (18:17). This may reflect the Jewish character of Matthew's community, since in some sense it sees Gentiles as outsiders. Yet elsewhere in the Gospel, Gentiles are seen quite positively.

Jesus calls the church's authority to retain or eject a member binding and loosing. See 16:19, where the power was given to Peter. Here it belongs to the church as a whole. The passage describing this process ends with Jesus' words, "If two of you agree on earth about anything you ask, it will be done for you by my Father in heaven. For where two or three are gathered in my name, I am there among them" (18:19-20). Jesus is present in the church. The presence of the risen Jesus, to whom God has given all authority, is the foundation of the church's authority (see 28:18-20).

The discourse ends with a section on forgiveness (18:21-35). Peter asks whether he must forgive as many as seven times, and Jesus answers that he must do so seventy-seven times. In other words, there is no limit to forgiveness. Jesus illustrates the point with a parable about a servant whom his master forgives an astronomical debt. When the servant refuses mercy to one who owes him a comparatively piddling sum, the master reinstates the first servant's debt and imprisons him. This recalls an explanation added by Matthew to the end of the Lord's Prayer: "For if you forgive others their trespasses, your heavenly Father will also forgive you; but if you do not forgive others, neither will your Father forgive your trespasses" (6:14-15). For Matthew, God shows mercy to those who practice it.

BOOK V

Narrative (19:1–23:39)

19:1-2: Summary. In chapters 19 and 20, Jesus moves from Galilee to the other side of the Jordan and then heads toward Jerusalem. These chapters also contain a mixture of conflict with authorities and teaching about the new community. The section begins with yet another summary, and as with the previous one, only healing of large crowds is mentioned.

19:3-12: Divorce and Celibacy. Responding to a challenge from the Pharisees, Jesus prohibits divorce on the grounds that in Genesis God declares husband and wife to be one flesh. While Jesus' prohibition of divorce in Mark is absolute, Matthew makes an exception for "unchastity," perhaps meaning unfaithfulness. This accords with one Pharisaic school of thought and may indicate Matthew's knowledge of some subtleties of Jewish legal interpretation. Jesus goes on to speak of those who are "eunuchs," meaning celibates, for the kingdom. This means that they give up marriage and sexual relationships to dedicate themselves to working for God's kingdom.

19:13-30: The Cost of Discipleship. Jesus teaches about the demands of following him. Jesus asserts that the kingdom belongs to those who are like children. He demands of the rich young man that he give up all his goods to follow him, and when the man finds this impossible, Jesus says that it is hard for the rich to enter the kingdom.

When Peter asks what he and his companions will receive for giving up everything, Jesus' answer differs a bit from that in Mark. Matthew puts the emphasis on future reward, omitting Mark's statement that in this life Christians will receive new relatives and property, as well as persecution. Matthew speaks of eternal life. But he also says that the Twelve will sit on thrones judging the twelve tribes of Israel, a Q tradition. So Matthew's Jesus subscribes to the traditional Jewish idea that when God sets the world straight, Israel will consist of twelve tribes. Then Jesus' inner circle will judge Israel, fulfilling the prediction that the "first will be last, and the last will be first" (19:30).

20:1-16: Parable of the Laborers in the Vineyard. There follows the parable of the Laborers in the Vineyard, unique to Matthew, which further illustrates the saying in 19:30. In fact, he repeats the saying at the end of the parable (20:16). A vineyard often symbolizes Israel itself (see, for example, Isa 5). In the parable, workers who toil for an hour at the end of the day receive the same wages as those who toiled all day. The parable does not fully fit the saying, for in the parable all the workers end up being equal. The parable illustrates God's generosity and opposes self-righteousness. It proposes a sort of justice that cuts across the grain of what would normally be considered just.

20:17-28: Third Passion Prediction and a Mother's Request. In 20:17, Jesus heads for Jerusalem, providing the occasion for the third passion prediction. The mother of James and John asks that her sons sit at Jesus' right and left hand in the kingdom. Jesus responds that they will share his suffering and death, that positions in the kingdom are distributed by the Father, and that those who wish to lead in the kingdom must become servants of all. He repeats Mark's declaration that "the Son of Man came not to be served but to serve, and to give his life a ransom for many."

20:29-33: Cure of Two Blind Men. The section on the trip to Jerusalem ends, as it does in Mark, with the curing of blindness on the road to Jericho. However, in Mark Jesus cures only one man, while in Matthew he cures two.

21:1-11: Entry into Jerusalem. Matthew's story of Jesus' victorious entrance into Jerusalem reflects that of Mark (11:1-11). Mark's version of the entrance alludes to Zech 9:9, where the Messiah comes to Jerusalem riding on a donkey. Matthew makes the reference explicit by turning it into a formula quotation. He is overly literal about the fulfillment. Where Zechariah uses synonymous parallelism, speaking about the Messiah riding on "a donkey, / on a colt, the foal of a donkey," meaning that the donkey and the colt are the same, Matthew takes them as two different animals and Matthew has Jesus ride on both of them simultaneously.

Mark is reticent about the title Son of David, but Matthew showcases it. Mark has the crowd shout, "Blessed is the coming kingdom of our ancestor David," while Matthew has them shout, "Hosanna to the Son of David," more directly identifying Jesus as Davidic Messiah. In a scene unique to Matthew, the entire city of Jerusalem asks who this is, and the crowds answer that it is the prophet Jesus.

21:12-17: Cleansing of the Temple. As in Mark, Jesus' first act upon entering Jerusalem is to cleanse the temple by attacking the money changers and animal merchants. Matthew embellishes this scene substantially. He agrees with Mark that Jesus defends the temple's nature as a house of prayer, and that the merchants' presence makes it a den of robbers. He then adds, "The blind and the lame came to him in the temple, and he cured them" (21:14). This corresponds to Matthew's customary emphasis on Jesus as healer. It is also a powerful image that Jesus actually performs cures in the temple itself. Jesus, Son of God, the one who has come to his people Israel to be Emmanuel, "God with us," heals in his Father's house.

Matthew adds that the chief priests and scribes see Jesus healing and hear children proclaiming him Son of David, and they get angry. They confront him, and he quotes Ps 8:2 to the effect that from children's mouths will come the truth. So Matthew again connects Davidic messiahship and healing, and he makes this the central issue between Jesus and the priests and scribes in the temple itself. Matthew does not lose this opportunity to make Christology the central issue.

21:18-22: Cursing the Fig Tree. On the next day, as he returns to Jerusalem, Jesus curses a fig tree for having no fruit. Matthew omits Mark's puzzling comment that it was not the season for figs. In Mark, the fig tree does not wither until the next day. This allows Mark to frame the cleansing of the temple with the fig tree episode. As the fig tree withers, so will the temple leaders who have not borne fruit. Matthew makes the same point but forgoes the framing technique. Instead, the fig tree withers "at once," showing Jesus' power. As in Mark, Jesus uses the incident to teach about the power of faith. With faith, the disciples too can achieve wonders.

21:23-27: Jesus' Authority Challenged. The chief priests and elders question Jesus about his authority for his actions in the temple (21:23-27). Jesus answers a question with a question, asking the authorities whether or not John's baptism was of God. They refuse to answer, fearing the people who believed in John. The scene reinforces the connection between Jesus and John.

21:28-32: Parable of Two Sons. One son says he will work in the vineyard, as the father requests, but does not do so, while a second son rebuffs the father's request but then does what the father wishes. As noted above, the vineyard is a frequent symbol for Israel. Jesus gets the priests and elders to admit that the son who initially rebuffs his father is the one who really does his will. He applies the parable to them. They seem to do the Father's will. But when John the Baptist, an emissary from the Father, preaches righteousness, they do not believe him. In contrast, tax collectors and prostitutes believe John and so will enter the kingdom ahead of the religious authorities. Again Matthew reinforces the bond between Jesus' mission and that of John. He also attacks the self-righteousness of his opponents. They purport to represent God, but by rejecting John and Jesus they prove unfaithful. Matthew delegitimates them.

22:1-14: Parable of the Banquet. Jesus tells the parable of the Great Banquet from Q (see Luke 14:16-24; *Gos. Thom.* 64). As we can tell from a comparison with Luke, Matthew heavily redacts this parable so that it becomes an allegory of salvation history. The parable is so heavily allegorized that the narrative in its present form does not make a lot of sense. The original form of the parable was fairly simple. A man gives a banquet. When his invited guests refuse to come, he invites others. The point is that the kingdom is like a banquet full of unexpected guests. Those one would expect to see there are missing.

Matthew transforms the parable into one about a king who gives a marriage feast for his son. References to God (the father), Jesus (the son), and the messianic banquet are clear. Matthew sends out slaves (note the plural), while Luke has a single slave. The slaves go to the invited guests twice in Matthew, while Luke has only one summons. When in Luke the guests refuse to come, the master simply invites others. In Matthew, the guests kill the second group of messengers.

Matthew alludes here to God's sending of many prophets to Israel's leaders, whom they reject and kill. The king "sent his troops, destroyed those murderers, and burned their city." At this point the allegory is taking over the plot. The murdered servants are the prophets, and the destruction of Jerusalem is the result of a history of Israel's leaders' refusal to accept God's invitation, culminating in rejection of Jesus.

The king sends his servants into the streets to bring into the banquet whomever they find. The hall is filled with guests, "both good and bad," a rather strange way to refer to them within the story world. Matthew's real point is that those who respond to God's invitation become the church, and the church is composed of good and bad people. This reiterates the point of the parables of the Weeds and of the Net (13:24-30; 36-43; 47-50).

Matthew adds a section to the parable that makes sense only if allegory drives the story. The king comes to examine his guests and finds one without a wedding garment. He commands that the offender be cast "into the outer darkness, where there will be weeping and gnashing of teeth." How can the king expect the guests, whom he has dragged off the streets, to be properly clothed? And why such a drastic punishment for a seemingly minor transgression? The parts of the story that do not seem to make sense serve Matthew's allegorical purposes. This is an allegory for

An Introduction to Jesus and the Gospels

the last judgment. The king (God) comes to judge, and the unprepared face eternal perdition. Matthew draws the phrase about the outer darkness from Q, where it occurs once. Matthew uses it six times, reflecting his stress on the last judgment. For Matthew, membership in the church is no guarantee of salvation.

22:15-22: Taxes to Caesar. Conflict with religious leaders mounts as Pharisees confront Jesus, seeking to trap him with the question about paying taxes to Caesar.

22:23-33: Resurrection. Sadducees then try to trip him up concerning the resurrection, in which they do not believe (see Acts 23:8).

22:34-46: The Greatest Commandment. Finally, the Pharisees reappear, trying to trick him by asking him which is the greatest commandment in the Torah. This rewrites the story in Mark, where a scribe (not a Pharisee, as in Matthew) asks the question, not to test Jesus, but simply to learn from him. In Mark, Jesus ends up praising the scribe. In Matthew the questioner is hostile to Jesus, and the evangelist transforms the scene into a conflict. Jesus answers the Pharisees by quoting Deuteronomy concerning love of God and Leviticus concerning love of neighbor. The section ends as Jesus challenges them to recognize that the Messiah, although a son of David, surpasses David.

23:1-39: Condemnation of the Scribes and Pharisees. Jesus delivers a long diatribe against the scribes and Pharisees (ch. 23). Matthew constructs this powerful attack using material from Mark, Q, and his own sources, and he probably creates some of the chapter himself. Throughout this speech, Jesus accuses them of hypocrisy. Their teaching is not necessarily wrong, but they do not live up to it. Jesus tells his audience to do as the scribes and Pharisees say, but not as they do. They practice religion to improve their own status and power. They refuse to accept Jesus, who is from God, and they prevent others from doing so. Jesus opposes with some of their legal interpretations, too. He accuses them of "lawlessness" in 23:28. Finally, they plot against Jesus just as their ancestors plotted against and killed the prophets, a theme echoing the banquet parable.

The chapter ends with Jesus' lament over Jerusalem, the city that kills the prophets and rejects Jesus. The last prophet mentioned was, according to Matthew, killed "between the sanctuary and the altar." Not only do the leaders kill the prophets, they defile the temple as they do so. We must not take this unrelenting attack as based on simple fact, but rather recognize that it was shaped by Christian disappointment in the failure of most Jews to accept Jesus and by anger at the role some Jerusalem leaders played in Jesus' death.

Chapter 23 contains instructions for the church, while at the same time condemning some non-Christian Jewish leaders. They are not to practice religion for show, status, or power. They are not to use titles such as *rabbi*, *father*, or *teacher*. Their leaders will be their servants, and those who exalt themselves will be humbled. We must remember to read attacks on the Jewish leaders as conditioned by the rivalry between them and Matthew's community, as the evangelist conceives it. Again, we cannot read Matthew's characterizations as simple historical fact.

Fifth Discourse: Apocalypticism (24:1–25:46)

Matthew's apocalyptic discourse resembles Mark's. Both distinguish the destruction of the temple from the eschaton, but Matthew's phrasing of the disciples' question makes the distinction clearer. After Jesus predicts the temple's fall, they say, "When will this be, and what will be the sign of your coming (Greek: *parousia*) and of the end of the age?" (24:3). *Parousia* is a technical term for the official arrival of the emperor, here applied to Jesus' second coming, that is, his visible return to earth at some point after his death and resurrection. Matthew agrees with Mark that many events are part of the last days, including typically apocalyptic happenings such as earthquakes, famines, and wars. They agree that the end comes with cosmic disturbances that cannot be missed or mistaken. Both expect false prophets and messiahs, and persecution of Christians, and both demand that Christian witness continue during the tribulation. Matthew adds problems within the church: "Then many will fall away, and they will betray one another and hate one another. And many false prophets will arise and lead many astray. And because of the increase of lawlessness, the love of many will grow cold" (24:10-12). Given Matthew's interest in the Law, the use of the term *lawlessness* is significant. He has used it previously to designate "lawless" ones within the church (7:23; 13:41). In those passages, the NRSV translation, "evildoers," blunts the force of the Greek text, which reads literally "workers (or doers) of lawlessness (*anomia*)." In the Septuagint and the New Testament, the Greek word *nomos* is used to designate the Torah.

Matthew wants Christians to live mindful of the last judgment. He does not necessarily expect the eschaton to come soon—the judgment may be delayed. But Christians should be constantly vigilant, obedient to God's will as interpreted by Jesus. To make the point, Matthew brings to the end of chapter 24 a passage from Q (Matt 24:45-51). Comparing a Christian to a slave in charge of a master's house, a steward, he says that the faithful slave is one who continues to do his job diligently even in the master's absence. He cares for his fellow slaves. He does not say, "My master is delayed" and then mistreat his fellow slaves and become drunk. The slave who takes the latter course is bitterly surprised when the master returns unexpectedly. The master puts him with "the hypocrites, where there will be weeping and gnashing of teeth" (24:51). This last comment comes from Q where it occurs once, but in another context. Matthew's introduction of it here fits his interest in judgment.

Chapter 25 is comprised of two parables and one prophetic prediction with parabolic features. Two of these three units are unique to Matthew. The first is the parable of the Ten Bridesmaids, found only in Matthew. (*Bridesmaids* reflects the NRSV translation. The Greek says literally "virgins.") Five are wise and are prepared for the bridegroom's delay, while five expect no delay and so run out of oil for their lamps. The five wise ones gain access to the wedding banquet, while the five foolish ones are excluded. One must always be awake, ready for Christ's return as judge, whenever that may be.

The second parable is the Talents. It teaches that Christians must use the time before the judgment profitably. Those who do not will be thrown "into the outer darkness, where there will be weeping and gnashing of teeth" (25:30).

The final unit of the chapter describes the Last Judgment, the only clear description of it in the New Testament. The Son of Man sits on a throne judging "all the nations." Humanity is divided into sheep and goats, meaning the "righteous" and "accursed." The righteous are those who feed the hungry, give drink to the thirsty, welcome strangers, clothe the naked, care for the sick, and visit prisoners. In serving the needy they serve Christ himself. The accursed do not do such things. The word *righteous* is the adjective for the noun "righteousness," a favorite word of Matthew, denoting adherence to God's will. The righteous receive "eternal life," and the accursed suffer "eternal punishment."

CLIMAX: PASSION, DEATH, AND RESURRECTION (26:1–28:20)

Matthew uses Mark as a model in his description of Jesus' death and the events leading up to it. We concentrate here on what is peculiar to Matthew, rather than commenting on material that is substantially similar to what we have already found in Mark.

26:1-5: Transition to Passion. Matthew supplies the usual formulaic ending to the apocalyptic discourse and begins the passion narrative: "When Jesus had finished saying all these things, he said to his disciples, 'You know that after two days the Passover is coming, and the Son of Man will be handed over to be crucified'" (26:1-2). This amounts to a fourth passion prediction and shows that Jesus is aware of what is about to happen. It also notes that the passion happens during Passover. The Jerusalem authorities conspire to eliminate Jesus without rousing the crowds.

26:6-27:66: Overview of Passion and Death. Much of the narrative proceeds as in Mark. A woman anoints Jesus with costly oil, and he proclaims that she does so for his burial (26:6-13). Judas arranges to betray Jesus for thirty pieces of silver (26:14-16). The disciples enter the city and arrange for a room for Passover (26:17-19). Then comes the Last Supper (26:36-46). Jesus predicts his betrayal and institutes the Eucharist. They then go to the Gethsemane where Jesus prays, while his disciples fail to keep watch with him. Jesus is arrested, tried before the Sanhedrin and delivered to Pilate (26:47–27:2). He is tried before Pilate, sentenced to death, mocked by the soldiers, is crucified, and is buried (27:3-66).

26:6-16: A Woman Anoints Jesus. The story is substantially the same as in Mark.

26:17-35: Last Supper. Jesus reveals that one of the Twelve will betray him. Each disciple asks him incredulously if he is the one. Only Matthew has, "Judas, who betrayed him, said, 'Surely not I, Rabbi?' He replied, 'You have said so'" (26:25). The only occurrences of the word *rabbi* in Matthew are on the lips of Judas here and at Jesus' arrest (26:49), and in 23:7-8, where Jesus says that Jewish leaders love to be called rabbi but Christian leaders should reject the title.

In Mark, Jesus says he will drink wine in the kingdom, while Matthew emphasizes that he will do so with the disciples (26:29). Generally Matthew improves the depiction of the disciples he finds in Mark, but he retains Peter's denial of Jesus and Jesus' prediction of it during the Last Supper.

26:36-56: Betrayal and Arrest. Judas comes to betray Jesus. Jesus says to him, "Friend, do what you have come here to do," added by Matthew. One of the disciples draws his sword, but Jesus stops him, saying, "All who take the sword will perish by the sword" (26:52; only in Matthew). This fits Jesus' demand for nonviolence in 5:39 and presents Jesus as calm, in control, and ever the teacher. He says, "Do you think that I cannot appeal to my Father, and he will at once send me more than twelve legions of angels?" (26:53; only in Matthew). Jesus has God's power at his disposal. A *legion* is a division in the Roman army, containing as many as six thousand men. The concept of an angelic, heavenly army is common in ancient Judaism and Christianity. The biblical title *Lord of Hosts* refers to this, since *hosts* means great multitudes, in this case an army. Matthew is not content with the idea that Jesus is powerless before his enemies, as Mark's story might imply. Even as he faces his passion, he could call the overwhelming power of God down on his enemies. There follows the scene of Jesus before the high priest, Peter's denial of Jesus, and the handing over of Jesus to Pilate (26:57–27:2).

27:3-10: Judas's Suicide. Unique among the Gospels is Matthew's story of Judas's death. (There is a different version of his death in Acts 1:18-20.) He is remorseful about betraying Jesus, throws the silver into the temple, and hangs himself. The chief priests use the money to buy a field to bury foreigners. Matthew says all of this fulfills Jeremiah, but it actually loosely quotes Zech 11:13. Matthew may associate these events with Jeremiah because of Jeremiah's buying land in Jer 32:6-15 and his potter material in Jer 18–19.

27:11-26: Trial before Pilate. Only Matthew has Pilate's wife contact him during the trial (27:19). She tells him to have nothing to do with Jesus because she has had a nightmare about him. Pilate perceives the emptiness of the accusations against Jesus, and he finally washes his hands (alluding to Deut 21:6-8) and says, "I am innocent of this man's blood." In a chilling declaration that has helped to fire anti-Semitism through the ages, "the people as a whole answered, 'His blood be upon us and on our children!'" (27:25). Scholars argue whether by "the people as a whole" Matthew means all present or the entirety of the Jewish people. It is most likely that Matthew means just all the people present. Whichever is true, the consequences of this verse have been tragic. The verse has been used through history as a justification for blaming all Jews for Jesus' death and for countless forms of "retribution" against the Jews as a result, including persecution and pogroms.

27:27-31: Soldiers Mock Jesus. Pilate's soldiers mock Jesus as "King of the Jews."

27:32-44: Crucifixion. Throughout the Gospel, Jesus refers to God as his Father. Unlike in Mark, where the title Son of God is kept secret until the centurion's declaration at the cross, in Matthew it is a public title. Therefore, the crowds at the crucifixion use it to taunt Jesus, saying, "If you are the Son of God, come down from the cross" (27:40), and "He trusts in God; let God deliver him now, if he wants to; for he said, 'I am God's Son'" (27:43).

27:45-56: Death. In Mark, Jesus cries out that God has forsaken him, and then he screams and dies. The centurion declares Jesus to have been the Son of God when he sees how he dies (Mark 15:33-39). Matthew adds a good deal. At the moment of Jesus' death, the curtain of the temple is torn in two, as in Mark. But then there is an earthquake, tombs are opened, and:

> Many bodies of the saints who had fallen asleep were raised. After his resurrection they came out of the tombs and entered the holy city and appeared to many. Now when the centurion and those with him, who were keeping watch over Jesus, saw the earthquake and what took place, they were terrified and said, "Truly this man was God's Son!" (27:52-54)

Matthew is uncomfortable with having the centurion recognize Jesus' identity purely on the basis of his death. He rewrites this scene to reveal the full import of Jesus' death as an eschatological event, complete with earthquake and resurrections. By letting this concern determine his narrative, he produces a puzzling story. The centurion sees the earthquake, but Matthew implies that he also sees the resurrections of the saints. How is that possible, if those resurrected did not emerge from their tombs and appear to people until Easter?

Resurrection of the dead was integral to many Jewish eschatological scenarios. It is evident in Dan 12, for example (see also 2 Macc 7; *Jub.* 23; *Pss. Sol.* 3, 13, 14, 15; *2 Bar.* 49-51; *4 Ezra* 7). So when Jesus rises from the dead, he becomes the firstborn of the dead. Arguing against Corinthian Christians who deny resurrection of the body, Paul says that if there is no general resurrection from the dead, then Christ was not raised. The two go together. Just as Paul did not see Jesus' resurrection in isolation from the general resurrection, so Matthew links it to resurrection more generally. But should not Jesus' resurrection happen before that of the saints? Certainly. But Matthew allows himself poetic license in portraying Jesus' death as the beginning of the eschatological age. He wants the centurion to come to his insight not on the basis of just the death, but of the death and resurrection, and he sees this as the decisive eschatological event. He hedges his bets a bit by not having the risen saints appear until Jesus' resurrection. The result is a confused narrative.

27:57-66: Burial and Setting of a Guard. When Jesus is buried, the chief priests and Pharisees request that a guard be placed at the tomb "until the third day," so that Jesus' disciples cannot steal his body and claim that he has been raised from the dead. Pilate allows them to post their own guard (27:62-66).

28:1-15: Resurrection. Mark lacks resurrection appearances. Each of the other canonical gospels has them, but no single story occurs in more than one text. Therefore, all of Matthew's material concerning the resurrection except the empty tomb is peculiar to him. Although none of the canonical gospels describe the resurrection itself, Matthew comes closest (28:2-3). He does so with apocalyptic tones. There is a "great earthquake," and an "angel of the Lord" descends and rolls back the stone from the tomb's entrance. The angel's "appearance was like lightning, and his clothing was white as snow" (28:3). This description is like those of angels and of God in the biblical apocalypses of Daniel and of Revelation, and like the description of Jesus' transfiguration in the Gospels. The guards are terrified (28:4). Some report the events to the chief priests. The priests bribe them to spread the story that the disciples have stolen Jesus' body. "And this story is still told among the Jews to this day" (28:15).

Except for the commissioning of the disciples by the risen Jesus (28:16-20), these are the last words of the Gospel, an important location for making an impression on the reader. They are a serious indictment of the priests, who know what happened yet choose to hide it from others. It is also a forceful statement of the antipathy between Matthew's community and those whom he terms "the Jews." We discuss below exactly how we should interpret this.

28:9-10, 16-20: Resurrection Appearances. There are two resurrection appearances in Matthew. The risen Jesus appears to Mary Magdalene and "the other Mary" at the tomb on Easter morning and tells them to inform the disciples (28:9-10). He also appears in Galilee to the eleven disciples on a mountain, the usual place of special revelation in Matthew. He tells them that all authority on heaven and earth has been given to him. This is an exalted Jesus, exercising God's authority over creation. Because Jesus has received such authority (Matthew uses the word "therefore"), they are to make disciples of all nations and baptize them in the name of the Father, Son, and Holy Spirit, "teaching them to obey everything that I have commanded you" (28:19-20). This is the only time in the Gospel when the disciples are said to teach. They can now do so because they have finished their course of study, so to speak. They have heard Jesus' teaching, experienced his healings, exorcisms, and other miracles, and seen his death and resurrection. Only now can they understand fully. This does not make them perfect. Matthew allows that although they see and worship Jesus, some still doubt (28:17).

The disciples are commissioned to *make disciples*, and to *teach* them to *obey* all that Jesus has *commanded* them. This language parallels that of Deuteronomy with respect to Torah (for example, Deut 6:1). Torah is to be taught to those who must learn it (the root of *disciple* means "to learn"). They must obey (often translated "observe") the commandments in Torah. Now it is Jesus' teaching that must be learned and obeyed. For Matthew, Jesus' teaching does not replace Torah. It is the essence of Torah.

CHRISTOLOGY

Matthew begins his Gospel with Jesus' genealogy, proving Jesus to be a child of Abraham and a son of David, qualified to be Messiah. The infancy narrative takes shape around five formula quotations, showing that Jesus fulfills Scripture. He is the culmination of God's plan for Israel. He is Emmanuel, "God with us," a symbolic name that designates Jesus as the one through whom God approaches Israel and the world, the one in whom resides God's authority and power. His name, Jesus, indicates that he will save his people from their sins (1:21). At the end of the Gospel, the risen Christ proclaims, "All authority in heaven and on earth has been given to me" (28:18). Because that is the case, the apostles are sent out to make disciples of all nations and to teach them Jesus' commandments.

Jesus' authority to interpret God's will is evident throughout the Gospel and is particularly clear in the Sermon on the Mount (chs. 5–7). In the six antitheses (5:21-48), a pattern is repeated in which Jesus quotes a portion of Torah with the formula "You have heard that it was said . . ." and goes on to say, "But I say to you . . ." In our section below on Judaism, we explain that the substance of Jesus' rulings need not be seen as antithetical to Torah. Nonetheless, the form of the six antitheses indicates that Jesus has absolute authority over Torah interpretation, an authority exceeding that of Moses. He speaks for God.

In Matthew, Jesus is born of a virgin, something not present in Mark. It would be simplistic to think that the virgin birth makes Jesus the Son of God because God is somehow his biological father. The text does not say that, nor does later church doctrine. Rather, the point of the virgin birth is that Jesus embodies God's action in the world, and that Jesus has his origin in God.

Believers call Jesus "Lord" in the Gospel, while others call him "teacher" or "rabbi" or something else. *Lord* occurs mostly in direct address to Jesus, so it is a signal about the attitude of a person to Jesus rather than a title with clear content on its own, but it does in general designate Jesus' exalted status. In the Hebrew Bible, "Lord" often designates God.

Jesus is a prophetic figure in Matthew (23:34-39), although Matthew sees Jesus as more than a prophet. Jesus is the one to whom the ancient prophets point. Matthew inserts many formula citations of biblical texts, each of which claims that Jesus' person, words, and actions fulfill biblical predictions. Jesus is parallel to Moses, but he is greater than Moses. Jesus is Son of David, qualifying him to be the Davidic Messiah. For Matthew, this expresses itself most fully in Jesus' healings. As Son of David, Jesus brings salvation to his entire people, but especially to the sick. This is clearest when, toward the end of his ministry, he enters the temple, cleanses it, and heals the blind and the lame there. Matthew connects this closely to Jesus' status as David's son (21:12-17).

As does Mark, Matthew emphasizes the titles Son of God and Son of Man. He takes up Mark's meanings and enhances them. *Son of Man* is a title that embraces all three aspects of Jesus' work—his authoritative ministry, suffering, and return as judge. Matthew is particularly interested in the Last Judgment. He is the only one of the evangelists to describe it. He does so in chapter 25, where the supreme judge is the Son of Man who sits on his throne and separates the sheep from the goats. Matthew also gives Jesus as Son of Man a role between the resurrection and the parousia. In the parable of the Wheat and the Weeds, the world is designated as the kingdom of the Son of Man (13:41).

Matthew's key concept for understanding Jesus is "Son of God." For Mark, Jesus' status as God's Son is a secret before the death and resurrection. For Matthew, it is not. God proclaims Jesus to be the divine Son at his baptism, rather than saying this directly to Jesus, as in Mark. Mark makes this a private revelation to Jesus; Matthew transforms it into a public pronouncement. Jesus refers to God as his Father throughout the Gospel. His disciples recognize him as Son of God in 14:33. Matthew rewrites Peter's confession so that Peter calls him "the Messiah, the Son of the living God"

(16:16), rather than simply "the Messiah" as in Mark. Jesus reacts by saying that Peter could know this only through God's revelation and declares Peter to be the rock on which he will build his church. This means that recognition of Jesus as Son of God is foundational for the church. The transfiguration follows, in which God proclaims Jesus the divine Son.

In the Hebrew Bible, Israel is God's son (for example, Hos 11:1). Jesus recapitulates in himself the history of his people and their dealings with God, thereby proving himself God's faithful Son. Israel, called God's son in the Bible, repeatedly failed tests in the desert, but God, as God's Son, passes those tests. The Jerusalem leaders reject Jesus as king of Israel (2:1-23) and as Son of God (26:63-68; 27:40, 43). Their mocking of him during the passion is ironic, for it is as God's obedient Son that Jesus suffers. When Jesus reveals his divine power by walking on the water, his disciples proclaim him Son of God.

THE DISCIPLES

Matthew's view of discipleship has much in common with Mark's. Disciples accept Jesus as God's definitive representative. They must accept his death and resurrection as part of God's plan to bring history to its culmination. They must be willing to give up everything and follow, to become part of a new community with new rules, to incur hostility from religious and political authorities.

Matthew improves Mark's portrayal of the disciples. While in Mark the disciples prove dense right to the end of the Gospel, Matthew credits them with a higher level of understanding. He does not fully rehabilitate them, however. They are frequently slow of perception and need things explained. Nonetheless, they usually understand eventually. Some examples make the point. They understand the parables (13:51). In the second boat scene, they recognize Jesus as Son of God (14:33). Peter calls Jesus both Messiah and Son of God, and so becomes the church's foundation (16:16). The disciples understand Jesus' teaching about the yeast of the Pharisees and Sadducees (16:12). In all of these particulars, Matthew contrasts with Mark.

Mark's boat scenes stress the disciples' incomprehension. Matthew retains that aspect but uses the episodes to make broader points about discipleship and the church and to make the disciples look better. Matthew makes the first scene an allegory of the church and discipleship (Matt 8:18, 23-27; Mark 4:35-41). The storm symbolizes troubles the church undergoes. The church is composed of people of "little faith" who prayerfully turn to Jesus in the midst of adversity. Matthew adds entire section about Peter walking on the water to the second scene to make the same point. Matthew's disciples are not perfect. They have "little faith," but this is an improvement over Mark, where they have "no faith."

Mark's Gospel has no resurrection appearances, so we never see the meeting between the risen Jesus and the disciples in Galilee, although the angel points forward toward it. In Matthew, we witness the meeting. The same ambiguities emerge as are evident in the body of the Gospel. The eleven see Jesus and worship him, but some doubt. Then he sends them out to teach and make disciples of all nations.

The disciples are to pass on Jesus' teaching after his death and resurrection. To do that, they must understand. But they cannot teach until they have experienced the totality of Jesus earthly career and heard all of his teaching. During Jesus' mission they receive various tasks—to preach, heal, and cast out demons, but they do not teach. But only after the resurrection can they do so (28:20).

CHURCH

Matthew's pride of place as the first of the four gospels in the New Testament may be due to its usefulness for the church. It presents Jesus' teaching topically and in a format convenient for church teaching, it improves the picture of the disciples to make them better transmitters of the tradition and more suitable models for Christians, and it portrays Jesus as Lord of the church. It also attends more to the real-life church of its audience than do the other gospels, addressing such matters as proper behavior and church discipline and structure.

Only Matthew of the four canonical gospels uses the word *church*. It does so in chapter 16 when Jesus declares Peter to be the rock of the church, and again in chapter 18, Jesus' discourse on church. In chapter 18 Matthew gives practical guidance on how to handle recalcitrant members and on how to treat the "least," and he highlights the role of forgiveness in the community.

Matthew presents the church as a "mixed bag." It is not the community of the saved. It is a group trying to live by Jesus' teachings and awaiting Jesus' eschatological judgment. The parables of the Weeds (13:24-30) and that of the Net (13:47-48) express the mixed nature of the church, as does the redaction of the Great Banquet (22:1-14). Matthew often mentions the Last Judgment. The motif of weeping and gnashing of teeth found once in Q appears six times in Matthew. Only he supplies a detailed description of the Last Judgment (25:31-46), and there he supplies concrete criteria for judgment.

WOMEN

Matthew is similar to Mark in its view of women. He is basically androcentric. As in Mark, most of the main characters in Matthew are men. The twelve disciples are all men. The parables in which women appear, particularly that of the Leaven and that of the Ten Bridesmaids, reinforce traditional women's roles.

The infancy narrative supports this conclusion. While in Luke's infancy narrative Mary is the protagonist, in Matthew it is Joseph. In Matthew, neither God nor angel speaks to Mary. Nor do we ever hear from her. Joseph receives the divine communications. He makes decisions on the basis of them. Some, however, note that although the infancy narrative contains mainly male characters—Joseph, Herod, the magi, the leading figures of Jerusalem, Archelaus—Mary is integral to it, and the anomaly of Jesus being born of woman with no participation from man can foster liberationist readings.

It is surprising that there are four women in Jesus' genealogy (1:1-16). Rahab is a prostitute in Jericho when the Israelites invade under Joshua. She aids Israel, so her family is spared when Israel is victorious. Tamar is the daughter-in-law of Judah (one of the twelve sons of Jacob). She pretends to be a prostitute to trick him into sleeping with her so that she can bear a child to continue the line of her dead husbands, sons of Judah. Although her methods are unorthodox, Judah praises her for being more righteous than he. Ruth is a Gentile who marries an Israelite. After his death she remains faithful to her mother-in-law and remains within Israel instead of returning to her own people. Bathsheba is the wife of Uriah the Hittite. David seduces her and has her husband killed. She is Solomon's mother.

Matthew's genealogy traces Jesus' ancestry through males, so why are the women there? Perhaps Matthew wants to show that God works in unexpected ways. Later in the Gospel, Matthew says that prostitutes and tax collectors enter the kingdom before those who deem themselves righteous (21:32). That may explain why a prostitute, one who pretends to be a prostitute, a Gentile, and a seduced woman are included in Jesus' genealogy. This is something of a theological answer, but it could have powerful social consequences for which even Matthew may not be prepared. When God works through those outside the system, will they then be brought into the system, domesticated in some way, or will they jeopardize the system? The system in question is patriarchal, built on androcentrism. The male is the ideal. He has contact with God for the sake of the wider community. Women's participation is either forbidden, irregular, or strictly controlled.

The four women in Matthew's genealogy are in some sense irregular, outside the system, but Jewish and Christian tradition domesticates them. Rahab is a Gentile and a prostitute, but she facilitates the Israelite conquest of Canaan and reaps her reward. Judah recognizes Tamar's deception as righteous. She deceives him in order to obey the law that a dead man's brother must raise up children to his name, and by doing so she ensures the survival of Judah's line and the eventual birth of Jesus. Ruth is a Gentile who chooses membership in Israel. She is a convert, in a sense. Bathsheba becomes Solomon's mother and so ensures Jesus' birth. Although David's sin in seducing her results in problems in the royal succession, the Bible whitewashes him and holds him up as a model of piety and loyalty to God. Matthew's inclusion of these four women in Jesus' genealogy provides fertile ground for liberationist rereadings of the Bible. But it is doubtful whether Matthew himself intends the inclusion of these women here to signify the liberation of women. He remains well within his androcentric constraints.

One anomaly is not so easily explained. Matthew is one of two gospels that contains the virgin birth. (Luke is the other.) When the genealogy reaches the birth of Jesus, there is a sudden shift from the male line of descent: "And Jacob the father of Joseph the husband of Mary, of whom Jesus was born, who is called the Messiah" (1:16). Although Mary does not play the role that she does in Luke, it is of her that the Messiah is born, and Joseph is "husband of Mary." The Bible frequently identifies women through their husbands. It is much less common for men to be identified with reference to their wives.

As in the Bible, Matthew's legal pronouncements are addressed to men, but since the masculine form is used for groups which can consist of both males and females, it is sometimes possible that both are meant. Nonetheless, Matthew's androcentric mind-set is clear when he says that beyond avoiding adultery, people ought not even to have lustful thoughts about a woman (5:28). He says only that a man may not divorce his wife, not the converse. Some have explained the latter by noting that in Jewish law, women could not divorce their husbands, while in Roman law, they could. It is sometimes argued that Matthew is more conservative about women than Mark or Luke because he is Jewish. Recent scholarship avoids the pitfall of seeing Jewish society as more patriarchal than Gentile society (see Plaskow). The position of Jewish women was probably not much different from that of other women, including the ability to seek divorce (see Levine). We discuss women in Jesus' movement in our chapter on the historical Jesus.

Matthew reproduces the story of the beheading of John the Baptist by Herod (14:1-12). As in Mark, Herod's wife, Herodias, manipulates Herod to effect John's execution. She uses her daughter seductively to pressure Herod and to play on his concern for public status. Nonetheless, Mark places the blame for the Baptist's death more squarely on Herodias than does Matthew.

Throughout the Gospel, male figures and images dominate. But whenever Matthew speaks of crowds coming to Jesus, these must include women. Matthew makes this explicit in the feeding stories (14:21; 15:38) and when Jesus defines his true family (12:46-50). When we hear of disciples in general, it is probable that these include women. Matthew retains Mark's story of the curing of Peter's mother-in-law (8:14-15), the story of the healing of the woman with a hemorrhage (9:20-22), and the raising of the dead girl (9:18-19, 23-26).

Matthew retains and revises Mark's account of the Gentile woman who convinces Jesus to heal her daughter (15:21-28). As usual, Matthew increases the interaction between petitioner and Jesus. She shouts her request to him in public, using the title "Son of David," so familiar in Matthew, and he ignores her. Then she kneels before him and makes him respond. He insists his mission is only to Israel. Her persistence finally convinces him to do what she asks. So the woman gets him to fulfill properly Isaiah's prophecy that he will go to the Gentiles (Matt 12:18-21). Jesus praises her: "Great is your faith!" There may be a contrast here with the "little faith" of the disciples.

The Hebrew Bible frequently speaks of God's wisdom. The word *wisdom* is feminine in both Hebrew (*hokhmah*) and Greek (*sophia*). The wisdom of God is often a circumlocution for God, similar to other circumlocutions, such as God's glory, name, spirit, word, and so on. Wisdom is personified in several books: Proverbs, Sirach, Wisdom, Baruch. She is God's companion, present at the creation, through whom God created the universe (Prov 9). In Sir 24, she is identified with Torah. Personified wisdom may have developed in part out of a felt need for a feminine element in God. Wisdom later supplies Christians with an important means of interpreting Jesus, his work, and his relation to the Father. Christian views of Jesus that utilize this image of wisdom are called wisdom Christology. It is especially prominent in John's Gospel, as we shall see. It is also present in Matt 11.

In Matt 11, Jesus speaks of the rejection of both himself and John. Jesus contends, "Yet wisdom is vindicated by her deeds" (v. 14). The deeds of John and Jesus are those of wisdom. The verse comes from Q. Luke's version has "children" instead of "deeds," as do some manuscripts of Matthew. It is likely that Matthew changed children to deeds to form an *inclusio* (frame) with 11:2, which speaks of the deeds of the Messiah. Later in the chapter (vv. 28-30), Jesus uses language typical of wisdom to describe his teaching, work, and relationship with those who come to him (Prov 9:5; 11:1, 16; Sir 24:19; 51:23-27). Wisdom language appears again in the passion narrative (Matt 23:34-37). The association of Jesus with a feminine element of God has proved suggestive to feminist scholars, some of whom now speak of Jesus-Sophia.

In Mark, the disciples James and John ask Jesus for prominent positions in the kingdom, thus demonstrating their lack of understanding. Matthew puts the request on the lips of their mother, perhaps to improve the disciples' image (20:20). She does, however, end up witnessing the crucifixion, while her sons flee (26:56; 27:56). In this sense, she is a better disciple than they.

At the beginning of the passion narrative, an unnamed woman anoints Jesus (26:6-13), as in Mark 14. The incident forms the first part of a frame completed by the story of the women at the empty tomb toward the end of the narrative (28:1-10). Both are positive pictures, in contrast to the negative depiction of males throughout the passion—the authorities plot Jesus' death and the male disciples abandon him. When the woman pours costly ointment on Jesus' head, the disciples complain about the waste (26:6-13). This echoes their reaction to the Gentile woman in chapter 15, whom they try to get rid of. Jesus announces that the woman anoints him for burial, and since for Matthew death is related to messiahship, this probably also has messianic overtones. The woman's recognition of Jesus' messiahship contrasts with the authorities' rejection of it. Jesus says that where the gospel is preached, her action will be narrated as well, indicating its importance. Ironically, the story simultaneously gives a woman a prominent role in which she compares favorably with male characters and yet absorbs her into an androcentric narrative. She is not one of

Jesus' disciples. She says nothing. She plays no further role. We do not even know her name.

Women disciples witness the crucifixion (27:55-56), while the men flee (26:56). These women "followed Jesus from Galilee and had provided for (literally: served) him." The Greek for "served" here is *diakoneo*, the same root from which the word *deacon* is derived. The women are disciples. Women disciples go to the empty tomb and hear from the angel that Jesus has risen (28:1-10). They receive the mission to announce this to the disciples. They are the first to encounter the risen Jesus. They take hold of his feet and worship him. Jesus tells them not to fear and confirms their angelic commission. This is a crucial function. It is the women who remain faithful to Jesus throughout his passion, it is they who first witness the resurrection, and it is they who are to tell the disciples about it. In the end, however, the eleven who meet Jesus on the mountain in Galilee and are commissioned to preach the gospel to all nations are all male (28:16-20). Women are prominent; men remain dominant.

JEWS AND JUDAISM

Matthew is obviously concerned about his community's relationship to Torah. It is Jesus, and so Matthew's Christian community, who understand God's will expressed in Torah, not non-Christian Jews, and especially not the Jewish religious leadership, either in Jesus' day or his own. For Matthew, if one truly understands Israel's Scriptures, then one will accept Jesus.

Scholars dispute whether a decisive split has already occurred between Matthew's community and the synagogue. Matthew speaks of "your" synagogues or "their" synagogues, implying that he and his church do not belong to non-Christian synagogues. So there is a split, to be sure, but how exactly do Matthew on the one hand and non-Christian Jews on the other conceive of that split?

Matthew presents the synagogues and their leaders as hostile to Jesus, increasing the hostility to a point even beyond what we find in Mark and Q. This suggests that he saw synagogues and leaders of his own day as hostile to the Christian movement. But that does not disclose whether his community observes Torah. A variety of attitudes to Torah were held by the early Christians. Some thought it still fully binding. Some thought that because of Jesus' teaching, they did not have to obey all of Torah. Paul argues that God through Jesus brought about a new creation, and

Torah as a religious system belongs to the old creation. Although it is God's word, its value lies in the fact that it points to Jesus.

What is Matthew's place in this variety of positions? Does he expect his community to obey Torah? Does he believe that Jesus interpreted Torah so that many of its injunctions were no longer binding? Was Matthew's interest in Torah in its prophetic aspect alone? Would an outsider, neither Jewish nor Christian, discern a difference between Matthew's community and the neighboring synagogue?

Matthew presents the main lines of Jesus' teaching in the Sermon on the Mount (chs. 5–7). Concern with Torah and with Jewish piety is evident throughout the sermon and is particularly clear in 5:17-20, which occurs toward the beginning of the sermon, shortly after the Beatitudes. Jesus says, "Do not think that I have come to abolish the law (Torah) or the prophets; I have not come to abolish but to fulfill" (5:17). Apparently someone does indeed think that Jesus came to abolish Torah. The prominence of this saying in this crucial sermon indicates that this misconception about Jesus greatly concerns Matthew. What does the contrast between "abolish" and "fulfill" mean? One possibility is that fulfillment means eschatological realization. In this view, fulfillment would not be of the Torah's legal prescriptions but of messianic prophecies. In this view, paradoxically Jesus could change or even abrogate Torah as a legal system without "abolishing" it. Paul makes this argument (Rom 3:21, 31).

The next verses imply that Matthew wanted his church to obey Torah's injunctions, not just to believe that Jesus fulfilled its prophecies. Jesus says, "For truly I tell you, until heaven and earth pass away, not one letter, not one stroke of a letter, will pass from the law until all is accomplished" (5:18). Suppose, by way of illustration, that the Torah says, "Do not do it." Jesus is saying that not even the dot over the "i" of "it," nor the horizontal line crossing the "t" will change. It is noteworthy that Jesus puts the lack of change in terms of the written Torah here. It is not a question of the spirit of the Law contrasted with its letter. He speaks of the written text. Torah remains the same, even after Jesus' coming. What does "until all is accomplished" mean? Does it mean the rest of history until the second coming of Jesus, or does it mean only until Jesus' ministry, death, and resurrection are accomplished? If it is the latter, then Matthew's church is no longer bound by Torah. If the former, then Torah still binds.

The sermon continues, "Therefore, whoever breaks one of the least of these commandments, and teaches others to do the same, will be called least in the kingdom of heaven; but whoever does them and teaches them will be called great in the kingdom of heaven" (5:19). Jesus opposes the view that some of Torah's commandments need not be kept. An alternative interpretation would take "these commandments" as referring to Jesus' commandments. But it is hard to see how Matthew could categorize any of Jesus' commandments or legal interpretations as "least." They all deal with major issues, unlike the much more comprehensive collection of law in the Torah that took centuries to develop and that was meant to regulate an entire nation over time, covering a great variety of circumstances.

Jesus ends this section of the sermon with a demand that his followers outdo the Pharisees in righteousness (5:20). For Matthew, righteousness is not an abstract quality. It is always identified with God's will, particularly as found in Torah. Of course, for Matthew one cannot truly be in accord with Torah if one does not accept Jesus and his interpretations. This role for Jesus is not unlike the role of the Teacher of Righteousness in the community of the Dead Sea Scrolls. He also interpreted specific legal issues differently from the Jerusalem establishment and introduced new regulations not in Torah. He believed that Jews who did not accept his teaching—the vast majority of Jews—were not in accord with Torah.

The rest of the Sermon on the Mount also has to do with Jesus' interpretation of Torah. Chapter 5 contains six "antitheses" whose general form is a citation of scriptural commands introduced by the words "you have heard that it was said," followed by Jesus' own commands, introduced by the words "but I say to you." Three of the antitheses deepen or radicalize the demands of the Torah. One not only should not murder; one should not even get angry. One not only should not commit adultery; one should not even have lustful thoughts. One should not only love one's neighbor; one should love one's enemies. The other three antitheses forbid something that the Law permits—divorce, oaths, and retaliation. Some think that in these three cases Jesus changes the Torah, while others think that it is not contrary to Torah to be stricter than Torah and point to the interpretation of the Law at Qumran as an analog. The debate is whether Jesus puts himself above Torah or only claims to be its absolute arbiter.

Chapter 6 considers three important forms of Jewish piety in Jesus' day—prayer, almsgiving, and fasting. In all three cases, Matthew supports the practices but insists that they must be done not for public effect, as in the case of the religious authorities, but quietly and humbly. In the case of prayer, Matthew contrasts simplicity with what "the Gentiles" do (6:7).

Toward the end of the sermon, Jesus says, "In everything do to others as you would have them do to you; for this is the law and the prophets" (7:12). The phrase "law and prophets" summarizes God's revelation to Israel. In 22:40, Jesus says that the entirety of the Law and prophets is summed up in the command to love God (Deut 6:5) and neighbor (Lev 19:18). Matthew believes that the Christian way of life fulfills Torah.

Jesus' diatribe in Matt 23 against the scribes and Pharisees contains a surprise, given Matthew's antipathy toward those two groups: "The scribes and Pharisees sit on Moses' seat; therefore, practice and do whatever they teach you and follow it; but do not do as they do, for they do not practice what they preach." The rest of the chapter castigates these groups, so these verses stand out. They are often explained as vestiges from an earlier stage in the community's development, meaning that at one time the community recognized scribal and Pharisaic authority, which it later rejected because the authorities rejected Jesus. That solution leaves unresolved why the final editor keeps these verses in the Gospel. Another possibility is that although it has broken from the synagogue, is hostile to its leaders, and thinks that non-Christian Jews oppose God by opposing Jesus, the community still recognizes the legal expertise of the scribes and Pharisees. Things do not have to be all or nothing.

A later verse sheds light on this question: "Woe to you, scribes and Pharisees, hypocrites! For you tithe mint, dill, and cummin, and have neglected the weightier matters of the law: justice and mercy and faith" (23:23a). This verse reflects Pharisaic efforts to "build a fence around the Torah"—to make rules stricter than Torah to ensure that Torah itself is not violated. Jesus does the same when he forbids not only killing, but even anger. If one is not angry, one will not kill. The matter at hand in 23:23 is tithing. Torah prescribes giving a tenth of major agricultural produce to the temple. It does not cover small items such as mint, dill, and cumin. This verse assumes that the Pharisees tithe spices, thus going beyond what Torah demands. Christian readers, accustomed to hearing criticisms of Jewish concentration on minute legalities, may listen to these words with equanimity. They praise a Jesus who can distinguish important from unimportant, as if Jesus' contemporaries were unable to do so. Jesus' next words shake such complacency: "These you ought to have practiced without neglecting the others" (23:23b). Matthew's Jesus does not believe that concentration on justice, mercy, and faith obviates the "other" rules, even Pharisaic ones. One ought to do both. All three elements—justice (righteousness), mercy, and faith—are central to Matthew's Gospel. Righteousness is particularly evident in Torah, mercy is at the center of the Torah, and Matthew repeatedly stresses faith, especially faith in Jesus.

There are other indications that Matthew urges Torah observance. In chapter 15, Matthew rewrites Mark 7, a chapter where Jesus attacks the Pharisees and the scribes for their purity laws. Matthew omits Mark's explanation of Jewish customs (Mark 7:3-5), perhaps because his own community is more familiar with them than is Mark's. In Mark, the dispute over hand washing expands into a general discussion of pure foods. Jesus pronounces, "Whatever goes into a person from outside cannot defile. . . . It is what comes out of a person that defiles" (Mark 7:18, 20). Mark comments, "Thus he declared all foods clean" (7:19). For Mark, Jesus annuls Jewish dietary rules. Matthew drops these words. For him, Jesus does not invalidate dietary rules but only teaches that such rules are meaningless unless accompanied by a moral life. Matthew brings the focus back to hand washing through the final words of the section: "These (sins) are what defile a person, but to eat with unwashed hands does not defile" (15:20).

It may seem contradictory that when Jesus says that what goes in from the outside, food, cannot defile, he does not abrogate dietary rules. But elsewhere in the Bible we encounter the form "not ritual, but morality" where negation of ritual is not intended. In Isa 58, for example, the prophet says that God detests ritual practices, meaning that God will not accept them unaccompanied by social justice. Similarly, Jeremiah tells worshipers not to trust that God resides in the temple unless they follow God's commands (Jer 7:1-15). We look also to Ps 51, which says that God does not require sacrifice, but a contrite heart. In none of these cases does the prophet or psalmist annul liturgical practice. The idea is simply that without moral behavior, liturgy is useless. This is Matthew's logic, too.

Matthew's interpretations of Torah differed from those of other Jews. His belief in the supremacy of Jesus' authority would certainly not be accepted by non-Christian Jews. The situation is not unlike that of the Qumran community. They thought that they were the ones in accord with Torah, while all other Jews were transgressors. Jews not in the Qumran community thought the converse. The question is whether the status of Jesus in Matthew's community placed it outside Judaism, despite the variety that existed within Judaism. Many scholars claim that in Matthew's estimation it did not. It is more than likely that non-Christian Jews outside Matthew's community would say that it did.

CONCLUSION

Matthew greatly enhances the gospel as he inherits it from Mark. He uses Q and other sources to supplement what he finds there, and as he rewrites his sources he creates a coherent whole that both preserves key aspects of Mark and goes beyond it. His Gospel is particularly noteworthy for the importance it accords Torah and Israel, as well as for its attention to church, ethics, and Christology. Matthew creates a gospel that has been of great use to the church over the centuries, and that assumed pride of place as the first of the four canonical gospels.

BIBLIOGRAPHY

Allison, Dale C. *The New Moses: A Matthean Typology*. Minneapolis: Fortress, 1993.

Aune, David E., ed. *The Gospel of Matthew in Current Study*. Grand Rapids: Eerdmans, 2001.

Balch, David L., ed. *Social History of the Matthean Community*. Minneapolis: Fortress, 1991.

Betz, Hans Dieter. *Essays on the Sermon on the Mount*. Philadelphia: Fortress, 1985.

Bornkamm, Günther. "The Authority to 'Bind' and 'Loose' in the Church in Matthew's Gospel." Pages 37-50 in *Jesus and Man's Hope*. Edited by D. Hadidian and others. Vol. 2. Pittsburgh: Pittsburgh Theological Seminary, 1970.

Bornkamm, Günther, Gerhard Barth, and Heinz Joachim Held. *Tradition and Interpretation in Matthew*. Philadelphia: Westminster, 1963.

Brown, Raymond E. *The Birth of the Messiah: A Commentary on the Infancy Narratives in the Gospels of Matthew and Luke*. Garden City, N.Y.: Doubleday, 1993.

Carter, Warren. *Matthew and the Margins: A Sociopolitical and Religious Reading*. New York: Orbis, 2001.

————. *What Are They Saying about Matthew's Sermon on the Mount?* New York: Paulist, 1994.

D'Angelo, Mary Rose. "(Re)Presentations of Women in the Gospels: Matthew and Luke-Acts." *WCO*, 171-95.

Davies, W. D. *The Setting of the Sermon on the Mount*. Cambridge: Cambridge University Press, 1964.

Davies, W. D., and Dale Allison. *A Critical and Exegetical Commentary on the Gospel According to Saint Matthew*. 3 vols. Edinburgh: T. & T. Clark, 1988–1997.

Hare, Douglas R. A. "How Jewish Is the Gospel of Matthew?" *CBQ* 62 (2000): 264-77.

Harrington, Daniel J. *The Gospel of Matthew*. Collegeville, Minn.: Liturgical, 1991.

Ilan, Tal. *Jewish Women in Greco-Roman Palestine*. Peabody, Mass.: Hendrickson, 1996.

Kingsbury, Jack Dean. *Matthew: Structure, Christology, Kingdom*. Philadelphia: Fortress, 1975.

Levine, Amy-Jill. "Anti-Judaism and the Gospel of Matthew." Pages 9-36 in *Anti-Judaism and the Gospels*. Edited by William R. Farmer. Harrisburg, Penn.: Trinity, 1999.

――――. *The Social and Ethnic Dimensions of Matthean Salvation History*. Lewiston: Edwin Mellen, 1988.

Luz, Ulrich. *Matthew in History: Interpretation, Influence, and Effects*. Minneapolis: Fortress, 1994.

――――. *The Theology of the Gospel of Matthew*. Cambridge: Cambridge University Press, 1995.

Meier, John P. "Matthew, Gospel of." *ABD* 4:622-41.

――――. *The Vision of Matthew: Christ, Church, and Morality in the First Gospel*. New York: Paulist, 1979.

Murphy, Frederick J. "The Jewishness of Matthew: Another Look." Pages 377-403 in vol. 2 of *When Judaism and Christianity Began: Essays in Memory of Anthony J. Saldarini*. Edited by Alan J. Avery-Peck, Daniel Harrington, and Jacob Neusner. Boston: Brill, 2004.

Neusner, Jacob. *A Rabbi Talks with Jesus: An Intermillennial, Interfaith Exchange*. New York: Doubleday, 1993.

Overman, J. Andrew. *Church and Community in Crisis*. Philadelphia: Trinity, 1996.

Plaskow, Judith. "Anti-Judaism in Feminist Christian Interpretation." *STS* 1:117-29.

Saldarini, Anthony J. *Matthew's Christian-Jewish Community*. Chicago: University of Chicago Press, 1994.

Senior, Donald. *What Are They Saying about Matthew?* New York: Paulist, 1983.

Stendahl, Krister. *The School of St. Matthew and Its Use of the Old Testament*, 2d ed. Philadelphia: Fortress, 1968.

Suggs, M. Jack. *Wisdom, Christology, and Law in Matthew's Gospel*. Cambridge: Harvard University Press, 1970.

Wainwright, Elaine. "The Gospel of Matthew." *STS* 635-77.

Wilson, Robert R. "Genealogy, Genealogies." *ABD* 2:929-32.

CHAPTER FIVE

THE GOSPEL OF LUKE AND ACTS OF THE APOSTLES

INTRODUCTION

The author of Luke's Gospel also wrote Acts of the Apostles, as a glance at their openings shows. The Gospel begins with a dedication to Theophilus (1:1-4) and ends with Jesus being taken up to heaven, something recounted in none of the other gospels. Acts of the Apostles begins, "In the first book, Theophilus, I wrote about all that Jesus did and taught from the beginning until the day when he was taken up to heaven" (1:1-2). Acts then retells the story of Jesus' ascension (1:6-11).

There are many other contacts between Luke and Acts. The Gospel emphasizes the role of the Holy Spirit, precisely what we find in Acts, and both books associate the Spirit with prophecy. Each book features journeys occupying many chapters. In Luke, Jesus journeys from Galilee to Jerusalem. In Acts, Christian missionaries travel from Jerusalem to Rome. Jesus as prophet is a theme in both books. Both begin with the descent of the Spirit; in Luke it descends on Jesus and in Acts on the disciples. There are numerous parallels between Jesus in the Gospel and the disciples in Acts. Both do miracles. Both preach in the temple. The trials of Paul resemble those of Jesus. The death of Stephen is like that of Jesus. We could go on.

Luke's Gospel is the first volume in a two-volume work in which the second tells the story of the movement arising from Jesus. Charles Talbert finds this similar to the sorts of biographies in the writer Diogenes Laertius's *Lives of the Philosophers*, where there is an account of the philosophers' births and teachings, followed by the acts and teachings of their disciples.

Luke's work is "apologetic" history. The Hellenistic age saw tremendous growth in mutual knowledge between different cultures and resultant cultural competition. Native writers wrote histories of their peoples, sometimes for outsiders, and sometimes for their own people as part of an effort at self-definition in a new, broader world. Each wanted to claim for his own group a distinguished place in the world. Examples include Manetho of Egypt and Berossus of Babylonia. The most famous Jewish apologetic history was that of the first-century C.E. writer Josephus.

Gregory E. Sterling argues convincingly that Luke–Acts is apologetic history. Addressed primarily to insiders, it helps them to define themselves and understand their place in the Roman Empire, their relation to Judaism, and their role in world history. Since the church had recently come into existence, this was particularly urgent. The church needed first to prove its antiquity, for antiquity was a mark of legitimacy. Luke presents Christianity as a continuation of Judaism, whose antiquity was widely recognized. Jesus fulfills Israel's prophetic oracles. But this poses a theological problem. Israel as a whole did not accept Jesus. Rather, the movement increasingly consisted of Gentiles. How is this to be explained? And does this cast doubt on whether God truly fulfills divine promises? So Luke's work is also a defense of God. Such defenses were common in ancient Judaism (for example, *4 Ezra*, Job; see Crenshaw). The technical name for this genre is *theodicy*, which comes from the Greek words for "God" and "justice."

The Bible locates Israel within the history of the entire universe and then tells of how Israel relates to important nations such as Egypt, Assyria, Babylonia, and Persia. Luke continues in that tradition by locating Christianity with respect to Judaism and by special attention to the Roman Empire, as well as to Rome's proxy rulers in Jewish Palestine, the Herodians. Luke's genealogy of Jesus goes back not just to David and Abraham, as in Matthew, but all the way back to Adam and even to God, another claim to antiquity (3:23-38). As Christianity stepped onto the world stage, he needed to show that it was acceptable to Rome. Jesus is three times pronounced innocent by Pilate, and Roman officials in Acts uniformly find Christianity to be part of Judaism and no risk to the empire.

The ascription of the Gospel to Luke is from the second century. Early church tradition holds that the author was a companion of Paul, and possibly a physician (Col 4:14; 2 Tim 4:11; Phlm 24). All we know for sure about the author we glean from the text itself. He was well educated. He writes the best Greek of any of the evangelists. He knows the Bible in depth and is an excellent writer who composes a long, well-structured, and sophisticated narrative. He is at home in the Roman world and presents Jesus and his movement as having worldwide significance.

Like Matthew, Luke employs Mark and Q as sources. Unlike Matthew, he omits almost 50 percent of Mark's material (he leaves out Mark 6:45–8:26, called the "great omission," and 9:41–10:12, called the "little omission"). Matthew's special material (M) accounts for around a third of his Gospel, while Luke's (L) accounts for around half of his. These observations lead us to expect that Luke has a distinctive voice, and that is indeed what we find.

MATERIAL UNIQUE TO LUKE

Luke's special material contains some of the most memorable material in the New Testament. The following table is not exhaustive. It is meant to provide a quick overview of this material so as to give a feel for the distinctiveness of Luke's Gospel.

Material Unique to Luke

Prologue (1:1-4)
    Infancy and childhood narrative (1:4–2:40)
        • Parallelism of annunciations and births of John and Jesus
        • Angels in the sky and shepherds in the field
        • Role of Mary and Elizabeth
        • Canticles of Mary and Zechariah
        • Appearance of baby Jesus in Jerusalem and temple
        • Prophecies of Simeon and Anna
        • Jesus in the temple at twelve years old (2:41-52)
    Historical notes (Tiberius, Herods, Lysanius, Caiaphas) (3:1-2)
    John the Baptist's ethical teaching (3:10-14)
    Tracing Jesus' genealogy back to Adam and God (3:23-38)
    Extensive rewriting and moving of scene at Nazareth synagogue, using
        Isa 61 (4:14-30)
    Miraculous catch of fish, leading to call of Peter, James, and
        John (5:1-11)

Mediation of Jewish elders to cure of centurion's servant (7:3-5)
Raising of widow's son (7:11-17)
Rewriting and moving of story of the woman anointing Jesus (7:36-50)
Women accompanying Jesus and disciples and supporting them (8:1-3)
Beginning of journey and story of Samaritan villagers (9:51-56)
Jesus' words to the disciples after their mission (10:17-20)
Martha and Mary (10:38-42)
Blessing for Jesus' mother (11:27-28)
Galileans whom Pilate killed (13:1-9)
Healing of a crippled woman on Sabbath (13:10-17)
Jesus speaks of the death of prophets in Jerusalem (13:31-33)
Healing on Sabbath of a man with dropsy (14:1-6)
Table etiquette: taking the lowest place, and inviting the needy (14:7-14)
Condemnation of Pharisees for love of money (16:14-15)
Duties of a slave illustrating discipleship (17:7-10)
Healing of ten lepers, one a Samaritan (17:11-19)
Kingdom of God not coming with observable signs (17:20-21)
Zacchaeus, rich tax collector (19:1-10)
Jesus' lament over Jerusalem (19:39-44)
Jesus' words to Peter about Peter's denial (22:31-34)
Bringing purse, bag, and sword on missions (22:35-38)
Trial before Herod (23:6-16)
Pilate's three declarations of Jesus' innocence (23:4, 14-15, 22)
Women of Jerusalem on the way to Calvary (23:26-32)
The good thief (23:39-43)
Resurrection appearance on road to Emmaus (24:13-35)
Appearance to the disciples (24:36-49)
Ascension (24:50-53)
Parables
  • Good Samaritan (10:29-37)
  • Friend at Midnight (11:5-8)
  • Rich Fool (12:13-21)
  • Barren Tree (13:1-9)
  • Master Serving at Table (12:35-38)
  • Slave's Wages (12:47-48)
  • Builder (14:28-30)
  • King (14:31-32)
  • Lost Coin (15:8-10)
  • Prodigal Son (15:11-32)

- Unjust Steward (16:1-13)
- Rich Man and Lazarus (16:19-31)
- Unjust Judge (18:1-8)
- Pharisee and Tax Collector (18:9-14)

STRUCTURE

Matthew found the beginning and end of Mark inadequate to his purposes, and Luke felt the same way. Like Matthew, he added an infancy narrative and resurrection appearances. Matthew tends to follow Mark's Gospel and to distribute his use of Q throughout the Gospel, using much from Q to construct Jesus' discourses. Luke tends to use his source material in blocks. He uses mostly Mark in 3:1–6:1, 8:4–9:50, and 18:15–24:11, and mainly Q in 6:20–8:3 and 9:51–18:14. He places a large amount of material, taken mostly from Q and L, into a long journey narrative that brings Jesus from Galilee to Jerusalem (9:51–19:27). Since Luke's Gospel and Acts of the Apostles form a single, two-volume work, we supply a brief outline of both.

Gospel of Luke

Prologue (1:1-4)
Infancy and childhood narrative (1:5–2:52)
Preparation for Jesus' ministry (3:1–4:13)
Galilean ministry (4:14–9:50)
Journey to Jerusalem (9:51–19:27)
Ministry in Jerusalem (19:28–21:38)
Passion Narrative (22:1–23:56)
Resurrection and Ascension (24:1–53)

Acts of the Apostles

Prologue (1:1-2)
Preparation for church's mission (1:3–2:4)
Mission in Jerusalem (2:5–8:1*a*)
Mission extends beyond Jerusalem (8:1*b*–15:35)
Paul's journeys, ending ultimately in Rome (15:36–28:31)

OVERVIEW

Luke–Acts extends the biblical story. To know how God acts in Jesus and the church, one must know God's past actions in Israel's history. While Luke sometimes uses a formula quotation, as does Matthew, he usually prefers to let biblical patterns shape the narrative. He "shows" rather than "tells." Luke draws on various biblical books but is especially fond of Isaiah, particularly "Second Isaiah" (chs. 40–55; see below). We explore the influence of Isaiah on Luke in a later section.

When Luke looks at Scripture, he sees a liberating God—one who frees humans from all that separates them from God and from human fulfillment. Humanity's main problem is sin. Sin assumes diverse forms, but Luke is most concerned with social sin—the absence of social justice, oppression of the weak by the powerful and the poor by the strong. This concern is present in each of the Synoptic Gospels, but it is particularly prevalent in Luke.

Luke considers Israel God's chosen people and places great weight on God's promises of liberation for Israel. This encompasses liberation from enemies, freedom to worship God, pardon for Israel's transgressions, the coming of a Messiah, and relief for Israel's poor and sick. For Luke, the main message of all the prophets throughout history is that God will make good on these promises, and God fulfills all of these promises in Jesus.

The infancy narrative describes the fulfillment of God's promises and is full of joy and hope. However, at its end the prophet Simeon predicts that Jesus will cause division within Israel. Throughout the rest of the Gospel, Jesus is rejected by Israel's leaders and others, finally dying on the cross. So the basic line of the narrative is that of tragedy.

Things to Look For

- Jesus takes a special interest in the poor.
- Luke embellishes the miracles and sees them as legitimate public signs of Jesus' identity.
- Luke emphasizes Jesus as prophet.
- Jesus is the savior of the entire world, not just of Israel.
- Luke has more material concerning women than do the other Gospels.

- Luke presents Israel's story as tragedy, since it does not accept the fulfillment of God's promises to it in Jesus.
- The prophetic spirit is prominent in the infancy narrative, and Jesus possesses the spirit during the time of his ministry. In Acts, the Spirit guides the church and makes it grow.
- Luke mentions prayer more than any other evangelist. Jesus frequently prays at important points in the narrative.
- Luke shows interest in political issues such as the position of Christianity in the Roman Empire, and Jesus' meaning for structures of power.

SURVEY OF THE GOSPEL

PROLOGUE (1:1-4)

Luke–Acts begins, as would any good ancient history, with a prologue explaining his goal and method. It is addressed to Theophilus, a name meaning "lover of God" or "beloved of God." It is debated whether Theophilus is real or fictional. If the former, he would be a rich patron who would finance the distribution of Luke's work. If the latter, Luke may follow convention but use a symbolic name. Luke tells Theophilus that many have attempted to write this story using the testimony of eyewitnesses and of others not eyewitnesses whose job it was to preserve the tradition (a possible meaning of "servants of the word").

Theophilus is not being told about these things for the first time. Luke acknowledges that many have told this story before. But if Luke needs to write an "orderly" account that conveys the "truth," as he says, then he judges previous accounts adequate. Luke uses Mark and Q as sources. Although he makes extensive use of them, he is not shy about omitting, adding, and rewriting.

INFANCY AND CHILDHOOD NARRATIVE (1:5–2:52)

Infancy Narrative (1:5–2:40). The infancy narrative sets the stage for everything to follow. The Greek of Luke's first two chapters has a distinctly biblical tone and makes Luke's work a continuation of the biblical story.

The theme of these introductory chapters is fulfillment. Israel's essence was defined by its long relationship with God. At the time of Jesus' birth, Israel found itself under Roman domination. This continued a long history of domination by foreigners. But Israel's God was all-powerful and had promised Israel freedom from its enemies and had sworn to David that a member of his family would always sit on the throne of Israel. Hopes for release occasionally took hold of the people. Prophets and psalmists often captured and expressed such aspirations. The evangelists saw Jesus as the fulfillment of those hopes. Luke is particularly insistent on seeing all biblical prophecy as pointing forward to Jesus.

It is fitting, then, that Luke–Acts makes Jerusalem and its temple central to its concerns, for they symbolize God's presence among and commitment to Israel. The infancy narrative begins and ends in the temple. It begins when an angel appears to Zechariah, John the Baptist's father (1:5-23), and it ends as Jesus is brought to the temple to be offered to God as Mary's firstborn (2:21-38). Luke adds a scene from Jesus' childhood, where Jesus makes his first trip as a young adult to Jerusalem for Passover and then, without informing his parents, stays behind to discuss Torah with teachers in the temple, which he sees as his Father's house (2:41-51). After Jesus' death just outside Jerusalem's walls, the resurrection appearances all take place in or around Jerusalem (24:1-53; unlike Matthew and John where they occur in Galilee; see also Mark 16:7), and the Gospel ends as Jesus' followers worship in the temple (24:52-53). Acts begins in Jerusalem, where the disciples preach and cure. Then the message moves beyond Jerusalem and ultimately to Rome.

The infancy narrative uses one of Luke's favorite devices, parallelism. The annunciation and birth of the Baptist and Jesus are parallel, and they both echo similar stories in the Bible, such as that of Samson. The following table lays out the similarities between the three stories.

Announcement of the Baptist's Birth (Luke 1)	Announcement of Jesus' Birth (Luke 1)	Announcement of Samson's Birth (Judg 13)
1:5 In the days of King Herod of Judea, there was a priest named Zechariah, who belonged to the priestly order of Abijah. His wife was a descendant of Aaron, and her	1:26 In the sixth month the angel Gabriel was sent by God to a town in Galilee called Nazareth, 1:27 to a virgin engaged to a man whose name	13:2 There was a certain man of Zorah, of the tribe of the Danites, whose name was Manoah.

name was Elizabeth.

was Joseph, of the house of David. The virgin's name was Mary.

1:7 But they had no children, because Elizabeth was barren, and both were getting on in years.

(Mary is a virgin.)

His wife was barren, having borne no children.

1:11 Then there appeared to him an angel of the Lord, standing at the right side of the altar of incense.

1:28 And he came to her and said, "Greetings, favored one! The Lord is with you."

13:3 And the of the LORD appeared to the woman

1:12 When Zechariah saw him, he was terrified; and fear over-whelmed him.

1:29 But she was much perplexed by his words and pondered what sort of greeting this might be.

1:13 But the angel said to him, "Do not be afraid, Zechariah, for your prayer has been heard. Your wife Elizabeth will bear you a son, and you will named him John. 1:14 You will have joy and gladness, and many will rejoice at his birth, 1:15 for he will be great in the sight of the Lord. He must never drink wine or strong drink;

1:30 The angel said to her, "Do not be afraid, Mary, for you have found favor with God. 1:13 And now, you will conceive in your womb and bear a son, and you will name him Jesus. 1:32 He will be great, and will be called the Son of the Most High, and the Lord God will

and said to her, "Although you are barren, having borne no children, you shall conceive and bear a son. 13:4 Now be careful not to drink wine or strong drink, or to eat anything unclean, 13:5 for you shall conceive and bear a son. No razor is to come on his head, for the boy shall be a nazirite to

even before his
birth he will be
filled with the
Holy Spirit."

1:18 Zechariah
said to the
angel, "How
will I know
that this is so?
For I am an
old man, and
my wife is
getting on
in years."

1:19 The angel replied,
"I am Gabriel. I stand
in the presence of God,
and I have been sent
to speak to you and to
bring you this good
news. 1:20 But now,
because you did not
believe my words,
which will be fulfilled
in their time, you
will become mute,
unable to speak, until
the day these things
occur."

1:24 After those days
his wife Elizabeth

give to him the
throne of his
ancestor David.
1:33 He will reign
over the house
of Jacob forever,
and of his king-
dom there will
be no end."

1:34 Mary
said to the angel,
"How can this be,
since I am a
virgin?"

1:35 The angel
said to her, "The
Holy Spirit will
come upon you,
and the power of the
Most High will over-
shadow you; there-
fore the child to be
born will be holy; he
will be called Son of
God."

1:38 Then Mary
said, "Here am I, the

God from birth.

conceived, and for five months she remained in seclusion. She said, 1:25 "This is what the Lord has done for me when he looked favorably on me and took away the disgrace I have endured among my people."

servant of the Lord; let it be with me according to your word." Then the angel departed from her.

1:70 as he spoke through the mouth / of his holy prophets from of old, / 1:71 that we would be saved from / our enemies and from the hand of all who hate us.... 1:73 the oath that he swore to our ancestor Abraham, / to grant us 1:74 that we, being rescued from the hands of our enemies, / might serve him without fear.

1:54 "He has helped his servant Israel, / in remembrance of his mercy, / 1:55 according to the promise he made to our ancestors, / to Abraham and to his descendants forever."

It is he who shall begin to deliver Israel from the hand of the Philistines."

All three cases concern the announcement of the birth of one to play a special role in God's plans for Israel. As God acts in the Bible, so God acts in the time of fulfillment. The angel announces the birth and explains its significance. The one to be born will fulfill God's promises to liberate Israel from its enemies. The parallelism shows that what happens does so according to a pattern, and that God is its source. Parallelism between John and Jesus does not mean that they are equal, as will become clear when the two mothers, Mary and Elizabeth, meet. Even the ones to whom the announcements are made, John's father Zechariah and Jesus' mother Mary, are not equal, for Zechariah responds with skepticism and is punished (1:18-20) while Mary responds with acceptance and is praised (1:38, 45). This may at first be confusing, for both Zechariah and Mary respond to the angel's surprising announcement with questions. But Zechariah asks, "How will I know that this is so?" while Mary asks simply, "How can this be?" Mary is asking simply how what the angel announces will happen, while Zechariah is demanding some sort of assurance.

As in the Bible, God's miraculously overcoming infertility (or in Mary's case, virginity) is symbolic of God's ability to liberate humans despite obstacles. When Zechariah expresses skepticism, the angel assures him that his words, that is, God's words, "will be fulfilled in their time" (1:20). And the Spirit-filled Elizabeth says about Mary, "Blessed is she who believed that there would be a fulfillment of what was spoken to her by the Lord" (1:45). The angel Gabriel has already assured Mary that "nothing will be impossible with God" (1:37). Nothing can prevent the unfolding of God's plan.

After the annunciations to Mary and Elizabeth, Mary travels to visit her cousin. Elizabeth, inspired by the Holy Spirit, rejoices, as does the baby in her womb, because she realizes that Jesus is the "Lord." This prompts Mary to utter her canticle of praise to God, usually called the Magnificat, from its first word in Latin. The Magnificat is similar to the hymn of praise by Hannah, the mother of the famous biblical figure Samuel in 1 Sam 2. The following table indicates the similarities.

Mary's Magnificat (Luke 1:46-55)	Hannah's Hymn (1 Sam 2:1-10)
1:46 And Mary said, / "My soul magnifies the Lord, / 1:47 and my spirit rejoices in God my Savior, / 1:48 for he has looked with favor on the lowliness of his servant. / Surely, from now on all generations will call me blessed; / 1:49 for the Mighty One has done great things for me, /	2:1 Hannah prayed and said, / "My heart exults in the LORD; / my strength is exalted in my God. / My mouth derides my enemies, / because I rejoice in my victory. /

and holy is his name. /
1:50 His mercy is for those
who fear him / from
generation to generation.
/ 1:51 He has shown
strength with his arm; /

he has scattered the
proud in the thoughts of
their hearts. /

1:52 He has brought
down the powerful from
their thrones, / and lifted
up the lowly; /

1:53 he has filled the
hungry with good things, /
and sent the rich away
empty. /

1:54 He has helped his
servant Israel, / in remembrance of his mercy, / 1:55
according to the promise he
made to our ancestors, / to
Abraham and to his descendants forever."

2:2 "There is no Holy One
like the LORD, / no one besides you;
/ there is no Rock like our God. /

2:3 Talk no more so very
proudly, / let not arrogance come
from your mouth; / for the LORD is
a God of knowledge, / and by him
actions are weighed. /

2:4 The bows of the mighty
are broken, / but the feeble gird on
strength.... 2:7 The LORD makes
poor and makes rich; / he brings
low, he also exalts. / 2:8 He
raises up the poor from the dust; /
he lifts the needy from the ash
heap, / to make them sit with
princes / and inherit a seat of
honor.

2:5a Those who were full
have hired themselves out for
bread, / but those who were
hungry are fat with spoil.

2:10 The LORD! His
adversaries shall be shattered; /
the Most High will thunder in
heaven. / The LORD will judge
the ends of the earth; / he will
give strength to his king, / and
exalt the power of his anointed."

2:5b The barren has borne
seven, / but she who has many

> children is forlorn. / 2:6 The
> LORD kills and brings to life; / he
> brings down to Sheol and raises
> up.... 2:8c For the pillars of the
> earth are the LORD's, / and on
> them he has set the world. / 2:9
> "He will guard the feet of his faith-
> ful ones, / but the wicked shall be
> cut off in darkness; / for not by
> might does one prevail."

As God acts in the Bible, so God acts in the time of fulfillment. Mary's hymn of thanksgiving and praise alludes to that of Hannah, many centuries before. And as God's previous activity, as extolled by Hannah, results in liberation for the oppressed poor and punishment for the powerful rich, so also does God's activity in Jesus bring good news for the poor and bad news for the rich and powerful. In the Gospel, readers will hear of Jesus' mission to the poor and his criticism of the rich and powerful. The canticle's words are the more compelling on the lips of Jesus' mother. Jesus speaks for himself when he begins his public career at the synagogue in Nazareth (4:14-21). His speech there asserts that his coming fulfills Isa 61, where the prophet is to announce the good news of liberation to the poor and oppressed. Jesus and Mary agree on the significance of Jesus' coming. That there are contacts between Mary's speech, which echoes Hannah, mother of the prophet Samuel, and that of Jesus, who speaks as a prophet, is natural. So even in the infancy narrative, Jesus is portrayed as a prophet, since his mother is like Samuel's mother.

Other themes emerge in the annunciations that pervade the infancy narrative and prepare for the Gospel. Fulfillment of God's promises brings joy, an echo of the joy Israel feels when Isaiah announces God's salvation. The angel informs Zechariah that John's birth will bring joy to the people (1:14). Elizabeth and the baby in her womb rejoice at Mary's visit (1:41, 44). Mary rejoices that God has chosen her as an agent for the fulfillment of the promises to Israel (1:46-48). Neighbors and relatives rejoice when John is born (1:58). Angels tell shepherds in the field that Jesus' birth is good news of great joy to all the people (2:10). The shepherds visit the baby and return rejoicing (2:20). The result of God's intervention in history to fulfill the divine promises is called "salvation" and "peace."

A major function of the Holy Spirit in the Bible is prophecy, a key category for Luke. Those with God's Spirit know God's plans and can announce them with authority. So the angel tells Zechariah that John the Baptist will be filled with the Holy Spirit and will exercise his prophetic office in the spirit and power of the prophet Elijah (1:15-17). Overshadowing by the Holy Spirit makes Mary pregnant with Jesus (1:35). When Mary visits Elizabeth, Elizabeth is filled with the Holy Spirit and so can recognize that Mary is carrying her "Lord," so she rejoices (1:41-45). Later, when Elizabeth gives birth to John, Zechariah is filled with the Holy Spirit and prophesies (1:67-79). Simeon the prophet announces what God is doing in Jesus. Luke mentions the Holy Spirit three times in three verses to indicate Simeon's inspiration (2:25-27). Simeon prophesies not just the fulfillment of God's promises in Jesus but the negative response of many in Israel to Jesus and to the extension of revelation to the Gentiles. Simeon echoes Isaiah's language (see Isa 40:5; 42:1).

Luke uses the same language as Isaiah to describe the results of God's action through Jesus. It is "salvation," and it brings liberation from enemies and peace. The proper reaction is joy. God is therefore Israel's "savior," as is Jesus. The fulfillment in these exuberant chapters is for Israel, and for the Gentiles only through Israel. This is precisely the sort of universalism we witness in Isaiah as well. It is not that fulfillment in Jesus supersedes Israel or that God has now decided to ignore God's special relationship with Israel in favor of a relationship with the whole human race. Luke–Acts continues the biblical story and can be properly understood only as such. Salvation therefore comes to the Gentiles through the Jews. The coming in of the Gentiles signifies not discontinuity, but fulfillment of what God promised through the prophets and is part of the fulfillment of God's promises to Israel itself.

It is proper that the fulfillment centers on Jerusalem and transpires among Torah-abiding Jews. Zechariah and Elizabeth are "righteous before God, living blamelessly according to all the commandments and regulations of the Lord" (1:6). Jesus' parents bring him to Jerusalem for purification rituals and for the sacrifice of the firstborn, which Luke asserts three times is in obedience to the Mosaic Torah (2:22-24, 27). Luke stresses the piety of the two prophets who recognize Jesus on behalf of Israel, Simeon and Anna (2:25, 37).

Having fulfilled the prescriptions of Torah, Jesus, Mary, and Joseph return to Nazareth. There, "the child grew and became strong, filled with wisdom; and the favor of God was upon him" (2:40).

The Boy Jesus in the Temple (2:41-51). Luke is unique among the canonical gospels in supplying a story about Jesus when he was twelve years old. Jesus makes the Passover pilgrimage to Jerusalem with his parents, but when they leave, he stays behind, unbeknownst to them. They return and find him in the temple engaged in discussion with the teachers "and all who heard him were amazed at his understanding and his answers" (2:47). Questioned by his parents, he says that he must be in his Father's house.

In the ancient world, such stories about the prodigiousness of famous people were common. We have a parallel in Josephus's somewhat immodest report of his own childhood: "While still a mere boy, about fourteen years old, I won universal applause for my love of letters; insomuch that the chief priests and the leading men of the city used constantly to come to me for precise information on some particulars of our ordinances" (*Life* 9).

Summary of Jesus' Childhood (2:52). The rest of Jesus' childhood is summarized with a single verse. Jesus grows in wisdom and in age, and he is approved of by humans and God alike.

PREPARATION FOR JESUS' PUBLIC MINISTRY (3:1–4:13)

This section contains John the Baptist's ministry, Jesus' baptism, Jesus' genealogy, and Jesus' temptation by Satan. The section begins by situating John's activity within world history. It is dated with reference to the Roman emperor Tiberius, the Roman governor of Judea, Pontius Pilate, Herodian rulers, the ruler of Abilene (a neighboring territory), and the high priest Caiaphas. This fits Luke's concern to have his work considered legitimate history.

3:1-22: John the Baptist and Jesus' Baptism. Luke follows Mark in applying Isa 40 to John the Baptist—he is the voice crying in the wilderness to prepare the way of the Lord (3:4-6)—but he does not end the quote where Mark does. Instead, he includes the words from the Greek version of Isa 40:5: "And all flesh shall see the salvation of God." Extending the citation allows Luke to include the word "salvation" for God's action and to stress its universal nature. Following Q, Luke's John rejects the conviction that being children of Abraham ensures salvation. Q material also reinforces apocalyptic elements in John's message (3:7-9,

17). Luke adds a section unique to him where John gives concrete moral instruction (3:10-14). It involves redistribution of goods and an end to financial oppression of the people by tax collectors and soldiers. This reflects the kind of concern for social justice that is central to the Gospel.

Luke makes small but significant changes to the story of Jesus' baptism (3:21-22). First, Jesus is praying, as he does before many important junctures in the story. This indicates his dependence on and subjection to God. Second, the Spirit descends on Jesus in "bodily" form, emphasizing the reality of the Spirit's role in Jesus' ministry. As in Mark, God speaks to Jesus in words that allude to Gen 22:2, Ps 2:7, and Isa 42:1, 44:2 designating him as Son and commissioning him for ministry.

3:23-38: Genealogy. Matthew's genealogy trumpets the fact that Jesus is son of David and son of Abraham. Luke includes this, and he extends the genealogy beyond Abraham all the way back to Adam, who is "son of God." The entire human race comes from God, and God cares for all humanity.

4:1-13: Jesus' Temptation. Like Matthew, Luke draws on Q for Jesus' temptation. He changes Q's order so that the third of the three temptations occurs in Jerusalem. Luke's redaction of this passage and the following one, Jesus' rejection in the Nazareth synagogue, emphasizes the Holy Spirit. In Mark 1:12, the Spirit "drives" Jesus to the desert, evoking the image of spirit possession. Luke rewrites this: "Jesus, full of the Holy Spirit, returned from the Jordan and was led by the Spirit in the wilderness" (4:1). Mark says nothing of the Spirit when Jesus begins his ministry, whereas Luke has, "Jesus, filled with the power of the Spirit, returned to Galilee ..." (4:14). The public ministry begins with Jesus quoting Isaiah to the effect that he has been "anointed" with the Spirit (4:18). The Spirit is now upon Jesus, the same Spirit who inspired the biblical prophets, all of whom predicted Jesus, and the Spirit who inspired Zechariah, Elizabeth, and Simeon in the infancy narrative. During his ministry, only Jesus is said to have the Spirit. He is the focus of God's activity in the world.

GALILEAN MINISTRY (4:14–9:50)

4:14-30: Rejection at Nazareth. A programmatic scene is one that tells us what is to happen. Luke presents such a scene in the synagogue of Nazareth, Jesus' hometown (4:14-30). He finds the episode in Mark 6, where it occurs well into Jesus' ministry, and makes it the first event, rewriting it extensively. (Remember that Mark has no infancy narrative and is just over fifteen chapters long, and that Jesus' public ministry in Galilee ends in ch. 8, so Mark locates the Nazareth scene well into Jesus' career.) In all of the Synoptics, the scene in Nazareth signifies Jesus' rejection by his own people, even his fellow villagers. Luke moves it to the beginning of the ministry because it is a paradigm for Jesus' rejection by the Jews and acceptance by the Gentiles. It is not unlikely that Jesus ran into opposition in Nazareth, but as the story reads in Luke, it is probably more an expression of his theology than of history.

Jesus enters the synagogue and is invited to read. He chooses a passage from Isaiah: "The Spirit of the Lord is upon me, / because he has anointed me to bring good news to the poor. / He has sent me to proclaim release to the captives / and recovery of sight to the blind, / to let the oppressed go free, / to proclaim the year of the Lord's favor" (quoting Isa 61:1-2, with an allusion to Isa 58:6). Jesus puts down the scroll, returns to his seat, and says, "Today this scripture has been fulfilled in your hearing" (4:21). The word *today* occurs several times elsewhere in the Gospel with the sense that God's liberating power is present here and now (5:26; 13:32-33; 19:9; 23:43).

Jesus proclaims the meaning of his mission. He applies to himself the prophet's self-description and so implies that he, too, is a prophet. The Bible often says that God's Spirit comes upon the prophets, but Isa 61 is the only biblical passage in which being commissioned as a prophet is equated with anointing (see Acts 10:38). Luke does not empty the title Messiah of royal content, but he associates it with prophecy. All of the Synoptics begin with the descent of God's Spirit on Jesus, but Luke emphasizes the role of the Spirit in Jesus' career and then in the life of the church. Luke repeats the connection between Spirit, messiahship, and miraculous power to exorcise and heal in Acts 10:38, where Paul proclaims "how God anointed Jesus of Nazareth with the Holy Spirit and with power; how he went about doing good and healing all who were oppressed by the devil, for God was with him." The Spirit in Luke–Acts is above all the Spirit of prophecy. When people receive the Spirit, they usually *speak*, often immediately. Since God's Spirit is upon him, Jesus can both speak and act for God. His first public act is to preach the good news, a prophetic act, reminiscent of Isaiah.

Prophets preach doom or salvation to the people. Jesus' message is "good news," but it is good news to the poor. Throughout Luke, Jesus criticizes social and economic inequities. Release for captives may mean freeing those in prison for debts. Jesus, following the Greek version of Isaiah, also speaks of blindness and oppression. As God's liberating agent, Jesus performs physical cures. Luke imports the element of "oppression" from Isa 58:6 where it refers to social oppression resulting from economic disparities. Finally, Jesus proclaims "the year of the Lord's favor." This refers to the Jubilee Year. In the Jubilee Year, celebrated every fiftieth year, the land was given rest from planting, debts were forgiven, and Israelites freed slaves who were fellow Israelites. The Greek word used for "release" of the captives and making the oppressed "free" (*aphesis*) appears in the Greek Bible in Lev 25:10 in connection with the Jubilee Year, where the land and its inhabitants receive "release." It is a word that in both Testaments of the Christian Bible means forgiveness.

Isaiah's message was not just for Israel, but for the nations. The same holds for Jesus. When the synagogue congregation acclaims him for the power of his words, Jesus says, "No prophet is accepted in the prophet's hometown" (4:24), and he states that Elijah and Elisha aided Gentiles, not Jews. The people want to kill him, but he escapes miraculously. The meaning of this scene is that although Israel might initially accept Jesus, it will soon reject and kill him.

4:31-37: Exorcism. Luke follows Mark in narrating an exorcism in Capernaum's synagogue. As in Mark, it indicates Jesus' attack on demons, his authority in teaching, and his spreading fame.

4:38-39: Cure of Peter's Mother-in-Law. In Mark "they told him about her," while in Luke "they asked him about her." This enhances Jesus' knowledge. Only in Luke does Jesus "rebuke" the fever, treating it like a demon.

4:40-41: Summary. Luke's summary is similar to Mark 1:32-34. He retains Mark's notice that Jesus would not permit the demons to speak because they knew him. Generally, Luke does not subscribe to the messianic secret, but here it underscores what the demons know. He adds that they shout, "You are the Son of God," and that Jesus does not permit them to reveal that he is the "Messiah."

4:42-44: Departure from Capernaum. As in Mark, Jesus tells Peter that he must move on. While Mark's Jesus says that he must "proclaim the message" elsewhere, whereas Luke's is more specific: "I must proclaim the good news of the kingdom of God."

5:1-11: Call of the First Disciples. Mark distrusts miracles as a foundation for faith. When Jesus calls the first disciples in Mark, they immediately leave their former lives and follow him. No motivation is explicit. In Luke, Jesus encounters the future disciples after they have spent a fruitless night fishing. He instructs them to lower their nets again, and they haul in a miraculously large catch (cf. John 21:4-8). Peter throws himself at Jesus' feet, acknowledging Jesus' lordship and his own sinfulness. Jesus then enlists them as followers and says that from now on they "will be catching people." Where Mark considers Jesus' miracles potentially misleading, Luke confidently portrays Jesus as the sort of wonderworker who would attract many in the Hellenistic world.

5:12-16: Cleansing a Leper. Luke retains the idea that Jesus' fame spreads without saying that it was the cured leper who does it, thus avoiding the element of disobedience in Mark 1:45. Luke turns this into a summary, where crowds flock to him "to hear him and be cured of their diseases." He avoids the impression created by Mark, that crowds come to Jesus just to be cured. They also wish to "hear him." Typical of Luke is the following: "He would withdraw to deserted places and pray" (5:16).

5:17-26: Cure of a Paralytic. As in Mark, this story combines healing with forgiveness of sin. Luke's introduction is noteworthy: "One day, while he was teaching, Pharisees and teachers of the law were sitting near by (they had come from every village of Galilee and Judea and from Jerusalem); and the power of the Lord was with him to heal" (5:17). This places the following story in a much richer context than in either Mark or Matthew. Teaching and healing are explicitly connected. The source of Jesus' power is clear.

5:27-39: Fellowship and Fasting. As in Mark, Jesus associates with the "wrong" people and does so for the same reason—he has come not for the "righteous" but to call sinners to repentance. Jesus' position on fasting here is the same as in Mark—it is inappropriate while he is present, but the church will fast later. Only Luke ends with the saying, "No one after drinking old wine desires new wine, but says, 'The old is good.' " Luke is preoccupied with people's failure to accept Jesus. They are too comfortable in their "old" ways. Repentance is a major theme in Luke and Acts. The Greek word for "repentance" is *metanoia*, which literally means a change of mind or thinking. To repent is to see the world in a new way, to leave one's old assumptions behind. Luke and Acts demonstrate the richness of what that means for Luke.

6:1-11: Controversy over the Sabbath. As in Mark, Jesus insists that human need overcomes Sabbath rules about work.

6:12-16: Call of the Twelve. Luke adds that Jesus spends the night in prayer before calling his disciples.

6:17-49: The Sermon on the Plain. Q contains a short sermon by Jesus that supplies the core of both Matthew's Sermon on the Mount and Luke's Sermon on the Plain. Luke's sermon, fashioned from this section of Q, is much shorter than Matthew's. Both begin with the Beatitudes. Matthew has nine, while Luke has only four. To these Luke adds four woes. In Matthew, the Beatitudes are in the third person, but Luke's Jesus addresses them directly to his disciples. Matthew's Jesus blesses those who hunger and thirst for righteousness and whose poverty is spiritual. Luke's Jesus focuses squarely on concrete economic circumstances. Jesus' disciples are the poor, hungry, and those who weep. They suffer as did the prophets before them. Luke adds woes that describe economic circumstances. He pronounces woe on the rich, the full, and those who laugh. They enjoy approval as did the false prophets.

The rest of the discourse expresses a radical ethic of love of enemies, nonresistance to oppression, following the golden rule, mercy, being nonjudgmental, and producing good works.

7:1-10: Cure of the Centurion's Servant. A centurion, a Gentile, wants Jesus to cure his servant. The story is from Q. In Luke's version, Jewish elders mediate, asking Jesus to grant the request, saying, "He is worthy of having you do this for him, for he loves our people, and it is he who built our synagogue for us" (7:5). There were Gentiles in the ancient world who admired Judaism. Some even worshiped the Jewish God, though they did not convert. These are sometimes called "God-fearers," and Acts presents them as ripe for Christian proselytism.

7:11-17: Raising a Widow's Son. The next episode is unique to Luke. Jesus raises a widow's only son. This echoes a similar action by the prophet Elijah (1 Kgs 17). In response, the people proclaim, "A great prophet has risen among us," and, "God has looked favorably on his people" (7:16). Although they do not know Jesus' full identity, they are not wrong. Jesus is for Luke a great prophet, and his presence indicates that this is indeed "the year of the Lord's favor" (4:19, quoting Isa 61).

7:18-35: Jesus and John the Baptist. Luke, like Matthew, incorporates a body of material from Q in which John sends disciples to question Jesus about his activities. This presents an opportunity for Jesus to praise John, yet to claim that God's action has now entered a new phase: "The least in the kingdom of God is greater than he" (7:28).

Luke adds a section not present in Matthew: "And all the people who heard this, including the tax collectors, acknowledged the justice of God, because they had been baptized with John's baptism. But by refusing to be baptized by him, the Pharisees and the lawyers rejected God's purpose for themselves" (7:29-30; cf. Matt 21:32). The word for "purpose" or "plan" of God (Greek: *boule*) does not occur in the other Gospels. In Luke, it occurs here and in 23:51, where it denotes the Jerusalem leaders' evil plan against Jesus. This usage carries into Acts. There the word designates God's plan four times (2:23; 5:38; 13:36; 20:27) and human plans opposing those of God one time (4:28). To reject God's plan for the world is to reject salvation.

7:36-50: Forgiveness of a Sinful Woman. A sinful woman approaches Jesus at dinner in a Pharisee's house and washes his feet with her tears, dries them with her hair, and anoints his feet with oil. The Pharisee is scandalized and is sure that Jesus cannot be a great prophet since he obviously does not know that this woman is a great sinner. Otherwise, he would not let her touch him. Jesus responds with a parable whose point is that the one forgiven more loves more. This woman loves God more than the Pharisee, who supposedly has less to be forgiven. When Jesus allows himself to be touched by a sinful woman, it does not prove he is not a prophet. It proves the opposite. It is as God's prophet that Jesus forgives the woman and pronounces her closer to God than the Pharisee. This story may derive from the one in Mark 14:3-9. We discuss below the significance of Luke's changes for women.

8:1-3: Women Disciples. Immediately after this story, Luke notes that there were women among Jesus' disciples, and he gives three of their names—Mary of Magdala, Joanna the wife of Herod's steward, and Susanna (8:1-3). These provide for the disciples out of their resources.

8:4-15: Parable of the Sower. Luke does not have a parable chapter, as do Mark and Matthew. His parables appear throughout the Gospel. Luke's additions to this parable improve style and make some clarifications. The "word" sown becomes the "word of God" (8:11). Satan takes away the word "so that they may not believe and be saved" (8:12).

8:16-18: Sayings on Discipleship. Luke reproduces several parabolic sayings on discipleship from Mark.

8:19-21: Jesus' True Family. Luke rewrites Jesus' words about his true family to remove the implicit criticism of his biological family. In Mark, when Jesus hears that his family is outside asking for him, he says, "Who are my mother and my brothers?" He then looks at those gathered around him and says, "Here are my mother and my brothers!" (Mark 3:31-35). Luke removes these words. Told that his family is seeking him, Jesus says merely, "My mother and brothers are those who hear the word of God and do it" (8:21). Mark sets up a parallel between the family standing "outside" and those "outside" who cannot receive the secret of the kingdom. Luke breaks the parallel. When Luke tells the story of Jesus being accused of casting out demons by Beelzebul's power, he omits that some think Jesus insane and that for this reason his family seeks to seize him (Luke 11:14-15).

Luke presents a very positive view of Jesus' mother. In the infancy narrative she delivers a definitive commentary on God's action in Jesus (1:46-55). At the beginning of Acts of the Apostles, she and Jesus' brothers are with the apostles and other disciples in Jerusalem and receive the Spirit along with them (1:14). Jesus' brother James is also a positive figure. He leads the Jerusalem church and makes the momentous decision allowing Gentiles into the church without being subject to Torah (Acts 15). For Luke, Jesus' family are disciples.

In addition to these changes, Luke adds "hear the word of God" to the idea of doing God's will (8:21). Hearing the word of God is a theme in the Gospel and in Acts.

8:22-25: Calming the Storm. Luke makes minor changes. He removes any idea that the disciples accuse Jesus of not caring about their plight. He does not have Jesus accusing them of having "no faith." Rather, Jesus simply asks them where their faith is.

8:26-39: The Gerasene Demoniac. The story is essentially the same as in Mark.

8:40-56: Woman Healed and Girl Raised. Luke makes only minor changes to these intertwined stories that he finds in Mark. Unlike Matthew, Luke sees no problem with power flowing from Jesus when the woman touches him, but Jesus knows that someone has accessed his power: "I noticed that power had gone out from me." Then the woman declares "in the presence of all the people" that she was cured. The word for "people" here is a favorite of Luke (Greek: *laos*). It can carry the connotation of God's people. The woman's testimony is therefore to all Israel.

9:1-6: The Mission of the Twelve. Mark 6:7 says that Jesus gave his disciples authority to cast out demons. Luke adds that Jesus gave them "power." These two words—authority and power—repeatedly characterize Jesus' exorcisms and healings (4:36; 5:17; 6:19; 8:46). The disciples share in Jesus' ministry. They go out and cure diseases "everywhere," an adverb added by Luke. Luke adds that they are to proclaim "the kingdom of God."

9:7-9: Herod. Luke omits the story of John's beheading from Mark 6 but retains the idea that Herod is interested in Jesus. Luke's Herod realizes that Jesus is not John. Herod tries to see Jesus but apparently fails. He will interview Jesus later, during the passion.

9:10-17: Feeding the Five Thousand. Mark and Matthew have two feedings; Luke has but one. He omits all of Mark 6:45–8:26, a section that contains the second feeding. In Luke, the feeding occurs in the town of Bethsaida, not in the wilderness. Perhaps this has to do with public witness to Israel. While in Mark it is "the disciples" who are with Jesus and help him, in Luke it is "the twelve." Luke is especially concerned for the institution of the Twelve, for he considers it a firm foundation for the church as well as an important symbol of continuity between Israel and Christianity. In Acts, the first action of the eleven is to elect someone to take Judas's place.

9:18-36: Peter's Confession and the Transfiguration. Luke makes important revisions to Peter's confession. First, Peter does not rebuke Jesus for his teaching about his passion, and Jesus never calls Peter "Satan." Second, Jesus says that the disciples must take up their crosses "daily." He turns the cross, taken literally in Mark, into a symbol for Christian life. The numerous ways in which one may suffer in Christian discipleship (forgoing the privilege of riches, taking the risk of family problems caused by discipleship, dedication to mission, and so on), along with the many ways in which humans suffer (poverty, oppression, sickness) may all be what Luke has in mind. Third, at the transfiguration, Luke has God call Jesus "my Son, my Chosen," language from Isaiah, where "chosen" applies both to the prophet and to Israel.

Fourth, only Luke tells us that Elijah and Moses "were speaking of his departure, which he was about to accomplish at Jerusalem" (9:31). The Greek word for "departure" here is *exodus*, an allusion to God's rescue of Israel from Egypt. Here it refers to the death, resurrection, and ascension of Jesus, by means of which he travels to God in heaven, the ultimate goal of Jesus' impending journey. There is irony in the fact that the original exodus was from slavery in Egypt and Israel's ultimate goal was Jerusalem, while Jesus' exodus is from Jerusalem itself. Ultimately the church takes the message from Jerusalem to Rome and the Romans destroy Jerusalem because it did not receive Jesus as God's prophet.

Luke omits the conversation between Jesus and the disciples that transpires in Mark immediately after the transfiguration. That conversation identifies John the Baptist as Elijah, implicitly in Mark and explicitly in

Matthew. For Luke, John accomplishes his ministry in the spirit of Elijah, but Elijah influences aspects of Jesus' career, too, so Luke does not want the identification to be univocal. The omission also removes the disciples' failure to understand resurrection.

9:37-43a: Exorcism of a Boy. Luke abbreviates this episode, and he removes Jesus' instruction of the disciples concerning the proper way to expel the demon. Jesus bemoans the faithlessness of the present generation and performs the exorcism. "And all were astounded at the greatness of God." Emphasis is on the amazing power of God at work in Jesus.

9:43b-45: Second Passion Prediction. As in Mark, the disciples do not understand, but Luke exonerates them: "Its meaning was concealed from them, so that they could not perceive it."

9:46-50: Failings of the Disciples. Jesus' disciples argue over who is the greatest. Luke's Jesus is miraculously "aware of their inner thoughts" and exhorts them to humility. He stops them from hindering those outside their group who exorcise in Jesus' name.

JOURNEY TO JERUSALEM (9:51–19:27)

Most of the material in this section derives from Q and L. Luke depends on Mark in only a few instances. The section is not highly structured, so after we treat the beginning of the journey and the journey theme in general, we examine the section thematically.

Beginning of the Journey (9:51-56). Luke begins his account of Jesus' journey with a passage unique to him, perhaps of his own creation. The journey is announced solemnly: "When the days drew near for him to be taken up, he set his face to go to Jerusalem" (9:51). Only in Luke is Jesus "taken up" into heaven (24:51; Acts 1:2, 11, 22). The expression "set his face to go" is as strange in Greek as in English. It conveys Jesus' strength of purpose and invites the reader to see the entire journey in the light of its goal.

Samaritan villagers do not want Jesus and his companions to pass through their region since they are headed to Jerusalem. There was often tension between the Samaritans and the Jews. Jesus' disciples ask whether they should call down fire from heaven on the village. This recalls Elijah calling down fire on the soldiers of the king in 2 Kgs 1:10. Jesus declines and they circumvent the village. Jesus' disciples misunderstand. Jesus is indeed like Elijah and Elisha, but concerning such things as the raising of the widow's son, not destruction of enemies.

The Journey Continues. There are reminders in subsequent chapters that Jesus is on his way to Jerusalem. The most important indication is 13:31-35. Pharisees tell Jesus that Herod is after him. Jesus says he will carry on his ministry of exorcism and healing, and that he must continue his journey, "because it is impossible for a prophet to be killed outside of Jerusalem." In a prophetic pronouncement against Jerusalem, he calls it "the city that kills the prophets." For him, God's ultimate chosen prophet is Jesus, and his death in Jerusalem testifies to his prophetic status.

Other indications that Jesus and his disciples are on a journey are 9:57; 10:1; 13:22; 14:25; 17:11; 18:31, 35; 19:1, 11, 28. Jerusalem is specifically mentioned as the journey's goal in 9:51; 13:22; 17:11; 18:31; and 19:11, 28.

Material from L

Economics and Social Justice. A quick inventory of the L material from the journey narrative reveals Luke's interests. One theme is Luke's attention to what we call economics. In ancient society there was no middle class as we know it. Those whom we might consider middle class were retainers. That is, their reason for existence was to serve and support the ruling class and upper class. This description covers groups such as certain levels of scribes, soldiers, and artisans. The upper classes were small and the lower classes, who struggled, often at a subsistence level, were large.

The parable of the rich fool (12:13-21) demonstrates the foolishness of dedicating one's life to acquiring material things. To use a modern proverb, "You can't take it with you." In chapter 14, Jesus counsels inviting the poor, maimed, blind, and lame to dinner rather than those who can repay the invitation. The chapter also contains Luke's version of the parable of the Great Banquet, symbolizing the kingdom of God. Only in Luke's version are the invited guests replaced by the poor, lame, blind, and maimed (cf. Matt 22:1-14). In 16:14-15, Jesus condemns the Pharisees for their love of money. Luke follows this with the parable of the Rich Man and Lazarus where the rich man goes to hell and the poor Lazarus to heaven (16:19-31). Finally, toward the end of the journey, Jesus encounters the rich tax collector Zacchaeus (19:1-10). The reader expects Zacchaeus's condemnation, because he is rich. Instead, Jesus approves of him because he gives half of his possessions to the poor and restores fourfold what he has taken unjustly.

Samaritans. Luke has a special place for Samaritans. It is in this section of the Gospel that we read the parable of the Good Samaritan

(10:25-37). In chapter 1, we offered the Good Samaritan as an example of the shocking nature of Jesus' parables—Jesus, a Jew, tells a story to his fellow Jews in which a priest and a Levite are presented in a negative light, being unwilling to help a man who has been attacked and injured, while a Samaritan comes to his aid. Samaritans and Jews often did not have good relations, and, indeed, the travel narrative begins with the Samaritans wishing to prevent Jesus and his disciples from passing through their territory, since they are Jews on the way to Jerusalem to celebrate Passover (9:51-56). Jesus calls on people to reevaluate their ideas of who is good and bad, to change their way of thinking, to open themselves to see things as God does.

We also hear in Luke's travel narrative of ten lepers cured by Jesus, of whom one was a Samaritan (17:11-19). Only the Samaritan returns and offers Jesus thanks, and Jesus remarks on that and contrasts him with the others, who did not return to thank him. In Acts of the Apostles, Luke describes early Christian missionary activity in Samaria (Acts 1:8; 8:1-14; 9:31; 10:15).

Women. Women also receive attention in these chapters. Here we find the story of Martha and Mary, both close friends of Jesus, to be examined below (10:38-42). To the parable of the Lost Sheep, found in Q, Luke adds that of the Lost Coin, where a woman is a model for God who drops everything to find the lost (15:3-10).

Forgiveness. The leaders do not receive forgiveness, for they do not think they need it. The parables of the Lost Sheep and the Lost Coin illustrate God's desire to bring back those who have strayed (15:3-10). The Prodigal Son exhibits God's eagerness to forgive even those who do not particularly deserve it (15:11-32). The parable of the Pharisee and the Tax Collector demonstrates that God values true repentance more than religious observance, especially if observance is coupled with self-satisfaction and judgment of others (18:9-14).

Discipleship. The story of Martha and Mary shows that the one necessary thing is listening to Jesus' teaching (10:38-42). A couple of parables—the Friend at Midnight and the Unjust Judge—teach perseverance in prayer (11:1-8; 18:1-8). Jesus warns his disciples not to rejoice in their power to heal and exorcise but rather to look forward to their heavenly reward (10:17-20).

The parable of the Master Serving Table and the parable of the Slave's Wages (17:7-10) make two complementary points—disciples who serve God simply do their duty and merit no special reward, and Jesus models this by being servant to all. Another parable compares discipleship to servanthood or even slavery in warning that one must always attend to one's duty, for one never knows when the accounting will come due (12:47-48). Christian discipleship is hard, and the parables of the Builder and the King Going to War warn that one should take stock to determine whether one is prepared to pay the price (14:28-33). The parable of the Unjust Steward, long a puzzle to the church because Jesus praises the steward's dishonest actions, teaches the necessity of action (16:1-8). Jesus contrasts the purposeful and effective action of those who pursue worldly goals with the less energetic actions of those whose goals are heavenly. All of these passages show that although Luke's Jesus presents a God who is almost limitless in forgiveness, and from whom come liberation and healing, God makes great demands and will ultimately demand an accounting.

Material from Q

Luke's choice of Q material to include in the journey narrative is in harmony with the L material surveyed above. The cost of discipleship comes through in the sayings about the Son of Man having nowhere to lay his head and about not taking time to bury one's father before following him (9:57-60). To these Luke adds that one may not even take leave of one's family, for "no one who puts a hand to the plow and looks back is fit for the kingdom of God" (9:62). The demands of discipleship are radical.

In chapter 10, Jesus sends the disciples on a mission, as in Matt 10 and Mark 6. Mark's version is short; Matthew and Luke flesh it out with Q material describing an itinerant mission like Jesus' ministry. Luke's Twelve have already gone on a mission in chapter 9, and in chapter 10 he says Jesus sends out seventy. Some speculate that the missions symbolize the mission to Israel (twelve tribes) and to the nations (seventy nations, Gen 10). That fits the overall scheme of Luke–Acts, where the message of salvation comes first to the Jews and then to the Gentiles.

Disciples must be fearless in preaching, disregarding danger (12:2-12). They are to trust God's care for them and relinquish all care for themselves (12:22-34). Disciples will not only suffer persecution but will experience trouble with family because of their discipleship (12:49-56; 14:53). Entering God's kingdom is like going through a narrow door, and many do not get through (13:22-30). The demands on the disciples are great, but they are blessed because of what they see (10:23-24). The disciples are taught the Lord's Prayer (11:1-4) and assured that their prayers will be effective (11:9-13). Jesus insists on the importance of being in the light rather than in darkness (11:33-36). The Son of Man will come unexpectedly as judge, and disciples must be ready (17:22-37). They must use the intervening time to bear fruit, as the parable of the Pounds illustrates (19:11-27).

Material from Mark

Luke uses little material from Mark to construct his journey narrative. He does include Jesus' assertion that loving God and loving neighbor are the most important commandments in Torah (10:25-28). Jesus' exorcisms symbolize the inauguration of God's kingdom, and one must side with Jesus in the battle with Satan (11:14-23). Disciples can be sure that although they are a seemingly powerless and oppressed minority now, the kingdom will grow as a mustard seed or as leaven in bread (13:18-21). Christians must not scandalize "little ones" (17:1-2), and children are models, for they occupy the bottom of society's hierarchy (18:15-17). Disciples must give up all possessions to follow Jesus (18:18-30). Luke finishes the journey with the same elements found in Mark as Jesus approaches Jerusalem. He cures the blind man at Jericho (18:35-43), and he enters Jerusalem riding on a donkey (19:28-38).

General Characterization of Material Included in the Journey to Jerusalem

Most of what is in the journey to Jerusalem relates to Jesus' teachings on discipleship and on proper conduct in general, what we might call ethics. Within that context, Luke lays emphasis on both God's forgiveness and God's demands. He criticizes religious leaders, too. He is especially interested in issues of social justice and in Jesus' approach to the poor and marginalized of society. By "marginalized" we mean those who are in some sense on the edges of society, particularly as concerns power, economic, and social relations. For Luke, the poor have been marginalized, for they are oppressed by a society in which they have little say and little ability to improve their lot, since the wealthy have a powerful interest in the status quo. Women, although we now know that they participated in positions of power and influence more than was once thought, do not have the same access to such positions as do men, and for many of them their social place is still determined to some degree by their gender. Samaritans were marginal in Jewish society (just as Jews were marginal in

Samaritan society—see the episode in 9:51-56). Lepers were marginal, since their affliction isolated them socially and ritually.

MINISTRY IN JERUSALEM (19:28–21:38)

Approach to and Lament over Jerusalem (19:28-44). In all of the Gospels, Jesus enters Jerusalem riding on a donkey (an allusion to Zech 9:9), with the crowds acclaiming him. Only in Luke do the Pharisees intervene as the crowds come near Jerusalem, ordering Jesus to stop them. Ironically, they wish to prevent the crowd from recognizing Jesus as the fulfillment of Israel's hopes. But for Luke, nothing can stop God's purpose. Jesus says that if the crowd were to be silent, the very stones would cry out.

As he nears the city, Jesus utters a lament over it unique to Luke (19:41-44). He weeps, saying, "If you, even you, had only recognized on this day the things that make for peace!" "Peace" recalls the Hebrew *shalom*, the state of being right with God and with the world, and of having the entire universe be as God intended. Luke implicitly challenges the emperor Augustus's boast that he brought peace to the world and the Roman claim that only under their rule is peace possible. "Peace" echoes God's promise to Israel through Isaiah, especially Second Isaiah (52:7; 54:10; 55:12). And it brings to mind the way the Gospel begins, as Zechariah and Mary extol God for fulfilling the divine promises to Israel and bestowing peace upon it. Jerusalem has not recognized the things that make for peace. So Jesus foretells its destruction. The details of the prediction are sufficient to convince many that Luke writes with hindsight. The world has already seen Jerusalem's destruction at the hands of the Romans. This has happened, for Luke, because Jerusalem "did not recognize the time of (its) visitation from God."

In 70 C.E., in the midst of a Jewish revolution, the Romans took the city, did it great damage, destroyed its temple, killed great numbers of men, women, and children, and sold many into slavery. The horror of the event was overwhelming. The thought that all this happened because God was punishing Israel for not accepting Jesus as Messiah is a terrible judgment and depicts God in stern, almost vindictive tones. Only recently have Christians begun to reconsider and regret such condemnation of Israel.

In all three Synoptic Gospels, Jesus drives the money changers and animal merchants out of the temple. The priestly authorities begin to look for a way to kill him. They are hesitant because, as Mark says, "The whole crowd was spellbound by his teaching" (11:18). Luke moves the notice about teaching deeper into the passage so that it follows immediately on Jesus' action and precedes the priestly plot. He says, "Every day he was teaching in the temple"

(19:47). Luke retains Mark's comment about the crowd being "spellbound" and changes "the whole crowd" to "all the people *(laos)*," a word used for Israel in the Bible (19:48). He makes the same change in 20:6. Luke's subtle changes highlight the importance of Jesus' teaching Israel in the temple and make it more central to why the priests plot against him.

Later, the Jerusalem authorities confront Jesus in the temple. Mark says Jesus was "walking" there, while Luke has, "He was teaching the people in the temple and telling the good news" (20:1). At the end of the apocalyptic discourse, just before Luke begins the passion narrative, he adds, "Every day he was teaching in the temple, and at night he would go out to the Mount of Olives, as it was called. And all the people would get up early to listen to him in the temple" (21:37-38). Luke's temple scenes at the end of the Gospel form a frame with the scene when Jesus was twelve years old, sitting in the temple, discussing religious matters with teachers, amazing them with his understanding (2:41-51).

Much about these chapters is close to Mark, but Luke provides a few important touches in addition to the ones we have noted. Jesus' enemies try to trap him with the question about paying taxes to Caesar (20:20-26). Luke adds, "So as to hand him over to the jurisdiction and authority of the governor." Luke references Roman power in legal tones. Luke adds, "They were not able in the presence of the people to trap him by what he said" (20:26).

PASSION NARRATIVE (22:1–23:56)

22:1-6: Introduction. Mark's Passion Narrative begins with the story of the woman who anoints Jesus, an anointing he interprets as preparation for his burial. Luke transfers this story to early in the ministry and changes it into a lesson of God's forgiveness (7:36-50). Luke begins his Passion Narrative with a note that Judas was conspiring with the authorities to betray Jesus. The other Synoptics have this, but only Luke says that this happens after Satan enters Judas.

22:7-38: Last Supper. There are important differences from Mark in Luke's Last Supper. One involves the institution of the Eucharist. In Matthew and Mark, Jesus speaks over the bread and gives it to his disciples, and then he does the same with the wine. In Luke, there are two cups of wine, one before the bread and one after it. Perhaps because of this difference, some textual difficulties developed in the tradition. The best manuscripts (those most likely to preserve the most original readings) have the sequence cup-bread-cup. Some textual witnesses, particularly what is called the Western tradition, leave out verses 19*b*-20. The following table lays out the major differences, passing over minor discrepancies in word order.

Textual Criticism at Work—The Eucharist

Mark 14:22-25	Best Witnesses (Luke 22:15-20)	Western Text (Luke 22:15-19)
14:22 While they were eating, he took a loaf of bread, and after blessing it he broke it, gave it to them, and said, "Take; this is my body." 14:23 Then he took a cup, and after giving thanks he gave it to them, and all of them drank from it. 14:24 He said to them, "This is my blood of the covenant, which is poured out for many. 14:25 Truly I tell you, I will never again drink of the fruit of the vine until that day when I drink it new in the kingdom of God."	22:15 He said to them, "I have eagerly desired to eat this Passover with you before I suffer; 22:16 for I tell you, I will not eat it until it is fulfilled in the kingdom of God." 22:17 Then he took a cup, and after giving thanks he said, "Take this and divide it among yourselves; 22:18 for I tell you that from now on I will not drink of the fruit of the vine until the kingdom of God comes." 22:19 Then he took a loaf of bread, and when he had given thanks, he broke it and gave it to them, saying, "This is my body, which is given for you. Do this in remembrance of me. 22:20 And he did the same with the cup after supper, saying, "This cup that is poured out for you is the new covenant in my blood."	22:15 He said to them, "I have eagerly desired to eat this Passover with you before I suffer; 22:16 for I tell you, I will not eat it until it is fulfilled in the kingdom of God." 22:17 Then he took a cup, and after giving thanks he said, "Take this and divide it among yourselves; 22:18 for I tell you that from now on I will not drink of the fruit of the vine until the kingdom of God comes." 22:19 Then he took a loaf of bread, and when he had given thanks, he broke it and gave it to them, saying, "This is my body."

The omission of "for you" with respect to the body and the complete omission of the second cup can be seen as depriving the passage of elements for interpreting Jesus' death as salvific. Earlier in the Gospel, Luke omits words Mark attributes to Jesus: "The Son of Man came not to be served but to serve, and to give his life a ransom for many" (10:45). Did a scribe add the second cup as well as the additional words over the bread to bring Luke's account into conformity with Mark and Matthew? The fact that the best manuscripts have the longer version suggests a different solution. Perhaps scribes wished to conform Luke to the simpler bread-cup sequence in the other Synoptics. This is a passage that attests to the importance of textual criticism. Before we can interpret a text, we must decide on just what the text is.

In each Gospel, Jesus foretells Peter's betrayal. In conformity with his tendency to improve the image of the disciples, Luke has Jesus tell Peter about this gently. Jesus says Peter will be able, from his experience, to strengthen his fellow disciples (22:31-34). Luke adds Jesus' words to the effect that although he told his disciples to pursue their mission with no purse or sandals while Jesus was alive, they must now bring both, and that they must buy swords as well (22:36). This makes Christians more "real-istic" than they perceive Jesus to have been. Jesus also predicts that he will be "counted among the lawless," in fulfillment of Isa 53:12, one of the passages about the Isaian suffering servant. (See the section below on Isaiah's influence on Luke–Acts.)

22:39-53: Gethsemane. Some manuscripts of Luke have Jesus sweating blood in Gethsemane (22:43-44). This scene was not originally part of the Gospel, judging by the best manuscripts. The passage does not really fit Luke's portrait of Jesus, in any case. While Mark emphasizes Jesus' suffering and feeling "abandoned" by God, Luke is different. Jesus is always calm and in control. As a prophet, he knows full well what must happen and it does not overwhelm him. Luke omits Mark's description of Jesus as distressed and agitated: "I am deeply grieved, even to death" (Mark 14:33-34). Luke's portrayal of Jesus' noble death draws on pictures of righteous martyrs, both inside Judaism (for example, 2 Macc 7) and in the broader Hellenistic world (see Seeley).

In Mark, the disciples fall asleep three times when Jesus goes to pray. Jesus grows frustrated and blames them. Luke softens this. He comes to the disciples but once, and he "found them sleeping because of grief" (22:45). Why they should be so grief-stricken is unclear. Jesus has pre-dicted his betrayal and death, but they do not seem to have understood, and, if they are so concerned, one would think that they would stay awake with Jesus. So Luke's version is awkward. His interest in improving the picture of the disciples overrides his concern for a smooth narrative.

When a crowd comes to arrest Jesus, a disciple attacks one of them and cuts off his ear. Only in Luke does Jesus pick up the ear and heal the man. Jesus is ever the healer, ever in control. In Matthew and Mark, the temple authorities send a crowd to arrest him. In Luke, the officials of the temple come themselves, thus making the confrontation between God's prophet and those in charge of the temple more direct. He says to them, "This is your hour, and the power of darkness." This is Luke's addition, and it recalls Satan entering into Judas earlier. The temple establishment arrays itself on Satan's side when God sends his prophet to defeat Satan and declare the people's liberation. Jerusalem's religious authorities make a tragic choice.

22:54-71: Jesus before the Sanhedrin. In the trial before the Sanhedrin in Mark and Matthew, the high priest alone questions Jesus. Luke claims that all present ask Jesus whether he is the Son of God (22:70). The entire temple establishment is complicit in Jesus' death.

23:1-5: Jesus before Pilate. Luke changes the trial before Pilate significantly. The charge against Jesus is overtly political: "We found this man perverting our nation, forbidding us to pay taxes to the emperor, and saying that he himself is the Messiah, a king" (23:1). Luke presents an accusation that no Roman administrator could ignore. The Romans had a vested interest in stability. Anyone disturbing the tranquility of a province was an enemy of the Roman order. Jesus' detractors go further. He not only threatens Rome by perverting the nation, he attacks Rome directly by telling others not to pay Roman taxes. A generation before Jesus' trial, Judah the Galilean led a tax revolt against Rome and was executed. Finally, Jesus' accusers translate "Messiah" for the Gentile Pilate in political terms, ones that he cannot mistake.

Pilate asks Jesus one question: "Are you the king of the Jews?" Jesus offers an ambiguous answer: "You say so." Pilate takes this to indicate Jesus' innocence of any charge worthy of Roman punishment: "I find no basis for an accusation against this man."

The accusers persist, charging, "He stirs up the people by teaching throughout all Judea, from Galilee where he began even to this place." Luke reminds us that Jesus' ministry began in Galilee and brought him to Jerusalem. Again, the word Luke uses for "people" calls to mind the covenant relationship between God and Israel.

23:6-12: Jesus before Herod. Pilate seizes on the mention of Galilee as a pretext to send Jesus to Herod Antipas, who is in Jerusalem for Passover. Herod's interest in Jesus is superficial. He hopes to see a miracle but is disappointed. The chief priests and scribes accuse Jesus before Herod, but Herod does not pronounce a verdict on Jesus. Herod sends Jesus back to Pilate, and Luke says, "That same day Herod and Pilate became friends with each other; before this they had been enemies" (23:12). In the other Gospels, Roman soldiers mock Jesus, ridiculing the notion that he is a king (they dress him in a crown of thorns and a royal robe) and a prophet (they strike him and demand that he prophesy). Luke, perhaps because he is offended by the mocking of Jesus' royal and prophetic roles, omits these details. Such a scene would also clash with the idea that Pilate considers Jesus innocent of the charges brought against him. Luke simply has Herod's soldiers mock Jesus and put an elegant robe on him.

23:13-25: Jesus Sentenced to Death. When Jesus appears before Pilate again, Pilate again declares him innocent. He does so solemnly.

> Pilate then called together the chief priests, the leaders, and the people, and said to them, "You brought me this man as one who was perverting the people; and here I have examined him in your presence and have not found this man guilty of any of your charges against him. Neither has Herod, for he sent him back to us. Indeed, he has done nothing to deserve death. I will therefore have him flogged and release him." (23:13-16)

Pilate assembles the leaders and the people. He repeats the main charge against Jesus—he perverts the people, leading them astray. Pilate declares that neither he nor Herod finds any basis for the charges. It is highly ironic that Pilate, a Roman, a non-Jew, recognizes that Jesus is not leading the people astray, while the leaders have gone to great lengths to get this charge to stick before both Pilate and Herod. The moment of truth and of decision has come, and the Jerusalem leadership betrays the people by refusing to recognize God's Messiah and prophet. It is they who lead the people astray, not Jesus.

Jesus' accusers are still unsatisfied. They demand his crucifixion. Pilate objects one last time: "Why, what evil has he done? I have found in him no ground for the sentence of death." But they insist, and he imposes the death sentence.

Pilate declares Jesus innocent three times and tries to release him, but Jerusalem's religious authorities insist on his execution. Luke knows that Jesus could die only by decree of Rome, delivered through its administrator, who alone would have the "power of the sword," the power to inflict capital punishment. But he is convinced that Jesus dies because Israel rejects him, as it did the prophets before him. So he shifts the blame for Jesus' death from Pilate to the Jewish leaders.

In Acts of the Apostles, Luke continues to portray Roman administrators as benign observers of the conflict between Jesus' followers and non-Christian Jews. In Acts they appear yet more favorably disposed toward the Christians. This is called Luke's Roman apologetic. The historical fact is that Pilate considered Jesus a threat to order, so he executed him. But Luke would have us believe that Pilate is sympathetic to Jesus and that Roman administrators depicted in Acts are guiltless or even praiseworthy in their treatment of Christians. This is typified by Gallio, Roman proconsul of the province of Achaia, which covered the southern part of the Greek peninsula. He deals with a civic disturbance caused, according to Luke, by Jewish opposition to Paul's evangelizing. Gallio's judgment is: "If it were a matter of crime or serious villainy, I would be justified in accepting the complaint of you Jews; but since it is a matter of questions about words and names and your own law, see to it yourselves; I do not wish to be a judge of these matters" (Acts 18:14-15).

23:26-56: Suffering and Death. In Luke, Jesus epitomizes the confident martyr. Even as he is led to his death, having already been savagely beaten, Jesus fulfills his prophetic function (23:27-31). On the way to the place of execution, women of Jerusalem are "beating their breasts and wailing for him." The Jerusalem leaders cause Jesus' execution, but its women recognize the tragedy unfolding before them. Jesus stops and says, "Do not weep for me, but weep for yourselves and for your children" (23:28). He then predicts the devastation to come upon Jerusalem. He comforts the women, not the converse. The entire scene is unique to Luke.

When Jesus is crucified, he says, "Father, forgive them; for they do not know what they are doing" (23:34). Only in Luke does Jesus speak these words.

As in the other Gospels, Jesus is crucified with two criminals. Only in Luke do they speak to one another. One rails against Jesus, while the other admits his own execution is justified and maintains Jesus' innocence. The "good thief," as he is often called, asks Jesus to remember him when he enters into his kingdom. Jesus responds, "Truly I tell you, today you will be with me in Paradise."

Luke omits Jesus' cry, quoting Ps 22:1, "My God, my God, why have you forsaken me?" This does not fit his view of Jesus' death. And while in Mark we hear only that Jesus cried out in a loud voice and breathed his last, in Luke Jesus says, "Father, into your hands I commend my spirit." Jesus is in control to the last.

When Jesus dies in Mark, the centurion declares him to be Son of God. This is the climax of Mark's careful use of that title. No human can say this of Jesus until the death. Luke does not preserve Mark's handling of the title Son of God. So he uses the centurion's confession for another purpose. The centurion, a Roman soldier, declares Jesus righteous (*dikaios*). The NRSV translates this as "innocent," so that the centurion declares Jesus guiltless, as Pilate has done three time earlier. But *dikaios* has the stronger sense of "righteous" elsewhere in the Gospel, with the religious sense of one truly in tune with God's will (1:6, 17; 2:25; 5:32; 12:57; 18:9; 20:20; 23:50). It is ironic that the Roman centurion recognizes Jesus' righteousness, while the temple authorities have worked to bring about his execution. Luke adds, "When all the crowds who had gathered there for this spectacle saw what had taken place, they returned home, beating their breasts" (23:48). The crowds, like the Jerusalem women earlier, perceive the tragedy, and, like the women, they mourn. Neither Mark nor Matthew recount any such reaction.

RESURRECTION AND ASCENSION (24:1-53)

24:1-12: The Women at the Tomb. All of the canonical gospels have an empty tomb scene. There are no resurrection appearances in Mark, and those in Matthew, Luke, and John are independent of each another. In Mark, although the women at the tomb are told to inform the disciples that Jesus has risen, they tell no one, for they are afraid. In Luke, they do inform the apostles, but "these words seemed to them an idle tale, and they did not believe them" (24:11). Peter runs to the tomb and finds it empty.

24:13-35: Appearance to the Two Disciples Walking to Emmaus. Luke's first resurrection appearance is to two disciples walking to Emmaus from Jerusalem. At first they do not recognize him. When he asks them why they are sad, they are amazed that he has not heard about the events concerning Jesus in Jerusalem. They explain to the stranger about "Jesus of Nazareth, who was a prophet mighty in deed and word before God and all the people." So these disciples see Jesus as a prophet, which is accurate.

The disciples blame the chief priests and leaders for handing Jesus over. They hoped that Jesus was the "redeemer" of Israel, applying to him a title used only in Luke. They tell Jesus of the women's report, confirmed by the visit of others to the tomb. Jesus rebukes them for not believing the words of the prophets. He says that the prophets foretold his suffering, and then he shows how everything in Scripture, "beginning with Moses and all the prophets," was fulfilled in him. Emphasis on biblical prophecy about Jesus and on the prophetic status of Jesus himself, is typically Lukan. It is worth noting here that the Jewish Scriptures say nothing about a suffering messiah. After sharing with them a meal that clearly alludes to the Eucharist, Jesus disappears, and they finally recognize whom they have encountered.

24:36-49: Appearance to the Disciples. The next resurrection appearance is to the eleven and their companions in Jerusalem. Jesus eats fish to prove his bodily resurrection. Then he repeats his lesson that "the law of Moses, the prophets, and the psalms" are fulfilled in him. He opens "their minds to understand the scriptures," and says that his suffering was foretold, "and that repentance and forgiveness of sins is to be proclaimed in his name to all nations, beginning from Jerusalem" (24:47). All of this is typical of Luke—fulfillment of Scripture in Jesus, especially the prophets, repentance, forgiveness of sin, the universal nature of forgiveness, and the centrality of Jerusalem.

24:50-53: Ascension. The Gospel ends with the ascension, found only in Luke. He goes up to heaven and his disciples worship him. Before Jesus leads the disciples out to Bethany, where he ascends to heaven, he orders them to remain in Jerusalem until they are "clothed with power from on high" (24:50), a reference to the coming of the Holy Spirit in Acts 2. After the ascension takes place (24:51), they return to Jerusalem "with great joy; and they were continually in the temple blessing God" (24:52-53). The ending is like the beginning. It occurs in the temple in Jerusalem and is full of joy. The stage is set for the proclamation of God's forgiveness, beginning in Jerusalem and extending to all nations. But much has transpired since Luke's opening chapters. Jerusalem has already rejected Jesus once. Now the question is whether it will do so again, and whether the Gentiles will be open to divine forgiveness.

BRIEF SURVEY OF ACTS OF THE APOSTLES

We do not give the same attention to Acts as to the Gospel. But we must at least see where Luke's narrative goes from here.

Acts opens as the Gospel closes. Jesus appears to his disciples in Jerusalem and its environs, teaches them, and ascends into heaven. Luke's placement of the ascension both at the end of the Gospel and at the beginning of Acts ties the two works securely together. Among Jesus' teachings at the beginning of Acts is a programmatic verse: "You will receive power when the Holy Spirit has come upon you; and you will be my witnesses in Jerusalem, in all Judea and Samaria, and to the ends of the earth" (1:8). They are to preach the gospel, beginning in Jerusalem and extending in ever-widening circles. Much of Acts takes the form of journeys to carry out this commission. The end of the book pictures Paul in Rome, preaching to the Gentiles. The gospel, now at the "center" of the world, is positioned to reach the "ends of the earth."

The apostles choose another person to make the twelfth member of their group, to take Judas's place (1:12-26). This gives the church the solid foundation of twelve apostles and signifies that God's desire to save all Israel—twelve tribes—is not to be surrendered easily. Acts chronicles the church's efforts to missionize Israel.

At Pentecost, a feast fifty days after Passover celebrating the wheat harvest and commemorating the gift of Torah, the Holy Spirit descends on the disciples (2:1-47). As the Gospel begins with the descent of the Spirit on Jesus, its sequel begins with the descent of the Spirit on the church. In Acts the Spirit frequently directs the church's mission. Since the Spirit is the Spirit of prophecy, the apostles speak when they receive it. Their audience is Jews from all over the empire, who speak many different languages. The disciples proclaim what God has done in Jesus, and, miraculously, everyone hears them in his or her own language. This is programmatic. The message is preached to Jews first but is destined for all nations. As missionaries traverse the empire, they approach the Jews of each place first. From there, they widen their mission to include Gentiles. The pattern is always the same—to Israel first, and then to all nations.

Many Jews accept the message, and the apostles instruct them to repent and receive God's forgiveness and God's Spirit. However, subsequent chapters show that although many of the Jewish people accept the message, their leaders generally do not. Still, Luke claims that many priests and Pharisees do accept the message (6:7; 15:5). This seems contradictory, but Luke holds two points in tension. The first is that many Jews, even leaders, see Jesus as God's true prophet. The second is that Israel as a whole, and especially its leaders, does not accept Jesus. The tension persists throughout Acts, but at crucial points it becomes clear that the message will be accepted primarily by Gentiles.

Peter and the other apostles preach in Jerusalem and attract the opposition of the temple establishment (chs. 2–5). They face questioning in a couple of scenes that are like Jesus' trial before the Sanhedrin. Things culminate in the case of Stephen, a Greek-speaking Jew who accuses Israel of rejecting God's prophet Jesus as it did Moses, and who even questions the centrality of Jerusalem's temple to God's plans. He becomes the first martyr (ch. 7).

The church in Jerusalem is persecuted and many flee Jerusalem (8:1). They enter Gentile territory, "And they spoke the word to no one except Jews" (11:19). Then Greek-speaking Jewish Christians preach to Gentiles and find a receptive audience. At this point church members begin to be called *Christian*, that is, followers of Christ, Greek for "Messiah." So *Christian* means something like "messianist." Until Gentiles entered the church, non-Jews, perhaps some Jews as well, saw followers of Jesus as a group within Judaism. When nonobservant Gentiles entered the community in substantial numbers there had to be another way to identify them. This was a watershed for the church.

The gospel spreads to Samaria in chapter 8, and in chapter 10, Peter commands that Gentiles be baptized. In response to a vision, Peter visits the household of Cornelius, a Roman centurion. As he speaks to them about Jesus, the Spirit descends on his audience. Peter is forced to admit that God is signaling divine approval of Gentiles entering the church, so he orders them to be baptized. Christians today may think it obvious that the church was meant for Gentiles, too, but this was not clear to the first Christians, all of whom were Jewish and did not see the Jesus movement as a new religion. Jewish Christians of the Jerusalem church demand an accounting from Peter for this innovation (11:3). Foremost among the Christians who seek an explanation are Christian Pharisees. A meeting is held in Jerusalem (ch. 15). When Peter explains, they are convinced, and James, Jesus' brother and head of the Jerusalem church, declares that the acceptance of the Gentiles is God's will, foretold by the prophets, and further, that Gentile Christians need not obey all of the commandments of the Torah. They need only refrain from sexual immorality, from eating blood, and from eating what has been sacrificed to idols. This meeting is often called the *Council of Jerusalem*, and it probably took place in 48 C.E. It was a defining moment.

Paul—Jew, Pharisee, and persecutor of the church—experiences a vision of the risen Jesus and becomes a member of the church (9:1-31; see Gal 1:13-24). Much of the rest of Acts (chs. 13–14, 16–28) concerns Paul's missions. When entering new territory, he always goes to the Jews first. The usual pattern is that they listen with some interest and then become divided in their reactions. Some Jews convert, but most try to hinder the gospel and harm the missionaries. Frustrated, Paul declares at one point, "It was necessary that the word of God should be spoken first to you. Since you reject it and judge yourselves to be unworthy of eternal life, we are now turning to the Gentiles. For so God has commanded us, saying, 'I have set you to be a light for the Gentiles, / so that you may bring salvation to the ends of the earth' " (13:46-47). Paul quotes Second Isaiah (Isa 49:6). The disbelief of the Jews precipitates the mission of the Gentiles, but the mission accords with God's will as Isaiah announced it. Nonetheless, Paul continues to approach Jews first each time he enters new territory.

When Paul attempts to deliver a collection of money from the Gentile churches to the Jerusalem church, he encounters antagonism from hostile Jews and is arrested (21:17-36). Appealing to the emperor, he travels to Rome. Upon arriving, he again preaches to Jews, but again meets a mixed reaction. Paul again quotes Isaiah, this time to the effect that God foretold the disbelief of the Jews (28:25-27; Isa 6:9-10), and concludes, "Let it be known to you then that this salvation of God has been sent to the Gentiles; they will listen." Paul then lives in Rome for two years, preaching the gospel "with all boldness and without hindrance" (28:31).

We do not hear of Paul's final fate. Christian tradition has it that he perished in Nero's persecution of Christians in 64 C.E. Luke ends his narrative with unhindered preaching of the gospel in the heart of the Roman Empire. Scholars debate whether Luke means that the message will now be preached only to Gentiles, or that preaching to the Jews continues beyond the period covered by Acts. Whichever is the case, the reader gets the impression that Israel rejects salvation foretold by its prophets, and that the Spirit directs the church to the Gentile mission.

CHRISTOLOGY

PROPHET LIKE MOSES

Luke retains Jesus' titles and functions found in Mark. Jesus is Son of God, Son of Man, Davidic Messiah, and so on. Luke adds his own characteristic stamp to the material about Jesus. Central to Luke's presentation of Jesus is prophecy. Jesus is God's eschatological prophet who in word and deed announces and effects the fulfillment of God's promises to Israel. Through Jesus, God makes available liberation from enemies, freedom from oppression, release from sickness, and forgiveness of sins. All of this is encompassed by the word *salvation*. Both God and Jesus are called saviors (1:47, 69; 2:11). Those who accept Jesus as God's prophet form the true Israel, and those who reject him cut themselves off from God's people. God's salvific message is not for Israel alone, but for all humanity, through Israel.

Jesus stands squarely within Israel's prophetic tradition. More specifically, he is the prophet foretold by Moses whose work follows the pattern of Moses himself. This is clearest in Acts of the Apostles, but it is reflected in the Gospel as well. Peter's speech in Acts 3:12-26 is instructive. He speaks as a Jew to other Jews within the Jerusalem temple, addressing his audience as "Israelites." He notes that they rejected Jesus, but he attributes that to ignorance. Their ignorance furthered God's prediction through the prophets that Jesus should suffer. Now Israel has a second chance. Their Messiah, Jesus, is waiting for "the time of universal restoration that God announced long ago through his holy prophets" (3:21). When that time comes, Jesus will return. Israel should prepare through repentance and acceptance of the church's message.

All of this fulfills Moses' prediction in Deut 18. Peter quotes, "Moses said, 'The Lord your God will raise up for you from your own people a prophet like me. You must listen to whatever he tells you. And it will be that everyone who does not listen to that prophet will be utterly rooted out of the people'" (Acts 3:22-24). Jesus is that prophet. Peter says that all previous prophets foretold this day. Jews are "the descendants of the prophets and of the covenant that God gave to your ancestors, saying to Abraham, 'And in your descendants all the families of the earth shall be blessed.'" God sent Jesus to Israel first to urge them to repentance. All who do not heed him are cut off from the people. Israel is thus redefined.

The parallel between Jesus and Moses is laid out in more detail in Stephen's speech in Acts 7. Stephen is the church's first martyr, killed in Jerusalem after speaking critically of Israel and the temple. He reminds Israel of the exodus, when they were "unwilling to obey" Moses. The speech ends with the accusation that Israel has a history of opposing the Holy Spirit and persecuting the prophets who foretold Jesus' coming, and that it has now betrayed and killed Jesus. Moses' significance for Jesus is both that he foretold Jesus' coming (Acts 3:22-24), and that now Israel's rejection of Jesus parallels its rejection of Moses. Moses performs signs and wonders to prove that he is from God, as do Jesus and church members (Deut 34:11; Acts 2:22, 43; 4:30; 5:12; 6:8; 7:36; 14:3; 15:12). Jesus' rejection also recalls the suffering servant of Isaiah, as explained above.

John the Baptist and Jesus both appear as prophets reminiscent of Elijah and Elisha. The canticle of Zechariah, father of John the Baptist, prophesies that the Baptist is a Spirit-filled prophet whose mission is to declare to Israel that the fulfillment of God's promises is happening in Jesus (Luke 1:68-79). John operates in the spirit and power of the prophet Elijah. Jesus begins his public ministry in the synagogue at Nazareth. He reads from the prophet Isaiah a passage where the prophet describes himself as anointed with the Spirit to bring good news to the poor, sick, and oppressed of Israel. Jesus declares that the passage is fulfilled in himself and his work. John, Jesus, and then the church preach the word of God, as do all prophets (3:2; 8:11; Acts 19:20). The scene in the synagogue is programmatic, for just as the prophets Elijah and Elisha work wonders for Gentiles, so Jesus will ultimately be preached to the Gentiles through the church. Jesus anticipates his rejection by Israel (4:23-24), saying that prophets are honored outside one's own native land but not within it. This teaching turns those in the synagogue against him. Details of Jesus' ministry recall Elijah and Elisha as he heals a Gentile (7:1-10), raises the son of a widow (7:11-15), and multiplies loaves (9:10-17). Jesus' ministry continues throughout the Gospel to consist of bringing good news to the poor, which evokes the opposition of the rich, powerful, and self-righteous. Jesus interprets his own death as a result of opposition among the Jerusalem elite aroused by his prophetic work (13:31-35). Luke takes this as part of Jerusalem's history of killing of God's prophets (11:47-51).

Prophecy permeates Luke–Acts. All of the ancient prophets foretold the fulfillment of God's promises in Jesus. Prophecy surrounds the births of Jesus and John. In the infancy narratives, Mary, Elizabeth, Zechariah, Simeon, and Anna receive the Spirit of prophecy. Jesus is depicted as God's prophet and ultimately dies as such. The early Christians receive the Holy Spirit, which enables them to carry on Jesus' prophetic mission. Israel's rejection of the message and its acceptance by the Gentiles is all foretold by Israel's prophets. It is no wonder that Luke derives his basic paradigm for divine activity from a prophet—Second Isaiah.

The careers of Christian missionaries resemble that of Jesus. Stephen's death parallels that of Jesus. The apostles, filled with the spirit, preach the

same message as Jesus, and they cure the sick and exorcise. Paul's appearances before the high priest and Sanhedrin in Jerusalem and the Roman
governor there recall the trials of Jesus, including such details as Paul's
being struck for supposed insolence to the high priest. The work of the
church continues that of Jesus.

ATONEMENT

It is debated whether Luke views Jesus' death as atoning. Many find significant that Luke omits one of the two verses from Mark that could support this interpretation—Mark 10:45, where Jesus says that his life must
be given as a ransom for many. At the Last Supper, Jesus says, "This cup
that is poured out for you is the new covenant in my blood" (Luke 22:20).
(Note that there are textual problems with this passage in Luke.) The
covenant sacrifice and blood alluded to here, the one in Exod 24, is not
a subisitutionary one or even a sin offering. Rather, it is a "peace offering,"
a celebratory rite involving a feast, in which the blood is ceremoniously
sprinkled on altar and people to symbolize the bond between Israel and
God.

Some point to the fact that the curtain of the temple is torn in two
before Jesus dies, which differs from Mark. That may mean that the death
itself does not signify the end of the Jewish cult as the means of forgiveness of sins, as in Mark. Another detail is that when Jesus dies the centurion does not pronounce him the Son of God, but rather as "righteous."
This might mean that the death is not as central to Jesus' divine sonship
as in Mark. Rather, it makes Jesus the noble martyr. At the end of Luke's
Gospel and in Acts of the Apostles, Christians continue attending the
temple.

ISAIAH'S INFLUENCE

Luke reads the Bible through the lens of Isaiah, and particularly of
Second Isaiah (Isa 40–55). Scholars divide the book of Isaiah into three
parts, which come from three different historical periods. Second Isaiah
comes from a prophet living in the Babylonian exile in the sixth century
B.C.E., an exile interpreted by many Jews as punishment for Israel's sin.
Isaiah's message is that God will soon liberate the people from exile and
return them to Judah to rebuild Jerusalem and its temple. It calls this "salvation," and in chapter 40, God orders the prophet to tell Jerusalem to
"preach" the "good news" of this salvation to Judah. The book is filled

with joy and eager expectation. This mighty act of liberation will catch the attention of all nations and turn them to the true God. The Gentiles will then join Israel to worship God.

All three Synoptic Gospels draw on Isaiah, but Luke is especially fond of that prophet. Luke is the only one of the Four Gospels to use the noun "salvation," a favorite word of Isaiah. Isaiah calls himself and Israel God's servant and chosen, and Luke applies the terms *prophet, servant,* and *chosen* to Jesus. Isaiah speaks of a servant who suffers and is esteemed—rejected by God but whom God then vindicates. This is especially evident in Isa 52:13–53:12. It was an important passage for early Christian reflection on Jesus' death. A clear echo of this suffering image is found in Luke 22:37, where Jesus is reckoned among the lawless. Acts 8:32-35 directly quotes Isa 53:7-8 and applies it to Jesus.

Isaiah was anointed by the Holy Spirit (Isa 61:1), and Luke stresses Jesus' relation to the Spirit. In fact, Jesus quotes Isa 61:1 in the synagogue at Nazareth and apples it to himself (4:16-21). Isaiah is a joyful book because of the salvation it announces, not just to Israel but also to the nations. Luke identifies Jesus' coming with the advent of salvation for all humanity, which is greeted with great joy in the infancy narrative.

Many times throughout Luke–Acts, Luke subtly alludes to Isaiah. For example, Second Isaiah begins with God's call to the prophet to "comfort" Israel and speak tenderly to Jerusalem by declaring the end of the exile. In Luke, when the prophet Simeon is introduced, he is said to be one who was "looking forward to the consolation of Israel" (2:25). The word for "consolation" here is the noun form of the verb "to comfort" in Isa 40. When he sees Jesus, Simeon identifies him as God's Messiah and says, "My eyes have seen your salvation, / which you have prepared in the presence of all peoples, / a light for revelation to the Gentiles / and for glory to your people Israel" (2:30-32), words that recall Isa 40:3-5; 49:6; 52:10. Simeon identifies Jesus with salvation, a favorite word of Isaiah.

The following table lists many of the parallels between Luke–Acts and Isaiah. Neither the themes nor the citations are exhaustive.

Parallels between Luke–Acts and Isaiah

- We have detailed the allusions to Isaiah in Simeon's words (Luke 2:29-32).
- Jesus quotes Isa 61 and applies to himself the prophet's words about himself (Luke 4:18-19).
- Jesus is called "prophet," "servant," and "chosen," as is Isaiah.

- At Jesus' baptism, God's words recall Isa 42:1, one of the scenes in Isaiah where God commissions him.
- Luke–Acts ends with Paul quoting Isa 6.
- Luke–Acts and Isaiah see God's message of salvation as addressed especially to the poor and marginalized (Isa 58, 61; Luke 4, 6, 7:22).
- Isaiah speaks of God as Israel's "savior" and "redeemer" (Isa 43:14; 52:9; Luke 24:21). Only Luke of the evangelists uses these terms of God. It also calls Jesus "savior," a title unique to Luke.
- Both Luke and Isaiah speak of God's offer of pardon (Isa 55:7; Luke 5:21), peace (Isa 59:8; Luke 1:79; Acts 10:36), and God's light shining on the people (Isa 60:1; Luke 1:78). Isaiah says that God's peace is for those near and far (57:19), and Luke takes that to mean Jews and Gentiles (2:14; Acts 2:39).
- Both Luke and Isaiah say that Israel is slow to believe the prophets (Isa 53; Luke 24:25).
- Jesus puts his opponents to shame (13:17; the only use of the expression in the Gospels), as in Isaiah Israel's opponents are put to shame (45:16).
- In Isaiah, a figure called "the servant," probably meaning Israel, suffers and is humiliated, and then is lifted up by God and marveled at (see 52:13). Jesus also suffers and is then exalted by God in Luke–Acts.
- Isaiah expects that even eunuchs will be allowed into the temple to praise God (Isa 56:3-7), and the apostle Philip evangelizes a eunuch in Acts 8:26-39.
- God is near to those who call on God in Isa 55:6 and Acts 17:27.
- Both Isaiah and Luke use beatitudes (Isa 65:13; Luke 6).
- Both Isaiah and Acts state that an earthly sanctuary cannot contain God (Isa 66:1; Acts 7:49).

Many of the themes and points in this table are not unique to Isaiah and Luke. But the sheer volume of contacts between the two works suggest that for Luke, Isaiah furnished a way to focus the biblical message and see how it applied to the "new thing" (see Isa 43:19) that God was doing in Jesus.

DELAY OF THE PAROUSIA

The Lukan introduction to the parable of the Pounds reveals another of Luke's concerns: "He went on to tell a parable, because he was near

Jerusalem, and because they supposed that the kingdom of God was to appear immediately" (19:11). They are mistaken. The parousia is not just around the corner. The parable enjoins using the intervening time fruitfully so as to be ready for a final accounting.

Mark expects imminent persecution in which every Christian must be ready to endure crucifixion (8:34); Luke turns the cross into a metaphor for daily suffering (9:23). Mark's Jesus says that some of his hearers will see the kingdom of God come with power (9:1), while Luke softens this to say that they will see the kingdom of God. Elsewhere, Luke indicates that the kingdom is in some sense present in Jesus' ministry (10:9-11; 11:10; 17:21). At his trial before the Sanhedrin in Mark, Jesus tells the high priest that he will " 'see the Son of Man / seated at the right hand of the Power,' / and 'coming with the clouds of heaven' " (14:62). Luke's Jesus simply says, "From now on the Son of Man will be seated at the right hand of the power of God" (22:69).

Luke's subtle changes to his sources suggest that for him the parousia is further off than for Mark. Luke directs his readers to social justice and to the spread of the church. To these ends, he writes his second volume, Acts of the Apostles. At the same time, Luke retains Mark's basic apocalyptic viewpoint. He has an apocalyptic discourse in chapter 21. Eventually, the cosmos will be disturbed, and the glorious Son of Man will come on the clouds.

WOMEN IN LUKE–ACTS

Luke has more material involving women than any other Gospel. Scholars often portray Luke as more open to recognizing women's importance to the life of the church. Others contend that although Luke contains more material about women, he portrays them in conventional, gender-determined roles and at times weakens aspects of his sources that take a more progressive stance. Here we sketch some of the features that make Luke noteworthy and some of the reasons scholars take the positions they do.

The enhanced role of women is evident in Luke's first chapters. In Matthew's infancy narrative, Joseph is the main character. It is he who gets messages through angels in dreams, and it is he who makes decisions that lead the plot in certain directions. We never hear from Mary.

The situation is reversed in Luke. Luke's infancy narrative says next to nothing about Joseph, except that Mary was betrothed to him and that he brought his family to Bethlehem to register in the census. (It is doubtful whether a census such as Luke describes could have taken place. We discuss this in chapter 8, with reference to the historical study of Jesus.) The angel Gabriel announces Jesus' birth to Mary, not Joseph (1:26-38). She is perfectly open and obedient to God and receptive to the surprising news the angel brings. Luke contrasts her with Zechariah, John the Baptist's father, a Jerusalem priest. He is a prominent figure in society, a religious leader. He is dubious when told that his wife Elizabeth will conceive, since she is old and has always been infertile (1:18). Mary, a young woman in an out-of-the-way Galilean town, is open to God's salvific action. She offers herself as God's servant, even when it means accepting such an unbelievable thing as the virgin birth. Gabriel tells her, "Nothing will be impossible with God" (1:37), while Zechariah is punished by being unable to speak until John's birth (1:20).

Mary visits Elizabeth, her relative. When she arrives, Elizabeth is filled with the Holy Spirit and so recognizes that Mary is pregnant with the "Lord." She praises Mary: "Blessed is she who believed that there would be a fulfillment of what was spoken to her by the Lord" (1:45). Elizabeth acts as a prophet. Through the Spirit she discerns and announces God's actions. She bestows what is the highest praise for Luke, that Mary believes in the fulfillment of God's promises. Mary, a righteous Jewish woman, typifies how Israel ought to respond.

Mary utters a hymn of praise traditionally called the Magnificat, which we analyze in some detail above. Here Mary acts as a prophet, and her task is to interpret God's most significant action, the fulfillment of all promises in Jesus.

Eight days after Jesus' birth, his parents bring him to the Jerusalem temple. There the prophet Simeon declares him the Messiah. Simeon's words reveal Jesus' significance for Israel and for the nations, and also for Mary, who will be pierced by sorrow. Luke does not end the scene here. Jesus has been acclaimed by a male prophet. Now he is also recognized by a female prophet, Anna. Anna, an elderly woman who is a widow who has dedicated her life to prayer and fasting in the temple, begins "to praise God and to speak about the child to all who were looking for the redemption of Israel" (2:38). Jesus' significance has now been confirmed by three female prophets—Elizabeth, Mary, and Anna. Anna has the same name as Hannah, the originally infertile mother of Samuel the prophet, who recited the hymn of praise that is the model for Mary's Magnificat (see our analysis above).

Luke pairs males and females throughout the Gospel. We list the main ones in the following table.

Luke's Pairing of Males and Females

- Mary compares favorably with Zechariah. She exemplifies how to receive God's word, and Zechariah demonstrates the opposite (1:5-38).
- Simeon the prophet discloses the meaning of Jesus, and immediately afterward Anna the prophet does the same (2:25-38).
- In the programmatic synagogue scene in chapter 4, Jesus cites two instances where Elijah and Elisha help Gentiles. One is the case of the male Naaman, and the other is that of the widow of Zarephath (4:25-27).
- Jesus raises a widow's son from the dead and then raises Jairus's daughter from the dead. There is symmetry between raising the son of a mother and the daughter of a father (7:11-17; 8:40-42a, 49-56).
- In an intertwined story, Jairus asks that his daughter be cured and the woman with a hemorrhage petitions Jesus on his way to Jairus and is cured (8:40-56).
- Jesus compares the stubbornness of his hearers to the receptivity of the men of Nineveh on the one hand and the queen of Sheba on the other (11:31-32).
- Jesus cures a woman on the Sabbath (13:10-17). He also cures a man on the Sabbath (14:1-6).
- Jesus brings salvation to a "son of Abraham" (19:9) and to a "daughter of Abraham" (13:16).
- The spread of the gospel is compared to a man sowing seed and to a woman kneading yeast into dough (13:18-21).
- God's concern for the lost is depicted as a shepherd seeking a lost sheep and a housewife seeking a lost coin (15:3-10).
- The end of the world comes suddenly—on men sleeping and on women grinding meal (17:34-35).
- The women are the first to see Jesus' empty tomb, and then Peter does so (24:1-12).

Although these pairings result in more material about women, much of it leaves women in traditional roles. It is surely significant that Mary is superior to the Jerusalem priest Zechariah. However, Mary is not every woman, and Luke might not intend for this to reflect on all women. The prophetic role of women in the infancy narrative gives them a key role in God's salvific plan, true, but Mary is an exception and is a virgin, Elizabeth is an infertile elderly woman, and Anna is an elderly widow. So none of the three represent women as a whole.

The two pairings in which Jairus is involved can be evaluated similarly. Whereas Jairus approaches Jesus publicly and confidently, the woman with the hemorrhage approaches him fearfully and surreptitiously. Jesus raises Jairus's marriageable daughter from the dead, and he raises and gives back to the widow her son without whom she would be in distress in a culture where women's place in society is often determined by their relationship to men. The woman kneading yeast, the woman searching for a coin within the house, the women grinding, and the women who go to the tomb to embalm Jesus all play conventional roles.

A passage that has received a great deal of attention for what it might tell us about Luke's attitude toward women is that of Martha and Mary. They are close friends of Jesus. When he visits their house, Martha serves and feeds him, a traditional role. Mary sits at Jesus' feet in the posture of a disciple (see Acts 22:3). When Martha objects, Jesus says that Mary has chosen the better part, which will not be taken from her. This seems an affirmation that women can be full disciples, choosing to listen to Jesus' word rather than to do more conventional things. Attention to Jesus' word can mean that they justifiably "neglect" their gender-defined chores. On the other hand, Mary plays a passive role and there is no indication that she then goes out and preaches the message publicly, as do the men.

Only Luke has the story of the sinful woman who approaches Jesus in a Pharisee's home and anoints his feet (7:36-50). In her humility and repentance, she contrasts favorably with the self-righteous Pharisee who is shocked that Jesus allows her to touch him. The contrasting parallel calls to mind the parable of the Pharisee and the Tax Collector, unique to Luke (18:9-14). So much for the positive. Luke's story may depend on the story of the woman who anoints Jesus for his burial in Mark 14:3-9. If so, he has taken a story in which a woman, not a sinner, has more insight into Jesus' impending suffering than do the disciples, and turned it into the story of a notoriously sinful woman.

Mark notes that there are women present at the cross who followed Jesus and provided for him in Galilee and who came up with him to

Jerusalem. We never hear about these women in the body of the Gospel. Luke at least gives us a short notice in 8:1-3:

> He went on through cities and villages, proclaiming and bringing the good news of the kingdom of God. The twelve were with him, as well as some women who had been cured of evil spirits and infirmities: Mary, called Magdalene, from whom seven demons had gone out, and Joanna, the wife of Herod's steward Chuza, and Susanna, and many others, who provided for them out of their resources.

Although Luke takes a step forward by putting this notice within the narrative of the ministry itself, there are other things to consider. For example, he omits Mark's statement that they were "following" Jesus, a word often indicating discipleship. Saying that Joanna has connections to Galilee's ruler may be Luke's way of stressing that these are women of means. It was not unusual in antiquity for women to exercise influence by using their material resources to support men of whom they approved. That the women have been cured by Jesus makes us wonder if Luke thinks there were women among Jesus' entourage for whom he had not done such a service. But Peter, James, and John also follow Jesus after seeing a miracle (ch. 5). It is also in accord with Luke's view that Jesus brings the marginalized into his movement. The women are doubly marginalized—they are women and were possessed.

In Mark, the angel at the tomb tells the women that Jesus is risen and instructs them to inform Peter and the other disciples. They say nothing to anyone, for they are afraid (16:1-8). Luke reads very differently. First, he specifies that the women did not go to the tomb immediately because "they rested according to the commandment" (23:56). Luke is ending as he began. The women disciples observe Torah strictly. Then Luke adds words of the angel: "Remember how he told you, while he was still in Galilee, that the Son of Man must be handed over to sinners, and be crucified, and on the third day rise again" (24:6-7). The word *you* is key. The angel implies not only that the women were with Jesus in Galilee, but that his teaching about his death and resurrection was directed toward them, not just toward the men. Even though the angel does not tell the women to carry the news to the disciples, they do so. The men are skeptical. "But these words seemed to them an idle tale, and they did not believe them" (24:11). Women were thought less reliable than men and more apt to carry idle tales. Peter visits the tomb and finds that their report is true. On the one hand, Luke seems to reinforce cultural

241

prejudices here. Who believes women? On the other hand, the context proves the women reliable, and the men wrong to doubt them. It also shows women as the first bearers of the news of the resurrection. The two disciples on the road to Emmaus credit the women with being the first to convey the news, not mentioning that they initially met with disbelief (24:22-24). The two disciples in question may be a man and a woman.

There is an ascetic streak in Luke that relates to gender. Luke implies that it may be necessary for men to leave their wives to follow Jesus (14:26; 18:29). This is aimed at men, but it may also leave women free to dedicate themselves to things other than domestic chores, raising children, and caring for husbands. Widows or virgins are prophets in 1:44-45, 2:36-38, and Acts 21:9. Anna, the temple prophet, lived most of her life as a widow, fasting and praying. Widows are provided for, according to Acts 6:1 (see 9:39, 41). A New Testament text with a more conventional view of gender roles, 1 Timothy, tries to regulate widowhood in the early church. He is afraid that young widowed women who wish to remain such will be disruptive because of their uncontrollable passions and their tendency to be idle, to gossip. Luke does not stereotype women in this denigrating way. He holds up celibacy for men and women as an ideal state, as does Paul in 1 Cor 7. Luke shows awareness of Paul's ascetic preferences in Acts 24:24-25.

Mark 10:1-12 forbids divorce. Luke does not preserve this. He seems more interested in preventing further marriage after divorce or losing a spouse (16:18).

JEWS AND JUDAISM

A driving force behind Luke's two-volume work is the theological problem that Israel does not accept Jesus as Messiah and prophet. The infancy narrative presents Jesus as the realization of all of Israel's hopes, the completion of all of God's promises, the fulfillment of all prophecies. Luke's first two chapters are replete with joy, the appropriate reaction to the coming of salvation. Characters inspired by the Holy Spirit point to unfolding events as God's definitive intervention in Israel's (and the world's) history. God's "plan" is for the liberation of Israel and the whole human race. But at the end of the infancy narrative, the prophet Simeon predicts that Jesus will mean the fall and rising of many in Israel and that a sword of sorrow will pierce Mary's heart. Mary's hymn of praise, the Magnificat, tells of social disruption to come—the lowly lifted up, the powerful brought down, the hungry filled, the full sent away empty. The rejection of Jesus is ultimately a rejection of his vision of a socially just society. Vested interests—religious, economic, political, social—will be disrupted.

Jesus' programmatic appearance in his hometown synagogue, transferred to the beginning of his ministry, ends with the villagers seeking his death (4:14-30). Jesus cites the precedents of Elijah and Elisha as paradigms for things to come—Israel will not accept God's prophet, but the Gentiles will. The rest of the Gospel proves the former—Israel will not accept Jesus. The picture is not unrelievedly bad; some in Israel do respond positively—the disciples, for example. And many common people come to Jesus as one who can heal them. But Israel's leaders are hostile, and the synagogue scene hints that Israel as a whole will follow their lead.

Much of Luke's Gospel is in the form of a journey to Jerusalem (9:51–19:27). Jesus says that he must go there, for "it is impossible for a prophet to be killed outside of Jerusalem" (13:33). He addresses Jerusalem as the one that "kills the prophets and stones those who are sent to it" (13:34). He says that he has desired to protect Jerusalem as a hen protects her brood, but the city was unwilling. At the end of the journey, Jesus again addresses the holy city directly, this time predicting its utter destruction because it did not recognize the time of its "visitation from God" in the person of Jesus (19:44). Jesus' trip to Jerusalem results in his complete rejection by the religious establishment. Pilate protests that he is innocent, but the Jewish leadership uses the Roman administrator to make sure that this troublesome prophet is eliminated. But even at the end there is some sign of hope. When they see him die, the Jewish crowd "returned home, beating their breasts" (23:48).

Jesus rises from the dead and meets two of his disciples walking to Emmaus (24:13-35). They see Jesus' death as the end of Israel's hopes. He reveals that God's plan included his suffering and death, as foretold by Israel's prophets. Again, hope is renewed. Jesus tells them to wait in Jerusalem for the coming of the Holy Spirit, and then he ascends into heaven. The Gospel ends with them in the temple, blessing God (24:53).

Acts of the Apostles opens after the resurrection but before Jesus ascends to heaven. His disciples ask him whether he will now "restore the kingdom to Israel" (1:6). There is no sign that they misunderstand God's plan, nor does Jesus correct them. The promises to Israel are still pending, despite Israel's rejection of Jesus. Jesus tells the disciples that when they receive the Holy Spirit, they are to bring the message of salvation to the world, beginning with Jerusalem. After Pentecost, Peter preaches to Israel (2:14-36; 3:12-26). He says that God made the one whom they rejected Lord and Messiah (2:36). Many repent and join the disciples. In chapter 3, Peter says that their rejection of Jesus was due to ignorance and that God is giving them a chance to repent. If they do so, Jesus will come again as their Messiah. If they do not, they cut themselves off from God's people, now defined as those who accept Jesus, the prophet like Moses predicted by Moses in Deut 18.

In the rest of Acts, the Christians continue to carry out a mission to Israel. Although many Jews do believe, Israel as a whole continues to reject God's plan. They even oppose Christians speaking to Gentiles, for, according to Luke, they are jealous of their success. Although the point is disputed, the end of Acts seems to give up on the mission to Israel. Quoting Isa 6:9-10, Paul says that the Holy Spirit predicted the Jews' recalcitrance. He then says, "Let it be known to you then that this salvation of God has been sent to the Gentiles; they will listen" (28:28). So, ironically, the salvation that fulfills the promises to Israel is accepted not by Israel but by the Gentiles.

Luke leaves us with a negative view of Israel. It betrays its own heritage by ignoring the fulfillment of the words of its prophets. It opposes God's plan for itself and for the world. In the words of Moses in Deuteronomy, quoted by Peter, though Israel is God's people, it cuts itself off from the people of God (3:23).

We must remember that these are Luke's thoughts and attitudes (if we have interpreted them correctly). Christians all accept the Bible as the word of God, but many Christians think that it is necessary to read it critically. If we judge Luke to be anti-Jewish in any sense, that does not mean that we must follow him down that road. We need not "take the bad with the good." Rather, Christians today, by recognizing anti-Jewish tendencies in various theologies in the New Testament, can identify them, analyze them, and not allow them to continue to support views of Judaism that, in the end, are inimical to both Judaism and Christianity.

CONCLUSION

Like Matthew, Luke rewrites Mark. Like Matthew, he draws on the sayings source Q. And again like Matthew, he produces a genuinely new work that builds on what has gone before, transforms the tradition it inherits, and creates a new and unique portrait of Jesus. In rewriting

Mark, Luke leaves out more material than does Matthew. The material he does include he rewrites. He abbreviates, improves style, and idealizes Jesus, the disciples, and Jesus' family.

Luke holds in tension continuity and discontinuity between Israel and the church. Major categories by which he does so are prophecy and salvation. He conceives of salvation in terms drawn from Second Isaiah, and his notions of prophecy depend a good deal on Jewish traditions about Moses, on the book of Isaiah, and on biblical conceptions of the Holy Spirit. Luke's God is a God of liberation, one who frees humans from poverty, oppression, sickness, and sinfulness. God's prophet, Jesus, comes, as foretold by all the prophets, to fulfill all of God's liberating promises to Israel. Although many in Israel believe, the majority do not. From that point of view, Luke's story is tragedy. However, the Gentiles do believe, and so God's message goes out to all the world. From that standpoint, Luke tells a tale of joy, of good news.

BIBLIOGRAPHY

Arlandson, James M. *Women, Class, and Society in Early Christianity: Models from Luke–Acts*. Peabody, Mass.: Hendrickson, 1997.

Baltzer, Klaus. "The Meaning of the Temple in the Lucan Writings." *HTR* 58 (1965): 263-77.

Brawley, Robert L. *Luke–Acts and the Jews*. Atlanta: Scholars, 1987.

Carroll, John T. "Luke's Portrayal of the Pharisees." *CBQ* 50 (1988): 604-21.

Carter, Warren. "Get Martha Out of the Kitchen." *CBQ* 58 (1996): 264-80.

Cassidy, Richard J. *Jesus, Politics, and Society: A Study of Luke's Gospel*. Maryknoll, N.Y.: Orbis, 1978.

Conzelmann, Hans. *The Theology of St. Luke*. New York: Harper & Row, 1960.

Crenshaw, James L. "Theodicy." *ABD* 6:444-47.

D'Angelo, Mary Rose. "(Re)Presentations of Women in the Gospels: Matthew and Luke–Acts." *WCO*, 171-95.

Darr, John. *On Character Building: The Reader and the Rhetoric of Characterization in Luke–Acts*. Louisville: Westminster John Knox, 1992.

Evans, Craig A., and James A. Sanders. *Luke and Scripture: The Function of Sacred Tradition in Luke–Acts*. Minneapolis: Fortress, 1993.

Fitzmyer, Joseph A. *The Gospel According to Luke* in AB, vols. 28-28A. Garden City, N.Y.: Doubleday, 1981–1985.

Gaventa, Beverly Roberts. *Acts of the Apostles*. Nashville: Abingdon, 2003.

Jervell, Jacob. *Luke and the People of God: A New Look at Luke–Acts*. Minneapolis: Augsburg, 1972.

Johnson, Luke Timothy. *The Gospel of Luke*. Vol. 3 of Sacra Pagina. Daniel J. Harrington, gen. ed. Collegeville: Liturgical, 1991.

———. "Luke–Acts, Book of." *ABD* 4: 403-20.

Josephus. Translated by H. St. J. Thackeray et al. 10 vols. LCL. Cambridge: Harvard University Press, 1930–1965.

Klauck, Hans-Josef. *Magic and Paganism in Early Christianity: The World of Acts of the Apostles*. Minneapolis: Fortress, 2003.

Kodell, Jerome. "Luke's Use of Laos, 'People,' Especially in the Jerusalem Narrative (Lk 19:28–24:53)." *CBQ* 31 (1969): 327-43.

Kopas, Jane. "Jesus and Women: Luke's Gospel." *JNTS* 26 (1986): 192-202.

Kurz, William. *Reading Luke–Acts: Dynamics of Biblical Narrative*. Louisville: Westminster / John Knox, 1993.

Levine, Amy-Jill (ed.; with Marianne Blickenstaff). *A Feminist Companion to the Acts of the Apostles*. London: T. & T. Clark, 2004.

Martin, Clarice J. "The Acts of the Apostles." In *STS*, pp. 763-99.

Moxnes, Halvor. *The Economy of the Kingdom: Social Conflict and Economic Relations in Luke's Gospel*. Philadelphia: Fortress, 1988.

Nickelsburg, George W. E. *Resurrection, Immortality, and Eternal Life in Intertestamental Judaism*. Cambridge: Harvard University Press, 1972.

Powell, Mark Allan. *What Are They Saying about Luke?* New York: Paulist, 1989.

Reid, Barbara. *Choosing the Better Part?: Women in the Gospel of Luke*. Collegeville, Minn.: Liturgical, 1996.

Sanders, J. T. "The Salvation of the Jews in Luke–Acts." Pages 104-28 in *Luke–Acts: New Perspectives from the SBL Seminar*. Edited by Charles Talbert. New York: Crossroad, 1984.

Schüssler Fiorenza, Elisabeth. "A Feminist Critical Interpretation for Liberation: Martha and Mary: Luke 10:38-42." *Religion and Intellectual Life* 3 (1986): 21-36.

Seeley, David. *The Noble Death: Graeco-Roman Martyrology and Paul's Concept of Salvation*. Sheffield: JSOT Press, 1990.

Seim, Turid Karlsen. *The Double Message: Patterns of Gender in Luke–Acts*. Nashville: Abingdon, 1994.

———. "The Gospel of Luke." In *STS*, pp. 728-62.

Sim, David C. "The Women Followers of Jesus: The Implications of Luke 8:1-3." *HeyJ* 30 (1989): 51-62.

Smith, Dennis E. "Table Fellowship as a Literary Motif in the Gospel of Luke." *JBL* 106 (1987): 613-28.

Sterling, Gregory E. *Historiography and Self-Definition: Josephos, Luke–Acts and Apologetic Historiography*. Leiden: Brill, 1992.

Talbert, Charles. *Readings Acts: A Literary and Theological Commentary on Acts of the Apostles*. Macon: Smyth & Hellways, 2005.

Tannehill, Robert A. "Israel in Luke–Acts: A Tragic Story." *JBL* 104 (1985): 69-85.

————.*The Narrative Unity of Luke–Acts.* 2 vols. Philadelphia: Fortress, 1986.

Tiede, David L. *Luke.* Augsburg Commentary on the New Testament. Minneapolis: Augsburg, 1988.

————. *Prophecy and History in Luke–Acts.* Philadelphia: Fortress, 1980.

Tomson, Peter J. *Presumed Guilty: How the Jews Got Blamed for the Death of Jesus.* Minneapolis: Fortress, 2005.

CHAPTER SIX

THE GOSPEL OF JOHN AND LETTERS OF JOHN

INTRODUCTION

The ascription of this Gospel to John tells us little. Early church tradition believed that John, one of the twelve apostles, was the author. Some identify the author with a disciple the Gospel calls the one "whom Jesus loved" (the "beloved disciple"; 13:23; 19:26; 20:2; 21:7, 20). At the end of chapter 21, the narrator says, "This is the disciple who is testifying to these things and has written them, and we know that his testimony is true" (21:24). There are various suggestions about the identity of this person—the Apostle John, Lazarus (whom Jesus raised from the dead), Nicodemus, or Mary Magdalene. No one really knows who it was. It is possible that the community that produced the Gospel was founded by or greatly influenced by this disciple. In this sense he or she would be ultimately responsible for the Gospel, but not its actual author. It is unlikely that an eyewitness wrote it. Most believe that the synoptic portraits reflect historical reality more closely than John's, because John's Jesus seems to be a more otherworldly, all-knowing figure. There is evidence that the Gospel has gone through several editions and represents extensive theological development of Jesus' story.

Gnostics found John's Gospel congenial. They found appealing John's notion of Jesus as a figure from the heavenly realm, sent into the world of darkness to bring light to those who received him. But the Gospel may in fact have been written to counter the idea, held by some Gnostics, that Jesus was not fully human, but only appeared to be so (a position called *Docetism*), or that salvation can be found within oneself (see our treatment of the *Gospel of Thomas*) rather than in complete dependence on Jesus.

John's Gospel contains interesting textual difficulties. The most famous is a passage present in many manuscripts but not part of the original gospel—the story of the woman caught in adultery, found in many manuscripts as John 7:53–8:11. By law, the woman should be stoned. Jesus, however, says that the one without sin should cast the first stone. The woman's accusers all depart, and Jesus tells the woman to sin no more. Scholars agree that the passage is not part of the original gospel. It is not in the earliest Greek manuscripts. Where it is present, it is not always in the same spot. Sometimes it appears in the Gospel of Luke. So it floats around in the New Testament and is absent in some of the best manuscripts. We should not use the passage to shed light on John's Gospel. That does not detract from its beauty and significance for Christians, of course. It is a story near to the hearts of many Christians, because it condemns self-righteousness and is a marvelous example of God's forgiveness.

John employed oral tradition, as did the other evangelists. Many hypothesize that he also used written sources. The two most common theories are that he used a source consisting of signs (miracles) or one containing discourse material. Support for the use of a signs source comes from the fact that the miracle at the wedding feast of Cana is counted as "the first of his signs" (2:11), while the curing of the royal official's son is called "the second sign that Jesus did after coming from Judea to Galilee" (4:54). But 2:23 claims that between these two miracles Jesus did other signs, in Jerusalem during Passover. At the end of chapter 20, we hear that "Jesus did many other signs in the presence of his disciples, which are not written in this book," hinting that there may be a larger collection from which John draws (20:30). Further support for such a source comes from the fact that only John refers to the miracles as "signs." If John did use a "signs source," it can no longer be reconstructed with any confidence. Whatever material John used, it completely integrated into the Gospel, both linguistically and theologically.

Some propose that a saying source lies behind the Fourth Gospel. Again, the homogeneous nature of the Gospel hinders reconstruction of any such sources, so they remain speculative. No source theory has won general acceptance.

RELATIONSHIP TO THE SYNOPTIC GOSPELS

The relationship of John to the Synoptics is a thorny problem. John is like Matthew, Mark, and Luke in many ways, but it is also unlike them in numerous ways. We can view the Synoptics side by side and see that they often correspond closely, even verbally, so that some theory of literary dependence is required, but a comparison of John with the Synoptics does not yield the same results. It is tantalizingly like the Synoptics, but the similarity does not necessarily imply literary dependence.

Let us begin with the similarities. Both the Synoptics and John are prose narratives about Jesus' public life, beginning with his association with John the Baptist and extending to his death. Matthew and Luke preface this with infancy narratives. John's prologue brings the narrative all the way back to the creation of the world, or even before that. Matthew, Luke, and John have resurrection appearances, a feature absent from Mark. All four canonical gospels depict a relationship between Jesus and the Baptist. In all, Jesus teaches, does miracles, gathers disciples, enters Jerusalem at the end of his career in a triumphal fashion, eats the Last Supper with his followers, is betrayed by one of his disciples, and is crucified under Pontius Pilate. In all four, Jesus is raised from the dead.

There are significant differences between John and the Synoptics as well. In the Synoptics, John the Baptist baptizes Jesus. Not so in John's Gospel. In the Synoptics, Jesus says little about himself. In John, he speaks of little else. What he says about himself in John is distinctive, for he says he came down from heaven, sent by the Father. He says no such thing in the Synoptics. Jesus' teaching in the Synoptics is in short units—even Matthew's long sermons are constructed by assembling shorter sayings and parables. John's Jesus delivers long discourses, sometimes in dialogue with others and sometimes as monologues. A common form in the Synoptics is the parable, in the sense of a short story. There is not a single parable by this definition in John. A major topic of Jesus' synoptic teaching is the kingdom of God. In John, it is mentioned in only one episode.

There are other differences. Exorcisms are prominent in the Synoptics; John contains none. John tells of three visits by Jesus to Jerusalem during his ministry, while the Synoptics have but one. John places Jesus' cleansing of the temple at the beginning of the ministry, while in the Synoptics it is at the end. The Synoptics say Jesus dies on Passover, while in John it happens the day before. The Synoptics do not recount simultaneous missions by John the Baptist and Jesus, while John does. John frequently speaks of those who oppose Jesus as "the Jews," while this is not so in the

Synoptics. In general, there is much that is somewhat familiar, but that it all looks rather different.

Some Features of the Synoptics Not Found in John
- Infancy narrative
- Virgin birth
- Birth in Bethlehem
- Baptism by John
- Temptation in the wilderness
- Exorcisms
- Parables
- Messianic secret
- Transfiguration on the mountain
- Institution of the Eucharist at the Last Supper
- Prayer by Jesus in Gethsemane asking for cup of suffering to be taken away
- Trial before the Sanhedrin
- Conviction for blasphemy at a trial before the Sanhedrin

STRUCTURE

John prefaces his Gospel with a poetic prologue presenting Jesus as the eternal Word of God, present with God at creation, through whom God creates the universe, and who becomes incarnate in Jesus. After the prologue, John's Gospel is in two main parts, the Book of Signs (chs. 1–12) and the Book of Glory (chs. 13–20). For John, the words and deeds of Jesus' public ministry are "signs" pointing to his true identity. He returns to heaven through his passion and death. The heavenly world is the place of glory, so Jesus' death and resurrection are his glorification and the part of the Gospel containing his passion and death is the Book of Glory. At the end of the Book of Signs, Jesus says, "The hour has come for the Son of Man to be glorified" (12:23).

The Book of Signs opens with John the Baptist's testimony to Jesus and Jesus' calling his first disciples (1:18-51), the first of whom are drawn from among John's disciples. The rest of the Book of Signs is composed partly of units each containing a sign and subsequent discourse (for example, 5:1-47, healing on the Sabbath; 6:22-65, multiplication of bread; 9:1-34, curing of a blind man; 11:28-53, raising of Lazarus). Hostility grows between Jesus and "the Jews," a fairly undifferentiated group consisting of all Jews, most of whom do not believe in Jesus (although there are exceptions). The Book of Signs is punctuated by three sayings about the Son of Man echoing the three passion predictions in the Synoptic Gospels (3:14; 8:28; 12:32-34). The Book of Glory contains the Last Supper, stretching for five chapters (chs. 13–17), the passion narrative proper, and resurrection appearances.

John contains evidence of having been composed over time, probably with multiple editions. For example, the last verse of chapter 20 seems to end the Gospel, but then there is another chapter, chapter 21, often called the *Appendix* or the *Epilogue*. The ending of chapter 14 concludes the Last Supper discourses, but they continue for three more chapters. Chapters 5 and 6 seem in reverse order because of geographical contradictions in the present arrangement. Although these observations are valid, we analyze the Gospel in its present form.

Prologue (1:1-18)
Book of Signs (1:19–12:50)
Gathering disciples and giving signs (1:19–4:54)
    John's Witness: Jesus' Title and First Disciples (1:19-51)
    Wedding at Cana (2:1-12)
    Cleansing of the Temple (2:13-25)
    Dialogue with Nicodemus (3:1-15)
    The Son Comes into the World (3:16-21)
    John's Testimony Continues (3:22-36)
    The Samaritan Woman (4:1-42)
    Cure of the Official's Son (4:43-54)
Jewish Feasts (5:1–10:42)
    Sabbath (Shabbat) (5:1-47)
    Passover (Pesach) (6:1-71)
    Booths (Sukkoth) (7:1–10:21)
    Dedication (Hanukkah) (10:22-42)
The Hour Approaches (11:1–12:50)
    Raising of Lazarus (11:1-54)
    The Hour Has Come (11:55–12:36)
    Conclusion of the Public Ministry (12:37-50)
Book of Glory (13:1–20:31)
    The Last Supper (13:1–17:26)
        Meal, foot washing, betrayal (13:1-38)
        Discourse (14:1–17:26)

The Passion Narrative (18:1–19:42)
    The Garden (18:1-11)
    Jesus before Annas and Caiaphas (18:12-27)
    Iesus before Pilate (18:28–19:16)
Crucifixion and Death (19:16-42)
The Resurrection (20:1-29)
Conclusion (20:30-31)
Epilogue (21:1-25)

OVERVIEW

John believes this world to be a place of darkness, alienated from God. Humans cannot reach God on their own. Jesus has come down from heaven to make access to the Father possible. He is the only bridge from the world below to the world above. Jesus is the incarnation of the Word, which existed with God before creation. John goes so far as to say that Jesus is God, although he does not mean that Jesus is the Father. The divine Word, through whom God created the universe, has become flesh, incarnate, fully human, in Jesus. In Jesus, the world of light penetrates the world of darkness. All who come to Jesus come to the light. Jesus is the only way to reach the light; to reject Jesus is to reject the light.

Jesus offers salvation to the world and most of the world rejects it. Those who accept it become a different kind of humanity, born again. Those who do not, the majority, have no real connection with God. This basic scheme structures the entire Gospel.

John's language reflects the opposition between heaven and earth, God and unbelieving humanity. He uses a series of binary opposites that reinforce each other, including light/darkness, heaven/earth, truth/falsehood, up/down, spirit/flesh, love/hate, disciples/world, Jesus/world. The language reflects not only John's theology, it also reflects the experience of his community as alienated from society at large and perhaps even from other Christians. It also helps to create that separation. Language creates a barrier—socially, theologically, psychologically—between community and world. John enlists the devices of riddles and double meanings to the same end. Those who grasp the truth are insiders, and only they can understand what Jesus says. All others remain in darkness.

Things to Look For
- Jesus' identity is central to the Gospel, in a way that goes beyond the other gospels. Those who accept that he comes from God are saved, those who do not remain in darkness.
- There are degrees of faith.
- "Witness" is an important term in the Gospel. The world puts Jesus on trial, but ironically, it really puts itself on trial. Witnesses for Jesus include John the Baptist, Jesus himself, the Father, Torah, and Jesus' deeds.
- The Gospel is permeated with irony. The readers know more than the characters. The characters often say things that are true in ways they do not suspect.
- Miracles are "signs" of who Jesus is. This contrasts with the Synoptics, where Jesus refuses to grant signs. Mark thinks the miracles can mislead.
- John frequently uses the term "the Jews," mostly negatively. "The Jews" are almost always hostile to Jesus.
- Jesus replaces Judaism. Access to God comes not through Moses, the Torah, and the feasts but through Jesus.
- John uses symbolism liberally. He also uses double meaning, riddles, and misunderstanding.

SURVEY OF THE GOSPEL

PROLOGUE (1:1-18)

John prefaces his Gospel with a prologue in the form of a poem revealing Jesus' true identity and explaining his earthly career (1:1-18). We treat the background of the prologue in a separate section below. The prologue is a key to the Gospel. The reader who understands it will be an "insider"—one who understands who Jesus is, what he talks about, and why he does what he does. He or she will have attained the sort of faith in Jesus that is the goal of Jesus' ministry and of the Gospel itself. The prologue does not mention Jesus. It speaks of the Word. It is clear both from the prologue itself as well as from its placement at the beginning of the Gospel, the Word become flesh is Jesus Christ. The Word is present with God "in the beginning," at the creation. The Word is with God and *is* God (1:1-2). Through the Word, God created everything (1:3). Jesus is the incarnation of the Word (1:14). "Incarnation" means enfleshment, made flesh. "Flesh" is used in the biblical sense of a full human being, Jesus. So the prologue conveys the belief that Jesus is both divine and human.

Jesus' coming into the world is a matter of cosmic significance. The very one through whom the world came to be now comes into the world as a human. He comes to humanity, and to Israel in particular. Ironically, although the world was created through him, the world does not accept him (1:10). And although Israel, the people closest to God, should be in the best position to recognize and accept Jesus, it does not do so (1:11). The few people who do accept Jesus are born again and become a new humanity comprised of God's children (1:12-13). Humanity as a whole cannot claim to be God's children. Only those who accept Jesus have access to life and light. The rest of humanity remains in darkness (1:8-9).

The prologue ends with an explicit reference to Judaism. God gave Israel the Torah through Moses. But, for John, that did not give Israel access to God. That can come only "through Jesus Christ" (1:17). What the Torah promised, grace and truth, Greek terms that correspond to God's covenantal qualities of loving-kindness and faithfulness to Israel (Exod 34:6, for example, and many other places in the Jewish Scriptures), come not through Moses but through Jesus, the "only Son."

Two passages in this poem refer to John the Baptist (1:6-9, 15). They are polemical, insisting that John is not the light, but only its witness. If it is necessary to assert that John is not the light, then it is reasonable to assume that someone says that he is and that the evangelist corrects this misunderstanding. The polemic concerning the Baptist continues in chapters 1, 3, and 4.

BOOK OF SIGNS (1:19–12:50)

Gathering Disciples and Giving Signs (1:19–4:54)
1:19-51: John's Witness: Jesus' Titles and First Disciples. In each of the four canonical gospels, John the Baptist appears in advance of Jesus and announces his coming. For all of them, both John's mission and Jesus' career fulfill Scripture. In the Synoptics, John baptizes Jesus, but the Fourth Gospel omits Jesus' baptism. The evangelist did not want Jesus' superiority to John compromised in any way. The Baptist's task is simply to "witness" to Jesus.

In a scene unique to John, "the Jews" send priests and Levites from Jerusalem to ask John the Baptist who he is (1:19-28). Priests and Levites in Jerusalem were the leaders of the Judean community. It is strange that "the Jews" send their leaders to ask something—one would not expect "the Jews" to send their leaders on errands. As we shall see, John creates a collective character called "the Jews" and presents them as a fairly monochromatic group that is generally hostile to Jesus.

The Baptist responds to these emissaries: "He confessed and did not deny it, but confessed, 'I am not the Messiah'" (1:20). The fourth evangelist is so anxious to deny that John is the Messiah that he writes awkward prose: "He confessed and did not deny it, but confessed." It is hard to imagine that no one thought John to be the Messiah when the evangelist refutes it so forcefully. The Baptist also denies that he is Elijah, a contradiction of Matt 11:14 and 17:10-13 (see also Mark 9:11-13). He also says that he is not "the prophet," perhaps meaning an eschatological prophet of the sort the Samaritans and the community of the Dead Sea Scrolls expected.

The Baptist tells his questioners that he is "the voice of one crying out in the wilderness, / 'make straight the way of the Lord,'" so he fulfills Isa 40:3, as the Synoptics also claim. The Baptist informs his audience that among them is someone whom they do not know and who is much greater than he (1:26-27). Such ignorance about Jesus pervades the Gospel.

The next day John sees Jesus and declares him "the Lamb of God who takes away the sins of the world" (1:29). Only in John is Jesus so designated. The lamb imagery probably refers to the Passover lamb. Only in John's Passion Narrative does Jesus die at the same moment that the Passover lambs are slaughtered in Jerusalem. The Baptist continues, "I myself did not know him." Even John does not immediately grasp Jesus' true identity, but once he observes the Spirit descend on Jesus, he can say, "I myself have seen and have testified that this is the Son of God" (1:34). Here we have the Gospel's characteristic language of witness. ("To witness" and "to testify" are the same in Greek, as are "witness" and "testimony.") The evangelist does not tell us when John saw the Spirit descend on Jesus, perhaps because it would have been at Jesus' baptism, which John omits.

The following day, John again calls Jesus the Lamb of God, and two of John's disciples follow Jesus and stay with him, becoming his first two disciples (1:35-39). This may reflect historical reality—that Jesus drew his first disciples from among the ranks of John's followers. It also illustrates that John prepares the way for Jesus. Once Jesus is present, one should follow him, not John. The two call him "rabbi," which the evangelist translates as "teacher." One of the two is Andrew, Simon's brother. He summons Simon, saying, "We have found the Messiah," and the evangelist adds, "which is translated Anointed" (1:40-42). Jesus renames Simon "Cephas," which the narrator explains is translated "Peter" (see Matt 16:17-18). "Cephas" is Aramaic for "rock," while "Peter" is the Greek form. It is likely that Simon was called Cephas, and that the Greek-speaking church changed that to Peter.

Next to be called is Philip, who calls Nathaniel, saying, "We have found him about whom Moses in the law and also the prophets wrote, Jesus son of Joseph from Nazareth" (1:45). Nathaniel at first is skeptical, until Jesus demonstrates miraculous knowledge, and then he proclaims Jesus rabbi, Son of God, and king of Israel (1:49).

At this point we should take stock of what is said about Jesus in the few verses we have already read (1:19-49). He is Lamb of God, Son of God, rabbi (Teacher), Messiah (Anointed), king of Israel, and the one about whom Moses, the Law, and the prophets wrote. This extensive catalog of titles and descriptions shows that Jesus fulfills all Jewish hopes.

These titles, though true, do not do justice to the evangelist's view of Jesus. He brackets the insights of the Baptist, Andrew, Philip, and Nathaniel with the prologue on one side, which says that Jesus is the Word, God, and instrument of creation, and Jesus' words to Nathaniel in 1:50-51 on the other. Jesus says, "Do you believe because I told you that I saw you under the fig tree? You will see greater things than these.... Very truly, I tell you, you will see heaven opened and the angels of God ascending and descending upon the Son of Man." This alludes to Jacob's dream at Bethel in Gen 28:10-22. Jacob dreams of a stairway (often translated "ladder") joining heaven and earth, on which angels ascend and descend. When he awakens, he realizes that the site is a point of contact between heaven and earth, so he names it "Bethel," meaning "House of God," declaring the place to be "the house of God" and "the gate of heaven." Jesus signifies that he himself is the true point of connection between heaven and earth. There is no way to God except through him. Jesus uses the phrase "Son of Man" in this context because the specific content that John attributes to that title is that Jesus comes from heaven and will return there.

2:1-12: Wedding at Cana. Chapter 2 contains two episodes that illustrate Jesus' relation to Judaism. In the first, Jesus attends a wedding feast at Cana of Galilee and turns the water meant for Jewish purification rites into high-quality wine. This symbolizes Jesus' replacement of Jewish institutions—in this case Jewish water rites for purification. The narrator concludes, "Jesus did this, the first of his signs, in Cana of Galilee, and revealed his glory; and his disciples believed in him" (2:11). In sharp contrast to the Synoptics, where Jesus refuses to give a sign, John terms Jesus' miracles "signs" that reveal his "glory," that is, his origin in the Father. The disciples believe because of a sign.

2:13-25: Cleansing of the Temple. In the second story, Jesus cleanses the temple at Passover by ejecting the money changers and animal sellers. When "the Jews" ask him for a sign proving his authority to do this, he says, "Destroy this temple, and in three days I will raise it up" (2:19). His hearers take him literally, but the reader learns that Jesus refers to his body, which will be raised three days after his death. The use of double meaning in John is common; here we have literal and symbolic meanings. In the Synoptics, the incident occurs at the end of Jesus' career; John moves it to the beginning, making it programmatic. John's attitude toward Jewish institutions is that they cannot provide the access to God available only in Jesus. At best, Jewish institutions such as the Torah and the temple point to Jesus. Only the insiders see this.

The narrator comments in verses 23-25 that Jesus' signs cause many to "believe" in him, but he does not trust them, because he understands humans. For John there are levels of belief; belief that relies on signs is imperfect. It can progress to a deeper knowledge of Jesus but does not necessarily do so.

3:1-15: Dialogue with Nicodemus. A Jewish leader, Nicodemus, comes to Jesus "by night," symbolizing that he is not fully in the light. Nicodemus admits, "Rabbi, we know that you are a teacher who has come from God; for no one can do these signs that you do apart from the presence of God" (3:2). The "signs" convince Nicodemus and his unidentified colleagues, probably other Jewish teachers, that Jesus is from God. There is irony in Nicodemus's words, for his assertion that Jesus is "from God" is truer than he imagines. Jesus responds that no one can see the kingdom of God "without being born from above." The English translation hides a double meaning. The word translated "from above" is *anothen*, which means either "again" or "above." Nicodemus takes it to mean "again" and so inquires how one can be born a second time. Jesus does mean "again," though not in Nicodemus's literal fashion. Believing in Jesus is to be born a second time, into a new humanity composed of God's children (1:12-13). It is also to be born from above. It is to become a member of the world of light above, and to be removed from the world of darkness here below.

Jesus clarifies what it means to be born "again" or "from above." It means to be born of water and the Spirit (3:5). Water refers to baptism (possibly a later addition to the text, if, according to some commentators, John is not interested in the sacraments—Christian rituals such as baptism and the Eucharist; note that water does not occur again in the discussion). Spirit is one side of the dualism flesh/spirit. Participation in the Spirit means to belong to God's realm, the light, the world above, while the flesh is in darkness. The dualism is absolute, for as Jesus says, "What is born of the flesh is flesh, and what is born of the Spirit is spirit" (3:6). He continues his explanation through a riddle: "The wind blows where it chooses, and you hear the sound of it, but you do not know where it comes from or where it goes. So it is with everyone who is born of the Spirit" (3:8). The key to the riddle is knowing that the word for "spirit" and "wind" are the same, *pneuma*. One could translate it as "spirit" throughout, or as "wind," or one could mix the translations. Jesus uses an example from nature here to make a point. In the ancient world, wind was not understood scientifically. Some texts, some Jewish apocalypses for example, speak of rooms at the edge of the world where the winds are stored until needed. As Jesus notes, people do not know where the wind comes from; they just see its effects. It is the same with the Spirit and those born of the spirit. Outsiders, unbelievers, cannot know where the Spirit comes from or comprehend the world to which people of the Spirit belong, for they have no access to it.

Nicodemus is puzzled: "How can these things be?" (3:9). Jesus' answer encapsulates the evangelist's attitude toward Jewish leaders of his own day: "Are you a teacher of Israel, and yet you do not understand these things?" (3:10). Jesus asserts, "We speak of what we know and testify to what we have seen; yet you do not receive our testimony" (3:11). The sudden shift to "we" suggests that circumstances in the evangelist's own time determine how he tells the story. John's community is the "we." They "testify" or "witness" to what they have seen—Jesus, the one come down from heaven. Their non-Christian Jewish contemporaries do not accept this. This explains their incomprehension. Perceiving the things of the Spirit ultimately means that they must accept Jesus, because "no one has ascended into heaven except the one who descended from heaven, the Son of Man" (3:13).

Deuteronomy, the fifth book of the Torah, says that Israel is fortunate because there is no need to ascend to heaven to ascertain God's will. Israel knows God's will through Torah. John's Jesus puts himself in place of Torah. The will of God in heaven can be known only through the unique one who comes down from heaven.

Jesus' words can also be read against the backdrop of Jewish and Christian stories about people who ascend to heaven. Elijah ascends in 2 Kgs 2:11. The mysterious figure of Enoch, seventh generation from Adam, does not die but is "taken" by God (Gen 5:24). He becomes the hero of an extensive apocalyptic literature based on the conviction that he went to heaven, received secrets, and returned to earth to share them (*1* and *2 Enoch*). The Apostle Paul claims he visited heaven and received secrets that he cannot tell (2 Cor 12:1-5). The book of Revelation says that a Christian seer named John made a trip to heaven and learned eschatological secrets (Rev 4:1 and throughout). Against all this, the fourth evangelist denies that anyone has ever gone to heaven. Jesus, the one who has come down from heaven, is humanity's only link to the world above.

Enoch, Paul, the seer John, and other apocalyptic seers and visionaries begin as human beings on earth, make a trip to heaven, and return to share their knowledge with an elect. Jesus' trip is in reverse. He is first of all the eternal Word of God, with God in the world of glory, and he must descend before he ascends. The second part of the trip, the ascension, takes place, ironically, in the crucifixion. That is how Jesus goes back to the glory of heaven. (John has no separate narrative of the ascension, as does Luke.)

It makes sense that in the Nicodemus dialogue, which stresses Jesus' heavenly origin, we hear the first prediction of Jesus' death: "Just as Moses lifted up the serpent in the wilderness, so must the Son of Man be lifted up, that whoever believes in him may have eternal life" (3:14-15). The term "lifted up" occurs three times in the Gospel to indicate Jesus' crucifixion (3:14; 8:28; 12:32). It has a double meaning, since it also means "exalted." Jesus' crucifixion is identical with his exaltation, for through the crucifixion he returns to the world of glory. Those who behold the crucified Jesus and understand this can take advantage of the connection to heaven that his descent and ascent establish. The evangelist says that this is foreshadowed in Num 21, where the people suffer a plague of serpents. Moses fashions a bronze serpent and lifts it up on a pole, and all who look at it are saved. For John, this is a type of Jesus crucified.

Nicodemus appears two more times in the Gospel. In 7:50-51, he challenges the chief priests and Pharisees by saying that it is not lawful to judge a person without giving him a hearing. In 19:39, he works with Joseph of Arimathea, another Jewish leader, to ensure Jesus a proper burial. He is a fascinating figure, in that he may illustrate a progression in faith.

3:16-21: The Son Comes into the World. The following verses sum up the significance of Jesus' descent into the world of darkness. His descent makes possible human participation in the light and offers salvation. Those who do not believe are already condemned, having rejected their only way to God. This is "realized eschatology." The condemnation that the Synoptics reserve for the last judgment takes effect or is "realized" in the very decision for or against Jesus.

3:22-36: John's Testimony Continues. John the Baptist reappears. The passage begins, "After this Jesus and his disciples went into the Judean countryside, and he spent some time there with them and baptized" (3:22). John is baptizing nearby, and some of his disciples tell him that Jesus "is baptizing, and all are going to him." John again insists that he is not the Messiah and says that he must decrease as Jesus increases. There follows another section (3:31-36) affirming Jesus' heavenly origin, the truth of his "testimony," his status of being above all, the fact that he gives the Spirit, and the idea that those who believe in Jesus will have eternal life and those who do not will experience God's wrath. It is unclear whether this summarizing passage is from the Baptist's lips or from the narrator.

4:1-42: The Samaritan Woman. The story of the Samaritan woman at the well appears only in John (4:5-42). It is introduced by the notice that the Pharisees know that Jesus makes and baptizes more disciples than John, causing Jesus to go back to Galilee through Samaria. Jesus' dialogue with the woman is driven by her misunderstandings. Jesus leads her step-by-step into deeper comprehension. The two meet at a well where she has come to draw water. Jesus reveals that he is the living water, a spring gushing up into eternal life. Thinking that he speaks of physical water that will never fail, she asks for it. Jesus discloses that he knows her past. Impressed by his miraculous knowledge, she concludes that he is a prophet, and she asks him to settle the dispute between the Samaritans and the Jews about whether one should worship on Mount Gerizim in Samaria, as do the Samaritans, or in Jerusalem, as do the Jews. Jesus says the Jews are right but that it no longer matters, since now all should worship in the Spirit. She says that she knows the Messiah is coming. Jesus reveals to her that he is the Messiah. She brings her fellow villagers to Jesus, and they come to believe that he is the "Savior of the world" (4:42).

4:43-54: Cure of the Official's Son. The section concludes with the curing of the royal official's son at Cana of Galilee, forming a frame with the wedding miracle earlier. The story portrays those who believe because of signs. Jesus implies that this is an inferior sort of faith, even if it is genuine: "Unless you see signs and wonders you will not believe" (4:48). This is one of the few stories in John with a close synoptic parallel (Q 7:1-10).

Jewish Feasts (5:1–10:42)

John structures this section around Jewish feasts—Sabbath, Passover, Booths, Hanukkah.

5:1-47: Sabbath (Shabbat). Chapter 5 takes place during a Jewish feast, though John does not specify which. The setting is a Sabbath during the feast. The chapter follows the pattern of miracle followed by discourse. Jesus performs a cure, and "the Jews" object that he does work forbidden on the Sabbath. Jesus says, "My father is still working, and I also am working" (5:17). The narrator adds, "For this reason the Jews were seeking all the more to kill him, because he was not only breaking the sabbath, but was also calling God his own Father, thereby making himself equal to God" (5:18). In the discourse, Jesus identifies his work with that of the Father, for the Father reveals the Father's deeds to Jesus. Those who believe will have eternal life. The Father has also appointed Jesus as judge, and Jesus' judgment is God's judgment. Jesus lists the persons and things that testify to him—John the Baptist, his own deeds (identical to the work of the Father), the Father, Scripture, and Moses (through Scripture).

Ironically Jesus' work on the Sabbath, forbidden by Torah, does not violate God's will. Rather, it discloses that he is God's Son who does God's work on the Sabbath. In a sense, he replaces the Sabbath. For his detractors, even Sabbath becomes a hindrance to recognizing God's work through him.

6:1-71: Passover (Pesach). The events of chapter 6 take place near the Passover. The chapter begins with the multiplication of loaves and fish (6:1-15), followed by Jesus walking on the water (6:16-21). The Synoptics contain the same sequence (Mark 6:30-52 and parallels), which raises the issue of the relationship between John and the

Synoptics. Possibly they both depend on oral tradition. Both miracles echo the exodus. God supplied Israel with miraculous bread in the wilderness, and God led Israel safely through the Red Sea. This leads to Jesus' discourse on the bread from heaven. He accuses the crowd of following him not because of his signs, but only because they ate their fill of the loaves. He tells them they must do the works of God. Doing God's works is equivalent to believing in Jesus. Ironically, they ask for a sign. Jesus has been doing signs throughout the Gospel, and he says that they have not been paying attention to them.

The crowd reminds Jesus that Moses gave a sign, manna from heaven. Jesus responds, "Very truly, I tell you, it was not Moses who gave you the bread from heaven, but it is my Father who gives you the true bread from heaven. For the bread of God is that which comes down from heaven and gives life to the world" (6:32-33). His hearers take him literally and ask for this bread. This recalls the Samaritan woman's request for physical water. Jesus states, "I am the bread of life. . . . I have come down from heaven, not to do my own will, but the will of him who sent me" (6:35, 38). Jesus contrasts himself with the manna: "I am the bread of life. Your ancestors ate the manna in the wilderness, and they died. This is the bread that comes down from heaven, so that one may eat of it and not die" (6:48-50). So again, Moses at best witnesses to Jesus. Those who rely on just Moses miss God's true approach to humanity in Jesus.

Jesus insists that his hearers must eat his flesh and drink his blood, a reference to the Eucharist (6:51-58). Some scholars think the verses were added later, since John does not show much interest in sacraments. The institution of the Eucharist is absent from the Last Supper, for example. It is striking that despite the emphasis on eating Jesus' flesh in this passage, Jesus tells Peter, "It is the spirit that gives life; the flesh is useless" (6:63). This lends further weight to the proposal that verses 51-58 are not original. If the verses are excised, the passage still flows smoothly. If the verses are secondary, then the discourse focuses more firmly on Jesus as revealer of the Father.

"The Jews" say, "Is this not Jesus, the son of Joseph, whose father and mother we know? How can he now say, 'I have come down from heaven'?" (6:41-42). The scene corresponds to the synoptic incident where Jesus visits his hometown synagogue and the people do not accept him as a prophet, since they have known him since childhood (Mark 6:1-6). Here it is transformed in a typically Johannine way. It is not merely Jesus' prophetic claim that alienates the crowd, it is his assertion that he came down from heaven. When some disciples take offense, Jesus says, "Does this offend you? Then what if you were to see the Son of Man ascending to where he was before?" (6:61-62).

Some abandon Jesus, and he asks the rest if they, too, will leave. Peter says, "Lord, to whom can we go? You have the words of eternal life. We have come to believe and know that you are the Holy One of God" (6:68-69). This recalls Peter's confession in the Synoptics (Mark 8:29). It has a Johannine twist, since Jesus has the "words of eternal life."

7:1–10:21: Booths (Sukkoth). In chapter 7, Jesus' brothers urge him to travel to Jerusalem for the feast of Booths so that all can know him. The narrator explains that not even his brothers believe in him, so their advice is insincere. Jesus declines, because his hour has not yet come—the hour of his passion and return to the Father. Later Jesus does go, secretly. Before he arrives, "the Jews" debate whether Jesus is a good man or a deceiver, yet they cannot debate openly "for fear of the Jews" (7:11-13). This exposes the convoluted nature of John's usage of the term "the Jews."

The rest of chapters 7–8 is a long interchange between Jesus and "the Jews" occurring over the several days of the feast. As usual, discussion ultimately centers on Jesus' identity, which for John equates to his divine origin. "The Jews," though their traditions should equip them to understand who Jesus is, fail to do so. Chapter 9 continues Jesus' stay in Jerusalem for Booths. Jesus cures a man born blind, and this raises the question of his identity and the conflicts between the cured man, his parents, and the leaders. Chapter 10 ends the period of Booths with Jesus' famous declaration that he is the good shepherd. The following paragraphs summarize these chapters.

7:14-18. "The Jews" marvel at Jesus' teaching and wonder where he got it (cf. Mark 6:1-6). Jesus says it comes from the one who sent him.

7:19-24. Jesus castigates "the Jews" for not keeping the Mosaic Torah. Torah permits circumcision on the Sabbath, a kind of physical work that benefits the recipient. How much more then does it permit healing on the Sabbath. This recalls Jesus' Sabbath healing in chapter 5 and the discussion there.

7:25-31. Some wonder whether Jesus might be the Messiah, but they are unsure since they believe that no one will know where the Messiah comes from, while they do know Jesus' origin. Assumed are Jewish traditions about the hiddenness of the Messiah or his origins (for example, *1 En.* 46, 48; *4 Ezra* 7:28; 13:32; *2 Bar.* 29:3; *b. Sanh.* 97a). Ironically, although the people know the village from which Jesus comes, they are ignorant of his ultimate origins. Jesus expresses the paradox: "You know me, and you know where I am from. I have not come on my own. But the one who sent me is true, and you do not know him. I know him, because I am from him, and he sent me" (7:28-29). The authorities try to arrest him but are unable, for his hour has not yet come. Temporal power is useless against Jesus. Physical force counts for nothing against him. He can be arrested only when he consents to it. Despite Jerusalem's hostile environment, many believe him because of his signs (7:31).

7:32-36. The authorities try again to arrest Jesus, unsuccessfully. Jesus says that they cannot do so because he must be with them a while longer to complete his mission, but then he will return to the Father. He says, "You will search for me, but you will not find me; and where I am, you cannot come" (7:34). "The Jews" puzzle over this. They wonder whether he means that he will go to the Greeks. Ironically, Christians ultimately do evangelize the Gentiles (Greeks). Indeed, in John 12:20-23, the sign that Jesus' hour has come is that some Greeks want to speak to him. Jesus' mission is not to the Greeks, so when they approach, he knows that the next phase of the Father's plan is near and that his own mission is finished. The section ends as "the Jews" wonder what Jesus means when he says, "Where I am, you cannot come."

7:37-39. On the festival's last day, Jesus cries out that all who are thirsty should come to him and drink, and that from the believer's heart will come rivers of living water, a reference to the Spirit. The narrator explains further, "As yet there was no Spirit, because Jesus was not yet glorified." Jesus is God's presence, and when Jesus returns to the Father, the Spirit becomes the presence of Jesus and the Father among believers.

7:40-44. The crowds again debate whether Jesus is the prophet, or perhaps the Messiah. Some object that Scripture says the Messiah is to come from Bethlehem, while Jesus comes from Galilee. This contradicts the conviction voiced earlier that the Messiah's origins will be mysterious (7:27). There were a variety of messianic beliefs current in first-century Judaism. John addresses two that are mutually contradictory. Neither the crowds nor the evangelist himself shows awareness that Jesus was born in Bethlehem.

7:45-52. The authorities argue about Jesus. Challenged about why they have not taken the situation in hand, the temple police tell the priests and the Pharisees that they have not arrested Jesus because "never has anyone spoken like this." Nicodemus objects to the leaders judging

Jesus without a hearing. Some leaders say Jesus is from Galilee and so cannot be the Messiah. Ironically, they claim that they know the Torah.

8:12-20. Jesus declares himself light of the world, recalling the prologue. The Pharisees accuse him of testifying on his own behalf. He answers that he must do so because he alone knows his origin. The Father also testifies for him. The Pharisees, misunderstanding, say, "Where is your Father?" Jesus replies, "You know neither me nor my Father. If you knew me, you would know my Father also." The religious leaders do not really know Jesus' Father, God. The only way to know God is to accept Jesus.

8:21-30. Jesus again asserts that he is soon to depart. "The Jews" wonder whether he might kill himself. This is ironic, for in chapter 10 Jesus claims to lay down his life of his own accord. Jesus responds, "You are from below, I am from above; you are of this world, I am not of this world" (8:23). This encapsulates the central message of the Gospel and explains both why Jesus is the only hope of humanity and why they do not receive him. Jesus says, "I am he." The Greek is *ego eimi*, which could be translated simply, "I am," but it means more in this passage. It alludes to God's name in Exod 3, "I AM," or "I AM WHO I AM." It is a claim to divinity. Jesus proclaims that they will recognize him when they have "lifted up" the Son of Man, another passion prediction using a verb simultaneously indicating crucifixion and exaltation.

8:31-59. The tone of the conversation between Jesus and "the Jews" rapidly deteriorates. The final section starts well enough. There are "Jews" who believe and are even disciples (8:31). But soon Jesus accuses them of plotting his death. They are therefore untrue to their father Abraham. Their real father is Satan, father of lies, for they do not accept the truth. They accuse him of being a Samaritan and having a demon. "The Jews" begin to realize the magnitude of the claims Jesus makes about himself. He claims to have existed before Abraham and to be able to protect from death those who believe in him. Finally, Jesus says, "Before Abraham was, I am" (8:58). Recognizing the allusion to the divine name (Exod 3), they attempt to stone him, but he hides himself and leaves the temple. If Jesus' claim is false, they rightly seek to stone him for blasphemy, but the reader knows the claim to be true.

Chapter 9. Chapter 9 brings no change of time or place, so we are still in Jerusalem during the feast of Booths. Jesus cures a blind man on the Sabbath, and the chapter describes the consequences. This is one of the most carefully crafted parts of the Gospel. It is a miracle followed by successive dialogues. According to Moloney, it contains eight sequential scenes, each featuring an interaction between two characters (counting groups as characters). The scenes are as follows: (1) Jesus and the disciples; (2) Jesus and the man born blind; (3) the blind man and his neighbors; (4) the blind man and the Pharisees; (5) the blind man's parents and the Pharisees; (6) the blind man and the Pharisees; (7) Jesus and the blind man; (8) Jesus and the Pharisees.

(1) *9:1-4.* Jesus' disciples wonder who has sinned, the man or his parents, to cause his blindness, but Jesus says the man's blindness is simply an opportunity for him to do another sign. The sign perfectly illustrates Jesus' claim to be light of the world (9:5).
(2) *9:5-7.* Jesus cures the man, who then departs.
(3) *9:8-12.* The man is questioned by his neighbors. They debate whether he is really the one who was blind. He insists that he is and declares that Jesus cured him.
(4) *9:13-17.* The Pharisees hear of it, summon the man, and accuse Jesus of breaking the Sabbath, proving himself a sinner. The man insists that Jesus is a prophet, an inadequate insight but one that points in the right direction.
(5) *9:18-23.* "The Jews" summon the parents of the healed man, who ask the leaders to consult the man himself about his cure. "His parents said this because they were afraid of the Jews; for the Jews had already agreed that anyone who confessed Jesus to be the Messiah would be put out of the synagogue" (9:22). This verse hints at the situation of John's church. Its members have been ejected from the synagogue for their christological claims.
(6) *9:24-34.* The leaders confront the man again. They declare Jesus a sinner, but the man insists that Jesus cured him. The leaders claim knowledge of Torah and say that they trust in Moses, while they do not know where Jesus comes from. The cured man boldly calls it astonishing that they do not know where he comes from, even though he cures the blind. The man sees the cure as proof that Jesus is from God. He wonders how it can be that they, having full knowledge of Torah, have no comprehension of a person clearly doing God's work. The leaders angrily throw the insolent man out.
(7) *9:35-39.* The man encounters Jesus, who reveals that he is the Son of Man.
(8) *9:40-41.* The chapter ends with Jesus telling the Pharisees, "If you were blind, you would not have sin. But now that you say, 'We see,'

your sin remains" (9:41). The Pharisees claim to know Torah, and Torah testifies to Jesus, so their sin is the greater.

This chapter indicts the Pharisees for their stubborn refusal to see what is before their eyes. They reject evidence that the less educated see clearly. Their hostility is dangerous to Jesus and to his followers, including the later church.

10:1-21. Chapter 10 continues the feast of Booths, which finally ends at 10:21. In this section, Jesus describes himself as the Good Shepherd, an image based on Ezek 34. In Ezek 34, God rejects Israel's shepherds, their kings, because they care only for themselves. God decides to rule the people directly. Jesus now fulfills this divine role. Of course, his hearers do not understand (10:6). Jesus uses the image to predict his death on behalf of the sheep. His death is voluntary and is proof of his love. The section and the feast end with another accusation that Jesus is possessed.

10:22-42: Dedication (Hanukkah). At this feast Jesus proclaims that he does the works of the Father, and that he and the Father are one. "The Jews" again take up stones to throw at him because of his blasphemy. Jesus insists that his works prove him to be one with the Father. Again they try unsuccessfully to arrest him. Jesus retreats to the other side of the Jordan, where many believers join him.

The Hour Approaches (11:1–12:50)

11:1-54: Raising of Lazarus. In the Synoptics, Jesus' attack on the temple leads to his death. For John, the precipitating factor is Jesus' raising of Lazarus from the dead. It is as the one who brings life and light to the world that Jesus is rejected.

When he hears that his good friend Lazarus, brother of Martha and Mary, is ill, Jesus stays away. (The sisters Martha and Mary are an interesting echo of Luke 10:38-42.) Jesus deliberately gives Lazarus time to die, so that he can raise him and thus perform a magnificent sign (11:4-6, 15). When he finally arrives, Martha says that had he been present, Lazarus would not have died. She expresses confidence that even now God will do whatever Jesus wants. Jesus says that Lazarus will rise from the dead. Martha takes this as an expression of conventional eschatology of the type found in the Synoptic Gospels. She agrees, professing faith in this traditional belief in resurrection "on the last day." Jesus then offers a riddle: "I am the resurrection and the life. Those who believe in me, even though they die, will live, and everyone who lives and believes in me will never die" (11:25-26). The key to the riddle is that death and life are used in two different ways. There is physical death and life, and spiritual death and life. Believers in Jesus, even if they die physically, will live eternally, and if they live physically and believe in Jesus, they will never die spiritually. This is John's realized eschatology. He affirms eschatological resurrection, but it is anticlimactic. The resurrection is already present in Jesus, so physical death loses its importance.

The next scene transports us to a fateful meeting of the Sanhedrin (11:45-53). The chief priests and Pharisees fear that the Romans will come and destroy their city and nation because of Jesus' growing following. A couple of generations later, the Romans did destroy city and temple (70 C.E.), and many Christians blamed it on Jewish refusal to accept Jesus. The high priest declares, "It is better for you to have one man die for the people than to have the whole nation destroyed" (11:50). The narrator explains that the high priest says this because his office invests him with prophetic powers.

11:55–12:36: The Hour Has Come. Things begin hastening toward Jesus' death. Passover approaches and the crowds wonder whether Jesus will come, since the leaders plan to arrest him (11:55-57). A woman anoints Jesus' feet, and he says that it is for his burial (12:1-8; see Matt 26:6-13 and Mark 14:3-9). Only John says that the woman is Mary—not Mary Magdalene, but the sister of Martha and Lazarus. We learn that the leaders also plan to kill Lazarus, since on his account many are believing in Jesus (12:9-11).

Jesus enters Jerusalem triumphantly, as in the Synoptics (12:12-19). The narrator says that his disciples fail to understand the implications of what is happening until after Jesus' death (see also 2:22). The crowd comes to meet Jesus because of his raising of Lazarus, a "sign." The Pharisees despair of controlling Jesus, for "the world has gone after him."

At this point, some Greeks seek to see Jesus, and when Jesus hears of it he knows that "the hour has come for the Son of Man to be glorified" (12:23). Jesus says that his impending death is glorification for God and for him. God's voice comes from heaven affirming that God is about to glorify God's name. Jesus explains that the voice comes not for him but for those around him (12:30). It is a sign. Jesus has no need for such signs. Jesus says that now the ruler of this world (Satan) will be cast out, and when the Son of Man is lifted up (crucified/exalted) he will draw all people to himself (12:31-34). This is the third of the passion predictions using the phrase Son of Man. The crowd objects that the Torah says the

Messiah will remain forever—an obvious misunderstanding of Torah, in John's view. Jesus warns them to walk by his light while they have him.

12:37-50: Conclusion of the Public Ministry. Jesus hides from the crowd. The lines are drawn. People have made their choices, and most have rejected Jesus, despite the signs. Their unbelief fulfills the prophecy of Isaiah, who foresaw Jesus' career (12:38-41). Nonetheless, John asserts that many, even some leaders, do believe in him but will not admit it for fear of being put out of the synagogue (12:42; see 9:22). They value human glory over divine. Jesus' public ministry ends with one last proclamation summarizing the Gospel's essence: God has sent Jesus; one who sees him sees God and whoever hears him hears God; those who reject him remain in darkness, and disbelief brings judgment (12:44-50).

BOOK OF GLORY (13:1–20:31)

The Last Supper (13:1–17:26)

13:1-38: Meal, Foot Washing, Betrayal. Unlike in the Synoptics, John's Last Supper is not a Passover meal. Jesus' death in this Gospel coincides with the time of the slaughter of the Passover lambs, emphasizing the parallel between Jesus and the lambs and recalling the Baptist's title for Jesus—Lamb of God. So for John the Last Supper takes place on the day before Passover. (The Jewish day goes from sunset to sunset.) There is no institution of the Eucharist in this account. There is, however, the story of Jesus washing his disciples' feet, found only in John.

John prefaces the Last Supper with a statement of Jesus' awareness of the significance of what is to happen: "Jesus, knowing that the Father had given all things into his hands, and that he had come from God and was going to God ..." (13:3). Knowing that he is to leave them, Jesus says, "By this everyone will know that you are my disciples, if you have love for one another" (13:35). This command is not the same as the one in the Sermon on the Mount, where Jesus commands love of enemies. Love here is for "one another," for members of the community. This fits the picture of John's community as a small minority in the midst of a hostile world. John stresses inner support and cohesion, not acceptance of outsiders. Similarly, in chapter 15, Jesus combines instruction to love one another with teaching that the world hates him and the disciples.

Jesus foretells Peter's betrayal but with a Johannine twist (13:36-38). He speaks of his impending departure, and Peter asks where he is going, showing that even the disciples do not fully understand Jesus' origins.

271

Jesus answers indirectly, saying that Peter cannot go with him now but will do so later. Peter says that he will follow Jesus anywhere and is willing to lay down his life for him. This is ironic, since Peter does not remain true to Jesus during the passion, and it also shows Peter's ignorance of where Jesus is going.

14:1–17:26: Discourse. The rest of the Last Supper is a long discourse by Jesus, interspersed with a few questions from his disciples (chs. 14–17). The discourse developed in stages. The last words of chapter 14 look like an ending: "Rise, let us be on our way," but then Jesus continues talking for three more chapters! So it looks as though the original discourse did end with chapter 14 and that what follows was added at a later time or times.

In chapter 14, Jesus informs the disciples that he must go away, and that he will prepare a place for them where he is going and will come back for them. Thomas objects that they do not know where he is going or the way to get there. Jesus responds, "I am the way, the truth, and the life. No one comes to the Father except through me. If you know me, you know my Father also. From now on you do know him and have seen him" (14:6-7). These verses present John's Gospel in a nutshell. Philip still does not understand and asks to see the Father. Jesus tells him that he is in the Father and the Father in him, so they have already seen the Father. Later in the chapter, Jesus says that he is in the disciples and they in him (14:20). The Father, Jesus, the Spirit, and the believers are closely connected, in a way that can be described as "indwelling." Believers have been made participants in the inner life of God, a notion that was to prove rich for later Christian theologians. Although the Gospel says that Jesus is God, Jesus tells the disciples, "The Father is greater than I," so they should be glad that he is going to the Father (14:28). Chapters 15–16 go back over some of the same themes as chapter 14, making it seem a later reflection on the same material.

Chapters 14–17 show that the Holy Spirit's presence in the community continues Jesus' work. The same Spirit descends on Jesus and remains with him during his ministry (1:32). When Jesus dies, he gives up his Spirit (19:30), so together with 1:32 this forms a frame for the Gospel. In 14:17, Jesus tells the disciples that the Spirit will come and abide with them. It is the Spirit of truth, and the world cannot receive it. In 14:26, the Spirit is called the *paraclete*, a Greek word meaning "advocate." The Spirit is from God and Jesus. The Spirit will come in Jesus' name and will teach them everything and will remind them of all Jesus has told them.

Several times the evangelist says that after Jesus' death and resurrection the disciples remember things that Jesus said and comprehend them for the first time. Now we learn that this happens through the Spirit. In 15:26, Jesus says that when the Spirit comes, it will testify on Jesus' behalf, as will the disciples. Finally, in 16:12-15, we learn that Jesus cannot tell his disciples everything yet. When the Spirit comes, it will guide them into "all truth." It will not speak on its own, but will speak what it hears, meaning that what it teaches it receives from Jesus and God.

Chapter 17 is a prayer of Jesus, reflecting on the interrelationships between Jesus, the Father, and the believers, anticipating the time when Jesus will no longer be on earth. Jesus prays, "Glorify me in your own presence with the glory that I had in your presence before the world existed." He restates the mutual indwelling of Jesus, the Father, and the believers. He asks for God's protection of believers and asserts that they do not belong to the world, any more than Jesus himself does. Therefore, the world hates them. He prays for the unity of believers and that they may also come to the world of glory to which Jesus is going.

THE PASSION NARRATIVE (18:1–19:42)

In its main lines, the passion of Jesus resembles that found in the Synoptics, but there are major differences. Mark is bleak, while Luke makes Jesus the admirable martyr, calm and in charge of his own fate. John goes further than Luke in exalting Jesus. The passion is Jesus' transition back to the Father.

18:1-11: The Garden. As in the Synoptics, Jesus is arrested in the garden, but in John he does not pray to be delivered from his suffering. Jesus is very much in charge in the garden scene. He asks those sent to arrest him whom they seek. When they say "Jesus of Nazareth," he says, *ego eimi*, "I am," another allusion to the divine name. When he says this, they step back and fall to the ground. He again says *ego eimi* and demands that they release his disciples. Then one of Jesus' disciples cuts off an ear of one of those sent to arrest him. Only in John is the disciple identified as Peter and the one attacked as Malchus, a slave of the high priest. Only in John does Jesus say, "Am I not to drink the cup that the Father has given me?"

18:12-27: Jesus before Annas and Caiaphas. There is no general trial before the Sanhedrin. Rather, Jesus appears before Annas, father-in-law of the high priest Caiaphas. John adds that the beloved disciple gains Peter access to the high priest's court. Jesus says more in this hearing than in his synoptic trials. He stresses the public nature of his teaching. In John there is no messianic secret. Jesus is sent briefly to the high priest Caiaphas and then directly to Pilate.

18:28–19:16: Jesus before Pilate. John substantially enhances this part of the narrative. He carefully fashions the trial before Pilate into seven scenes, each focusing on the interaction between two characters (or groups). The form recalls that of chapter 9, the story of the man born blind. "The Jews" are unwilling to enter Pilate's quarters, lest they incur impurity, preventing them from celebrating Passover. Therefore the scenes alternate between Jesus and Pilate inside the praetorium, and Pilate and "the Jews" outside the praetorium. Pilate's interactions with "the Jews" center around Pilate's realization that they have no case against Jesus. The conversation between Pilate and Jesus is remarkable, particularly given their sparse communication in the Synoptics. The sevenfold episode breaks down as follows.

(1) *18:28-32.* "The Jews" demand Jesus' death. Pilate thinks this is a matter of their Torah and should not involve him.

(2) *18:33-38a.* Pilate asks Jesus if he is king of the Jews, and Jesus answers his kingdom is not of this world. Jesus shifts the discussion from kingship to truth, and says that those who desire the truth listen to him. Pilate utters the famous question, "What is truth?" This is ironic, since he is asking the only person on earth able to tell him what truth is, but he is not open to see that.

(3) *18:38b-40.* Pilate tells "the Jews" that Jesus is innocent and offers to release him, but the crowd demands Barabbas instead.

(4) *19:1-3.* Pilate allows his soldiers to mistreat Jesus. They mock him, ironically, as "King of the Jews."

(5) *19:4-7.* Pilate brings Jesus, beaten and humiliated, before "the Jews." The priests and police demand his crucifixion. Pilate insists that he finds no case against Jesus. "The Jews" respond, "We have a law, and according to that law he ought to die because he has claimed to be the Son of God" (19:7). There is no explicit law cited here, nor is there one. Rather, Jesus' claim is considered an affront to God and so blasphemous (see our discussion of Mark 2:1-12). The biting irony of this is evident.

(6) *19:8-12.* Pilate and Jesus again speak privately. Pilate reminds Jesus of his power over him. Jesus retorts that Pilate can have power over him only if God allows it, and he says that those who accuse him are

guilty of a "greater sin." This continues the tendency found in the Synoptics to exonerate the Romans and blame the Jews for Jesus' death. Verse 12 attests to an extended struggle between Pilate, trying to release him, and "the Jews," bent on his execution.

(7) *19:13-16a.* Pilate presents Jesus to "the Jews" again as their king. They protest, "We have no king but the emperor." As he puts these words on the lips of "the Jews," the evangelist is aware that countless Jews suffered and died just a few decades later in a war against Roman power, and that many did so to defend God's sovereignty. Finally, Pilate delivers Jesus "to them" to be crucified. Of course, in reality, Roman soldiers crucified Jesus, not Jewish authorities.

Only John records a dispute between Pilate and "the Jews" when he puts the inscription on the cross saying that Jesus is king of the Jews. They ask him to alter it to "This man said, I am King of the Jews" (19:19-22). Pilate refuses. "The Jews" have insisted on the execution of their true king, and Pilate will not lessen the irony.

19:16b-42: Crucifixion and Death. Unique to John is that when Jesus hangs on the cross, he entrusts his mother and the beloved disciple into each other's care. This illustrates his control of the situation, concern for his mother and beloved disciple, and trust in them both, and care for those he leaves behind. He says that he is thirsty, and the evangelist explains that he does so to fulfill Scripture. Then he says, "It is finished," bows his head, and gives up his spirit. We are far from Mark's scene, where Jesus asks God why God has forsaken him, and then cries out and dies. We are much closer to Luke's presentation.

"The Jews" ask Pilate to remove the bodies before sunset, the beginning of Passover. It was Roman practice to break the legs of the crucified when they wanted to hasten death, but Jesus is already dead. He is stabbed with a spear to make certain. This serves several purposes for John. First, Jesus dies as the Passover lambs are slaughtered. Second, Jesus' bones are not broken, since the Torah says not to break the lamb's bones (19:36; Exod 12:46; Num 9:12; Ps 34:20). Third, the incident fulfills Zech 12:10, which John quotes in 19:37, concerning the piercing of Jesus' side. Finally, the blood and water that flow from Jesus' side may have symbolic significance. The water may represent baptism and the blood Eucharist. Some think that the water symbolizes the Spirit, as in chapter 4. Nicodemus now makes his last appearance in the Gospel, accompanying Joseph of Arimathea to secure the body for burial.

The Resurrection (20:1-29)

The synoptic narratives diverge from each other after the death of Jesus. None of their stories correspond directly. It is not surprising then that John's resurrection accounts do not correspond to the synoptic accounts. Mary Magdalene goes to the tomb alone. When she finds it empty, she runs to tell the other disciples. Peter and the beloved disciple run to the tomb. The beloved disciple arrives first, but waits for Peter. When they enter, the beloved disciple believes (20:8). Mary Magdalene has already borne witness to the resurrection, and apparently his visit to the tomb convinces the beloved disciple. But full understanding of this in light of Scripture is still in the future for the disciples (20:9). The contrast between Peter and the beloved disciple may reflect tension between John's church and the broader church. Peter may represent the mainstream church while the other disciple symbolizes John's church. Although the beloved disciple accords Peter the respect due to one of greater authority, the disciple has greater insight.

Jesus appears to Mary and commissions her to tell the disciples that he is going back to God (20:11-18). He then appears to the disciples, who are hiding behind locked doors "for fear of the Jews" (20:19-23). He imparts the Spirit to them and gives them power to forgive sins. Thomas is not present and later says that he will not believe unless he can handle Jesus' risen body. A week later he gets his chance (20:24-29). He declares, "My Lord and my God," a faith confession that brings us back to the beginning of the Gospel where the Word is said to be God. Jesus says, "Have you believed because you have seen me? Blessed are those who have not seen and yet have come to believe" (20:29). Throughout the Gospel, Jesus has done visible deeds, signs, attesting to his identity. He has also portrayed faith resulting from such signs as just the beginning of adequate faith. He acknowledges Thomas's faith but prefers faith that does not rely on visible signs. There must be a reference to John's own church here, which contains many people, probably the vast majority, who never saw Jesus in person and who perhaps never directly experienced miracles through his power.

Conclusion (20:30-31)

Chapter 20 ends with what sounds like a general conclusion to the Gospel (20:30-31). It says that what the Gospel contains is only some of what Jesus said and did, and that they have been written so that "you may come to believe that Jesus is the Messiah, the Son of God, and that through believing you may have life in his name."

EPILOGUE (21:1-25)

Chapter 21 appears to be a later addition. Again it associates and contrasts Peter and the beloved disciple. In this chapter, Jesus entrusts the care and leadership of the church to Peter. The chapter may have been written partly to encourage John's community to respect Peter's authority and to cooperate with the mainstream church that looked to Peter as one of its original leaders. Another reason for adding the chapter was to explain the beloved disciple's death. Some thought that Jesus had promised that the disciple would not die before the parousia. "Yet Jesus did not say to him that he would not die, but, 'If it is my will that he remain until I come, what is that to you?'" (21:23).

The Gospel ends with the information that it is the beloved disciple who "is testifying to these things and has written them, and we know that his testimony is true" (21:24). Few commentators think that one of Jesus' disciples composed this Gospel. The beloved disciple may have founded the Johannine community or at least been a prominent member of it. He or she was a primary link to Jesus for them. He or she passed on information to the church that eventually took form in the Gospel as we have it.

CHRISTOLOGY

The whole point of this Gospel is its Christology. Even more than the Synoptics, it focuses on Jesus. Gone are Matthew's sweeping and radical ethical demands, Mark's mysterious parables, and Luke's insistence on economic justice. Or if not gone, at least not expressed explicitly. Instead, this Gospel presents a Jesus who is a stranger from heaven. He is God and Son of God. Through him God made the universe.

John conceives of this world as one of darkness and alienation from God. The Word comes down from the world of glory to bring divine light to this world. He is humanity's one chance to establish life-giving contact with God. He is a lifeline stretching from God to humanity. Those who do not see this remain stranded here below. More than that, they hate those who do join themselves to Jesus. There is a deep abyss between Johannine Christians and non-Christians, a gap that is the difference between light and dark, truth and falsehood, God and Satan.

How does Jesus save? For John, Jesus saves by being the eternal Word incarnate. The salvific event is the incarnation itself. In the earthly Jesus, salvation and resurrection is already present. Those who cleave to Jesus are already removed from the world and belong to the world above. There is no need for a sacrificial death to remove sin. Jesus' death is his return to the Father. Ultimately, Jesus will return and bring all who belong to him into the glorious realm, where a place has been prepared for them.

BACKGROUND OF THE PROLOGUE

Mark begins his Gospel with the Baptist's career; Luke and Matthew start it just before Jesus' birth. John begins at the creation: "In the beginning." "Beginning" alludes to the opening words of the first book of the Bible, Genesis: "In the beginning when God created the heavens and the earth." John says, "In the beginning was the Word, and the Word was with God, and the Word was God.... All things came into being through him" (1:1). As the prologue progresses, it is clear that the Word is Jesus himself. So John makes the remarkable claim that Jesus is God, that he was present at creation, and that God created everything through him. This goes well beyond anything that the other canonical gospels say about Jesus.

John draws on Jewish wisdom speculation here. In the ancient world, "wisdom" could mean many things. In Israel, it could mean folk wisdom, the sort preserved in proverbs. It could also mean wisdom resulting from a good education enjoyed by the elite so as to serve the royal court. For kings, it meant the ability to rule well (1 Kgs 3:12, 28). In the postexilic period, when written scriptures were produced, wisdom came to be identified with Torah (Sir 24:23). Finally, *wisdom*, a feminine noun in both Hebrew (*hokhmah*) and Greek (*sophia*), was personified. It is with personified Wisdom that the prologue finds many parallels (see Tobin, pp. 353-54). She was present with God "in the beginning," at creation (Prov 8:22-23; Wis 9:9; Sir 24:9), she fashioned all things (Wis 7:22), humans find life (Prov 8:35; Wis 8:13) and light (Wis 6:12; 7:26) in her, Wisdom is superior to the light since she is never conquered by darkness (Wis 7:29-30), Wisdom is at work in the world (Prov 8:30-31; Sir 1:15; Wis 8:1), no one knows the way to her (Bar 3:31), Wisdom comes to Israel (Sir 24:10; Bar 3:37–4:1), Israel forsakes wisdom (Bar 3:12; Prov 1:20-30), Wisdom passes into souls and makes them God's friends and prophets (Wis 7:27), and Wisdom lives among humans (Bar 3:37).

Jesus is masculine, so John speaks not of "wisdom" but of "word." "Word" is masculine in both Hebrew (*dabar*) and Greek (*logos*), and it is one of many circumlocutions for God in Jewish texts. In order to say that

God is both active in the world and transcendent, Jewish texts use circumlocutions such "God's word," "spirit," "name," "glory," and so on. "God's glory" appears in the temple, for example. God creates in Genesis by uttering words. For example, "God said, 'Let there be light'; and there was light" (Gen 1:3). John combines all of this by portraying Jesus as God's Word through whom God created everything.

John may also draw at least indirectly on Greek philosophical notions here. Judaism was part of the Hellenistic world, and Jewish thought interacted with that world for years before the advent of Christianity. The Logos was an important concept to the Jewish philosopher, Philo of Alexandria, who flourished during the first half of the first century C.E. Philo sees the Logos as equivalent to wisdom, but it is as the Logos that the figure is the subject of most of his attention. The parallels between John's prologue and Philo's works include the following (Tobin, p. 354): it existed with God before creation (*Opif.* 17, 24); it is called "God" but without the definite article ("the"), which distinguishes it from the one, unoriginate God (*Conf.* 146); it is connected with the "beginning" (*Conf.* 146) and God creates through it (*Cher.* 127); it is associated with light (*Somn.* 1.75; *Opif.* 33; *Conf.* 60-63); and it is connected with humans becoming God's children (*Conf.* 145-46).

John goes beyond Jewish thought when he identifies the Word with Jesus, a human being. Later Christian thinkers would strive mightily to understand how Jesus could be both divine and human. The Gospel of John does not consider the matter theoretically, and so it remained open to docetic and Gnostic interpretation.

JESUS AND JOHN THE BAPTIST

Right at the beginning, in the prologue, the Gospel alerts the reader that the relationship between Jesus and John needs special attention. Verses about John disrupt the prologue's smooth, poetic flow, and they insist that John is not the light: "There was a man sent from God, whose name was John. He came to testify to the light, so that all might believe through him. He himself was not the light, but he came to testify to the light. The true light, which enlightens everyone, was coming into the world" (1:6-9). The careful reader wonders whether there is motivation for such insistence. Do some assert that John is the true light? Later in the prologue we hear of John again: "John testified to him and cried out, 'This was he of whom I said, "He who comes after me ranks ahead of me because he was before me"'" (1:15).

After the prologue, John appears, baptizing. "The Jews" send priests and Levites to ask him who he is. "He confessed, and did not deny it, but confessed, 'I am not the Messiah'" (1:20). The narrator stresses John's denial to the point of awkwardness of prose. John also denies being Elijah or "the prophet." When pressed further, John says that he is but the forerunner of the one to come, whom the reader knows to be Jesus (1:26-34). John calls Jesus the "Lamb of God" and says that he saw the Spirit descend on him. Since in the Synoptics the Spirit descends on Jesus at his baptism, it is striking that the evangelist records no baptism of Jesus by John. Two of John's disciples follow Jesus and become his disciples (1:35-39).

The Baptist appears again in chapter 3. There Jesus and John carry on simultaneous missions in which they baptize (3:22-24). John's disciples, alarmed that Jesus is becoming more popular than John, inform him. John testifies, "He must increase, but I must decrease" (3:30). John thus accepts his subordinate role. Only in this gospel do Jesus and John carry on simultaneous missions, and only in this gospel is Jesus said to baptize. But even here there is ambivalence: "Now when Jesus learned that the Pharisees had heard, 'Jesus is making and baptizing more disciples than John'—although it was not Jesus himself but his disciples who baptized" (4:1-2). So the Gospel says both that Jesus baptized and that he did not. The likeliest explanation of this contradiction is that Jesus did baptize, but the Synoptics erased any hint of it so as to distinguish Jesus from John and assert Jesus' superiority to him.

This substantial body of material concerning John reinforces the idea that John's significance is purely as witness to Jesus. The evangelist seeks to put to rest any hint that John has importance in himself.

REALIZED ESCHATOLOGY

When John uses traditional terms, such as "judgment," they assume a different meaning than in the other gospels. Matthew, Mark, and Luke expect a Last Judgment. John does not completely give up on that scenario (see 5:25-29), but it is superseded by what has been called realized eschatology. Where the other gospels expect eschatological judgment, John's eschaton is here already. One is saved or not by the very decision whether or not to believe in Jesus. Belief establishes life-giving contact with God. Disbelief leaves one separated from God. This is well expressed in a passage where it is difficult to decide whether the words belong to John the Baptist or the evangelist:

> God did not send the Son into the world to condemn the world, but in order that the world might be saved through him. Those who believe in him are not condemned; but those who do not believe are condemned already, because they have not believed in the name of the only Son of God. And this is the judgment, that the light has come into the world, and people loved darkness rather than light because their deeds were evil. (3:17-19)

For John, belief in Jesus has specific meaning—acceptance that Jesus has come from the Father and is going back to the Father, and that it is only through Jesus that one can reach the Father. Those who do not believe condemn themselves.

WOMEN

John is no less androcentric than the other three canonical gospels. For all of them, Jesus is male, his inner group of disciples is male, and the majority of the other characters are male. Jesus is not an advocate for women's equality in any of them. That being said, some features of the Fourth Gospel are worthy of note. First is the general point valid for all of the Gospels, and all of early Christian literature, for that matter. It is that ancient Greek usually used the masculine form when mixed-gender groups were designated. When a group is in question and it is not explicitly said to be made up of only males, we cannot assume that the masculine plural means simply males.

John's prologue is an instance of wisdom Christology, meaning that it builds upon the picture of personified Wisdom to understand Jesus. It is possible that the figure of wisdom was appealing because it expresses God and God's activity in female terms. It is unclear whether Wisdom's gender played any role in the fourth evangelist's adoption of wisdom Christology. Today's readers can see this Christology as opening an avenue for seeing Jesus as the incarnation of a God for whom both male and female terms and conceptions are appropriate. Some find this a fruitful way to speak about Jesus in ways that are less gender-bound than usual.

Jesus' mother makes her first appearance in this gospel at a wedding feast in Cana of Galilee (2:1-11). When the hosts run out of wine, she asks her son to help. He says, "Woman, what concern is that to you and to me? My hour has not yet come." The address "woman" may sound disrespectful, but it is doubtful that the evangelist intends it that way. ("Woman" is also used as an address in 4:21, 19:26, and 20:13, 15.) Although Jesus seems to rebuff his mother's (John never names her) request at first, he does turn water into wine, thus performing the first of his signs, one that inspires faith in his disciples. It is remarkable that, although at first he resists doing this, he eventually does it at his mother's behest. Jesus' mother succeeds in rearranging the divinely ordained schedule of Jesus' ministry.

Chapter 4 presents an extended dialogue between Jesus and a Samaritan woman. Both the woman and the disciples are surprised that he speaks to her, both because she is a woman and because she is from Samaria. Jesus defuses both issues. Such well scenes, sometimes including a woman offering a man water, are often sexually charged and result in betrothal. It quickly becomes obvious that this is not the point in this case, as Jesus turns the discussion from physical water to what it represents, the Spirit and eternal life. When Jesus shows miraculous knowledge of the woman's married life, she recognizes his prophetic status. The scene becomes one in which the divine revealer brings a human being to truth.

Like Nicodemus in chapter 3, the Samaritan woman misunderstands much of what Jesus says. Unlike him, each misunderstanding leads to greater understanding, until she finally recognizes him as Messiah and eschatological prophet. She then becomes a missionary to her fellow Samaritans. Her missionary role is signaled not only by what she does, but by the context. When Jesus' disciples return and are amazed that he is speaking to a woman, he speaks to them about the fields being ripe for the harvest. That is mission language. Since the evangelist deliberately turns the reader's attention to the woman's gender, it cannot be by chance that Jesus engages her in a discussion of such deep subjects, central to the purpose of the Gospel, and that she ultimately becomes the bearer of the truth to her fellow villagers. She assumes an active role in revealing the light.

The incident of the woman caught in adultery that appears as John 7:53–8:11 in some manuscripts is probably not an original part of the Gospel. It is a memorable story, a condemnation of self-righteousness and willingness to judge others. Nonetheless, Jesus does not critique double standards. It is still the woman who is held to account. One wonders what happened to the man. It is noteworthy, however, that Jesus makes a point about self-righteousness and mercy in the case of a woman, specifically on the matter of adultery.

In chapter 9, Jewish leaders question both parents of the man born blind. They do not restrict themselves to the father. And it is the decision of both not to risk putting themselves in jeopardy.

In the raising of Lazarus in chapter 11, we meet Martha and Mary again, known to us from Luke's Gospel (Luke 10:38-42; John 11:17-44). The women are Jesus' close friends. They interact in a respectful, yet active and familiar way with Jesus. There is a hint of reproach in Martha's voice as she tells Jesus that he could have saved Lazarus, and there is an implicit request to him to do something about it now. Jesus discusses the nature of resurrection with her, revealing that his presence is equivalent to resurrection. The evangelist thinks it appropriate that Jesus impart the essence of his message to a woman. When Mary comes to Jesus, she also says that had he been there in time Lazarus would have survived.

At the beginning of chapter 12, Mary anoints Jesus. Judas protests that the money for the ointment should have been given to the poor, and Jesus defends Mary. The episode corresponds to the anointing of Jesus at the beginning of the passion narrative in Mark. Mark does not record the woman's name, but John does. But in Mark, it is not clear that the woman acts with this conscious intention. John says that she bought the ointment deliberately to anoint Jesus for burial. In John the male disciple of Jesus, Judas, compares poorly with Jesus' friend Mary, whose story introduces the passion narrative.

To find the next relevant passage, we must go to the Gospel's end, to the resurrection. As far as we can tell, John does not picture anyone at the Last Supper except Jesus and his closest male disciples. Women may be present, but John does not mention them.

As in the Synoptics, women are the first to learn about the empty tomb. In the Synoptics, several women go to the tomb, and an angel (or angels) informs them that Jesus is risen. In John, Mary Magdalene goes to the empty tomb first. She sees no angel there. She mistakenly thinks that someone has stolen Jesus' body, so she runs to the other disciples to tell them (20:1-10). In Luke, when the women tell the other disciples about the empty tomb, they do not believe them. There is no hint in John that they do not believe Mary, but they do run to the tomb. The evangelist explains, "As yet they did not understand the scripture, that he must rise from the dead" (20:9). This applies to all of the disciples, not just Mary. None of them expect the resurrection. All are surprised by it.

Mary returns to the tomb, manifesting admirable persistence, proving her loyalty to Jesus (20:11-18). Jesus appears to Mary. John contrasts the male disciples, who have just left the tomb without seeing Jesus, and Mary who stays and sees him. She mistakes him for the gardener but recognizes him when he speaks her name. This corresponds with John's theme of misunderstanding leading to deeper understanding. It also fits the fact that there is often an element of doubt or lack of recognition in resurrection appearances in each gospel (for example, Matt 28:17; Luke 24:13-26, 36-43). Jesus prevents her from holding on to him because he must ascend to the Father. He tells her to bring that information to the disciples. She does so. This makes her not only the first to know about the resurrection but also the first to tell anyone about it. She also is a missionary, a missionary to the disciples themselves. There is no hint that they doubt her.

Although there is not a lot of material in John concerning women, it is nevertheless striking. It is not that John presents women as equal to men. Mary the mother of Jesus exercises influence as a mother, and Mary Magdalene is messenger to the other disciples, who are more clearly leaders. Still, the material concerning women in John furnishes a foundation rereading the gospel tradition in order to do more justice to the role of women both in the early church and today.

JEWS AND JUDAISM

"The Jews" occurs sixty-three times in the plural, and three times in the singular in the Fourth Gospel. In Mark, the singular never occurs, and the plural occurs six times, five of which are at the crucifixion. In Luke, the singular never occurs, and the plural occurs three times. In Matthew, the singular never occurs, and the plural appears five times, three of which are at the crucifixion. Given the marked disparity between John and the Synoptics, it is clear that John has "a thing" about the Jews. Attempts to see "the Jews" as simply a designation for people from Judea, "Judeans" (the same Greek word means both "Jews" and "Judeans"), succeed in explaining only a portion of the occurrences. Although there is merit in reading the term as denoting Jewish leaders, the other gospels lump all of the Jewish leaders together and see them as opposing Jesus without using the term "the Jews." Generally, of course, the term "the Jews" goes well beyond just their leaders.

John's use of "the Jews" has a rhetorical effect. The reader forms a picture of a mostly homogeneous group, mostly hostile to Jesus. Even when they seem open to Jesus initially, they end up opposing him. By having Jesus debate with "the Jews," John sets Jesus over against Jews as a group. By portraying "the Jews" as Jesus' enemies, John makes them the enemies of his church as well. The overall effect is intensely negative.

John's problem with the Jews is that they do not accept Jesus as the ultimate revelation of God and as the one through whom one must approach God. Of course, for Jews to do this would be devastating to their religion, as the Gospel itself makes clear. It would entail a conviction that the Torah, although it points to Jesus, is inadequate as a way of relating to God. Paul the apostle makes this case, and it is no surprise that he was the apostle to the Gentiles, not to the Jews. John makes astonishing claims about the nature and status of Jesus. The Gospel says that Jews see that as blasphemy. Jews of the time accepted a variety of mediating figures between humans and God, some heavenly and some human, but none fit John's description of Jesus.

John's attitude to Jews and Judaism is contained in brief in the prologue. There it says that the one through whom the cosmos, including humanity, was made was rejected by the world when he became flesh. The prologue continues, "His own people did not accept him" (1:11). The prologue ends, "The law indeed was given through Moses; grace and truth came through Jesus Christ. No one has ever seen God. It is God the only Son, who is close to the Father's heart, who has made him known" (1:17-18). This is an unambiguous statement that access to God comes not through the Mosaic Torah, but only through Jesus Christ. The assertion at the end of the Torah that God spoke to Moses face-to-face is indirectly denied (Deut 34:10).

Jesus claims several times that the Torah and Moses witness to him (5:39-47). "The Jews" see it differently. In 9:28, they say to the man cured of blindness, "You are his disciple, but we are disciples of Moses." At the end of that episode, Jesus says to the Jewish leaders, "If you were blind, you would not have sin. But now that you say, 'We see,' your sin remains" (9:41). They condemn themselves out of their own mouths, since Torah testifies to him.

In the lengthy dialogue between Jesus and "the Jews" in chapters 7–8, things come to a head. Through the typically Johannine device of misunderstanding leading to deeper understanding, "the Jews" slowly come to appreciate and oppose the full import of Jesus' claims. During that process, Jesus calls them children of Satan, since they accept Satan's lies and because they seek to kill him. The scene climaxes in Jesus' assertion, "I am," a claim to divinity, at which they take up stones to throw at him (8:59). In the passion, John continues to treat "the Jews" as a coherent character, plotting and achieving Jesus' death. Even after Jesus' death and resurrection, "the Jews" remain an active character, now threatening the disciples. When Mary Magdalene discovers the empty tomb, the other disciples are hiding "for fear of the Jews" (20:19).

It is hardly surprising that John's group, consisting originally of Jewish Christians and believing what it does about Jesus, should earn the disapproval of the local synagogue. Three times the Gospel says that belief in Jesus results in expulsion from the synagogue (9:22; 12:42; 16:2). We do not know the extent of opposition to the Christian movement in ancient Jewish synagogues, but we need to keep in mind that what to a Christian might look like rejection of God's word to a Jew would look like reverence for God's word. And although the text presents the disagreement as having to do with belief about Jesus, we really do not know for sure that this is an accurate portrayal. Unacceptable attitudes toward Torah, treatment of various customs, and so on might also have also have played a role. James D. G. Dunn provides us with a nuanced study of the variety of things that separated Christians from Jews in different places at different times.

THE LETTERS OF JOHN

John is unlike the other three canonical gospels in that we have some written evidence about what happened to the community after the Gospel was written. First, 2, and 3 John share consistent thought, language, and situation, so we assume that for all practical purposes they were written by the same person. The language and conceptions in these letters are close to the Fourth Gospel. The Gospel and 1 John both begin with prologues that speak of "the beginning," the word, life and light, testifying to the light, the life that was with the Father and has now been revealed, and Jesus' sonship (John 1:1-18; 1 John 1:1-4). The letters speak of the command to love one another (a command aimed at love within the community, not toward enemies) and discuss it as in some sense new, of abiding in Christ and God, of an advocate (Jesus in the letters, the Spirit in the Gospel), hatred, the world as opposed to the community, the sending of the Son into the world by the Father, and so on. We are in the same social and theological environment here.

The marked similarity between Gospel and letters points to their origin in the same community. But few scholars still hold that Gospel and letters were written by the same person. There are important differences between them. A key theological divergence is that though the Gospel retains elements of future eschatology, it emphasizes realized eschatology, while the letters emphasize future eschatology. This brings the letters closer to the Synoptic Gospels. With the passage of time, the Johannine community may have drawn closer theologically to other forms of Christianity.

Most striking about the letters is the historical situation they imply. Love within the community was important to the Gospel, but it assumes center stage in the letters because the community has split over differing christologies. The letters' author sees this as not only a doctrinal difference, but as due to lack of love. The christological issue at stake in the letters is nothing less than Jesus' humanity. Most Christians today take for granted the christological formula arrived at in the middle of the fifth century at the Council of Chalcedon, in which Christ is said to be one person with two natures, fully human and fully divine. This formulation took centuries to develop, and there were serious disagreements along the way.

It is hardly surprising that christological argument erupted in the Johannine community. John's Christology, after all, is the highest of the four we have examined. Only he says that Jesus is God and that he was present with God at the creation. John's Jesus seems omniscient and omnipotent. He is the man from heaven who does not really belong here below. He is the only way to reach the Father. He and the Father are one and abide in one another. He who sees Jesus sees the Father. Such Christology is obviously open to misinterpretation. Second-century gnostics found this Gospel hospitable to their thought. Many gnostics were happy to affirm that Jesus was from heaven and did not really belong here below, and for some of them it made no sense to say that Jesus was human. They, and others, advocated Docetism, the belief that Jesus merely *seemed* to be human. Such Christology had no need to reconcile humanity and divinity in Christ.

We have seen that John's Gospel is not docetic, for it insists on the authentic humanity of Jesus. The prologue states it strongly: "The Word *became* flesh and lived among us" (1:14, italics added). "Flesh" is commonly used in the Bible to contrast humanity with God. Although Jesus is certainly unique, the evangelist never questions his true humanity. But that is exactly what some in the second century used John's Gospel to do.

The letters of John confirm that some members of the evangelist's community developed a docetic Christology shortly after the Gospel assumed its final form. We do not possess writings by them, but we can guess what they may have said by examining the arguments the letters mount against them. The offenders have left the community: "Many deceivers have gone out into the world, those who do not confess that Jesus Christ has come in the flesh; any such person is the deceiver and the antichrist!" (2 John 7). The author cannot imagine that any true believer could really leave the community: "They went out from us, but they did not belong to us; for if they had belonged to us, they would have remained with us. But by going out they made it plain that none of them belongs to us" (1 John 2:19).

In the Gospel of John, Jesus says that the world will hate the disciples as it has hated him (John 15:18-25). Similarly, the letters' author conceives of the world as a dangerous and hostile place (1 John 2:15-17; 3:13); "The whole world lies under the power of the evil one" (1 John 5:19). The world gladly receives those who abandon the community. The author explains it this way: "They are from the world; therefore what they say is from the world, and the world listens to them. We are from God. Whoever knows God listens to us, and whoever is not from God does not listen to us. From this we know the spirit of truth and the spirit of error" (1 John 4:5-6). Echoes of the Gospel are audible, but now the issue is not just the community against the world, but different ways in which the world treats the community and those who abandon the community. Apparently, the world is more amenable to a docetic Christ than to the Christ accepted by the author.

In the end, the author sees those who have left as violating Jesus' love commandment: "Those who say, 'I love God,' and hate their brothers or sisters, are liars" (1 John 4:20).

CONCLUSION

After two thousand years of Christian history, it is hard to imagine a New Testament without John's Gospel. In the first five centuries or so, Christian theology developed through theological struggles within Christianity and through engagement with the non-Christian world. In those developments, Christianity took the direction of John's exalted Christology. However, it did not for the most part retain John's attitude to the world. Although the late second-century thinker Tertullian could ask rhetorically, "What has Athens to do with Jerusalem?" meaning that Christianity was radically different from the intellectual and religious environment of its day, the church became more and more a part of the Roman world until it became the official religion of the Roman Empire in the early fourth century. In that same century, the Christian canon was settled, and John's Gospel had found in it an unchallengeable place.

BIBLIOGRAPHY

Ashton, John. "The Identity and Function of the *Ioudaioi* in the Fourth Gospel." *NovT* 27 (1985): 40-75.

———. *Understanding the Fourth Gospel.* New York: Oxford, 1991.

Barrett, C. K. *The Gospel of John and Judaism.* Philadelphia: Fortress, 1975.

Brown, Raymond E. *The Community of the Beloved Disciple: The Life, Loves and Hates of an Individual Church in New Testament Times.* New York: Paulist, 1979.

———. "The Gospel According to John." AB, vol. 29-29A. Garden City, N.Y.: Doubleday, 1966–1970.

———. *An Introduction to the Gospel of John.* Edited by Francis J. Moloney. New York: Doubleday, 2003.

Buell, Denise. "Rethinking the Relevance of Race for Early Christian Self-Definition." *HTR* 94 (2001): 449-76.

Bultmann, Rudolf. *The Gospel of John: A Commentary.* Translated by J. R. Beasley-Murray. Philadelphia: Westminster, 1971.

Culpepper, Alan. *The Anatomy of the Fourth Gospel: A Study in Literary Design.* Philadelphia: Fortress, 1983.

D'Angelo, Mary Rose. "(Re)Presentations of Women in the Gospels: John and Mark." *WCO*, 129-49.

Dodd, C. H. *The Interpretation of the Fourth Gospel.* Cambridge: Cambridge University Press, 1968.

———. *Historical Tradition in the Fourth Gospel.* Cambridge: Cambridge University Press, 1963.

Duke, Paul D. *Irony in the Fourth Gospel.* Atlanta: John Knox, 1985.

Dunn, James D. G. *The Partings of the Ways: Between Chrisianity and Judaism and Their Significance for the Character of Christianity.* Philadelphia: Trinity, 1991.

Fortna, R. T. *The Gospel of Signs.* London: Cambridge University Press, 1970.

Josephus. Philo. Translated by F. H. Colson, G. H. Whitaker, and R. Marcus. 10 vols. And 2 supplementary vols. LCL. Cambridge: Harvard University Press, 1922–1962.

Käsemann, Ernst. *The Testament of Jesus: A Study of the Gospel of John in the Light of Chapter 17.* Philadelphia: Fortress, 1968.

Kysar, Robert. *John the Maverick Gospel.* Atlanta: John Knox, 1976.

Levine, Amy-Jill, ed. *A Feminist Companion to John.* Cleveland: Pilgrim, 2003.

Martyn, J. Louis. *History and Theology in the Fourth Gospel*. 2d ed. Nashville: Abingdon, 1979.

Meeks, Wayne. "The Man from Heaven in Johannine Sectarianism." *JBL* 91 (1972): 44-72.

————. *The Prophet-King: Moses Traditions and the Johannine Christology*. Leiden: Brill, 1967.

Moloney, Francis J. *The Gospel of John*. Vol. 4 of Sacra Pagina. Edited by Daniel J. Harrington. Collegeville: Liturgical, 1998.

O'Day, Gail R. *Revelation in the Fourth Gospel*. Philadelphia: Fortress, 1987.

Perkins, Pheme. "The Gospel according to John." *JBC*, pp. 942-85.

————. "The Johannine Epistles." *JBC*, pp. 986-95.

Schnackenburg, Rudolf. *The Gospel according to St. John*. 3 vols. New York: Crossroad, 1982.

Segovia, Fernando. *The Farewell of the Word: The Johannine Call to Abide*. Minneapolis: Fortress, 1991.

Sloyan, Gerard S. *What Are They Saying about John?* New York: Paulist, 1991.

Smith, D. Moody. *John among the Gospels: The Relationship in Twentieth-Century Research*. Minneapolis: Fortress, 1992.

————. *The Theology of John*. Cambridge: Cambridge University Press, 1994.

Tobin, Thomas. "Logos." *ABD* 4:348-56.

CHAPTER SEVEN

OTHER GOSPELS

ORAL TRADITION

We live in a mostly literate culture. Reading is a basic skill taught from earliest age. Books are mass-produced; when we speak of a particular book, we can be confident that most are able to consult that same book. We think of the words and deeds of Jesus as being preserved in written texts called the Gospels, available in a book called the New Testament. Texts of noncanonical gospels are available in collections such as *New Testament Apocrypha*. But the world of early Christianity was one in which the ability to read was rare, when most communication was carried out orally. Oral tradition was crucial in remembering and passing on Jesus traditions. Most early Christians looked not to texts but to oral tradition for information about Jesus. Even educated Christians did so. The evangelists themselves drew on oral traditions.

Papias was a bishop from the early second century who claims that Mark got his material from Peter and that Matthew was originally written in Aramaic. He obviously knew written gospels. But he said that he trusted that information less than what he got from oral tradition. We must remember that oral tradition remained vibrant throughout the first and second centuries and even beyond, and that it formed part of the environment in which gospels were written, interpreted, and revised. As we look at the noncanonical gospels in this chapter, we should remember that they could also draw on oral tradition, and that alongside our written gospels, both canonical and noncanonical there was also material that was passed on orally, which we have now lost.

Noncanonical go: Some appear to be
the same genre as th‹ _____ gospels—a narrative covering the public
career, death, and resurrection of Jesus, prefaced in some instances with
an infancy narrative or account of Jesus' preexistence. Others are narratives but encompass a smaller period, usually Jesus' infancy and childhood. Still others are collections of sayings. There are also dialogue
gospels, where the risen Jesus interacts with a disciple or a group of
disciples.

SAYINGS GOSPELS

Q

We spoke of Q when we discussed the synoptic problem. We decided
that the best solution to the question of how the Synoptic Gospels—
Matthew, Mark, and Luke—relate is that Mark wrote first, and that
Matthew and Luke used Mark as a source. Matthew and Luke also
depended on another source, no longer extant, which we call Q.
Obviously, Q must predate Matthew and Luke. Most think that Luke
sticks closer to the original order of Q. Therefore, conventional citation
of Q uses Luke's chapter and verse. So, for example, Q 3:7-9, a passage
about the Baptist, is the same as Luke 3:7-9.

Is Q a gospel? That depends on one's definition of "gospel." Certainly
it is not a gospel according to the definition that we have been using till
now in this book. It is not a narrative, for example, but a collection
mostly of sayings. But we derived our definition of gospel from the four
canonical gospels. A variety of Christian works from the first few centuries of the common era call themselves gospels, even though they do
not fit our definition. The purpose of this chapter is to broaden our outlook, so that we see the canonical gospels in historical and theological
perspective, and so that we can get a wider picture of early Christianity
than is possible when we restrict ourselves to the canon. Very broadly
speaking, then, we can use as a working definition of gospel the following: a *gospel* is a text containing Jesus' words or deeds or both, intended
to be a guide to how people look at Jesus.

According to this broad definition, Q is a gospel. It has played an
important role in Christianity, in that it was used extensively by both
Matthew and Luke. Yet it has not survived. That has led to the hypothe-

sis that it was not meant to survive. In this view, Matthew and Luke co-opted Q by incorporating it into their own writings, thereby interpreting it both by changing the specifics of particular sayings and by placing it in the context of their narratives, narratives meant to guide the reader to proper interpretation. If that is true, then if there was a community that had Q as its foundational document, that community might have used these sayings differently and might have had a different take on Jesus than we get from Matthew and Luke. Even if it was not the intention of Matthew and Luke to co-opt Q, we can still ask whether a community based on Q would be a different form of Christianity than that behind the Synoptic Gospels.

Just about every aspect of Q has been the subject of debate. One factor in the debate is that the text is no longer extant, which leaves room for hypotheses about its exact contents and shape. Nonetheless, the great majority of scholars accept that fact that it did exist and agree on its main features. Q was a collection primarily of sayings and some parables of Jesus, with one miracle and some material about John the Baptist included. It began with the career of John the Baptist, went on to the threefold temptation of Jesus by Satan in the desert, included a long central section of mostly sayings, some parables, and a miracle (the curing of the centurion's servant), and ended with an apocalyptic discourse.

Sayings collections were common in the ancient world. Biblical examples are the book of Proverbs and Sirach (also called Ecclesiasticus). Philosophical groups sometimes gathered the sayings of their founder in such collections. So the genre of Q would be well known in its ancient context.

Scholars have analyzed Q in much the same way they have analyzed other ancient texts, particularly biblical texts. They have employed the various forms of criticism we have studied. In the past couple of decades, a good deal of energy has gone into dividing Q into redactional layers. Some have posited two, or even three stages of development for the text. The model supporting this sort of development is that biblical and related texts served communities that changed over time and that rewrote their traditions to correspond to, and at times to precipitate, those changes. However, in the case of Q, some find it futile to posit hypothetical stages of development for a text that is itself hypothetical.

John Kloppenborg offers one of the most widely debated stratifications of Q. His separation of the document into layers is based on literary considerations, and so if each of these layers then has its own tendencies and outlooks, it is not because he used those different outlooks as the criterion for the layers. That means that if each of the layers truly has its own character, then we can say something about the view of the person or people that composed it. Based on Kloppenborg's layers, one can make the case that the early layers of Q presented Jesus as a teacher of wisdom. His wisdom was critical of society, as was, for example, the philosophy of the Cynic philosophers, and the text advocated a lifestyle similar to that of the Cynics. Cynics were wandering street preachers who challenged society's dedication to such things as wealth, power, and status, and advocated a simple, even ascetic lifestyle. Over time, the community that cherished the original form of Q naturally encountered the hostility of the society of which it was critical. In response, Q incorporated apocalyptic elements and its Jesus began to assume the contours of an eschatological prophet, rejected by Israel, and his followers started to look more and more like rejected prophets themselves. Kloppenborg's analysis is hardly the only one available. A different analysis is supplied by Dale Allison, for example.

Some scholars have used Kloppenborg's analysis to support the idea that the historical Jesus himself was an antiestablishment wisdom teacher, and that as time went on the later church became more and more apocalyptic. We look at this issue in more detail in the next chapter. Here it is sufficient to say that eschatological elements are found even in Kloppenborg's earliest reconstructed layer, and that the later layers contain wisdom elements, so the outlook of each layer is not as clear as it might seem at first. Further, even if Q did go through a development of the sort suggested here, there is no firm evidence that this correlates with the postulated historical development of the Q community, itself hypothetical, or that it sheds any light on the historical Jesus.

Our discussion of research on Q reveals an obstacle for our interpretation of it. Its traditions are not of a piece. They demonstrate different points of view and are not fully harmonious with each other. But that is true of the canonical gospels, too. Writers who work with traditional material often end up with finished products containing tensions and contradictions. Apparently, those who composed these documents, and here we are often speaking of communities rather than simply individuals, were more tolerant of diversity within a text than are we. Given these observations, we can still offer a provisional sketch of Q's outlook.

In its present form as represented by most reconstructions, Q contains both wisdom and prophetic elements. Overall, it sees Jesus as the eschatological prophet. A mysterious Son of Man is coming soon to judge the world, and he will judge according to whether people have listened to Jesus' teachings. Jesus and many of his followers are to live an itinerant lifestyle, testifying to the fact that this world is soon to end. Members of this community find the world an inhospitable place, antagonistic to their message. Like John the Baptist and like Jesus before them, they expect to incur the displeasure of the authorities. But in the end the Son of Man will vindicate them. Other followers, perhaps better styled supporters, offer their hospitality to make possible the work of the more radical followers. The community appears to consist of Jewish Christians who maintain their observance of Torah. It is in Q that we find Jesus' prophetic saying, found at the beginning of Matthew's Sermon on the Mount, "Until heaven and earth pass away, not one letter, not one stroke of a letter, will pass from the law until all is accomplished" (5:18).

Much has been made of the fact that Q did not have a passion narrative. Jesus' death and resurrection, so important to the canonical gospels, as well as to the most of the rest of the New Testament, play no significant role in Q. Jesus' suffering and death, to the extent that it appears in the document, is the result of rejection by Israel, and it shows that Jesus belongs within the tradition of Israel's prophets. This point of view builds on a strand of interpretation both in the Bible and in texts from late Second Temple Judaism that speak of God's sending of prophets to Israel to exhort it to repentance and submission to God. In this tradition, Israel consistently rejects the prophets. Such a view lies behind Jesus' parable of the Great Banquet in Matt 22 and the parable of the Tenant Workers in the vineyard found at the beginning of Jesus' period in Jerusalem in all three Synoptics (Mark 12:1-12 and parallels). For Q, the death of Jesus is not redemptive, but is a function of his prophetic role.

It is not entirely clear whether we ought to posit an actual, historical community whose foundational document was Q. It is possible that Q was one text among several that existed in any of a number of communities, and that we should not extract from it a general theology and attribute that theology to a historical group. Further, no text encompasses the full range of oral tradition available to Christians in the ancient world. We may interpret Q in isolation and purely on its own merits, but early Christians may have read it in the context of an oral tradition whose outlook was broader than the document itself. The issue becomes more acute when the hypothetical layers of Q, read as complete wholes, are then thought of as several communities or several stages in the life of a single community. There are few controls on such interpretation and historical reconstruction.

The Gospel of Thomas

A Coptic (Egyptian) form of the *Gospel of Thomas*, contained in Codex II of the Nag Hammadi library, is considered by many to be the single most important document discovered there. In its present form, it dates from the early fourth century and consists of 114 sayings of Jesus. Some of the sayings are familiar from the Synoptic Gospels and others are not. At times those that are known from the Synoptics are in a form that may predate that preserved in the Synoptics. More often they have a peculiar twist. According to many, such "twists" are due to sayings material being recast within a gnostic context. Others find that, although the sayings have been transformed in the light of a worldview that has things in common with Gnosticism, they are not fully gnostic.

Fragments of this gospel had been found in a garbage dump near the Egyptian town of Oxyrhynchus and published around the turn of the twentieth century. The fragments are in Greek, the original language of *Thomas*. The earliest of the fragments dates to the beginning of the third century. The Greek fragments do not entirely agree with the Coptic translation of the text from Nag Hammadi. This is not surprising, since collections of sayings were particularly susceptible to being altered over time. Sayings could be added, dropped, and altered as new circumstances demanded. This raises the question of whether any overarching interpretation of the work as a whole is possible. In any case, the only full copy of the text that we possess, the one in Coptic from Nag Hammadi, is only one of many potential versions of the document. Nonetheless, most scholarly opinion holds that a collection such as *Thomas* does reflect the general point of view of the person or community that put it together in the first place, or received and adapted it to their purposes. So we look at the work as we have it, assuming that it can tell us something about how at least one Christian group viewed Jesus and Christian life.

The concept of authorship becomes problematic in a work like this as it is for Q, and perhaps for the other gospels as well. We should probably think more in terms of its preservation, transmission, and adaptation in a community. The claim at the beginning of the text that the sayings were written down by Didymus Judas Thomas (and the designation of the work as *The Gospel of Thomas* at its end) is a fiction designed to bolster confidence in the sayings' authenticity. This use of pseudonymity was extremely common in antiquity. It is not impossible that early in the history of some community for which this text was important someone named Thomas, perhaps even the apostle, was a prominent figure. But we cannot know that. Thomas comes from the word for "twin" in Aramaic, and Didymus comes from the word with the same meaning in Greek. Thomas is one of the twelve apostles in the canonical gospels. In the Gospel of John, he is called "the twin" (11:16; 20:24; 21:2). Thomas plays an important role in Christian literature from Syria, so it is possible that this work originated there. In a later Christian book, *Acts of Thomas*, Thomas is said to be Jesus' own brother. "Judas" is a Greek form of the Jewish name "Judah." Mark 6:3 lists four brothers of Jesus, among them Judas. It makes sense that later Christian tradition would claim that Jesus' words were recorded by his own brother.

The date of *Thomas* is disputed. Some date its oldest form early, perhaps as early as Q, and find in it important clues about the historical Jesus as well as about specific forms of earliest Christianity. Others think it to be second century at the earliest. Those who date it early consider it independent of the Synoptics, at least in its early form. As it was passed down, altered, and recopied, the synoptic tradition could have influenced it. Those who date it late think that it may get a good deal of its material from the Synoptic Gospels. There are no easy answers to such questions. Recently, Stephen Patterson has made the case that although the collection as presently constituted is late, the work contains a substantial number of sayings and parables that appear to be earlier than their counterparts in the Synoptics. He argues that redactional changes made to these units in the Synoptics are lacking in *Thomas*. From this he reasons that, although *Thomas* in its Coptic form may be later, there was an earlier form of *Thomas* that dates from the first century. For our purposes, we need not decide whether individual sayings are early or late, or even whether *Thomas* is dependent on the Synoptics or not. We simply treat *Thomas* as another sort of gospel produced and used by Christians within the first centuries after Jesus' death.

Thomas is a collection of sayings with just enough narrative to supply the context of Jesus speaking to his disciples. Like Q, it lacks a passion narrative. The text begins with the words, "These are the secret sayings that the living Jesus spoke and Didymos Judas Thomas recorded. And he said, 'Whoever discovers the interpretation of these sayings will not taste death' " (1; translations of *Thomas* are from Funk and Hoover). This opening conveys important hints about document's nature and its views.

First, the sayings of Jesus it contains are "secret." "Secret" here means both that the words Jesus speaks are spoken only to a select group and that their meaning is not obvious. One need only read a few of the sayings to see that they have a mysterious quality, and that their meaning is often opaque. That Thomas writes the words down guarantees their authenticity. Eternal life is promised to those who find the meaning of the words. The significance of Jesus, then, is in his teachings, not in his deeds or death or resurrection. Neither the teaching nor its interpretation is open to everyone. Jesus is a revealer, one who discloses what was previously hidden, but, ironically, even this disclosure is hidden from the general public. Even when one has the sayings, they still must be interpreted.

An obstacle to understanding the sayings in *Thomas* is that there is no context within which to interpret them. The sayings and parables stand for the most part as isolated units. No general frame of organization has been found for the sayings, except for occasional clusters of sayings gathered around a particular catchword, for example. Faced with this lack of context, we should try to find an interpretive context that makes the most sense out of the sayings. For many, that context is Gnosticism. A good many of *Thomas*'s sayings that at first glance are obscure become comprehensible when seen as gnostic. Of course, Gnosticism itself did not exist in a vacuum. It was part of its world and shared many elements with other ways of looking at the world. So if we concentrate on one or another element in *Thomas*, we can imagine it as belonging to any number of ancient contexts. Jewish mysticism and Jewish wisdom speculation have been suggested. And we have noted that the very notion of Gnosticism as a unified and coherent phenomenon may be misleading.

Positing a gnostic background for the *Gospel of Thomas* helps to explain why it is not Jesus' death that is important, but his revelation. In *Thomas*, Jesus does not have the usual titles, such as "Messiah," "Son of God," "Son of Man," and so on. He is simply the revealer. And the point of the revelation is not apocalyptic, as in the Synoptics, nor is he its object, as in the Gospel of John. The point of the revelation is understanding this world and one's place in it, as well as the lifestyle in concert with these insights.

Thomas manifests a fairly negative attitude toward the world. Its readers are to distance themselves from it: "If you do not fast from the world, you will not find the (Father's) domain" (27; see also 80). The way this is done is by cutting ties to this world, including ties of family and place (14, 16, 55, 86, 101, 105). Adherents are to wander, living in no settled place.

They are to give up their family relationships. This is probably the meaning of the enigmatic injunction "Be passers-by" (42). It is not surprising, then, that they experience the world as hostile to them (68, 69). It is debated whether their detachment from this world also involves asceticism. The text does not contain much about specific ascetical practices, and when it does mention them, it seems to have an ambivalent attitude toward them, even denigrating them in places (6, 14). *Thomas* does, however, speak against wealth: "Let one who has found the world, and has become wealthy, renounce the world" (110; see also 63). It also says, "Buyers and merchants [will] not enter the places of my Father" (64).

Sprinkled throughout *Thomas* are sayings dealing with the origin of Jesus' hearers, and of their ability to achieve some sort of enlightenment by looking within themselves. In saying 28, Jesus says that when he came "in flesh" (see John 1:14), he found people to be "drunk" and needing to "shake off their wine." This is a typically gnostic image for the state of spiritual humans before they are made aware of their origin and destiny. Their origin is made clear in saying 50: "Jesus said, 'If they say to you: "Where have you come from?" say to them, "We have come from the light, from the place where the light came into being by itself, established [itself], and appeared in their image" ' " (see also 84). In the same saying, they are called "the chosen of the living Father," suggesting that only a portion of the human race is spiritual. This impression is strengthened when Jesus says earlier in the collection, "I shall choose you, one from a thousand and two from ten thousand" (23).

Jesus says that when his hearers undress without being ashamed and put their clothes under their feet, they "will see the son of the living one and you will not be afraid" (37). This looks back to the story of the fall of Adam and Eve in Genesis, where, after eating the forbidden fruit, they come to know that they are naked and they are ashamed. So *Thomas* is alluding to a primal ideal state. But this goes well beyond Genesis. The putting off of clothes probably refers to the physical body, a metaphor widely known in the ancient world. So the saying means that regaining the primal state means putting off the body, in some sense. Putting it under the feet refers to understanding the body's inferior state as part of the physical world that entraps the divine spark (see also 21, 87, 112).

Thomas is not apocalyptic. Even those sayings that seem at first glance to have an apocalyptic meaning are turned in a nonapocalyptic direction (11, 18, 111). When asked when the kingdom will come, Jesus says it will not come with visible signs. Rather, it is "spread out on the earth and people do not see it" (113). This recalls Luke 17:20-21, where Jesus says that the kingdom is not coming with observable signs. In Luke, Jesus says that the kingdom is "within" or "among" you. How to interpret that has been debated by scholars for ages. It may mean that the kingdom is interior to the human being, a matter of attitude and heart (probably not what it meant for Jesus). Or it may mean that the kingdom of God is present, perhaps in the ministry of Jesus himself. In *Thomas*, it may mean that the kingdom consists of the collection of individual divine sparks, spread through humanity, whose presence is unsuspected by unspiritual persons, and even by the spiritual themselves, until awakened. A large part of salvation is knowing oneself, not in the modern sense of understanding one's own psychology, or in the Socratic sense of being critically self-aware, but in the sense of knowing oneself as belonging not to this world, but to the spiritual one. Jesus says that the kingdom is not in heaven or in the sea. Rather, "when you know yourselves, then you will be known, and you will understand that you are the children of the living Father. But if you do not know yourselves, then you live in poverty, and you are the poverty" (3).

When asked about when the resurrection will come, Jesus says, "What you are looking forward to has come, but you don't know it" (51).

The *Gospel of Thomas* and the Gospel of John show many points of contact. But recent research suggests that they are opposed on some basic points. Elaine Pagels lays out a powerful case for contrasting *Thomas* and John on the score of the role of Jesus and the way of salvation. *Thomas* advises its readers to find salvation within. It goes so far as to say that once one understands oneself, then one has no real need of Jesus. Jesus says, "Whoever drinks from my mouth will become like me. I myself shall become that person, and the hidden things will be revealed to him" (108). John, on the other hand, insists that one finds salvation only through Jesus. John speaks a good deal about accepting Jesus' word, but there is little that Jesus says that does not have to do with himself, his own nature, and his coming from and going back to heaven. John explains the fact that some believe in Jesus and some do not by saying, "People loved darkness rather than the light because their deeds were evil" (3:19). This is a general condemnation of anyone who does not believe that Jesus has come from the Father and is the only connection to the light above. But *Thomas's* Jesus points people to what is within themselves. *Thomas's* Jesus says, "There is light within a person of light, and it shines on the whole world. If it does not shine, it is dark" (24; see also 61). In John, there is an unremitting focus on Jesus as the sole source of light. In *Thomas*, each spiritual person is the light amidst the darkness.

NARRATIVE GOSPELS

Many of these gospels have been lost. We know of them through comments of early Christian writers, who sometimes quote short sections from them. Since we know them only secondhand through these writers, and since what we are told about them is not always consistent, conclusions about them must be tentative.

Tatian's *Diatessaron*

Some early Christians were not content with a multiplicity of gospels, and so they tried to create a single one by combining the ones they found most useful. The most well-known effort is the gospel harmony of Tatian, a Syrian Christian, produced in around 170 C.E. This was a harmonization of the four canonical gospels. It remained popular in Syria for several centuries. We know of other harmonies as well. According to Jerome, Theophilus of Antioch created one, and Eusebius tells us that Ammonius of Alexandria did, too. Justin Martyr, a famous second-century Christian apologist, appears to have used a harmony of the Synoptics. It is not clear that any of these harmonies was a real redaction of the Gospels in the sense that Matthew, for example, incorporated and redacted Mark and Q. Rather, they attest to the belief that the Gospels, or at least the Synoptic Gospels, all say essentially the same thing, and where they differ, one can simply harmonize them without doing violence to their thought.

The Gospel of the Nazareans

This gospel was written in Aramaic, perhaps around the turn of the second century. Early Christian writers describe it as similar to Matthew, some of them thinking that it was the original form of that gospel. Its extant fragments show a concern for Torah, as does Matthew itself. We have no explicit title for the work, but writers such as Jerome tell us that it was used by the Nazareans (or Nazoreans). The fourth-century Christian writer Epiphanius informs us that the Nazareans were a Jewish Christian sect that was completely Jewish and that saw Jesus as the Messiah. The sect existed in Syria or Palestine. Epiphanius says that they had the "whole" Gospel of Matthew, preserved in Hebrew letters, probably meaning that it was in Aramaic. We do not know what he means by this, but it is clear that they possessed a gospel similar to Matthew in some important respects, perhaps particularly in the emphasis it placed on

Torah. The gospel might actually be some form of Matthew, or it might have been simply a gospel similar to Matthew in content and tone.

If our general impressions of this gospel are correct, it is particularly frustrating not to have it, for it would provide us with valuable information about a segment of Christianity that remained Jewish. Discussions of Jewish Christianity have been plagued by a lack of solid evidence. It would be especially interesting to know more about how such groups observed Torah and what sort of Christology they held.

The Gospel of the Ebionites

We know of this gospel only through the writings of Epiphanius. The Ebionites were a Jewish Christian group that existed in the second through fourth centuries. They held that Jesus' death replaced the sacrifices of the temple. They were vegetarian, perhaps because meat became available mostly through sacrifice. According to Epiphanius, they denied that Christ was human, but they also denied his full divinity, since he was not begotten of God but was created like an angel. One interpretation of the gospel is that it sees the descent of the Spirit into Christ as the point where the heavenly Christ joins himself to a human, Jesus, although Epiphanius does not say that. For the Ebionites, Christ put to an end the sacrificial system. The gospel seems to have been a harmonization of the Synoptics, redacted to reflect the group's views. Epiphanius says it was an adaptation of the Gospel of Matthew, but James Edwards makes the case that it depends more on Luke. It perhaps was composed sometime in the second century. Its original language is unclear.

The Gospel of the Hebrews

This was another Jewish Christian gospel, originating in Egypt around the turn of the second century. The fragments preserved by early Christian writers suggest that it was independent of the canonical gospels. Like John, it posited Jesus' preexistence. It is interested in Jesus' brother James, recounting an appearance to him and claiming that he was present at the Last Supper.

Marcion's Gospel

Marcion was a Christian prominent in Rome in the middle of the second century. He rejected the God of the Old Testament, who was the creator, and whom he found harsh, demanding, and punitive. For him, Judaism is a false religion, created by the God of the Old Testament. Jesus comes to reveal the God of love, and so he is not an agent of the Jewish

God. Marcion rejected the Old Testament, and he accepted only a radically altered version of the emerging Christian Scriptures. He accepted the letters of Paul, but he thought they had been altered by the mainline churches to reflect more positively on Judaism and its God. He also accepted Luke's Gospel, but he thought that it too had been altered by those with a positive attitude to Christianity's Jewish heritage. He therefore used an expurgated version of Luke and of Paul's letters. His gospel is quoted by his rival Tertullian. Tertullian tells us that Marcion's Jesus says that he has come not to fulfill the Law, but to abolish it (*Against Marcion* 4:7). This is in direct contradiction to Matt 5:17. Marcion held a docetic Christology, that is, Jesus was not truly human but only appeared to be so.

The Gospel of Peter

This gospel was popular in some circles in Syria in the second century. We knew of it through Eusebius, but we possessed no passages from it until some pages from its end turned up in 1886 in an Egyptian monk's tomb. These pages begin in the middle of Jesus' trial before Pilate, so we do not know how comprehensive the gospel was originally. In the trial, it is Herod, not Pilate, who condemns Jesus to death, and Jews crucify him, not Romans. As in Matthew, Pilate literally washes his hands to symbolize his innocence in the affair. So this gospel furthers the tendency visible in the canonical gospels to shift blame for Jesus' death from the Romans to the Jews.

Where Mark has Jesus cry, "My God, my God, why have you forsaken me?" *Peter* has him say, "My power, O power, You have left me" (1; translation of Cartlidge and Dungan). Then it is said that he is "taken up," even though Jesus' dead body remains on the cross. This may reflect a Christology in which the Messiah descends on the human Jesus, probably at his baptism, and departs before his death. This is reminiscent of the *Gospel of the Ebionites*. During the crucifixion, Jesus is silent "as if he had no pain," perhaps because he is still in union with the heavenly Messiah.

When Jesus dies, the people panic, saying, "Woe, because of our sins; The judgment and the end of Jerusalem are at hand" (25). We noted the Synoptic Gospels blame the destruction of Jerusalem and its temple by the Romans in 70 C.E. on Jewish refusal to accept Jesus. Here that judgment is made by the Jewish people itself. In Luke 23:48, Jewish crowds mourn death immediately after he dies on the cross, but it is not said that they predict Jerusalem's fall.

The description of the resurrection in the *Gospel of Peter* is remarkable. The canonical gospels do not recount the resurrection itself, although Matthew and Luke contain resurrection appearances. Matthew's narrative comes closest to that found in *Peter*. In Matthew, the tomb is sealed and guards are set over it. The guards are the Jewish authorities' own, perhaps drawn from the temple police. They see and tremble at an angel who descends from heaven accompanied by an earthquake, rolls back the stone at the entrance to the tomb, and tells Mary Magdalene and the other women that Jesus has risen. The guards tell the Jewish authorities what they have seen and are paid to say that Jesus' disciples stole his body: "And this story is still told among the Jews to this day" (Matt 28:15).

In *Peter* the account of the sealing of the tomb is more elaborate. The stone blocking its entrance is huge, and it is sealed with seven seals by a centurion named Petronius and his soldiers, so these are Romans, not Jews. As the Sabbath dawns, a great crowd gathers, and they and the guard witness a great voice from the sky, the opening of the sky, and the descent of two angelic figures, who enter the tomb, whose stone has rolled away. When they emerge, their heads reach into the heavens, and they are supporting Jesus between them. His head rises above the heavens. Behind them follows the cross. A voice from the sky asks, "Have you preached to those who are asleep?" and the cross answers, "Yes" (41-42). This alludes to what is, in the fourth-century Nicene creed, called the descent into hell. According to this scheme, between his death and resurrection, Jesus went to preach to the dead, offering them an opportunity to have faith and thus gain entrance into heaven.

The heavens open again, and another angelic figure descends and enters the tomb. The soldiers inform Pilate about what has happened, concluding that Jesus is the Son of God. Pilate tells the Jewish crowd that they bear the blame for Christ's blood, not him. The crowd insists that Pilate command the soldiers to silence, saying, "It will be better for us . . . to bear the guilt of the greatest sin before God than to fall into the hands of the Jewish people and to be stoned" (48). Ironically, the crowd, which is undoubtedly Jewish, fears being stoned by "the Jewish people." This stretching of language recalls the Gospel of John's use of the term "the Jews" in defiance of historical reality. The text breaks off as Simon, his brother Andrew, and others go off to the sea, in an apparent preparation for the sort of resurrection appearance that we find in John 21.

Scholars debate many questions about the *Gospel of Peter*, including the shape of the original document, its theological tendencies, its stages of composition, and whether or not it depends on canonical accounts. *Peter* has achieved a level of prominence because of the work of John Dominic Crossan. He discerns layers of composition and deems his reconstructed earliest layer as earlier than the canonical accounts of the passion. Later layers develop in the direction of putting all the blame for Jesus' death on Jews rather than Pilate. Crossan believes that his reconstructed early form of *Peter* is of use in investigating the historical Jesus. In any case, *Peter* attests to the continuing tendency to play down the guilt of the Romans in Jesus' death and the corresponding effort to cast all blame on the Jews. It also may have had a Christology quite different from that of the canonical gospels and later orthodoxy. It satisfies curiosity about the resurrection by supplying a description of it in legendary terms.

INFANCY AND CHILDHOOD GOSPELS

There is obviously much about Jesus and his life that believers and historians would love to know. The gospels were clearly not written to answer many of our questions. But Christians of the second and subsequent centuries began filling in the gaps in our knowledge of Jesus by fanciful and pious stories. Early on, they began to tell stories providing detail about Jesus' infancy and childhood. Matthew and Luke add infancy narratives to the beginning of their gospels, something absent from Mark. Luke gives us the story of the twelve-year-old Jesus' trip to Jerusalem with his parents, where he stays behind in the temple and amazes people with wisdom. But these were meager fare for Christians anxious to know Jesus intimately.

The Infancy Gospel of Thomas

The *Infancy Gospel of Thomas*, dating to the second century, is more aptly termed a childhood gospel, for it does not deal with Jesus' birth or infancy. It aims to satisfy curiosity about Jesus' childhood. It caters to fascination with Jesus' miraculous powers, and it assumes that Jesus possessed and used these powers even as a child. If the attribution of this gospel to Thomas means that Judas Thomas, brother of Jesus, was its putative author, that is fitting, for Jesus' brother would have witnessed the events of his childhood. Thomas promises us knowledge of "the childhood and great deeds of our Lord Jesus Christ" (1:1; Cartlidge and Dungan). Jesus' childhood activities recounted here are "great" in terms of their miraculous nature, but they go to such lengths in ascribing unlimited power to the child that they present him as a bit of a monster. Several incidents seem to be built on stories or to incorporate versions of sayings found in the canonical gospels.

In the first story, Jesus fashions clay sparrows on the Sabbath. When "a certain Jew" observes this, he reports the violation of Sabbath law to Joseph. Joseph demands of Jesus, "Why do you do on the Sabbath what it is not lawful to do?" (2:4), echoing the kind of question posed by others in such passages as Mark 2:24. Jesus quickly hides the evidence by clapping his hands, causing the sparrows to come to life and fly away.

Another child, son of a scribe, breaks down the pools of water Jesus had collected, and Jesus hurls invective at him, calling him an "unrighteous, impious ignoramus," and kills him by causing him to wither like a tree that will no longer bear fruit (3:2; see Mark 11:12-14, 20-21). His parents confront Joseph: "What kind of child do you have who does such things?" (3:3). Characters in Mark ask the same sort of question, but for very different reasons.

Jesus then kills a boy who bumps into him, prompting his parents to say to Joseph, "Because you have such a boy, you cannot live with us in the village; your alternative is to teach him to bless and not to curse, for he is killing our children" (4:2). Jesus strikes his accusers with blindness. Joseph dares to admonish Jesus, and Jesus utters a veiled threat to him, as well, saying, "It is fitting for you to seek and not find" (5:3; compare Matt 7:7). A teacher volunteers to take the "smart child " under his wing. He soon regrets it, for Jesus runs circles around him intellectually and humiliates him (compare the story of the twelve-year-old Jesus in the temple in Luke 2:41-51). The teacher returns Jesus to Joseph, saying that Jesus is perhaps "a God, an angel" (7:3). Jesus reveals, "I am from above in order that I may curse them and call them into the things which are above, because he who sent me on your account ordered it" (8:1). Instantly, all whom Jesus has afflicted are healed. The words Jesus speaks about his origins from above and about the one who sent him recall John's Gospel. It is in that Gospel that Jesus uses miracles as signs, as he does here in *Thomas*, but in John they are signs of a very different nature.

This episode marks a turning point in the gospel. From now on, Jesus uses his powers for mostly salutary ends. He raises a boy killed by a fall from a roof (although he does so to prove he did not push him!). He cures a boy who injured his foot with an ax. He carries water in his garment after accidentally breaking the jar he had brought for the purpose. He causes grain sown by his father to yield miraculous amounts (see the parable of the Sower in Mark 4:1-8).

When Joseph cuts a board the wrong length, Jesus miraculously stretches it to the proper length. Then Jesus goes through two more teachers. The first was so foolish as to strike him for his impertinence, and Jesus curses him and he falls down, close to death. In the school of the second, Jesus demonstrates his divine knowledge of Torah, and the teacher acknowledges his wisdom. Then Jesus heals the first teacher. Next Jesus cures a snake bite incurred by James, raises a baby who has died, and raises a man killed on a construction project. The people come to realize that "this child is a God or an angel of God, because his every word becomes a finished deed" (17:2; 18:2). The text ends with the story about Jesus in the temple from Luke 2:41-51. Added to the end are words of the scribes and Pharisees to Mary saying that she is blessed among women and that God has blessed the fruit of her womb (see Luke 1:42). The gospel ends with the doxology, "Glory be to him forever and ever" (19:5).

Jesus' use of his powers in this gospel is entertaining, even if it makes him a dangerous character. Eventually he uses his powers for good, although he has to do a little growing up first. The general point of the gospel is to recognize his miraculous powers as signs of his origin and so to believe in him.

The Gospel of James (Protevangelium of James)

This is an early example (second century) of a work extolling the virtues of Mary, mother of Jesus. It claims James as its author, probably meaning Jesus' brother. It combines Matthew's and Luke's accounts with a good deal of noncanonical material, interweaving them all into a connected narrative. The work is often called a *protevangelium*, or a proto-gospel, because it mostly concerns what happens before Jesus' birth. It contains twenty-five chapters, and Jesus is born in the twenty-first. The book focuses on Mary, and one of its ancient titles was "The Birth of Mary," and another "The Story of the Birth of Saint Mary, Mother of God."

Mary's birth comes about in a way familiar to readers of the Old and New Testaments, and of other Jewish and Christian literature. Her parents, Joachim and Anna, are infertile, a condition considered a misfortune in the ancient world, and through the intervention of God they conceive and bear a child. Mary receives the highest blessings of the priests. As did Hannah, mother of Samuel, in 1 Sam 1–2, Anna gratefully dedicates her daughter to the temple's service. Mary spends from ages three to twelve there, but she cannot stay once she has reached puberty, lest she pollute the temple with blood. (Menstrual blood is considered defiling in the Hebrew Bible.) Joseph, an old man with children, is chosen by the priests as her husband in a way reminiscent of the choice of Aaron as head priest in Num 17—candidates are given rods, and a dove comes out of Joseph's rod and alights on his head. Joseph is embarrassed because he is so old and Mary so young, but he accedes to the wishes of the priests. The emphasis on Joseph's age and the detail that he already has children preserves the idea that Mary was a virgin throughout her life, despite her marriage to Joseph and that fact that the canonical gospels claim that Jesus had brothers and sisters (Mark 6:3 and parallels; John 7:3).

In Matthew, God's angel communicates with Joseph, not Mary. In Luke, the angel talks to Mary, not Joseph. *James* harmonizes the two by having the angel talk to both. When Mary first becomes pregnant, we hear Joseph's thoughts on the matter. He is in despair, thinking he has not protected the virgin he received from the sanctuary. He confronts Mary, reminding her of her temple upbringing. She pleads innocence. He ponders what he ought to do. The Law commands him to expose her, subjecting her to punishments. He does not wish to disobey the Law, but he wonders whether Mary's child is from the angels and does not want to be guilty of its death. The angel ends his agony by enlightening him. Thus the narrative embellishes the problems Mary's pregnancy causes, highlighting the fact that Mary conceives of the Holy Spirit and stressing her virginity.

When the angel reveals to Mary that she is to conceive of God, she asks, "Shall I conceive by the Lord, the living God? As all women do, shall I give birth?" (11:5). In Luke, Mary does not ask this question. It focuses attention on the physical aspects of the birth. The angel says, "Not thus," and goes on to say that Jesus will be Son of God and will save the people from their sins, a combination of what the angel says to Joseph in Matthew and Mary in Luke. Later in the work, we find out what the angel's "Not thus" means. Mary has not only conceived without knowing a man sexually, she also remains a virgin even after Jesus' birth. Salome, told by the midwife of the miraculous birth and informed that Mary remains a virgin, insists on examining her with her finger, a scene that recalls the similar demand of "doubting Thomas" in John 20. When she performs the examination and is convinced, her hand withers away. She prays, and the angel tells her to touch Jesus and she will be cured and have joy. She does so. The scene conveys the idea that Mary was not only a virgin after she conceived Jesus but before he was born, but that she remained a virgin after that. Salome's fate warns anyone from questioning such a holy mystery. Her cure stresses Jesus' holiness and origin in God.

This text testifies to the ongoing fascination of the stories of Mary and Jesus to Christians. Building on older texts, it embellishes them with legendary details in order to underscore Mary's special nature and function in God's plan, and to advocate belief in her perpetual virginity as a symbol of that nature and function.

REVELATION DIALOGUES AND DISCOURSES

A number of texts take the form of dialogues between the risen Christ and his disciples. Many involve long discourses by Christ. For the most part, these texts are found in the Nag Hammadi library and are gnostic. Gnostic teachers often claim that their views come from sources unavailable to others. We see that, for example, when the *Gospel of Thomas* declares itself to be "secret" teachings.

Dialogue of the Savior

A good example of this sort of text is the *Dialogue of the Savior*, from codex III of the Nag Hammadi library, probably composed in the second century. Unfortunately, the text is fragmentary. It seems to rely upon sources that have been reworked and incorporated in this new, complex work. Scholars have discerned a sayings source, perhaps similar to the *Gospel of Thomas*, from which sayings have been taken, reworked, embellished, and interpreted. There are other materials in the document, such as a creation myth modeled on Gen 1–2, a cosmological list, and an apocalyptic vision. It begins with an exhortation, a prayer, and an instruction about how to ascend through the heavenly spheres to the spiritual world above, making one's way through the heavenly powers whose purpose it is to keep spiritual persons imprisoned.

The *Dialogue* is in the form of a conversation between Jesus and his disciples. The main topic is eschatology, realized and future. Tension between present and future eschatology is present to some degree throughout Christianity. Christians generally believed that some eschatological events and goals were accomplished in Jesus' life, death, and resurrection, and that some remained to be accomplished. Such concerns are central to Paul's theology, for example, which is sometimes spoken of as an "already/not yet" tension in his theology. Romans 5 teaches that we have already been set right with God but that we still have to be saved from God's eschatological wrath. Pauline scholars sometimes speak of this as the "eschatological reservation" in Paul. John's Gospel emphasizes what we already have, so it features realized eschatology. However, it does retain aspects of future eschatology, as in chapters 5 and 11.

The *Dialogue of the Savior* grapples with similar problems, but with a gnostic slant. Through baptism the believers have already escaped this world in a sense. But they remain here to reveal the truth to others. Then they can attain full "rest," a term common in gnostic texts, indicating complete escape from this physical world and entrance into the world of pure light. Terms typical of Gnosticism, such as stripping off of the body and leaving behind the female works are employed to designate this transition. This reference to the female deserves attention. It assumes that the male is the ideal, and that the female is to some extent a defective form of humanity. Such an idea may be based on the second chapter of Genesis, where Eve is created only after Adam has been created and cannot find a proper companion among the animals. Such mythological attempts to explain the male/female dichotomy among humans are common in the ancient world.

Apocryphon of James

The *Apocryphon of James*, found in the first codex of Nag Hammadi, is in the form of a letter of James, probably the brother of Jesus. It was written in or near the second century. It tells of a dialogue between the risen Jesus, Peter, and James, in which Jesus teaches in the forms of parables, sayings, and beatitudes. The outlook of the book is not obviously gnostic, although it emphasizes knowledge and uses such typically gnostic language as "sleep" and "drunkenness." In the end, Jesus goes up in a "chariot of spirit," and the two disciples make a heavenly journey, typical of apocalypses and other revelatory literature.

Gospel of Mary

The *Gospel of Mary* has become popular recently. It is even mentioned by the best-selling novel *The Da Vinci Code*. The reason for such attention is the prominence accorded Mary Magdalene in this document. Mary was obviously a very important figure in Jesus' following, yet she is not given a leadership role in the canonical gospels or in any other documents from the New Testament or from other early Christian literature. This text is not part of the Nag Hammadi library. An incomplete manuscript of it was discovered in the nineteenth century in Egypt. A Greek fragment of the gospel dates to the early third century, so the gospel itself probably dates to the second century.

The gospel has two main parts. The first is a dialogue between Jesus and his disciples. Then Jesus departs and the disciples mourn, beginning the second main part. Then Mary comforts them, and Peter asks her to reveal to them what Jesus has told her privately. He says, "Sister, we know that the Savior loved you more than the rest of women. Tell us the words of the Savior which you remember—which you know (but) we have not nor have we heard them" (10:1-6; translation from Robinson, *Nag Hammadi*). Her revelation consists of an instruction of how to deal with the powers that try to hold the spiritual person captive as he or she ascends to the spiritual world. But once she teaches them, Peter resents her. He says, "Did he really speak privately with a woman (and) not openly to us? Are we to turn about and all listen to her? Did he prefer her to us?" (17:18-22). At first Peter seems open to revelation whatever its source. But then his patriarchalism takes over. Is he really to be taught by a woman? Can it be that Jesus told her something that he did not tell Peter? Levi puts Peter in his place: "Peter, you have always been hot-tempered. Now I see you contending against the woman like adversaries. But if the Savior made her worthy, who are you indeed to reject her? Surely the Savior knows her very well. That is why he loved her more than us" (18:7-15).

The *Gospel of Mary* raises questions about the role of women in the early centuries of the church. We have observed the androcentrism and patriarchalism of the canonical gospels and of other early Christian literature, and we have also discovered evidence that leads us to challenge the historical accuracy of their presentations. One can do the same for other early Christian literature, such as the letters of Paul or the book of Revelation. The beauty of the *Gospel of Mary* is that it makes strong claims for the role of Mary Magdalene in the early church that make us look more closely at the way Mary is portrayed in earlier texts and wonder whether she gets her due. Scholars have recently unmasked the ways in which Mary has been domesticated by the emerging orthodox church, which has painted her as a sinner and even as a prostitute, although this has no basis in the canonical gospels. One need not accept the historicity of precise events depicted in the *Gospel of Mary* to recognize that it raises questions about Mary and about other early Christian women that have yet to receive adequate answers.

CHRISTOLOGY OF THE NONCANONICAL GOSPELS

One of the factors leading to the creation of new gospels was interest in filling in aspects of Jesus' life for which the canonical gospels gave insufficient information. The interest is driven by a view of Jesus that emphasizes the miraculous. The *Infancy Gospel of Thomas* presents a view of the child Jesus that to moderns seems bizarre. It is not so much that Jesus has full miraculous powers at a young age. Few Christians today have probably given much thought to whether he had such powers or not. What seems odd is that he would use such powers in a childish, self-ish, and arbitrary way. We are accustomed to hearing about Jesus' miracles within the context of his ministry. The genius of the canonical gospels is that they contextualize each feature of their portraits of Jesus. They do not present just miracles, or just sayings, or just Jesus' suffering and death. Rather, they see each of these elements as part of a broader whole. By contextualizing each category of Jesus material in this way, they interpret such elements.

A good example of contextualization is Mark's treatment of the miracles. He does not deny that Jesus did miracles. He recounts many of them. But by placing the miracles in the context of gospel in which Jesus tries to keep them quiet, all the while teaching about the necessity of his suffering and death, he puts the miracles in proper context, from his point of view.

The *Infancy Gospel of Thomas* also contextualizes the miracles, but because it supplies a context so different from any of the canonical gospels, it makes us see them differently. As modern readers, we probably react negatively to this Jesus, and we might even think that God has been a bit reckless to trust such dangerous powers to an immature child. To deal with this, we will probably neutralize this negative image by doing just what the canonical gospels do—we will recontextualize these powers, reasoning that Jesus would use them only for what we consider to be legitimate ends. To do that, we will probably draw on the Four Gospels, and relate the miracles to Jesus' teaching there.

In awarding such powers to the child Jesus, the *Infancy Gospel of Thomas* is making an important contribution to the ongoing Christian reflection of just who Jesus is. If he has divine powers, when did they start? Do they say something about his very nature? If so, did Jesus have that nature from the beginning? Was he Son of God in this sense throughout his whole life? Even many of those who might not like the image of the child Jesus striking down his playmates might not agree if we limit Jesus' powers to his ministry, implying that he only had them for that time. The solution to this problem offered by this particular gospel may not satisfy us, but the sort of question it addresses is not entirely foreign to sober christological reflection, as is made clear by the debates about Jesus' person by the great theologians of the first five Christian centuries.

The *Gospel of James* also deals with Jesus' divine nature, but it does so by focusing on the virgin birth. Unsatisfied with the descriptions found in Matthew and Luke, this gospel weaves a legendary account, using the canonical narratives but going well beyond them. It is unafraid to make the virgin birth graphically physical, and it is a warning to anyone who would not affirm its physical reality. At the same time, it establishes the beneficent nature of this supernatural Jesus, as the woman punished for disbelieving the virgin birth is subsequently cured simply by touching the Christ child.

Reconciliation of the humanity and divinity of Jesus assumes a different form in the *Gospel of the Ebionites*, but precisely how it does so is unclear from the extant fragments. It may be that the gospel thinks of Jesus as a human being who is used by the divine figure of the Messiah, who descends on Jesus at his baptism. Christ is not really human, nor was he begotten of God. Rather, he was created like an angel. Division of the human and divine in Jesus (if indeed this is what the *Gospel* means) is forcefully rejected by later mainstream doctrine, which insists on the unity of the two natures—human and divine—in one person, Jesus Christ. Nor does later tradition accept that Jesus was a heavenly being but inferior to God.

The revelation gospels picture the risen Christ instructing his disciples. They stress the resurrection, the ongoing communication between Christ and the church, and the possibility of new revelation. Such gospels were particularly congenial to gnostic views. One of the most intriguing of such gospels is the *Gospel of Mary* because of the questions it raises about Jesus' relation to women in general and Mary Magdalene in particular, as well as about the role of women in the early Church.

Q and the *Gospel of Thomas* are similar in that they both consist mainly of sayings. Q presents them as public sayings of Jesus before his death, while *Thomas* presents them as secret sayings of the risen Jesus. In its present form, Q presents Jesus as the ultimate eschatological prophet. Heeding his teaching prepares one for the coming judgment. There is nothing here about Jesus' divinity, or about his death as salvific, or even about his resurrection. *Thomas* presents a Jesus more congenial to gnostic views. This Jesus teaches his listeners to discover their true selves, to distance themselves from this world, and to recover their true humanity. He is the ultimate revealer. Although this gospel does not have all the mythological trappings of some other gnostic texts, it accords with many of them in its emphasis on revelation and on knowledge of one's true self as the way to salvation.

BIBLIOGRAPHY

Allison, Dale. *The Jesus Tradition in Q*. Harrisburg: Trinity, 1997.

Cartlidge, David R., and David L. Dungan, eds. *Documents for the Study of the Gospels*. Rev. and enl. ed. Minneapolis: Fortress, 1994.

D'Angelo, Mary Rose. "Reconstructing 'Real' Women in Gospel Literature: The Case of Mary Magdalene." *WCO*, 105-28.

Edwards, James R. "The *Gospel of the Ebionites* and the Gospel of Luke." *NTS* 48 (2002): 568-86.

Ehrman, Bart D. *After the New Testament: A Reader in Early Christianity*. New York: Oxford University Press, 1999.

———. *Lost Christianities: The Battle for Scripture and the Faiths We Never Knew*. New York: Oxford University Press, 2003.

———. *Lost Scriptures: Books That Did Not Make It into the New Testament*. New York: Oxford University Press, 2003.

Elliott, Jack K., ed. *The Apocryphal Jesus: Legends of the Early Church*. New York: Oxford University Press, 1996.

Funk, Robert W., and Roy W. Hoover, eds. *The Five Gospels: The Search for the Authentic Words of Jesus*. New York: Macmillan, 1993.

Hedrick, Charles W., ed. *The Historical Jesus and the Rejected Gospels*. Vol. 44 of *Semeia*. Atlanta: Scholars, 1988.

King, Karen L. *The Gospel of Mary of Magdala: Jesus and the First Woman Apostle*. Santa Rosa, Calif.: Polebridge, 2003.

———. "The Gospel of Mary Magdalene." *STS* 2:601-34.

———. *What Is Gnosticism?* Cambridge: Harvard University Press, 2003.

Kloppenborg, John S. *The Formation of Q*. Philadelphia: Fortress, 1987.

Koester, Helmut. *Ancient Christian Gospels: Their History and Development.* Philadelphia: Trinity, 1990.

Levine, Amy-Jill. "Who's Catering the Q Affair?: Feminist Observations on Q Parenesis." *Semeia* 50 (1990): 145-61.

———. "Women in the Q Communit(ies) and Traditions." *WCO*, 150-70.

Pagels, Elaine. *Beyond Belief: The Secret Gospel of Thomas.* New York: Random House, 2003.

Patterson, Stephen J., James M. Robinson, and Hans-Gebhard Bethge. *The Fifth Gospel: The Gospel of Thomas Comes of Age.* Harrisburg, Penn.: Trinity, 1998.

Perkins, Pheme. "The Gospel of Thomas." *STS* 2:535-60.

Peterson, William L. "Ebionites, Gospel of the." *ABD* 2:261-62.

Robinson, James M. "The Image of Jesus in Q." Pages 7-25 in *Jesus Then and Now: Images of Jesus in History and Christology.* Edited by Marvin Meyer and Charles Hughes. Harrisburg, Penn.: Trinity, 2001.

———. "*Logoi Sophon*: On the Gattung of Q." In *Trajectories Through Early Christianity.* Philadelphia: Fortress, 1971.

———, ed. *The Nag Hammadi Library in English.* New York: Brill, 1996.

Schaberg, Jane. "The Infancy of Mary of Nazareth." *STS* 2:708-27.

———. *The Resurrection of Mary Magdalene, Legends, Apocrypha, and the Christian Testament.* New York: Continuum, 2002.

Schottroff, Luise. "The Sayings Source Q." *STS* 2:510-534.

Tuckett, Christopher M. "Q (Gospel Source)." *ABD* 5:567-72.

Turner, John D., and Anne McGuire, eds. *The Nag Hammadi Library after Fifty Years.* New York: Brill, 1997.

CHAPTER EIGHT

THE HISTORICAL JESUS

PRELIMINARY QUESTIONS

ARE THE GOSPELS TRUE?

For believers and for historians, the question of whether or not the Gospels are true is important. But often we are not clear on what we mean by "true." This chapter deals not with whether they are theologically true. The Christian church long ago made the decision that they are. Rather, we ask here about their historical accuracy. If I know that what the Gospels say that Jesus said and did is historically accurate, then I look at them one way. If I do not have this confidence, then I may see them another way.

However, this way of putting the question is simplistic and can condemn us to taking hardened positions with little possibility of dialogue. Remember our discussion of history in chapter 1. The modern study of history is a product of the Enlightenment. Modern historical study as it developed in the nineteenth century attempted to see the past as it actually was, to know "what really happened," and to be "objective" in the pursuit of that knowledge, using solid evidence and right reasoning. This simplified view of history has been challenged. Postmodern thinkers, sociologists of knowledge, feminists, and others have drawn attention to the vested interests inherent in any interpretation of texts and reconstruction of history. In a way, that should be obvious. Most of us can appreciate that in assessing reports about anything, we should consider the sources. But the point goes still deeper. It is truly difficult, probably impossible, to escape one's place in history and in society. We are always enmeshed in a world that limits us in countless ways of which we are aware only dimly if at all. To what degree is what we think affected by our place in society, the time in history in which we live, the presuppositions of the intellectual and social world in which we operate, the basic limitations of our knowledge, and the limits of our senses?

It is easy to lose patience with this line of thought. After all, is there not a "common sense" that all humans possess, and do we not have an intuitive and reliable sense of what is real and what is not, and that something either really did happen or really did not happen? Actually, even this "commonsense" approach is a philosophical stance. "Common sense" can mean just what almost everyone in a particular place and time agrees on. For example, "common sense" is obviously different for an upper-middle-class Christian person in the United States today than it is for a poor, jobless citizen of a nondemocratic, undeveloped country. Of course, we need not leave the United States to see such differences. In a globalized world, we cannot escape the realization that groups and nations do not share "common sense" with one another. We need to keep this in mind as we interpret gospel texts. Our "commonsense" interpretation is really interpretation that applies in an uncritical way the presuppositions and convictions of twenty-first-century Westerners from a limited range of social and economic class. That does not necessarily make something an "incorrect" interpretation, but it certainly means that our conclusions must be tentative and open to challenge.

Given all this, must we simply give up on "objective" historical research? Most scholars would answer "no." Most are aware of the serious issues surrounding any act of interpretation, but at the same time they do not deny that there are more and less adequate reconstructions of the past; some reconstructions are more true to what "actually happened" and some are less true. At the same time, they recognize that one can make a reliable judgment about a relatively simple question such as whether Augustus Caesar really did rule Rome from 31 B.C.E. to 14 C.E., but that as soon as one goes beyond a simple chronicle, one enters a realm of judgment and interpretation operating within specific communities of discourse. So the nature of Augustus's rule can be seen in any number of ways, depending on, for example, the historian's choice of and evaluation of evidence, the specific way in which that evidence contributes to an overview, and the way in which that overview depends on a specific way of viewing reality.

There is yet another complicating factor in this study. We are looking at texts that do not simply claim to convey history. They proclaim religious truth. They make statements about Jesus that go far beyond whether he lived at a particular period, or interacted with certain groups and individuals, or even did specific acts that were miraculous. They make claims that he is the Jewish Messiah, or that he is God come down to earth. Here we go well beyond what most historians would consider to be their expertise. We are in the realm of religious faith. But, of course, in a religion such as Christianity, focusing on a human being who walked the earth at a particular time and place, believers are accustomed to thinking that they have a firm historical foundation of what Jesus actually said and did on which to build their religion. Indeed, Christianity (and Judaism) have often been polemically compared to other religions as based on historical fact rather than on mythological fancy. If historical fact is challenged, then things tend to fall apart. It is either all true or all false, many often think. That makes the stakes of historical research extremely high. For some Christians, it makes biblical criticism sacrilegious.

FAITH AND HISTORY

The term "historical Jesus" can mislead. It is too often taken to mean "facts" about Jesus that debunk religious belief about him. It is true that over the past couple of centuries, some have aimed to discredit Christian beliefs, but they have not been the majority of Jesus scholars. Historical research may affect how one thinks about Jesus, but does not necessarily undermine faith. On the contrary, many consider it healthy for historical research to affect one's theology. Good history can make for good theology, and conversely, bad history has often produced regrettable results, as with, for example, negative portrayals of ancient Judaism by Christian scholars, theologians, and preachers, portrayals that have actually become active ingredients in theology and Christology.

Historians who study Jesus do not resolve historical questions by resorting to church dogma. Rather, they operate by the same rules of evidence and argument as do other historians. Many theologians, who reflect on faith from within the believing community, pay attention to what historians say and take account of it as they do theology. Their job differs from that of the historian. Historical reconstruction can support, nourish, and at times challenge contemporary Christian theology, but it does not for most theologians determine it. While historians concentrate on Jesus as experienced by his contemporaries, theologians also take into account later Christian reflection about Jesus, seen in the pronouncements of the great councils of the church, for example, as even more important for

Christology than what historical scholars may reconstruct about the earthly Jesus.

QUESTIONS BEYOND HISTORIANS' REACH

Some things are susceptible to historical investigation, others are not. Suppose we invent a time machine and send emissaries back through the ages to witness Jesus' crucifixion. When they return, we ask them, "Was Jesus of Nazareth crucified outside Jerusalem around 30 C.E. under the Roman administration of Pontius Pilate? And did he die for our sins?" What could they answer? They would be able to tell us the time and place of Jesus' execution and who was Roman administrator at the time. They might be able to tell us the Roman reasons for executing Jesus. Perhaps they could report on interpretations of Jesus' death, maybe including those of the disciples, of Jesus' enemies, and of neutral observers. They might even be able to shed light on how Jesus interpreted his own death. But they could not, based on their own observations, know whether through Jesus' death our sins are forgiven. This is a matter for faith and theological interpretation, not susceptible to proof or disproof either by eyewitnesses or historians. Jesus certainly died on a cross, and Christians believe he died for our sins, but these are two rather different sorts of truths.

What holds for our time travelers is even more true of modern historians. We can answer a range of questions through historical research, but historical study cannot prove or disprove theological claims. Historians can investigate and make judgments about whether people *said* that God did such-and-such, but they cannot as historians know whether they were right.

Our example raises another aspect of history. Even if we put theology aside as a way to explain things, history is not just a matter of chronicling events. It is also a matter of assessing cause and effect. So the philosophy and theology of the historian must have something to do with how she or he sees things. Here is where things get interesting.

IS HISTORY SCIENTIFIC?

Science depends on repeatable experiments, whereas history deals with one-time events. Historians draw analogies, look for patterns, make comparisons. They judge probability and hypothesize about cause-and-effect based on their views of human behavior, the nature of societies, the potential of technology, and other factors. They remain open to evidence that challenges their hypotheses and are willing to change their positions to fit the evidence better. But the events historians investigate are past and cannot be directly witnessed or repeated. We do not have the past; we have only stories about it, relics from it, testimonies left behind by eyewitnesses or by those who heard about it later. The evidence is often not clear or incontrovertible. The historian makes judgments about this evidence and assesses these interpretations from the past. This can be a somewhat "messy" business, resulting not in "solid fact" but in possible, plausible, or probable reconstructions.

Even if we could experience the past directly, there would still be no simple "truth" available, any more than there is in our assessment of current events. Interpretation is a part of our very experience of events. We experience everything in light of our past experiences, our beliefs, worldviews, attitudes, place in history and society, and so on.

This all means that despite their best efforts, historians can never be completely "objective." One must have some sort of worldview to make sense of anything. The answers one gets depend on the questions one asks, what one considers evidence, what methods one uses, what one's philosophy is, what one's experiences are. But this need not mean simply that one's ideology determines one's historical judgment. Most historians assume that some reconstructions are truer to the past than others, and that they should construct hypotheses that fit the evidence, not force the evidence into preconceived theories, and that they should be self-critical and willing to change their points of view in the light of new evidence or stronger arguments.

THE SEARCH FOR THE JESUS OF HISTORY

A classic in historical Jesus study is Albert Schweitzer's *Quest of the Historical Jesus*, published in 1906. It reviews the attempts to capture the historical Jesus by scholars of the preceding years, beginning with the posthumous publication in 1778 of parts of the work of H. S. Reimarus. It shows that these attempts always produced a reconstruction of Jesus with a striking resemblance to the interpreter. The interpreters generally subscribed to liberal Protestant theology, which thought that the church had been untrue to Jesus by espousing doctrines that he never would have accepted. Jesus, in their eyes, came to preach universal truths such as the fatherhood of God and the brotherhood of humans. He advocated a simple principle of love, not a complicated religion driven by dogma. In other words, Jesus was really a liberal Protestant.

The nineteenth-century lives display a universal tendency in both scholarship and Christology. We tend to see Jesus in our own image. What we approve of, he surely "must have" approved of. What we consider good, he "must have" thought good. Our Christology surely corresponds to what Jesus thought of himself. This certainly makes Jesus relevant. It is, however, open to serious historical debate.

Schweitzer's book brought to a close what came to be called the first quest for the historical Jesus. Significantly, the failure of his predecessors did not prevent Schweitzer from delineating his own historical Jesus. It pushed him to pursue more adequate methods and a more defensible portrait. While nineteenth-century lives of Jesus made him a liberal, nineteenth-century Christian, Schweitzer did the opposite. He adopted the insights of Johannes Weiss, who in 1892 made a strong case for an eschatological Jesus, who expected God's imminent intervention in history. Schweitzer's Jesus was apocalyptic, one so different from Schweitzer's contemporaries as to be barely comprehensible to them. The conviction that Jesus was an eschatological figure was immensely influential in the twentieth century. Toward the end of that century and into the present, scholars are divided over whether such terms do Jesus justice.

Schweitzer's work did not result immediately in a new quest. World War I undermined the optimistic view that history evolved and progressed, and in its wake the theology of Karl Barth, which presents God as totally other and God's word as confronting the world, contrasted markedly with liberal theology. The immensely influential New Testament scholar, Rudolf Bultmann, considered the quest to be futile. It was not possible to get back to Jesus because the church had altered and even invented traditions, and it was theologically wrong to base faith on historical research. James D. G. Dunn has suggestively called the first quest a flight from dogma and the reaction to it a flight from history.

In 1953, one of Bultmann's students, Ernst Käsemann, called for a new historical quest, insisting that to ignore the historical Jesus was to engage in a sort of Docetism, a bypassing of his true humanity and engagement in history. Thus investigating the historical Jesus was theologically necessary. The new quest recognized that historians could not write a biography of Jesus that revealed his inner life or that depended heavily on the narrative elements composed by the evangelists to frame Jesus' words and deeds. Instead, they laid emphasis on the continuity between the historical Jesus and the church's gospel proclamation, the technical term for which was *kerygma*, Greek for "proclamation."

Many consider that more recent studies constitute a third quest. It is distinctive in its emphasis on the Jewishness of Jesus, greater attention to recent advances in understanding late Second Temple Judaism, and interest in social-scientific insights into Jesus' milieu. Earlier scholarship often set Jesus over against other Jews and contrasted his teachings and practices with those of his Jewish contemporaries. Such contrasts always worked to denigrate Judaism and amounted to little more than Christian propaganda.

WHY BOTHER?

On just about every aspect of the historical study of Jesus there are disagreements. Many have deserted the quest, or never seriously engaged in it, because they see no potential for conclusive answers. Fundamentalists and other conservative Christians disapprove of the quest because they believe that biblical text is inerrant in all matters, including historical ones. But the quest will continue, for several reasons. For historians, how can they resist studying such a significant figure? For believers, how can they not ask about the human Jesus, if he speaks and acts for God? That there can be no absolutely reliable answers should not deter us. The same is surely true of theology and Christology as well. Christians have advocated a bewildering variety of interpretations of Jesus. If they were to look for absolute answers on which all could agree, they would stop talking about Christ altogether.

Finally, discussion of Jesus rests on countless assumptions about what is considered historical. It is too easy to accommodate the gospel narratives to our own views or assume that they present something close to a simple recording of events. To abandon this quest is to cease examining and debating those assumptions. We need to discuss and assess evidence, debate method, and engage in self-criticism and self-awareness. We will never reach universal agreement, but there is much to be said for the dialogue and debate.

SOURCES

The canonical gospels are the main sources for the historical Jesus. Mark is the earliest, and when Matthew and Luke get their material from Mark, we cannot consider them independent sources. Q is another source used by Matthew and Luke, and most consider it independent of Mark. Matthew's special material (designated "M") and Luke's ("L") are considered independent of Mark and Q. Therefore, Mark, Q, M, and L constitute independent sources for our work. Although there are important differences between these four sources, the Synoptics do not read as if they were stitched together from works radically different in tone and content. Material in these sources is fairly consistent in character. This is the more evident when we compare the Synoptics to the Gospel of John. There we do see striking differences in style, form, and content. It is hard to believe that Jesus was *both* as he is in the Synoptics *and* as he is in John.

The vast majority of scholars think that the Synoptics have greater claim to overall historical accuracy than does John. There is a general tendency in the early church to exalt Jesus, and Jesus is obviously more exalted in John than in the Synoptics. In John, he is God, present at the creation. His message on earth mainly concerns his own identity. He claims to be Son of God, Messiah, the light of the world, and so on. We see none of this in the Synoptics, where he spends most of his time talking about the kingdom of God and acting to bring it about. It is more likely that the Johannine tradition has exalted Jesus than that the Synoptic traditions have made him less godlike. Nonetheless, John's Gospel does supply some useful material for historical study.

The Synoptics are also theological interpretations of Jesus, as we have seen. They augment, subtract from, and rewrite the material they inherit. Each has a distinct slant on Jesus. We can use our insight into their distinctive views to aid us in historical judgment. Identifying the evangelists' redaction enables us to recover earlier forms of sayings or events. It can also suggest to what degree the evangelists or their communities produced stories or sayings, and whether or not such material departs from or is in continuity with earlier Jesus tradition.

Paul's letters also provide helpful material. Some confirm what we already know—that Jesus was a Jew and observed the Torah (Gal 4:4), was crucified (Phil 2:8), and that early Christians believed he had been raised from the dead (1 Cor 15:3-8). They also confirm what seemed likely—that he forbade divorce (1 Cor 7:10-11), had brothers, one of whom was James (Gal 1:19), had an inner circle of twelve (1 Cor 15:5), perhaps was betrayed by one of his own (1 Cor 11:23), and shared a final meal with disciples at which he spoke words taken to be the institution of the Eucharist (1 Cor 11:23-25). Paul reproduces little of Jesus' teaching. He has abundant opportunity to quote Jesus in dealing with church problems but seldom does so. Rather, Jesus' death and resurrection, interpreted in terms of his own theology, occupy Paul's attention.

Recently, noncanonical Christian documents have received more attention in historical Jesus study, especially the *Gospel of Thomas* and the *Gospel of Peter*. Scholars have eagerly scoured *Thomas* for relevant material. Much of *Thomas* may be gnostic and therefore more useful for understanding later Christian views than the historical Jesus. A couple of its sayings not in the canonical gospels may go back to the historical Jesus, but they tell us nothing new. There are some other sayings in *Thomas* that are in the Synoptics and that seem to be in a more original form in *Thomas*, since they do not show the Synoptics' redactional features. *Thomas* has also become important in discussions of whether Jesus thought apocalyptically. Some sayings that in the Synoptics have apocalyptic contexts are present in *Thomas* without such contexts. This raises the question of whether or not the sayings were originally apocalyptic.

Christians are apt to think that Jesus' life and death was the most important thing to happen in late Second Temple Jewish Palestine or even in the entire world. For Christians, he is. But Jesus is barely a blip on the radar screens of first-century Jews and Romans. Jesus was important enough to attract the attention of the Jerusalem authorities and of the Roman prefect. He was condemned to death by Pilate. However, many Palestinian Jews died at Roman hands during this period. Josephus tells us that around the time Jesus was born, a Roman administrator, Varus, crucified two thousand Jews. Indeed, two Jewish revolutionaries were crucified alongside Jesus. In this sense, Jesus is not unusual.

We hear almost nothing of Jesus in non-Christian literature of the first century, Jewish or otherwise. Josephus has a couple of short references to him. The Roman historians Tacitus and Suetonius, writing in the early part of the second century, mention him briefly but tell us nothing we did not already know and may get their information from Christian sources. A Roman governor in Asia Minor, Pliny the Younger, writes about Christians toward the beginning of the second century. He says that Christians met daily and sang hymns to Christ as a god. This tells us something about later Christian practice but possibly nothing about Jesus himself. (See Hurtado's study of worship of Jesus in the early church.) Rabbinic documents are too late to help us. The first of them to be written down, the *Mishnah*, was set in writing around 200 C.E. and says nothing about Jesus. The *Talmuds*, written between around 400 and 600 C.E., refer to him, but they are late and give no clearly independent information.

JOSEPHUS ON JESUS

Josephus's writings contain a paragraph about Jesus worth our attention. Josephus was not a Christian, so some parts of the paragraph are clearly Christian interpolations. We italicize Christian additions in the following quote.

> At this time there appeared Jesus, a wise man, *if indeed one should call him a man.* For he was a doer of startling deeds, a teacher of people who receive the truth with pleasure. And he gained a following both among many Jews and among many of Greek origin. *He was the Messiah.* And when Pilate, because of an accusation made by the leading men among us, condemned him to the cross, those who loved him previously did not cease to do so. *For he appeared to them on the third day, living again, just as the divine prophets had spoken of these and countless other wondrous things about him.* And up until this very day the tribe of Christians, named after him, has not died out. (*Ant.* 18.63-64; quoted from Meier, *Marginal Jew,* 1:60; italics added, based on Meier's analysis)

This passage shows how Jesus looked to a Jew outside his movement. For Josephus, Jesus was a teacher and someone who did extraordinary deeds. Pilate condemned Jesus to crucifixion on the basis of accusations made by Jewish leaders. Josephus knows of the ongoing Christian movement. Most of this confirms what we know from the Gospels. Josephus's belief that Jesus had Gentile followers may be influenced by his knowledge of the later Christian movement.

This is one of only two references to Jesus in Josephus. In the second, Josephus tells of the execution of James, "brother of Jesus, who was called Christ" (*Ant.* 20.200), by the high priest Ananus.

CRITERIA OF AUTHENTICITY

Scholars have developed a set of criteria to help determine what is historical. Some criteria have proved more useful than others, and all are subject to debate. None are sufficient in themselves, and there are problems with all of them. However, together, they supply guidelines and methods that help us get "behind" the Gospels to a plausible historical reconstruction.

Dissimilarity. This criterion excludes material that fits closely Judaism of Jesus' time or early Christianity, so it is sometimes called the principle of double dissimilarity. Taken too far, it dismisses from consideration anything that Jesus shares with his fellow Jews or supporting continuity between Jesus and the church. N. T. Wright has refined the criterion, suggesting that we look for material understandable within Jesus' Jewish context but distinctive within it, on the one hand, and things that are not identical with early Christian beliefs but make comprehensible how early Christian beliefs emerged, on the other hand. A limitation of the criterion is that there is so much that we do not know about early Judaism and early Christianity, so we can seldom be sure if something is distinctive.

Embarrassment. The principle of embarrassment identifies material that the early church would not have invented because of its embarrassing or problematic nature. For example, if the Gospels portray one of Jesus' disciples as a betrayer, then it probably happened that way. The early church would hardly have made it up. One problem with this criterion is that what a modern interpreter might find embarrassing, an ancient Christian might not. That vulnerability in the criterion can be lessened if the texts themselves show some discomfort with the material (as, for example, with Jesus' baptism by John, below).

Multiple Attestation. Multiple attestation means being attested in more than one independent source. Generally speaking, we think that the following sources are independent of one another: Mark, Q, John, M, L, Paul. Another sort of multiple attestation is that of form. When something is attested in a variety of forms, that bolsters the argument that it is authentic. For example, miracles are mentioned in sayings and narrated in stories. An argument against leaning too heavily on this criterion is that multiple attestation might indicate that the early Christians found something fairly helpful or congenial. This, then, would to some degree contradict the first criterion, that of dissimilarity.

Coherence. When something coheres with material isolated according to the previous principles, it may be authentic. The helpfulness of this criterion depends on the reliability of the earlier ones.

Linguistic and Environmental Context. Things that do not fit the context of early first-century Jewish society in Palestine should be excluded. Again, there are debates about just what does fit first-century Jewish society, and there is an unfortunate dearth of information about it.

Rejection and Execution. Reconstructions that cannot account for Jesus' execution at the hands of the Romans are inadequate. Most would find this valid, but there are scholars who think that Jesus' death could have been just an accident of history—he was in the wrong place at the wrong time—so speculations on how he came to be crucified would be misleading.

Result. The movement Jesus began continued after his death. There must have been aspects of Jesus' person and work that made that possible. This is not to say that Jesus intended to found a new religion, for most Jesus scholars maintain that he did not. Some would criticize this criterion because it assumes a continuity between Jesus and the church that is unproved.

A Combination of Principles and Methods. Authors such as Meier and Crossan begin with well-defined principles by which they judge the evidence, and they build up their image bit by bit. Sanders follows a different method. He thinks that on the basis of our knowledge of the times in which Jesus lived and the overall character of the Jesus traditions, one can hypothesize about the most appropriate interpretation of Jesus and then test that picture against the evidence. The evidence, for him, consists not primarily of the sayings material, whose authenticity is hard to prove and that is open to many interpretations. He prefers to assemble "virtually indisputable facts" and base his picture on them. Once he forms a picture of Jesus in this way, he can consider how sayings support or challenge that picture.

THE "FACTS" ABOUT JESUS

We begin with Sanders's "facts." We present the list, look at each item briefly and then examine several items in more detail. The list in this form is an adaptation of Sanders, taken from Murphy (pp. 336-37).

- Jesus was born ca. 4 B.C.E. near the time of the death of Herod the Great.
- He spent his childhood and early adult years in Nazareth, a Galilean village.
- He was baptized by John the Baptist.
- He was a Galilean who preached and healed.
- He called disciples and spoke of there being twelve.
- He taught in the towns, villages, and countryside of Galilee (apparently not the cities).
- He confined his activity to Israel.
- He preached "the kingdom of God."

- About the year 30 he went to Jerusalem for Passover.
- He engaged in a controversy about the temple and created a distur-bance in the temple area.
- He had a final meal with his disciples.
- He was arrested and interrogated by Jewish authorities, specifically the high priest.
- He was executed on the orders of the Roman prefect, Pontius Pilate, being crucified outside Jerusalem by Roman soldiers.
- His disciples at first fled.
- They saw him (in what sense is uncertain) after his death.
- As a consequence, they believed he would return to found the kingdom.
- They formed a community to await his return and sought to win others to faith in him as God's Messiah.
- At least some Jews persecuted at least parts of the new movement (Gal 1:13, 22; Phil 3:6), and it appears that this persecution endured at least to a time near the end of Paul's career (2 Cor 11:24; Gal 5:11; 6:12; cf. Matt 10:17; 23:34).

Born in 4 B.C.E. Both Matthew and Luke assert that Jesus was born in the reign of Herod the Great (40–4 B.C.E.). They do so independently, for the differences in the infancy narratives are so great that no reliance on a shared source is likely.

Raised in Nazareth. Nazareth does not appear in the Hebrew Bible, nor does Josephus mention it. There would be no reason for early Christians to claim that Jesus was raised there if it were not so.

Baptized by John the Baptist. This is independently attested by Mark, John, and Q, and as we shall see below, Christian tradition demonstrates embarrassment with it.

A Galilean Who Preached and Healed. That Jesus preached is widely attested in all of the Jesus material and in all forms in which it was passed down. Jesus' healing appears in multiple independent sources—Mark, John, Q, M, L.

Called Disciples and Spoke of Twelve. There is no doubt that Jesus had disciples. His movement would not have continued beyond his death without them. That there was an inner group of twelve is multiply attested—Mark, John, Q, and Paul (1 Cor 15:5).

Taught in Galilee's Countryside. Most of Jesus' active ministry took place in Galilee, much of it in the small villages. He did visit some larger towns, such as Capernaum on the shore of the Sea of Galilee (apparently a base for his operations in the area), but he is never said to enter a major city. Galilee's capital, Sepphoris, is only about four miles from Nazareth. It was a Hellenized city, often thought by scholars to be shunned by Jews. Recent research suggests a largely Jewish city. It is unclear whether Jesus did not go there because of its Hellenistic tone or for some other reason. He likely thought that he would get a more receptive audience in Galilee's villages and towns.

Confined His Activity to Israel. There are few concrete instances of Jesus interacting with Gentiles. General statements that he moved around in Gentile territory tell us little, because we do not hear much of what he did there.

Preached Kingdom of God. This is multiply attested and prominent in the traditions.

About 30 C.E. *Went to Jerusalem for Passover.* This is multiply attested (Mark and John) and explains a good deal about his death, as we shall see.

Details of Passion. The items in the list dealing with the passion—the final meal, the arrest, Jerusalem authorities deciding he must die, condemnation by Pilate, Jesus' death, flight of the disciples, disciples' belief that they saw him alive after his death, their conviction that he would return—all are multiply attested.

Christian Community. The establishment of Christian communities after Jesus' death is a matter of public record. In some places this aroused some Jewish opposition.

THE INFANCY NARRATIVES

Texts written in the second century and later concerning Jesus' birth and childhood are not good historical sources. We have found the *Infancy Gospel of James (Protevangelium of James)* and the *Infancy Gospel of Thomas* to be highly fanciful narratives, full of legendary elements. The infancy narratives of Matthew and Luke (Matt 1–2; Luke 1–2) are heavily theologically charged. For example, Matthew's narrative proves that Jesus fulfills five citations from Israel's prophets. It also draws parallels between Jesus and Moses. Luke has his own theological motivations. When we compare the two Synoptic infancy narratives, their differences are immediately apparent. Both Matthew and Luke have Jesus born in Bethlehem and raised in Nazareth, but they do so by different means. In Matthew, Jesus' family lives in Bethlehem. He is born in a house there. They flee to Egypt because Herod is trying to kill Jesus. When Herod dies, an angel warns Joseph not to return to Judea because Herod's son Archelaus now rules there. They go to Nazareth instead. In Luke, Joseph and Mary are natives of Nazareth and go to Bethlehem to register in a census decreed by Caesar Augustus. There is no room at the inn, so Jesus is born in a manger. After a visit to Jerusalem, they return to Nazareth. The differences between Matthew and Luke are apparent. It is also impossible to reconcile Matthew's idea that Herod was seeking to kill Jesus with Luke's scene of Jesus being publicly acclaimed in the temple eight days after his birth.

Luke's census is highly questionable. Such an undertaking for "the whole world" would be without precedent—nor has this extraordinary event left any trace in historical sources. A census requiring everyone to travel to the city of one's ancestors would be unworkable even today, with modern modes of transportation. If such an unusual census of worldwide proportions had actually taken place, we would expect it to leave some sort of record in historical documents. The only census of which we know that affected Jewish Palestine at this time was the one that took place when Judea passed from the administration of Herod's son Archelaus to direct Roman administration. That took place in 6 C.E. But Luke (and Matthew) tells us that Jesus was born under the reign of Herod the Great, who died in 4 B.C.E. Luke seems to be somewhat confused on his dating of events here.

Note that Luke is not saying that Joseph was actually from Bethlehem. It is just that he was a descendant of King David, whose home village was Bethlehem. Here Luke's theological motivation stands out. The evangelist John shows no knowledge of Jesus' birth in Bethlehem. He mentions that people expected the Messiah to be born in Bethlehem but knew that Jesus was *not* born there (7:41-43).

All in all, Matthew's and Luke's infancy narratives tell us little of historical worth. They do agree, however, that Jesus was born under Herod the Great (died 4 B.C.E.), so most accept that. Also, they both say that Jesus grew up in Nazareth. There is no reason to make that up, so most scholars accept that as well. Matthew and Luke agree on the virgin birth as well, but that is something which historians cannot judge.

JESUS' CHILDHOOD

We know nothing of Jesus' childhood. Luke provides one anecdote about the twelve-year-old Jesus amazing teachers of the Law in the temple with his knowledge. This is the sort of story one would expect concerning an important figure in the ancient world. In his autobiography, Josephus says that he also was treated as an expert in the Torah when he was only fourteen years old (see our discussion of Luke 2:41-51 and the quote from Josephus there).

JESUS AND JOHN THE BAPTIST

Mark tells us that John was in the wilderness by the Jordan River, "proclaiming a baptism of repentance for the forgiveness of sins," and that Jesus was baptized by John (1:4-5). Matthew omits the phrase "for the forgiveness of sin," perhaps because for him forgiveness of sin cannot occur before Jesus' ministry (Matt 1:21; 26:28). Josephus tells us that John's baptism was meant not to wash away sins but as a sign that one had repented (*Ant.* 18.116-19). Modern Christians are familiar with baptism for the forgiveness of sins, but how would John's baptism be understood in his own context?

John was a prophet, preaching in the wilderness, attracting crowds and baptizing them. In Q, John predicts an imminent fiery judgment to overtake the wicked and warns his listeners to prepare (Q 3:7-9). This makes John an eschatological prophet. For him, history was reaching a climax and God was about to intervene to set things straight.

The Gospels paint John in the colors of Elijah, the ninth-century Israelite prophet who railed against the idolatry of the Israelite king Ahab and his wife Jezebel (1 Kgs 17–19, 21; 2 Kgs 1–2). Elijah ascended to heaven in a fiery chariot (2 Kgs 2:11-12), so he did not die. This caught the attention of the postexilic prophet Malachi, at the end of whose book is the prophecy, "Lo, I will send you the prophet Elijah before the great and terrible day of the LORD comes. He will turn the hearts of parents to their children and the hearts of children to their parents, so that I will not come and strike the land with a curse" (4:5-6; the chapter and verse numbering here is that of the *NRSV*, which follows the Greek; in Hebrew it is 3:19-24). The "day of the LORD" means judgment day. Discord between parents and children indicates a society that ignores God's will and implies that the world is falling apart. Malachi expects Elijah to warn Israel before God comes to judge so that it has a chance to repent. In the Synoptics, John the Baptist resembles Elijah in the place of his dwelling, the wilderness, in his dress and food, and in his function and message (2 Kgs 1:8; Mal 4:5-6; Mark 1:6).

John was not alone in his hopes. We know of at least three other prophets like him. During the administration of the Roman governor Fadus (44–46 C.E.), Theudas and his followers went to the Jordan River and predicted that it would split and allow them to cross. This would repeat what happened in the days of Joshua, an event that itself echoed the miraculous crossing of the Red Sea (Exod 14; Josh 3). Fadus dispatched cavalry, killed many, captured Theudas, and executed him. About a decade later (ca. 56 C.E.), a Jewish prophet from Egypt whose name has been forgotten led a crowd to the Mount of Olives east of Jerusalem and proclaimed that at his command Jerusalem's walls would fall, allowing entrance into the city. This recalls the battle of Jericho in Josh 6, where God causes the walls to fall so as to deliver the city to the Israelites. Again the Romans attacked them, although this time the prophet escaped, never to be heard from again. A similar episode occurred among the Samaritans in the 30s. A prophet led a crowd up the Samaritan sacred mountain, Gerizim, convinced that God would reveal the hidden sacred vessels from the first Samaritan temple, thus signaling eschatological restoration. Pilate responded with such force that even his Roman superiors disapproved, resulting in his removal from office in 36 C.E.

All of these incidents involved prophets who kindled hope that God would intervene on behalf of Israel as in the past. In all cases the Romans reacted repressively. The wilderness setting is significant for these prophets and for John the Baptist as well. It was fraught with meaning in Israel's history. At the exodus, Israel fled from Egypt to the wilderness. There they were tested by God, benefited from God's mercy and protection, and received the Torah. In the eighth century, the prophet Hosea speaks of God bringing Israel back to the wilderness where, like a suitor seeking a bride, he will woo Israel. There God will purify and renew Israel. The prophet Elijah, pursued by the idolatrous queen Jezebel, flees to the wilderness and eventually goes to Mount Sinai (called Horeb in northern kingdom traditions) to find refuge and be recommissioned by God (1 Kgs 19). At various times in Israel's history, it found refuge from its enemies in the desert.

Both the Gospels and Josephus say that Herod Antipas executed John (Mark 6:14-29 and parallels; *Ant.* 18.116-119). In Mark, Herod's wife Herodias instigates his death, because John condemned her marriage as violating Torah. In Josephus, Herod eliminates John because he fears his influence over the people. John's fate is the same as that of the other three eschatological prophets. They operated in territory under direct Roman administration. John worked in an area controlled by Herod, so Herod executed him. In each case, an eschatological message brought unwelcome attention from the authorities, who saw it as a threat.

John differs from these prophets in that he baptized. Washing with water was a common Jewish ritual, effecting ritual purity. It was especially important when entering the temple, where a high degree of purity was required, or when the priests were to engage in their sacred duties, which called for a still higher degree of purity. Ritual washing was important in the community of the Dead Sea Scrolls. Maintenance of purity was key for them, both because they believed that God's angels were among them, and because God and God's angels were soon to intervene in human history.

In these other cases, washing was repeated. In rites outside of Qumran, washing had nothing to do with sin. The Qumran community may have thought of sin as ritually defiling and therefore have seen water rituals as related in some way to cleansing oneself from the defilement of sin. John's baptism was a one-time affair, unlike Jewish purification rituals. God would judge the people soon, and baptism signified repentance and cleansing in preparation for judgment. In his association of washing with sin, John may have been closer to the Qumran community than to other Jews.

Christians generally believe that Jesus was sinless (Heb 4:15), so this raises the question of why he would have to repent. Individual sin may not be the best model for understanding John's baptism or the reason that Jesus accepted it. The ancients were less individualistic than we, and their identity was more dependent on membership in groups than is ours. Jesus' coming for baptism may have less to do with a personal sense of sinfulness than with an identification with Israel. As Israel prepared itself through repentance for God's judgment, Jesus expressed solidarity with his people.

Why accept Jesus' baptism and relationship with John as historically accurate? The criterion of embarrassment applies here. Matthew, Luke, and John found aspects of Jesus' relationship with John problematic. Matthew rewrites Mark's version of Jesus' baptism. Matthew says, "John would have prevented him, saying, 'I need to be baptized by you, and do you come to me?' But Jesus answered him, 'Let it be so now; for it is proper for us in this way to fulfill all righteousness'" (3:14-15). These words appear in no other canonical gospel (Epiphanius tells us that the *Gospel of the Ebionites* rewrites them, so that John begs Jesus to baptize him and Jesus refuses). They assume that the greater baptizes the lesser. Jesus tells John that his baptism accords with God's will. It is just "for now." It does not signify Jesus' subordination to John.

Luke takes a different tack. He never says that John baptizes Jesus, although his narrative implies it. Instead, he says simply that Jesus "was baptized" (3:21). And he puts off saying that until he says that Herod imprisoned John (3:20). This is subtle, but in the infancy narrative Luke makes John's subordination to Jesus clear. There Luke recounts the annunciations and the births in parallel, and there is no question that John's significance is purely as one who prepares the way for Jesus.

John's Gospel devotes the most attention to this issue. In this Gospel, the Baptist never baptizes Jesus at all! He says he saw the Spirit descend on Jesus but does not say when (1:29-34). The prologue to John's Gospel contains two references to John the Baptist (1:6-9, 15). They interrupt the prologue's poetic flow, so they seem to be added to a preexistent piece. The essence of the insertions is contained in the words, "He (John) himself was not the light, but he came to testify to the light" (1:8). This raises the possibility that someone thought that the Baptist was himself the light.

John's Gospel proper opens with "the Jews" questioning John about his identity. "He confessed and did not deny it, but confessed, 'I am not the Messiah'" (1:20). The Baptist also denies that he is Elijah or "the prophet" (1:21). He then says he is merely the forerunner of Jesus. In 3:26, a disciple of the Baptist complains that Jesus baptizes nearby and that everyone is going to him. John explains again that he himself is not the Messiah, merely his forerunner, and "he must increase, but I must decrease" (3:25-30). Finally, we get the inconsistent statements in chapter 4: "The Pharisees had heard, 'Jesus is making and baptizing more disciples than John'—although it was not Jesus himself but his disciples who baptized" (4:1-2). It may be that Jesus baptized for a time, but that to differentiate Jesus from John, that information was suppressed except for John 3:26 and 4:1. Even as the evangelist preserves this detail, he negates it. If the evangelist expends so much effort to rebut claims about John, chances are the relationship between John and Jesus is problematic.

Clearly the canonical gospels have trouble handling the idea that John baptized Jesus. The problem as perceived by the evangelists suggests that Jesus began his public career by being baptized by John and perhaps joining John's following. At some point, Jesus left John and began an

independent career. John 1:35-37 suggests that he took some of John's followers with him. John 3:26-30 indicates that this caused rivalry with
John's remaining disciples. A second block of Baptist material in Q (the
first has to do with Jesus' baptism) preserves hints of the breakup (Matt
11:2-19; Luke 7:18-35). John hears of Jesus' activities and sends disciples
with the question, "Are you the one who is to come, or are we to wait for
another?" This is an odd question if John has already recognized Jesus as
the one who is to come. But a close reading reveals that none of the
Synoptics actually says that John acknowledges Jesus as such. Only the
Fourth Gospel does so. There are two ways we could read the Baptist's
question. Either John has already accepted Jesus as the one to come and
Jesus' actions now make him doubt, or John has not previously accepted
Jesus and now Jesus' actions make him think that Jesus might be the one.
Jesus' response to John make the former more likely, at least from Q's
point of view. Jesus lists his accomplishments and then says, "And blessed
is anyone who takes no offense at me" (Q 7:23). This implies that Jesus'
actions, such as healings, might cause offense. Since he says this to John,
it suggests that John is in fact offended.

How could anyone object to these acts? The key lies in Jesus' other sayings in this passage. Jesus criticizes those who accept neither his message
nor John's. He notes that John came living an ascetic lifestyle and was
accused of being possessed. Jesus "came eating and drinking, and they say,
'Look, a glutton and a drunkard, a friend of tax collectors and sinners!'"
(Matt 11:19). Early Christians did not invent this accusation. It is likely
that Jesus did something to invite such criticism, even if it is untrue. The
Gospels are replete with stories of Jesus eating. He used banqueting to
symbolize the kingdom. And he also drinks. He does so at the Last
Supper, and he tells his disciples that he will drink with them again in the
kingdom. So John and Jesus led radically different lives. If John thought
that his lifestyle was part of his message, then Jesus' lifestyle may have
offended him.

Jesus worked in the towns, John in the wilderness. John was a stern,
hellfire-and-brimstone preacher. Jesus delivered some harsh judgments,
but this was not his general tone. He emphasized the positive side of the
kingdom—liberation of the poor, oppressed, and suffering, healing, and
forgiveness. John baptized; if Jesus did so, he stopped early in his ministry.
While John was in the wilderness preaching a baptism to wash away sins,
Jesus was in the villages using meals to symbolize God's generosity, forgiveness, and care for the marginalized. Jesus performed healings, while

John did not. Jesus saw his ministry as an extension of John's; John may have seen it differently.

Like many who progress beyond their teachers, Jesus respected John. He says that John is a prophet and "more than a prophet." He also says, "I tell you, among those born of women no one is greater than John; yet the least in the kingdom of God is greater than he" (Q 7:28). This expresses Jesus' high estimation of John but places him in an earlier stage of God's dealings with Israel.

Jesus' association with John tells us much. Jesus began his career moved by John's eschatological message. He agreed with John that God was about to act definitively to change the world. This form of thought is often considered apocalyptic. Apocalypticism was a feature of early Christian thought, very prominent in the New Testament. If Jesus began his career by receiving John's eschatological baptism, and if the early Christian movement was apocalyptic, it becomes likely that Jesus thought in apocalyptic terms. This helps to explain Jesus' death, for each of the eschatological prophets we have studied experienced violent repression.

THE END, IN JERUSALEM

No one doubts that Jesus was crucified by the Roman administrator of Judea, Pontius Pilate, around the year 30 C.E., just outside Jerusalem. Jesus died a criminal's death. This is not the kind of thing a religious group fabricates about its founder. So it must have been so.

Crucifixion was a horrible, inhumane punishment. It was meant to be. The Romans used crucifixion to instill terror. They crucified those of whom they wished to make examples. Crucifixions were public, carried out in places where they could be witnessed by large numbers of people. The Romans reserved this extreme penalty for criminals who were most disruptive to their rule and prosperity—hardened criminals, slaves, and political offenders. Jesus was neither a hardened criminal nor a slave. In the trials before Pilate, three charges are made against Jesus. One relates to his threat against the temple, a second to his claims to kingship, and a third to his claims to be Son of God.

When Pilate crucifies Jesus, he affixes a sign to the cross reading "The King of the Jews" (Mark 15:26). This detail may be authentic. Romans sometimes did this, but not always. The title "King of the Jews" was not one that the early Christians revered. They did make "Messiah" a central category for understanding Jesus. Since a messiah was often a king, this is how Pilate would have interpreted it. Even if Jesus did not explicitly call himself a messiah, his proclamation of the kingdom of God could arouse such suspicions. And Pilate would have been quick to act on such charges during Passover in Jerusalem. The population of Jerusalem swelled dramatically during this pilgrimage feast, some estimate to four times its usual size. Passover commemorated the exodus, an event of national liberation. Roman administrators generally resided in Caesarea on the coast, not in Jerusalem in the inland hill country. They came to Jerusalem when necessary. Passover was one of those times. This explains Pilate's presence and his vigilance concerning disturbances.

Another of the charges against Jesus was that he threatened the temple. When Jesus arrived in Jerusalem, he created a commotion in the temple. According to Mark, "He entered the temple and began to drive out those who were selling and those who were buying in the temple, and he overturned the tables of the money changers and the seats of those who sold doves" (11:15). He prevents anyone from carrying anything through the temple. He then quotes a combination of Isaiah and Jeremiah: "Is it not written, / 'My house shall be called a house of prayer for all the nations'? / But you have made it a den of robbers" (11:17).

As Mark tells the story, Jesus was upset at commerce in the temple. It is not clear, however, whether the point is that buying and selling itself has no place in the temple, or that the sellers and money changers are dishonest. It is difficult to see how the business of the temple, where animal sacrifice was central, could be carried on without commerce, especially when pilgrims came from afar. Money offerings would have to conform to certain standards as well. The Ten Commandments forbade images of animals and humans, so coins with the image of the emperor would not do and had to be exchanged for coins without such images.

Commercial exchange occurred in the Court of the Gentiles, the temple's outermost court. It did not take place in the holier temple precincts. Some who were stricter might not have been satisfied with this. A text from among the Dead Sea Scrolls speaks of the day when the entire city of Jerusalem will be holy, to the extent that no sexual activity takes place within it (CD XII), and Zechariah looks forward to a Jerusalem so holy that even everyday items like horse trappings and daily cookware will be sacred (14:20-21). Zechariah says, "There shall no longer be traders in the house of the LORD of hosts on that day." Jesus may have been deeply concerned for the temple's purity, but elsewhere he shows little interest in such matters.

Sanders takes a different tack. He regards overturning the tables as a symbolic act, the kind of sign performed by prophets. Overturning symbolizes destruction. Therefore, Jesus foretells the destruction of the temple. Indeed, in all four canonical gospels Jesus does speak of the temple's destruction: "Not one stone will be left here upon another; all will be thrown down" (Matt 24:2; Mark 13:2; Luke 21:6). In John's Gospel, Jesus says, "Destroy this temple, and in three days I will raise it up" (2:19). John interprets this figuratively, taking it to refer to the resurrection (2:21). "The Jews" take him literally, saying Jesus could not possibly build the temple in three days, but they misunderstand. The narrator explains, "He was speaking of the temple of his body" (2:21). The same issue arises at Jesus' trial before the high priest. Mark claims that "false witnesses" say that Jesus exclaimed, "I will destroy this temple that is made with hands, and in three days I will build another, not made with hands" (14:55-58). Matthew alters this slightly. There Jesus is accused of saying, "I am able to destroy the temple of God and to build it in three days" (26:61). Talking about the destruction about the temple would be dangerous. Temple priests administered Jerusalem and surroundings for the Romans, so prophecy against the temple undermined Roman order.

Many scholars are skeptical that Jesus uttered the combined quotation from Isaiah and Jeremiah when cleansing the temple, though most agree that his temple action was prophetic and symbolic. It is hard to believe that Jesus performed that act without remembering Jeremiah's prophecy against the temple (Jer 7 and 26). Jeremiah prophesies at the temple that unless worshipers obey God's will regarding social justice and idolatry, God will destroy the temple (Jer 7:1-15). In Jer 26:8, priests, prophets, and "all the people" react to Jeremiah's prophecy by saying, "You shall die!" Jeremiah is put on trial in Jerusalem. Powerful members of Judean society defend him, and he survives. Another man prophesies the same thing as Jeremiah at the same time, and he is condemned to death and executed (Jer 26:20-23).

In 62 C.E., four years before the Jewish rebellion against the Romans, another Jesus prophesied against Jerusalem. He went about the city shouting about "a voice against Jerusalem and the sanctuary" (Josephus, *Jewish War* 6.300-309). The leading citizens had him arrested, punished, and released. He persisted, so they seized him again and dragged him before the Roman governor, who scourged and released him. He persisted, and he finally died during the war. Parallels with Jesus of Nazareth are intriguing: prophecy against Jerusalem, trials before Jewish officials and Roman governor, scourging. This other Jesus escaped execution, perhaps because he did not have a following as did Jesus of Nazareth.

The connection with Jer 7 may be key to Jesus' prophetic action. Jeremiah tells the people to not trust in the temple to protect them, if they are not doing God's will: "If you truly amend your ways and your doings, if you truly act justly one with another, if you do not oppress the alien, the orphan, and the widow, or shed innocent blood in this place, and if you do not go after other gods to your own hurt, then I will dwell with you in this place, in the land that I gave of old to your ancestors forever and ever" (7:5-7). Jeremiah lists other sins of which his hearers are guilty—murder, adultery, false oaths, and, again, idolatry. All are "abominations," that is, defilements. Jeremiah continues, "Has this house, which is called by my name, become a den of robbers in your sight?" (7:11). Josephus testifies to the great wealth of the temple as positive (*Jewish War* 5.210-11, 222-24; *Ant.* 14.110; 15.395). But not all felt that way. The Qumran community accuses the Jerusalem establishment of amassing wealth, often at the expense of the poor (1QpHab VIII-XII; CD VI).

In Mark 7, Jesus criticizes the practice of dedicating property to the temple so as to avoid supporting parents. Mark 13 contains a discourse that begins with Jesus' prediction of the temple's destruction. The setting is the temple. Jesus tells his listeners to beware of the scribes, meaning Jerusalem's establishment scribes. He speaks of their desire for social status and says, "They devour widows' houses" (12:40). Immediately following this, he observes a widow depositing two small copper coins into the temple treasury. Jesus comments, "Truly I tell you, this poor widow has put in more than all those who are contributing to the treasury. For all of them have contributed out of their abundance; but she out of her poverty has put in everything she had, all she had to live on" (12:43-44). The already-rich temple, full of self-satisfied, rich donors who benefit from their "generosity," devour the widow's living.

TITLES

Researchers once looked to the titles of Jesus in the Gospels as keys to how he thought of himself. Over time, the limitations of this approach became evident. First, titles such as "Son of God" and "Messiah" did not have a fixed content in Second Temple Judaism. "Son of Man" was prob-ably not a title at all. "Son of David" was clearer. In addition, Christian texts construed these titles in their own ways, ways that did not neces-sarily reflect Jesus' views. Most significantly, in the Synoptics Jesus never says clearly, "I am the Messiah" or something similar, whereas in John he claims all sorts of titles for himself. In the Synoptics, the closest he comes to using a title is when he answers, "I am," to the high priest's question, "Are you the Messiah, the Son of the Blessed One?" (Mark 14:62-63), but in Matthew and Luke his answer is less clear: "You have said so" (Matt 26:64); "If I tell you, you will not believe, and if I question you, you will not answer" (Luke 22:67-71). In any case, there is no single *saying* in the Synoptics where Jesus says this of himself. As time went on, Christians may have used titles as ways of reflecting on Jesus' function and identity that departed from Jesus' explicit claims. Whether or not these were legit-imate developments from an implicit Christology that could be attributed to Jesus is a matter of debate. The fact remains, however, that if these titles express the later theology of the church, we cannot simply assume without careful examination that they shed light on the historical Jesus. This does not mean that they are theologically false or indefensible as ways of understanding the Jesus of faith.

ESCHATOLOGICAL PROPHET

A title that Jesus accepts, even in the Synoptics, is "prophet." Rejected in his hometown synagogue, Jesus says, "Prophets are not without honor, except in their hometown, and among their own kin, and in their own house" (Mark 6:4). Jesus' action in the temple is prophetic, in the tradi-tion of Jeremiah and Isaiah. Jesus begins his career by following an escha-tological prophet, John the Baptist.

Mark, John, and Paul attest independently that there was a special group of twelve among Jesus' followers. Paul's testimony is early and comes from one who had personal contact with Peter, James, and others from among Jesus' followers (1 Cor 15:5). The New Testament contains little information about most of the Twelve. We hear a good deal about Peter. He and two others, James and John, were close to Jesus. About the others we know next to nothing. In fact, our lists of the Twelve do not even fully correspond (Matt 10:2-4; Mark 3:16-19; Luke 6:14-16; Acts 1:13). What is far more important than the individuals is that they were twelve in number.

A saying of Jesus indicates why he chose the Twelve. As they approach Jerusalem, Jesus says to his disciples, "You who have followed me will also sit on twelve thrones, judging the twelve tribes of Israel" (Matt 19:28). The saying has a strong claim to authenticity. It is hard to imagine the early church producing it, knowing that one of the Twelve was Judas, who betrayed him. The act of judging may mean judicial activity, but it may mean simply "ruling," on the analogy of Israel's leaders in the book of Judges, whose activities were not judicial. Jesus' saying and his choice of the Twelve assume a reconstituted Israel encompassing all twelve tribes. So his eschatology must be Jewish restoration eschatology, of which we have many other examples.

Jesus' prohibition of divorce fits his being an eschatological prophet. Mark, M, and Paul independently attest to this prohibition. In Mark 10, Pharisees ask Jesus whether divorce is lawful. Jesus says that Moses allowed divorce because of the people's hardness of heart, "But from the beginning of creation, 'God made them male and female.' 'For this reason a man shall leave his father and mother and be joined to his wife, and the two shall become one flesh.' So they are no longer two, but one flesh. Therefore what God has joined together, let no one separate" (10:6-9). Jesus quotes Gen 1–2, concerning Adam and Eve before the fall. Social arrangements should be as God originally planned. Matthew 5:31-32 has Jesus forbid divorce without scriptural warrant, but in that chapter Matthew stresses Jesus' authority as reliable revealer of God's will. In Matt 19:8, Jesus' prohibition of divorce is because "from the beginning it was not so." This refers to humanity's beginning, when God created the first humans and placed them in Eden. This fits the apocalyptic principle that the end is like the beginning.

There are other indications that Jesus was a prophet of Jewish restoration. When Jesus speaks of the destruction and rebuilding of the temple, he is subscribing to ideas found in Jewish texts. His preaching of repentance and forgiveness also fits such scenarios.

MILLENARIANISM

Many religious phenomena occur not just in one culture or period, but in many. Cross-cultural comparison can be a powerful tool for understanding religious phenomena, as long as differences of circumstances, culture, and history are respected. Recently Allison has compellingly defended the picture of Jesus as a millenarian prophet. In the following table reproduced below, are the elements of Jesus' program that he finds to be typically millenarian (Allison, 61-64). Practically every element listed is represented in Jesus' teaching and activity and in the movement that he began.

Characteristics of a Millenarian Movement

- Addressed the disaffected or less fortunate in a period of social change that threatened traditional ways and symbolic universes; it indeed emerged in a time of aspiration for national independence
- Saw the present and near future as times of suffering or catastrophe
- Was holistic, that is, envisaged a comprehensive righting of wrongs and promised redemption through a reversal of current circumstances
- Depicted that reversal as imminent
- Was both revivalistic and evangelistic
- May have promoted egalitarianism
- Divided the world into two camps, the saved and the unsaved
- Broke hallowed taboos associated with religious custom
- Was at the same time nativistic and focused upon the salvation of the community
- Replaced traditional familial and social bonds with fictive kin
- Mediated the sacred through new channels
- Demanded intense commitment and unconditional loyalty
- Focused upon a charismatic leader
- Understood its beliefs to be the product of a special revelation
- Took a passive political stance in expectation of a divinely wrought deliverance
- Expected a restored paradise that would return the ancestors
- Insisted on the possibility of experiencing that utopia as a present reality
- Grew out of a precursor movement

THE DEEDS OF JESUS

Sanders includes miracles among the "facts" about Jesus. He is not asserting that the miracles actually happened, nor does he deny it. Historians can judge only whether Jesus and those around him thought that he was doing miracles. The general consensus is that they did. The miracles are multiply attested and are mentioned even in non-Christian sources.

The ancients thought about miracles differently than we do. We tend to think that there are laws according to which the universe operates. Many ancients thought that unseen forces, often personal (God, angels, demons, for example), caused things that we would now explain scientifically. Sickness could be caused by demons. The sun rose and set because God assigned it an angel to make it do so. Much that happens in the universe results from what we call "supernatural" agency. But the term "supernatural" here is misleading. Unseen and superhuman forces were at work everywhere. Humans could travel to heaven, a place above the earth, and return to tell about it. Hell was a specific place under the earth or at its farthest reaches. These unseen, personal forces were part of "nature," broadly conceived. For the ancients, then, miracles were not the breaking of natural laws but the special manifestation of unseen power. The word the New Testament uses for "miracle" is *dynamis*, which means "act of power." We derive the word "dynamic" from it. Both Testaments present God's mighty acts as "signs," ways that God gets our attention, proves something to us, cares for, or warns us.

NATURE MIRACLES

Jesus' miracles fall into three categories—exorcisms, healings, and nature miracles. Historians are skeptical about what are often called *nature miracles*—calming the sea, walking on water, multiplication of loaves, raising the dead, and turning water into wine. Historians always deal with probability. Reports of healings and exorcisms were relatively frequent in the ancient world and are common even today, in segments of society and various parts of the world. Claims of nature miracles of the sort attributed to Jesus are less common, even in the ancient world.

Nature miracles are not frequent activities of Jesus. He walks on the water once, calms the sea once, and turns water into wine once (only in John, where it has a symbolic meaning). Scholars consider the two accounts of the multiplication of loaves variations on a single story. The raising of Jairus's daughter in the Synoptics is, of course, a one-time event (it does not appear in John). Jesus raises someone from the dead once in Luke (the widow's son of ch. 7), and once in John (Lazarus in ch. 11). In contrast, there are many stories of Jesus' exorcisms in the Synoptics and of his healings in the Synoptics and John.

Nature miracles may have been attributed to Jesus in later tradition both because they exalt his image and because they have special meaning in Jewish tradition. Elijah and Elisha multiplied loaves and raised the dead. The following story is an example:

> A man came from Baal-shalishah, bringing food from the first fruits to the man of God: twenty loaves of barley and fresh ears of grain in his sack. Elisha said, "Give it to the people and let them eat." But his servant said, "How can I set this before a hundred people?" So he repeated, "Give it to the people and let them eat, for thus says the LORD, 'They shall eat and have some left.'" He set it before them, they ate, and had some left, according to the word of the LORD. (2 Kgs 4:42-44; see 1 Kgs 17:8-16, a more distant parallel)

This incident shares the following elements with the gospel stories (Mark 6:35-44; 8:1-10; and parallels): possession of food by only one person in a crowd, command of the man of God to distribute this food, objection in the form of a question by the follower(s) of the man of God, repetition of the order to feed the crowd, eating, and leftovers. The story about Elisha multiplying loaves shaped the one involving Jesus. Similarly, the story about Jesus raising the widow's son (Luke 7) has a counterpart in 1 Kgs 17:17-24, where Elijah raises a widow's son, and 2 Kgs 4:18-37, where Elisha does the same.

The calming of the storm at sea depicts Jesus as having divine powers. Psalm 107 says, "They saw the deeds of the LORD, / his wondrous works in the deep. / For he commanded and raised the stormy wind, / which lifted up the waves of the sea. / ... Then they cried to the LORD in their trouble, / and he brought them out of their distress; / he made the storm be still, / and the waves of the sea were hushed" (vv. 24-25, 28; see also Ps 65:7; 89:9). Jesus' walking on the water recalls Ps 77:19: "Your way was through the sea, / your path, through the mighty waters; / yet your footprints were unseen." Job says God "trampled the waves of the Sea" (9:8; see 38:16).

EXORCISMS

There are more exorcisms in the Synoptics than any other kind of miracle. In Mark, the very first miracle story is an exorcism (1:21-28). Reactions to the exorcisms are recorded in Mark 3:19-30. The scene is composite—that is, it is composed of originally independent elements—but most of the parts have strong claim to authenticity. In this scene, people say that Jesus is insane, and his family tries to seize him. Christians would not have invented either the characterization of Jesus as insane or the fact that his family either believed it or was sufficiently embarrassed by it to try to quash his activity. Then religious authorities accuse Jesus of being possessed by Satan and of exorcising through him. Again, these charges are not the fabrication of the church. It seems likely then, that Jesus' exorcising aroused strong feelings in those around him. Jesus points out the absurdity of Satan casting out Satan and then interprets his exorcisms as binding Satan so that his "house can be plundered." Plundering Satan's house means freeing those bound to him. As Mark's Jesus puts it, Satan's end has come. In other words, part of Jesus' work as an eschatological prophet is to defeat Satan, breaking his power over individuals and over God's creation. The binding of evil powers, angels in particular, is known from Jewish tradition. It plays a major role in Book of the Watchers, for example, a work incorporated into the larger apocalyptic composition we call *1 Enoch* (*1 En.* 1–36).

Jesus preaches the inbreaking of the kingdom of God, which for him is an eschatological reality. The coming of the kingdom will change the world decisively and will happen not through God's will and strength, not human effort. It is common for ancient holy men to be exorcists, but what is unique to Jesus here, and therefore probably historical, is his interpretation of his exorcisms as eschatological events signaling the end of Satan's rule and the beginning of God's kingdom.

HEALINGS

Jesus cleanses lepers and cures the blind, lame, paralyzed, and deaf. Such acts lead John to question whether Jesus is in fact the one to come. No extant Jewish texts expect such a wonder-working eschatological figure, much less a wonder-working Messiah. One possible exception to this is found in a fragmentary text from Qumran. The text speaks of the "anointed one" (Messiah), to whom the heavens and earth will listen. It goes on to say that the Lord will be "freeing prisoners, giving sight to the blind, straightening out the twis[ted]. . . . He will heal the badly wounded and will make the dead live, he will proclaim the good news to the poor . . . and enrich the hungry" (4Q521; translated by Martínez and Tigchelaar). Some suggest that it is the Messiah who heals and raises the dead, but it is more likely God who performs these wonders. The text depends on Ps 146, which speaks of God who "executes justice for the oppressed; / who gives food to the hungry. / The LORD sets the prisoners free; / the LORD opens the eyes of the blind. / The LORD lifts up those who are bowed down." Isaiah also talks the blind, the deaf, and the lame being cured (35:5-6). Jesus' healings are of the kind mentioned in Isaiah and in 4Q521. What Jewish texts expect of God in the eschatological age, the Gospels say that Jesus does, or that God does through Jesus. It is natural that people beset by political oppression, poverty, and disease, whose sacred stories tell of an ideal past in which death and suffering did not exist, look to a future in which all is made right. There are examples of such hopes from other Jewish literature of the Second Temple period.

Few contest that Jesus was a wonder-worker, and that he cured the blind, deaf, lame, and paralyzed. On other grounds, we have found there is reason to think of Jesus as an apocalyptic prophet. For Jesus, the two things went together. Apparently, Jesus himself made this connection, one explicit in Q and adopted by Matthew and Luke. Jesus combines this healing activity with his own emphasis on including society's marginalized in the kingdom. Especially noteworthy is Jesus curing of lepers, something not mentioned in the Jewish texts we have discussed. Lepers were perhaps the most obviously marginalized of those suffering physical ailments. Jesus' choice to heal them was therefore a brilliant move, because it symbolized in one act both the healing power of the kingdom and the fact that it includes those once excluded.

JESUS' TEACHING

Scholars once meticulously analyzed every saying and parable of Jesus, thinking that through peeling away of later interpretation, application of rigorous criteria of authenticity, examination of Greek words and constructions with an aim of retranslation into Aramaic, and use of other such methods, they would arrive at a solid core of authentic Jesus material. Such analysis continues and has its place. It is not done with the same degree of optimism as before because of appreciation of the role of early Christian belief and of changing circumstances in transforming Jesus tradition. Scholars have also come to a sharper realization that context is crucial, even decisive, in interpretation and that a saying or parable uttered in one context can mean something different in another and we are usually not completely sure of the original contexts of Jesus' utterances. The complex interplay of text and context and the application of various methodologies by researchers holding different theologies, philosophies, and social locations means that the consensus that was once sought has become harder to attain.

At the same time, it is an exaggeration to say that everything is up for grabs. The tradition certainly shows that Jesus traditions were altered, transformed, lost, even invented. But it also reveals efforts to preserve Jesus' teaching, even when it did not support the tendency of a particular text in which it is now found. Preservation of future eschatology in John 5 is an example. Dunn has recently made a persuasive case for the importance of oral tradition, even in some of the changes in gospel tradition that we usually attribute to sources or redaction, and he has insisted on the conservative nature of much oral tradition based on analogies with similar situations in the world today. In any case, plausible reconstruction of the historical Jesus depends on careful argumentation, examination of assumptions, respect for evidence, and recognition of the limits of historical research.

KINGDOM OF GOD

There is general agreement that the kingdom of God was central to Jesus' teaching. It is prominent in the Synoptics. It is present in Mark, M, L, and Q, and so is multiply attested. Though neither Paul nor John make much of the kingdom of God, they preserve it. The book of Revelation, an apocalypse, uses the term, though not often. The term makes sense within a Second Temple Jewish context, yet Jesus' precise usage is unusual. Language about the kingdom "coming" and of one "entering" it are unique to Jesus.

What did Jesus mean by the "kingdom of God"? Is it this-worldly, or otherworldly? Does it mean an actual kingdom on earth, or is it really a kingdom that will exist only in heaven? Does it come by human effort, or is it purely God's doing, or it is a combination of the two? Is it individual conversion, or does it entail cosmic change? Are the positions of poor and rich reversed, or will there be equality for all? Who will get in? Who will be excluded? Will it come soon, or is it far off? Will Jesus be the Davidic king in this divine kingdom, or is he only the eschatological prophet who announces it? The questions are many, and they are important. Believers have found New Testament evidence for most positions, some of which are mutually contradictory. A good place to start is Jewish usage.

Although the phrase "kingdom of God" is not present in the Hebrew Bible and occurs in the Greek version of the Jewish Scriptures only in Wis 10:10, the idea that God reigns or is king is common, particularly in Psalms and in the prophets. It is also present in the Pseudepigrapha, that vast corpus of Jewish texts written from about the third century B.C.E.

onward, where the term takes on an increasingly eschatological tone. In the Hebrew Bible, the idea that God reigns is sometimes associated with the Israelite kingdoms (1 Chr 28:5), but its broader use denotes God's active and powerful action in the world. This is expressed in the following:

> They shall speak of the glory of your kingdom,
>   and tell of your power,
> to make known to all people your mighty deeds,
>   and the glorious splendor of your kingdom.
> Your kingdom is an everlasting kingdom,
>   and your dominion endures throughout all
>   generations. (Ps 145:11-13)

God's sovereignty over all creation is an axiom of Israelite and Jewish belief. God can use that authority and power to reward and to punish both Israel and the nations.

There is ample testimony in the Bible and in other Jewish literature that the rule of God can and should become concrete in Jerusalem.

> The LORD is king; let the peoples tremble!
>   He sits enthroned upon the cherubim; let the earth quake!
> The LORD is great in Zion;
>   he is exalted over all the peoples....
> Mighty King, lover of justice,
>   you have established equity;
> you have executed justice
>   and righteousness in Jacob....
> O LORD our God, you answered them;
>   you were a forgiving God to them,
>   but an avenger of their wrongdoings. (Ps 99:1-2, 4, 8)

God's throne on the cherubim is in the holy of holies in the Jerusalem temple. Zion is the holy hill on which the temple sits, or the sacred city as a whole. God's rule is not arbitrary, but has its foundation in justice and equity. God is both forgiving and willing to punish.

The rule of God is frequently connected with the Israelite monarchy in Jewish tradition. In a psalm probably used for the king's coronation, God says, "I have set my king on Zion, my holy hill," and the king responds,

"He (God) said to me, 'You are my son; / today I have begotten you" (Ps 2:6, 7). In 2 Sam 7, God tells David that his son, Solomon, will be God's own son. Since kings are anointed, this passage brings together, at least implicitly, the titles "Messiah," "King of Israel," "Son of David," and "Son of God."

Israel ideally consists of twelve tribes. In the tenth century B.C.E., Israel split into two kingdoms, and in the eighth century, the northern kingdom was exiled by Assyria and its tribes were lost. When the southern kingdom, Judah, was exiled to Babylonia in the sixth century, the Davidic kingship came to an end. Throughout the Second Temple period, then, Israel lived with the tension between an ideal—twelve tribes united under the Davidic monarchy, and the reality—foreign domination and most of the tribes lost. At times this tension gave birth to hopes of a restoration. We have discussed Jesus as a Jewish restoration prophet under the heading "Eschatological Prophet" above.

The kings were meant to be God's representatives on earth, but the prophets often castigated them for not governing justly. Instead of caring for the people, they pursued their own interests. Using the common ancient shepherd metaphor for a king, God says through Ezekiel, "You shepherds of Israel who have been feeding yourselves! Should not shepherds feed the sheep?... You have not strengthened the weak, you have not healed the sick, you have not bound up the injured, you have not brought back the strayed, you have not sought the lost, but with force and harshness you have ruled them" (34:2, 4). God promises that God will shepherd the sheep, judge "between sheep and sheep, between rams and goats" (34:17), and set up David as shepherd, who will feed God's sheep. Echoes of Jesus' parable of the shepherd who seeks the lost sheep, his ministry of healing, his criticism of oppression, his seeking out of the lost and marginalized, and his expectation of judgment between sheep and goats are evident. Like the ancient prophets, Jesus criticized the people's leaders for not fulfilling their proper roles.

Very quickly in Christian tradition Jesus was dubbed Son of David and Messiah. It is not clear that he claimed these titles for himself, since there are no direct words of Jesus in the Synoptics in which he does so. When others bring the topic up, he reacts ambivalently except for Mark 14:61-62 (Matt 27:11; Mark 8:27-33; 15:1-5; Luke 23:3). The connection in Jewish sources between God's rule and Davidic messiahship hints at how early Christians could have interpreted Jesus' role in this way, even if he made no such claims. But hopes in the Second Temple period were varied, and not all place the restoration of the Davidic monarchy at the center (see Collins). The book of Daniel expects the kingdom of God to come and smash the oppressive kingdoms of the earth (2:24-45) but expects no eschatological Messiah. Two apocalypses written around the turn of the second century C.E. (*4 Ezra* and *2 Baruch*) anticipate a Messiah who is a heavenly figure, also called the Son of Man. Where to locate Jesus in this landscape is no simple matter.

KINGDOM AS FUTURE

A central question is whether the kingdom is present or future. There is evidence for both. Scholars agree that the New Testament is full of future eschatology but disagree on how much of this goes back to Jesus. The following section looks at some key texts that point in one direction or another.

The Lord's Prayer is in Q. Luke has a shorter form than Matthew (Matt 6:9-13; Luke 11:2-4). Luke's form is closer to Q, although he has made changes in wording. The prayer is modeled on the Jewish Qaddish prayer but is remarkable for its brevity and directness. Perrin supplies the following version of the Qaddish:

> Magnified and sanctified be his great name in the world that he has created according to his will. May he establish his kingdom in your lifetime and in your days and in the lifetime of all the house of Israel, even speedily and at a near time. (Perrin, p. 28).

Luke's version of the Lord's Prayer is the following:

> Father, hallowed be your name.
> Your kingdom come.
> Give us each day our daily bread.
> And forgive us our sins
>   for we ourselves forgive everyone indebted to us.
> And do not bring us to the time of trial. (Luke 11:2-4)

The two prayers share sanctification (making "hallowed" or "holy") of God's name, and the petition for the advent of God's kingdom. The mention of God's will in the Qaddish may have influenced Matthew's definition of the coming of the kingdom as doing God's will on earth as it is done in heaven.

Even though there are many prayers and hymns in the New Testament and early Christian literature, the early church attributes only this one to Jesus. The direct and unadorned address to God at the beginning of the prayer recalls Jesus' use of the Aramaic word *Abba* (Mark 14:36). Many have taken this to be an intimate form of address, meaning something like "Daddy," but this has been proved unlikely. The fact that the Aramaic term *Abba* has been preserved in the Greek New Testament, and that it does not seem characteristic of Jewish prayers of the time or later Christian prayers, make it likely that Jesus' followers remembered him using this form of address to God. These considerations, along with the prayer's presence in an early source, Q, makes it likely that it goes back to Jesus.

The phrase "Your kingdom come" presents the kingdom as future and as brought in by God, not humans. The "trial" from which Jesus prays to be delivered may be apocalyptic in nature. Sufferings caused by the conflict between God and God's enemies in the end-time are sometimes called a test.

The Last Supper supplies more evidence for a future kingdom. That Jesus shared a final meal with his disciples enjoys multiple attestation (Mark, John, and Paul). It also accords with the prominence of meals in his ministry, also multiply attested. During the Last Supper, Jesus says that he will not drink wine again until he drinks "it new in the kingdom of God" (Mark 14:25). Most scholars accept the saying as authentic. It speaks of the coming of the kingdom without any specificity about Jesus' role in it, so it lacks this characteristically Christian perspective. It conceives of the kingdom as this-worldly, since it involves drinking wine. Jesus realizes that the end of his career is near and that the kingdom is imminent. He expects either that God will bring it in soon while he is still alive, or that he will be raised to participate in it when it comes.

A similar point is made in Jesus' saying from Q that "many will come from east and west and will eat with Abraham and Isaac and Jacob in the kingdom of heaven" (Matt 8:11). This future involves the raising of the patriarchs and assumes an earthly kingdom where there is eating and drinking.

Both Matthew and Luke consider the Beatitudes, found in Q, central to Jesus' message. Beatitudes were not common in the early church but occur frequently in Jewish sources. They are succinct ways of approving of particular modes of behavior or human qualities and appear in both wisdom and apocalyptic materials. They can be eschatological but need not be so. The Beatitudes assume different forms in the two gospels. Matthew has nine and Luke four. Luke follows them with four woes not present in Matthew. The following table illustrates the difference between the versions of the beatitudes as reflected in Luke's first three. Luke's fourth, corresponding to Matthew's ninth, is unlike the others. It is lengthy and reflects church experience.

Matthew 5	Luke 6
5:3 Blessed are the poor in spirit, for theirs is the kingdom of heaven.	6:20 Blessed are you who are poor, for yours is the kingdom of God.
5:6 Blessed are those who hunger and thirst for righteousness, for they will be filled.	6:21 Blessed are you who are hungry now, for you will be filled.
5:4 Blessed are those who mourn, for they will be comforted.	6:21 Blessed are you who weep now, for you will laugh.

Luke is probably closer to the original. Matthew's longer versions are less radical, more suited to an established church with mixed social classes, and, as is characteristic of that Gospel, more concerned with guidance for behavior. They also introduce one of Matthew's favorite words, "righteousness." Luke's announces that the future brings reversal of the lot of the poor and hungry, assuming that economic deprivation is unjust and will be rectified in the kingdom. This fits Luke's general attitude to economic issues. He adds woes against the rich, the full, and the happy. Most agree that economic issues played an important role in Jesus' prophetic preaching. They are multiply attested both in sources and forms. They also fit the theme of eschatological reversal evident in such sayings as "The last will be first, and the first will be last," used by each of the Synoptics in various contexts (Matt 19:30; 20:16; Mark 10:31; Luke 13:30).

KINGDOM IN THE PRESENT

Sayings about the presence of the kingdom are closely associated with Jesus' activity of preaching and performing powerful works. Jesus sees his exorcisms as raids on Satan's realm (Mark 3:20-30). Q's Jesus says, "If it is by the finger of God that I cast out the demons, then the kingdom of God has come to you" (Luke 11:20; cf. Matt 12:28). The phrase "finger of God" is unusual, and it occurs in this sense only here and in Exod 8:19. Its distinctiveness argues for authenticity. In Exodus the Egyptian magicians admit that they cannot replicate the deeds of power done through Moses, for they are truly God's work. By analogy, Jesus says that he casts out demons not by his own power, but by God's. The conflict between God and Satan is not resolved in a single incident but is ongoing.

A saying in Luke 17 seems anti-apocalyptic: "The kingdom of God is not coming with things that can be observed; nor will they say, 'Look, here it is!' or 'There it is!' For, in fact, the kingdom of God is among you" (17:21). The phrase "among you" could also mean "within you." Some commentators take this to mean that the kingdom is a matter of an inner personal state. There is little to recommend this view, given its lack of support in other Jesus materials. Instead, Jesus means that the kingdom is present in his own activity.

Other elements that point to the presence of the kingdom are the general characterization of Jesus' message as presented in Mark 1:15 and parallels—the kingdom of God has come near. In Luke 10:23-24, Jesus tells his hearers that prophets and kings of the past longed for what the hearers see and hear. Jesus' feasting and his rejection of fasting also indicate the kingdom's presence (Mark 2:18-22). When John the Baptist sends to Jesus, asking whether he is the one to come, Jesus points to his activities—healing, raising the dead, and preaching good news to the poor (Matt 11:2-6).

Although there is a strong case to be made that Jesus thought that the kingdom was in some sense near or even present in his ministry, there is also evidence that he refused to prove it. When Jesus is asked for a sign to prove his authority, he refuses: "No sign will be given to this generation" (Mark 8:12). Later Christians could not accept that Jesus refused a sign. In Q, Jesus says, "No sign will be given to it (this generation) except the sign of Jonah," which means his preaching (Matt 16:4; Luke 11:29-32). In the end, those who repented at Jonah's preaching will condemn Jesus hearers who do not repent. Jesus' hearers should recognize God's power in his prophetic activity. Matthew is not content to leave it there, for in another context he repeats the idea of the sign of Jonah, this time adding that Jonah's three days in the belly of the fish prefigure Jesus' resurrection (12:40). So the real sign will be the resurrection. Finally, the

Gospel of John insists that his public ministry is full of signs. These texts trace a development from a Jesus who refuses to grant signs to one whose entire public ministry is full of them. It is likely that this represents a chronological development, and that the historical Jesus was reluctant to give signs. The saying in Luke 17 fits this context. Jesus is saying that the sorts of signs his hearers are looking for are not the ones in which they should trust. They should recognize the power of God at work right in front of them, in his ministry. If they do not accept that, then they cannot see the kingdom.

THE PARABLES

Most think of a parable as a short story told to convey a lesson. Jesus' parables are more than that. They almost always contain something strange, a twist that brings hearers up short and makes them see the world differently. The Gospels associate many of the parables with God's kingdom. God's power at work means not just healings and exorcisms, but transformation of human society. Jesus' works of power are weapons against Satan and the effects of human alienation from God, and the parables are equally important instruments for bringing about the kingdom.

Major insights about the parables become possible when we view them apart from their gospel settings. The evangelists interpret the parables by framing them within specific contexts. In some cases this defuses them, neutralizing their surprise element. Crossan's analysis of the parable of the Good Samaritan (Luke 10:30-35) is a turning point in parable study (see ch. 1). Luke makes it an example story—one ought to behave as the Samaritan does. Crossan shows the real point to be that the Samaritan is good—a judgment hard for a first-century Jewish inhabitant of Judea to accept. This compels a rethinking of how the world works. It questions long-accepted categories of who is good and who is not. It changes the world.

The parable of the Lost Sheep is so familiar that we have trouble grasping how strange it is (Matt 18:10-14). Losing one sheep is bad. Losing ninety-nine is much worse. Why endanger so many to rescue one? Because this makes so little sense, it is probably authentic. For Jesus, who seeks out the lost and marginalized, God's love and forgiveness exceed expectations. Jesus' association with sinners carries the same implication of forgiveness, and his decision to associate with them satisfies the criteria of embarrassment and dissimilarity.

The Prodigal Son combines forgiveness with the theme that self-righteous people resent God's generous forgiveness and so put themselves outside God's good graces. When the prodigal returns, the father forgives him and arranges a feast. The dutiful son sullenly refuses to participate, thus excluding himself. The "good" people resent God's forgiveness of the "bad."

God prizes repentance and humility and condemns self-righteousness. In the parable of the Pharisee and the Tax Collector, the two characters pray in the temple. The Pharisee prays confidently, thanking God that he is such a good person, and looking down on those whom he judges to be morally inferior to himself. The sinful tax collector simply asks for mercy (Luke 18:10-14). Jesus says the sinner is justified, not the Pharisee. The same point is implied in the parable of the Lost Sheep, for the shepherd abandons those who stay around and follow the rules.

God's forgiveness, although generous, does not come without obligations. Jesus tells of a master who absolves a servant of a gigantic debt (Matt 18:23-34). When the servant refuses to forgive an infinitely smaller debt, the master reinstates the servant's original debt and imprisons him. This recalls the words at the end of the Lord's prayer in Matthew: "If you forgive others their trespasses, your heavenly Father will also forgive you; but if you do not forgive others, neither will your Father forgive your trespasses" (6:14-15). Matthew makes forgiveness central to Jesus' ecclesiastical discourse (Matt 18).

God's justice does not correspond to human justice, a theme related to God's generous forgiveness. Parables already discussed show this, since one expects that the righteous Pharisee or the dutiful son will be praised, in contrast to the sinful tax collector or the prodigal son. Matthew's Workers in the Vineyard, where some work all day and some for a single hour and all receive the same pay, seems unfair (20:1-16). What is "fair" to humans may not be "just" to God.

The parable of the Rich Man and Lazarus in Luke 16 condemns large disparities in wealth. When the two characters die, the rich man goes to hell and the poor man to heaven. No crime or virtue is attributed to either one. Such social inequality is itself unjust. This reinforces the point made by the Beatitudes, discussed above.

Jesus' teaching undermines conventional piety and social structure. Being rich is God's blessing, is it not? And doesn't God demand righteousness? If Jesus is right, then the kingdom must be a strange place that defies expectation. That is exactly the point of the Great Banquet (Matt 22:1-14; Luke 14:15-24). Matthew makes the parable an allegory of salvation history. Luke's form is more original, though he added the part about the poor, crippled, blind, and lame, taken verbatim from earlier in the chapter (v. 13). Without Luke's addition, the point is that those we expect to enter the kingdom do not, while those we expect to be absent are there. Luke preserves this idea but moves it in the direction of social justice by introducing the poor and the physically challenged.

A series of parables warns that one must prepare for an imminent accounting (Matt 24:43; Mark 13:34-36; Luke 12:35-46). This is typically apocalyptic and emerges in other parts of Jesus' teaching (for example, Matt 24:36-42). Servants must be ready for their master's return by attending to their duties in his absence. Parables carrying this message assume various forms and enjoy multiple attestation. Other parables make the same point—the Wise and Foolish Virgins, the Pounds, and the Last Judgment (which is more of a prophetic prediction with parabolic elements), all in Matt 25.

We have explored just a representative sampling of the parables. They are the creations of one not content with how things are, who regards society and religion as structured to maintain the privileges of the few by an elite who manipulate God to bless the status quo. They contrast human justice with God's justice. They reveal a deity who writes off the debts of flagrant sinners while critiquing the self-righteousness of those who follow the rules. They disclose a Jesus who prepares people for a definitive act of God that will call them to account for their actions and attitudes.

JESUS AND EATING

John the Baptist lived an ascetic lifestyle in the desert, while Jesus traveled the villages of Galilee and Judea, eating and drinking. In Q Jesus says, "John came neither eating nor drinking, and they say, 'He has a demon'; the Son of Man came eating and drinking, and they say, 'Look, a glutton and a drunkard, a friend of tax collectors and sinners!'" (Matt 11:18-19; see Deut 21:20). Jesus' opponents are the accusers, so we take this with a grain of salt. However, accusations frequently have some modicum of truth, which gives them credibility. The truth here is that Jesus made meals potent symbols of his message.

Food is a powerful symbol in all societies. The way food is handled, prepared, and eaten, with whom, and when, provides an interpretive key to any group. Food is used to express intimacy or friendship, to celebrate various occasions, and for religious purposes. That is certainly true of ancient Mediterranean societies. Judaism was known for its dietary rules, and purity rules concerning meals provided the Pharisees and others with devices for defining their groups and Israel as a whole. The Qumran community used access to the communal meal to incorporate new members into its ranks gradually; exclusion from communal food punished transgressors. The Pharisees adapted purity rules meant for temple priests and paid close attention to purity issues with food. That made it problematic for them to eat with those who did not share their rules.

Jesus also uses food to define community. He eats with the wrong people. The Pharisees criticize him for eating with tax collectors and sinners (Mark 2:15-17). Whether or not this is specifically a matter of purity is unclear. We remember that impurity and sin are not the same, so sinners and tax collectors were not necessarily ritually impure. There is a case to be made, however, that at Qumran, moral impurity incurred ritual impurity (Klawans). In any case, it is true to say that Jesus, the Qumran community, and the Pharisees all use food to define their communities.

Jesus answers those who condemn him, "I have come to call not the righteous but sinners." Jesus engages in table fellowship as a symbol of the kingdom. His dining with sinners symbolizes their inclusion in God's kingdom. Such behavior fits other material, such as the parable of the Great Banquet. It recalls Jesus' parable of the two sons—one says he will not do what his father asks but then does so, while the other quickly agrees to do it but then does not. Jesus' conclusion is, "The tax collectors and the prostitutes are going into the kingdom of God ahead of you" (Matt 21:31).

There is a strand of tradition expecting the culmination of history to include a feast, sometimes in the presence of the Messiah. This is known as the messianic banquet. That can be expressed negatively, as when Ezekiel and Revelation picture God's enemies as the feast's food (Ezek 38–39; Rev 19), or positively (Isa 25:6-8; *1 En.* 62:12-14). Jesus refers to such a banquet when he says, "Many will come from east and west and will eat with Abraham and Isaac and Jacob in the kingdom of heaven" (Matt 8:11). Similarly, at the Last Supper Jesus tells the disciples, "I will never again drink of the fruit of the vine until that day when I drink it new in the kingdom of God" (Mark 14:25). The banquet motif in the

Bible incorporates the element of judgment. Who is in and who is out spells salvation or condemnation. Jesus' meals express God's forgiveness and inclusiveness. Those with a more restrictive view of God's action ironically exclude themselves through their restrictions. This is a powerful social and religious critique.

It is not surprising that one of Jesus' last acts is to have a final meal with his disciples and to use that meal to point forward to the messianic banquet. It is a fitting culmination to his ministry.

RADICAL DEMANDS

Jesus preaches a powerful combination of forgiveness and radical demand. Although God's forgiveness is almost profligate, Jesus' God is not a "pushover." God's judgment is harsh on the self-righteous and judgmental. Jesus is particularly hard on certain types of sin, such as not responding to a person in need (Matt 25:31-46; Luke 16:19-31). Jesus makes stringent demands on everyone. The Sermon on the Mount (Matt 5–7) contains demands that exceed those of Torah. Where Torah says do not kill, Jesus says do not even get angry. Where Torah says do not commit adultery, Jesus says do not even have lustful thoughts. Jesus insists that his followers sell all of their goods and give them to the poor, and he says that it is easier for a rich person to pass through the eye of a needle than to gain access to the kingdom (Mark 10:17-27).

Christians often think that the Hebrew Bible portrays a harsh and unforgiving God while the New Testament presents a gentle and forgiving Jesus, but a different impression is created by such sayings as the following:

> If any of you put a stumbling block before one of these little ones who believe in me, it would be better for you if a great millstone were hung around your neck and you were thrown into the sea. If your hand causes you to stumble, cut it off; it is better for you to enter life maimed than to have two hands and to go to hell, to the unquenchable fire. And if your foot causes you to stumble, cut it off; it is better for you to enter life lame than to have two feet and to be thrown into hell. And if your eye causes you to stumble, tear it out; it is better for you to enter the kingdom of God with one eye than to have two eyes and to be thrown into hell, where their worm never dies, and the fire is never quenched. (Mark 9:42-48)

Jesus insists on absolute loyalty to him and his vision of the kingdom. Following Jesus precedes family responsibilities. In Q, when someone asks permission to bury his father before following Jesus, Jesus says, "Let the dead bury their own dead" (Matt 8:22). When another asks to take leave of his family, Jesus says, "No one who puts a hand to the plow and looks back is fit for the kingdom of God" (Luke 9:62). He also says, "Enter through the narrow gate; for the gate is wide and the road is easy that leads to destruction, and there are many who take it. For the gate is narrow and the road is hard that leads to life, and there are few who find it" (Matt 7:13-14). In another place he says, "Many are called, but few are chosen" (Matt 22:14).

The combination of forgiveness and radical demands typifies millennial movements. Also typical are demands for loyalty to the new way of life and dedication to the charismatic leader. All of this reinforces the point already made, that Jesus was an eschatological prophet, one inspired by Jewish hopes of restoration, one who thought in apocalyptic terms.

JESUS AND HIS FAMILY

Evidence about Jesus' relationship with his family is mixed. Some indicates a positive relationship; some suggests problems. Positive elements occur in the infancy narratives, but we have found those unhelpful for historical reconstruction. Matthew and Luke contain the virgin birth (not present in Mark, John, or elsewhere in the New Testament), something historians cannot judge, but neither Matthew nor Luke claims that Mary had no children after Jesus. Each mentions Jesus' brothers in a passage taken from Mark (Matt 12:46; Mark 3:31; Luke 8:19), and Matthew takes over another passage from Mark which mentions Jesus' brothers and sisters and names four brothers—James, Joses, Judas, and Simon (Matt 13:55-56; Mark 6:3). John's Gospel also speaks of Jesus' brothers (2:12; 7:3, 5, 10).

Those accustomed to think of Mary as ever-virginal will find problematic the idea that Jesus had siblings. Various scholarly solutions to this problem have been proposed. It is possible that when the Gospels say brothers (*adelphoi*) and sisters (*adelphai*) they mean "cousins." This raises the objection that the Greek words in question almost never mean cousin and that there is a Greek word for "cousin" not used here. However, translating back into Aramaic, Jesus' native language, the word for brother can be used in a wider sense to mean cousin, although that is not its more common meaning. The *Infancy Gospel of James* provides another solution. It claims that when Mary and Joseph wed, Joseph was elderly and already had children. Neighbors would have considered them Jesus' half-brothers and half-sisters, even though because of the virgin birth they would not be his blood relations.

If we evaluate the evidence purely as historians, and not through the prism of later doctrine, the most natural way to take what Matthew, Mark, Luke, and John say is that Jesus did indeed have siblings. Nonetheless, it is not unreasonable to reach another conclusion.

Mary is present at the foot of the cross in John's Gospel, but she is not there in the Synoptics. The Synoptic scene is more plausible. The Synoptics are generally more reliable than John, and it is more likely that Mary would be added to the scene than that she would be removed from it. In Acts 1, Mary is with the disciples as they await the descent of the Spirit. Luke wrote Acts, and it is Luke who presents the extremely positive picture of Mary in his infancy narrative. It is not entirely clear how much weight to give Acts assertion here. It may be right. We simply cannot decide for sure.

There is stronger evidence for the participation of James, Jesus' brother, in the nascent movement. He is the foremost authority in the Jerusalem church, according to Luke, for he makes the final decision not to require Torah observance of Gentiles who join the church (Acts 15). Paul calls James, brother of Jesus, a "pillar" of the Jerusalem church (Gal 2). He speaks of James, Peter, and John in that order, awarding pride of place to James (2:9).

Jesus' apparent insensitivity to family concerns as seen in the case of the man who wanted to bury his father also appears elsewhere. In Q, Jesus says that love for him must exceed love for family (Q 14:25-26). In Mark, Jesus' family agrees with the judgment of some that he is insane, for they try to seize him (3:21). Later in the same chapter, Jesus' mothers and brothers and sisters stand outside and ask for him while he speaks to his followers. His response is, " 'Who are my mother and my brothers?' And looking at those who sat around him, he said, 'Here are my mother and my brothers! Whoever does the will of God is my brother and my sister and my mother' " (3:33-35).

It is not uncommon for adherents of millenarian movements to be alienated from their families. It still happens today. Jesus will not allow one man to take leave of his family, and another may not bury his father. When Jesus commands the rich young man to sell everything and give the proceeds to the poor in order to follow him, the man sadly departs. Jesus' own disciples say, "Then who can be saved?" (Mark 10:26). Jesus declares that God can make it possible. Peter points out that the disciples have left everything to follow Jesus. Jesus responds, "There is no one who has left house or brothers or sisters or mother or father or children or fields, for my sake and the sake of the good news, who will not receive a hundredfold now in this age—houses, brothers and sisters, mothers and children, and fields, with persecutions—and in the age to come eternal life" (10:29-30). Q has similar passages. For example, Jesus says, "Whoever loves father or mother more than me is not worthy of me; and whoever loves son or daughter more than me is not worthy of me" (Matt 10:37). Luke's version is more radical: "Whoever comes to me and does not hate father and mother, wife and children, brothers and sisters, yes, and even life itself, cannot be my disciple" (14:26). It is reasonable to take the more radical version as more original, since tradition tends to "tame" such extreme elements.

If Jesus uttered words like those in the foregoing paragraphs, he may have done so as the founder of a millenarian movement and as one in the tradition of the prophets, who used hyperbolic language to preach strong messages. Jesus did not advocate hatred of family. Rather, he insisted that nothing should stand in the way of discipleship.

JESUS AND WOMEN

Some material hints at important roles for women in the Jesus movement and in early Christianity. At the same time, each text we have examined is constrained by some degree of patriarchalism and androcentrism. Our question now is how Jesus views women in his group and women in general.

Women were certainly among Jesus' followers. The evangelists did not make up the idea that women traveled with Jesus (Luke 8:1-3). Luke may portray them so that they fulfill certain acceptable roles in his society—providing for the men, for example—thereby lessening a negative impact on some readers. Most accept that some women disciples stayed close enough to watch his execution. Women were the first to witness his resurrection. Early Christians would not have fabricated this. Indeed, Luke tells us that they met with disbelief.

Mary Magdalene is prominent among the disciples. The *Gospel of Mary* claims that Peter is jealous of her closeness to Jesus. Although this text is late and imaginative, it focuses on a fascinating mystery—whatever happened to Mary and what role did she play during Jesus' life and in the early church? She was obviously important in Jesus' following, but we know nothing of her afterward. This forces us to admit that our sources are not adequate for a full understanding of women in the Jesus movement. Mary is later portrayed as a repentant prostitute, a characterization with no evidence to support it, so we see how the androcentric nature of the early church has skewed our perceptions.

Women sometimes play surprising roles in the Gospels. A Gentile woman bests Jesus in verbal jousting so that he consents to heal her child (Mark 7:24-30). An audacious woman approaches Jesus and touches his garment (Mark 5:25-34). The incident of the woman who anoints Jesus is intriguing (Mark 14:3-9). In Mark, Jesus assigns great significance to her action in light of his impending death, while Luke moves this incident to an earlier point in his Gospel and makes the woman a notorious sinner, grateful for forgiveness (7:36-50). There is no reason to question that Martha and Mary are good friends of Jesus. Their relationship with him is multiply attested (Luke and John). The story of Mary sitting at Jesus' feet while Martha busily makes the meal continues to be debated by those who see her as a full disciple and those who find troubling her submissive attitude (Luke 10:38-42).

We have names of other women disciples—Mary, mother of James and Joses, Salome; Joanna; Susanna (Mark 15:40; Luke 8:1-3). Luke tells us there were "many others" (8:3). True, we know little about them. This must be seen in light of the fact that the gospel narratives focus on Jesus. They do not reveal much about Jesus' disciples. When they do, it is the men they feature. We become familiar with Peter, less so with James and John. About the others we know next to nothing.

Women were among Jesus' disciples, but the Gospels do not depict them within the inner circle, that is, the group of twelve or the still smaller group consisting of Peter, James, and John. Many male church leaders opposed a public role for women, so they may have suppressed information about women in Jesus' inner circle.

Paul attests that some women held high offices in the church—apostles and prophets (Rom 16; 1 Cor 11), for example. We hear of that only in passing, since Paul does not focus on it. The Pastoral Epistles—1 and 2 Timothy and Titus—strongly attack the idea that women can be teachers and leaders in the church, and they do so in Paul's name, though most scholars do not think they are by Paul. The difference in the position of women between the authentic Pauline letters and the pseudepigraphical

Pastorals shows that women did attain important positions of leadership in some Pauline churches, and that there was a backlash against them.

Corley employs a comparative method to address these questions. She finds that in the Roman Hellenistic world of the first century, many women were taking more public roles. As they did so, they were slandered by those upset by their disturbing social order. Women with the audacity to attend banquets were labeled prostitutes, since according to the ethos of the time it was only courtesans that could socialize with men in such brazen fashion. Women taking on public roles in the early church also attracted criticism and slander, as the Pastorals demonstrate. A classic example of a prominent woman being labeled a prostitute is Mary Magdalene.

Corley contends women were indeed present among Jesus' disciples, and that he had a progressive attitude toward women. Nonetheless, the portrayal of Jesus as a champion of women's rights exceeds the evidence. Jesus' teaching does not focus on women's rights. This contrasts with his explicit teaching on economic justice. Perhaps because Jesus did not make this an issue, the early church could revert quickly to a more conservative stance, but this was not universal. Hints in the letters of Paul, the role of women in some gnostic communities, and their prominent place in other groups such as the Montanist movement of the second century, show variety in the early church.

JESUS AND TORAH

Scholars once widely held that Jesus violated Torah and defended himself for doing so. More recent readings cast doubt on this. Judaism of the time was not monolithic, nor was there a central authority defining proper behavior for all Jews. Second Temple Judaism is composed of *Judaisms*, in the plural (see ch. 2). Variety within Judaism comes less from doctrinal differences, as with later Christianity, and more from differences about how to interpret and obey Torah. Jesus debates with his contemporaries about purity, Sabbath observance, and dietary rules not as one who stands outside Judaism, but as a faithful, Torah-abiding Jew.

Food laws provide a test case of whether Jesus transgressed Torah. Mark has no stake in Jesus' adherence to the Torah, and he declares that Jesus annulled Jewish food laws: "Thus he declared all foods clean" (Mark 7:19). Significantly, Mark makes this an editorial comment. Apparently he has no direct words of Jesus to this effect. Matthew deletes this statement and rewrites the episode to make it an intra-Jewish discussion of hand washing, not of dietary rules (15:1-20). Acts of the Apostles attests that the issue is not settled by the time the Gentile mission begins. In Acts 10, Peter is told in a vision to eat impure food. He refuses, protesting that he has never eaten anything unclean. A heavenly voice tells him, "What God has made clean, you must not call profane" (10:15). This amazes Peter, for Torah itself declares some foods unclean. Acts associates the vision with admitting Gentiles into the church, for Peter is then told to preach to some Gentiles. When he does, they receive the spirit, and so Peter has them baptized without obligating them to take on Torah observance. His decision is ratified in Jerusalem in Acts 15. In the light of this struggle to determine the right course of action, it is hard to see how Jesus could have settled the issue. It is noteworthy that nowhere in Acts in the discussion of Torah observance does anyone cite relevant teaching of Jesus.

The Synoptics and John say that Jesus cures on the Sabbath. What modern readers often miss is that the gospel stories do not claim Jesus violated Sabbath by healing. They make the opposite point. Their claim is that Jesus defended curing on the Sabbath as in accord with Torah. Jesus also defends his disciples when they pluck grain on the Sabbath (Mark 2:23-28). His argument in both cases is that human need overrules the usual prohibition of work, and he cites legal precedent for his position. Jesus is not alone in addressing this question. Rabbinic texts and Qumran scrolls also raise the question.

In the antitheses in Matt 5, Jesus seems to place himself above the Torah. Six times he says "You have heard that it was said . . ." to introduce a quotation of the Law and then introduces his own interpretation with the words "But I say to you." Neusner points out that even though most of what Jesus says fits within Judaism, setting oneself above Torah in this fashion is unacceptable to a Jew. But the formulaic way in which this passage is constructed is Matthew's work. It is unique to Matt 5 and probably not how the historical Jesus spoke. In terms of content, Jesus does not change the Law so much as radicalize it. For example, the Torah forbids killing, while Jesus forbids getting angry. This is to engage in what the rabbis called building a fence around the Torah, making strict rules so that the Torah would be protected.

Jesus does violate Torah, according to Sanders (*Jesus and Judaism*, pp. 252-55), when he says to one who wishes to bury his father, "Let the dead bury their own dead" (Q 9:60). This violates honoring one's parents, one of the Ten Commandments. But even this is debatable. In extreme cases, rules of Torah yield to necessity, such as the priority of human need on the Sabbath. In the present case, following Jesus is so urgent that family obligations must be relaxed. In fact, alienation from one's family is likely if one joins the Jesus movement. An analogy is that of the Jewish freedom fighters, called the Maccabees, who, faced with an enemy who attacked on the Sabbath, ruled that self-defense was permissible. Another example is that of the Qumran community, which had to forgo the sacrifices demanded by Torah because they considered the sanctuary defiled. They thought of their refusal to sacrifice as adherence to Torah.

Association with Sinners

Jesus' association with sinners is multiply attested, and it fulfills the criterion of embarrassment. It is not simple, however, to determine what "sinners" means. On one occasion, Matthew's Jesus tells the leaders, "The tax collectors and prostitutes are going into the kingdom of God ahead of you" (21:31), since they believed the message of the Baptist. Luke describes a Pharisee's indignation when Jesus allows a notoriously sinful woman to touch him (Luke 7:36-50). In Mark 2:15-17, Pharisaic scribes are scandalized because he eats with tax collectors and sinners. He responds, "Those who are well have no need of a physician, but those who are sick; I have come to call not the righteous but sinners." The evidence supports the view that Jesus associated with those held in contempt by society. It is not unusual that a millenarian movement is antiestablishment and appeals to those labeled "sinners."

The issue of purity arises with regard to the Pharisees, who interpreted purity rules in their own way. Gospel readers frequently assume that anyone who did not observe Pharisaic purity rules was to them a sinner. But there is no evidence for this. A Pharisee was unable to eat with another Jew who did not observe purity rules regarding food, any more than an orthodox Jew today can eat with a Jew who does not keep kosher in the same way. That is a far cry from considering the other to be sinful. Jesus did oppose various purity rules and their social consequences. But he did not necessarily oppose purity rules per se. He may have singled out rules that oppressed individuals and groups.

It is a mistake to equate sin and impurity. Many purity rules had nothing to do with sin. For example, touching a dead body made someone ritually impure. Yet touching a corpse was not only necessary, it was required at times. Similarly, a woman's impurity during menstruation and childbirth was not sinful. Impurity was a state hindering participation in the cult or presence in temple precincts. We analyze purity in chapter 2 as a mechanism for organizing society and making sure that everything and everyone stays in its proper place.

Who were the sinners with whom Jesus associated? Were they public sinners—prostitutes, for example? Jesus mentions prostitutes in Matt 21, but only there. Even that reference is not present in Mark and Luke. The woman in Luke 7 may be a prostitute, but that story is Luke's revision of the story of the woman in Mark 14, who is not a prostitute, so not much weight can be placed on Luke's version. A complicating factor is that Jesus had women in his entourage, and women who assumed public roles were vulnerable to the accusation of being loose in morals. Jesus' association with prostitutes may be analogous to his being called a glutton and a drunkard. It is not exactly true, but it has some foundation in his practice.

Sinners with whom Jesus associated must have been outside the mainstream of society in some sense. Otherwise, his being with them would have elicited no comment. Whatever their offense, they were ostracized. Jesus' association with "sinners" may be part of his general social critique. He reveals God to be more interested in inclusion than exclusion, in forgiveness than in condemnation.

Sinners are often associated with tax collectors in the Gospels. Tax collectors are unpopular at any time and place, but in first-century Jewish Palestine, they were especially unpopular. Each Jew owed tax to the temple every year. Herodian rulers demanded taxes. The Romans had to be paid. Taxes are especially onerous for those on the edge of subsistence. Jesus speaks of day laborers forced to sell their labor because they possess no land, tenant farmers who turn over a large portion of the land's produce to the owner, destitute people, beggars, and so on. It would not be surprising if tax collectors were disliked and marginalized by many in society.

JESUS AND GENTILES

Today relatively few Christians are of Jewish descent. So it seems obvious that Jesus' mission included Gentiles. Yet the Gospels indicate the opposite. Jesus' mission was to Israel. He enters Gentile territory at times, but little is said about his activity there. There are only two stories dealing with Gentiles (other than the Roman governor) in the Synoptics. Both show that Jesus does not pursue a mission to them. When Jesus agrees to come and cure the centurion's servant, the centurion protests that he is not worthy for Jesus to come under his roof (Q 7:1-10). Jesus performs the cure from a distance. In Luke's version, a delegation of Jews persuades Jesus to do this favor for a Gentile by saying he has been sympathetic to Judaism.

The other story is the healing of the Gentile woman's daughter (Matt 15:21-28; Mark 7:24-30; not in Luke). Mark emphasizes the woman's Gentile origins: "The woman was a Gentile, of Syrophoenician origin." Jesus wants nothing to do with her. He says, "Let the children be fed first, for it is not fair to take the children's food and throw it to the dogs." She answers, "Sir, even the dogs under the table eat the children's crumbs." Jesus responds, "For saying that, you may go—the demon has left your daughter." This is a remarkable interchange. Jesus is cold, even disrespectful in this conversation. Even more remarkable is that the woman bests him, and he admits it. Ultimately, she persuades him to help her. She does so at the cost of accepting his designation of the Gentiles as dogs. Matthew's version of the story is even more striking (15:21-28). When the woman asks for help, Jesus refuses to answer her. His disciples request that he get rid of her. He says, "I was sent only to the lost sheep of Israel." Then the story continues more or less as in Mark.

A noteworthy feature of both stories—the centurion's servant and the Gentile woman's daughter—is that the cure happens at a distance. These incidents are hardly a convincing rationale for a Gentile mission. Jesus does perform the requested cures, but in neither case is it part of his normal activity, nor does it change Jesus' mind about the scope of his mission.

In Matthew's story of the centurion, Jesus marvels that he has not encountered such faith in Israel (8:5-13). Matthew brings to this spot the saying about people coming from east and west to feast with Abraham, Isaac, and Jacob, while the "children of the kingdom" are excluded (Luke has it elsewhere). Matthew takes this to mean that Gentiles will be with the Israelite patriarchs in the kingdom, while Jews will miss out. But in Jewish restoration eschatology, the most common meaning of people coming from east to west is that the dispersed Jews come back to the land of Israel and to Jerusalem. This may have been the original intent of the saying. Passages that contain the motif of the return of the exiles often also talk about Gentiles coming to Jerusalem to worship the true God.

This complex of ideas may be key to how Jesus thinks about the Gentiles in relation to God's kingdom. Many Jewish texts look forward to a time when the Gentiles will recognize the Jewish God as the true God and worship him, sometimes in Jerusalem (for example, Isa 2:2-4; 49:6; 56:3-8; Mic 4:1; Zech 2:11; 14:16; Tob 14:6-7). This theme is evident in Second Isaiah, written among the exiles in Babylonia in the sixth century

B.C.E. Jesus may have believed that once Israel accepted his prophetic work and turned to God, then God would favor Israel, causing the nations to acclaim Israel's God. Jesus needed no concrete plans for a Gentile mission. This would occur as the Jewish prophetic literature anticipated—through God's own action.

This explains the situation of the earliest church, as well. As depicted in Acts, the early church consisted entirely of Jews, who did not at first preach to non-Jews. Acts is twenty-eight chapters long, and by chapter 10, the church is still going only to Jews. Chapter 10 is a turning point, for there Peter brings the message to Gentiles. When he does, the Spirit comes upon them, and Peter recognizes that God is including them in salvation. Peter has them baptized. The church is shocked at what he has done. A crucial meeting occurs in Jerusalem (ch. 15). The leader of the Jerusalem church, James the brother of Jesus, decides that Gentiles will be admitted to the church, and that they need not observe Torah. To justify his decision, James quotes Amos 9. He quotes the Greek version of the prophecy, which says that the restoration of the dynasty is "so that all other peoples may seek the Lord— / even all the Gentiles over whom my name has been called" (Acts 15:17).

Luke–Acts was written at least partly to make the case that the traditional sequence of eschatological events—Israel's repentance and subsequent conversion of the Gentiles—was reversed because of Israel's refusal to accept its Messiah, Jesus. Faced with the reality of Gentile belief and Jewish unbelief, Luke makes the case that events have proceeded to the second step without the first being fulfilled. It is uncertain whether he thinks Israel will later come to belief. Paul is clear about this. He also sees the two steps as reversed, but he expects both to happen. He lays this out in Rom 11. He says that he converts as many Gentiles as possible so that Israel will know that it has "missed the boat" and will believe. Then the eschatological events will have been completed.

RESURRECTION

Many treatments of the historical Jesus do not deal with the resurrection. The historical Jesus is defined as Jesus from his birth to his death, as in the case of any human being. That is a valid approach. The point of historical Jesus research is, after all, to regard Jesus as he would have been seen by his contemporaries, preresurrection. Nonetheless, we naturally have questions about the historicity of the resurrection, so we make some very brief points about it.

Historians generally accept that the earliest Christians experienced something that they interpreted as the risen Jesus. We have a firsthand account by Paul to that effect, who also attests to the witness of others (1 Cor 15:3-11; Gal 1:15-16). It would be hard to explain the origins of the church without taking into account early Christian belief in the resurrection. However, to say that some Christians experienced what they thought was the risen Christ is not the same as having historical proof that Jesus was actually raised. Other explanations are possible, whatever weight one might attach to them.

Stories about what happened after Jesus' death fall into two categories—stories of the empty tomb and appearances of the risen Christ. We do not have more than one independent witness for any one story, and Paul is the only instance of Jesus appearing to a nondisciple. Paul is reticent about the details of his own experience (the accounts in Acts are somewhat self-contradictory and are perhaps later developments), so it is not entirely clear whether he is describing precisely the same sort of experience as related in the gospel stories. In 1 Cor 15, Paul associates Jesus' resurrection with the general resurrection of humans expected at the end of time in Jewish eschatological belief. Jesus is unique in that he is the first to be raised, but ultimately is the first among many to be raised. All, or many, other humans will also be raised. What Jesus' resurrection means is that the end-time events have been set in motion.

Jesus' death is not a resuscitation, as was his raising of Lazarus, Jairus's daughter, or the widow's son. It is not simply that he returns to the state he was in before his death, only to die again, ultimately. Still, it is a bodily resurrection in some sense. In some stories, the bodily character of the resurrection is stressed. Jesus can be touched and he eats. But he can also come and go miraculously, coming through locked doors in Acts, for example. The early church believed that when God raised Jesus (and this is what the New Testament usually says—Jesus did not raise himself), Jesus entered a new and glorious form of existence. Paul insists that, although Jesus has a "bodily" existence, it is of a completely different sort from ours (1 Cor 15:35-57).

Whether or not God raised Jesus from the dead is well beyond the purview of historical study. No amount of sifting of evidence or historical reasoning will ever solve the problem. It is a matter of faith.

The Gospels present Jesus as fully aware of his impending death and resurrection. We would expect this from those who observe Jesus from the point of view of Easter faith. If he had been so aware and had imparted that knowledge to his disciples, as the Gospels say, then it is hard to explain how the death and resurrection seems to surprise them. For example, when Jesus appears to two disciples walking to Emmaus, they say, "We had hoped that he was the one to redeem Israel" (Luke 24:21). This states clearly what other accounts suggest—that the disciples had not factored in Jesus' violent end, nor did they expect him to rise from the dead.

It seems likely that as Jesus went to Jerusalem during the volatile Passover period and determined to perform a provocative prophetic act in the temple, he would have realized how dangerous that was. He may even have expected his own death. He predicated his entire ministry on the conviction that the kingdom of God was near, and his words at the Last Supper indicate that he expected to be drinking wine with his followers in that kingdom, soon. As a prophet, he expected God's intervention in history. Whether he thought that was to come before or after his own death is not clear. But it is unlikely that he had the sort of detailed knowledge of what was to happen, including his disciples' experience of his resurrection.

CONCLUSION

In this chapter we attempt to move backward through Christian tradition, back behind the Gospels, all the way to the historical Jesus. The methods and conclusions of any such effort are subject to debate. Some would claim that the entire enterprise is invalid, because the Gospels tell the simple truth about Jesus (historically as well as theologically). Others, acknowledging that the Gospels present different pictures of Jesus and that none fully corresponds to the historical Jesus, nonetheless have decided that evidence is too unreliable, the methods inadequate, and the results too tentative to try to reconstruct the historical figure. Believers who do engage in this study have a range of goals. Some, probably a minority, find the historical Jesus incompatible with church doctrine. Many others think that this study enriches our experience of the Gospels, since it highlights their theological content and deepens our appreciation for Jesus' humanity. All, believers or not, can benefit from this study because it sheds light on one of the most influential people in world history and on the origins of one of the world's great religions.

To what degree the gospel portraits are continuous or discontinuous with the historical Jesus is another matter. Judgment on that depends at least partly on how continuity and discontinuity are defined. It is simplistic to discuss this merely in terms of whether or not Jesus literally made this or that claim for himself, or whether or not such and such an incident actually occurred precisely as narrated. Reconstruction of the historical Jesus in a particular way does not close the door to theological discussion. Rather, it serves as grounds for discussion and makes possible a richer appreciation of Jesus and of divine action in the world.

BIBLIOGRAPHY

Allison, Dale C., Jr. *Jesus of Nazareth: Millenarian Prophet.* Minneapolis: Fortress Press, 1998.

Banks, Robert. *Jesus and the Law in the Synoptic Tradition.* Cambridge: Cambridge University Press, 1975.

Borg, Marcus. *Meeting Jesus Again for the First Time: The Historical Jesus & the Heart of Contemporary Faith.* New York: Harper Collins, 1994.

———. "The Teaching of Jesus Christ." *ABD* 3:804-12.

Brown, Raymond E. *An Introduction to New Testament Christology.* Mahwah, N.J.: Paulist, 1994.

———. "The Pater Noster as an Eschatological Prayer." Pages 217-53 in *New Testament Essays.* New York: Paulist, 1965.

———, et al., eds. *Mary in the New Testament.* Philadelphia: Fortress, 1978.

Chilton, Bruce D., and Craig A. Evans, eds. *Studying the Historical Jesus: Evaluations of the State of Recent Research.* Leiden: Brill, 1994.

Collins, John J. *The Scepter and the Star: The Messiahs of the Dead Sea Scrolls and Other Ancient Literature.* New York: Doubleday, 1995.

Corley, Kathleen E. *Private Women, Public Meals: Social Conflict in the Synoptic Tradition.* Peabody, Mass.: Hendrickson, 1993.

———. *Women and the Historical Jesus: Feminist Myths of Christian Origins.* Santa Rosa, Calif.: Polebridge, 2002.

Crossan, J. Dominic. *The Historical Jesus: The Life of a Mediterranean Jewish Peasant.* San Francisco: HarperCollins, 1991.

———. *In Parables: The Challenge of the Historical Jesus.* New York: Harper and Row, 1973.

———. *Jesus: A Revolutionary Biography.* San Francisco: HarperSanFrancisco, 1994.

Davies, Stevan. *Jesus the Healer: Possession, Trance, and the Origins of Christianity.* New York: Continuum, 1995.

Dunn, James D. G. *Jesus Remembered.* Grand Rapids: Eerdmans, 2003.

Ehrman, Bart D. *Jesus: Apocalyptic Prophet of the New Millennium.* New York: Oxford University Press, 1999.

Evans, Craig A. "Opposition to the Temple: Jesus and the Dead Sea Scrolls."

Pages 235-53 in *Jesus and the Dead Sea Scrolls.* Edited by James H. Charlesworth. New York: Doubleday, 1992.

Fredriksen, Paula. *Jesus of Nazareth, King of the Jews: A Jewish Life and the Emergence of Christianity.* New York: Knopf, 2000.

Funk, Robert W., and Roy W. Hoover, eds. *The Five Gospels: The Search for the Authentic Words of Jesus.* New York: Macmillan, 1993.

Harvey, A. E. *Jesus and the Constraints of History.* Philadelphia: Westminster Press, 1982.

Harvey, Van Austin. *The Historian and the Believer: The Morality of Historical Knowledge and Christian Belief.* New York: Macmillan, 1969.

Horsley, Richard A. *Jesus and the Spiral of Violence: Popular Jewish Resistance in Roman Palestine.* Minneapolis: Fortress, 1993.

Hurtado, Larry W. *Lord Jesus Christ: Devotion to Jesus in Earliest Christianity.* Grand Rapids: Eerdmans, 2003.

Jeremias, Joachim. *The Parables of Jesus,* rev. ed. New York: Scribner's, 1963.

Johnson, Elizabeth. *Consider Jesus: Waves of Renewal in Christology.* New York: Crossroad, 1990.

Käsemann, Ernst. "The Problem of the Historical Jesus." Pages 15-47 in *Essays on New Testament Themes.* London: SCM, 1964.

Klawans, Jonathan. *Impurity and Sin in Ancient Judaism.* New York: Oxford University Press, 2000.

Kraemer, Ross Shepard, and Mary Rose D'Angelo, eds. *Women and Christian Origins.* New York: Oxford University Press, 1999.

LeBeau, Bryan F., Leonard Greenspoon, and Dennis Hamm, S.J., eds. *The Historical Jesus through Catholic and Jewish Eyes.* Harrisburg: Trinity, 2000.

Levine, Amy-Jill. "Jesus, Divorce, and Sexuality: A Jewish Critique." Pages 113-29 in *The Historical Jesus through Catholic and Jewish Eyes.* Edited by Bryan F. LeBeau, Leonard Greenspoon, and Dennis Hamm. Harrisburg, Penn.: Trinity, 2000.

———. "Second Temple Judaism, Jesus, and Women: Yeast of Eden." *BibInt* 2 (1994): 8-33.

Martin, Raymond, Joan W. Scott, and Cushing Strout. "Forum: Raymond Martin, Joan W. Cott, and Cushing Strount on *Telling the Truth About History*." *History and Theory* 34 (1995): 320-39.

Martínez, Florentino García, and Eibert J. C. Tigchelaar, eds. *The Dead Sea Scrolls Study Edition.* 2 vols. Grand Rapids: Eerdmans, 2000.

McClymond, Michael J. *Familiar Stranger: An Introduction to Jesus of Nazareth.* Grand Rapids: Eerdmans, 2004.

Meier, John P. "The Historical Jesus and the Historical Law: Some Problems within the Problem." *CBQ* 65 (2003): 52-79.

———. "Jesus." Pages 1316-28 in *NJBC.*

———. *A Marginal Jew: Rethinking the Historical Jesus.* 3 vols. New York: Doubleday, 1991–2001.

Meyer, Ben F. *The Aims of Jesus.* London: SCM, 1979.

―――. "Jesus Christ." *ABD* 3:773-96.

Miller, Robert J., ed. *The Apocalyptic Jesus: A Debate.* Santa Rosa, Calif.: Polebridge, 2001.

Murphy, Frederick J. "Jesus the Jew." Pages 328-75 in *Early Judaism: The Exile to the Time of Jesus.* Peabody, Mass.: Hendrickson, 2002.

Neusner, Jacob. *A Rabbi Talks with Jesus: An Intermillennial, Interfaith Exchange.* New York: Doubleday, 1993.

Oakman, Douglas. *Jesus and the Economic Questions of His Day.* New York: Edwin Mellen, 1986.

Patterson, Stephen. *The God of Jesus: The Historical Jesus and the Search for Meaning.* Harrisburg: Trinity, 1998.

Perrin, Norman. *Jesus and the Language of the Kingdom: Symbol and Metaphor in New Testament Interpretation.* Philadelphia: Fortress, 1976.

―――. *Rediscovering the Teaching of Jesus.* New York: Harper and Row, 1976.

Powell, Mark Allan. *Jesus as a Figure in History: How Modern Historians View the Man from Galilee.* Louisville: Westminster John Knox, 1998.

Riches, John. "The Actual Words of Jesus." *ABD* 3:802-804.

Rousseau, John J., and Rami Arav. *Jesus and His World.* Minneapolis: Fortress, 1995.

Sanders, E. P. *The Historical Figure of Jesus.* New York: Penguin, 1995.

―――. *Jesus and Judaism.* Philadelphia: Fortress, 1985.

Scott, Bernard Brandon. *Hear Then the Parable: A Commentary on the Parables of Jesus.* Minneapolis: Fortress, 1989.

Stegemann, Ekkehard W., and Wolfgang Stegemann. *The Jesus Movement: A Social History of Its First Century.* Minneapolis: Fortress, 1999.

Tatum, W. Barnes. *In Quest of Jesus.* Nashville: Abingdon, 1999.

Theissen, Gerd, and Annette Merz. *The Historical Jesus: A Comprehensive Guide.* Minneapolis: Fortress, 1996.

Weiss, Johannes. *Jesus' Proclamation of the Kingdom of God.* Philadelphia: Fortress, 1971. First published in German in 1892.

Wright, N. T. *Jesus and the Victory of God.* Minneapolis: Fortress, 1996.

―――. "Jesus, Quest for the Historical." *ABD* 3:796-802.

Vermès, Géza. *Jesus the Jew: A Historian's Reading of the Gospels.* Philadelphia: Fortress, 1973.

CHAPTER NINE

CANONIZATION

W e spoke briefly of the canon in the introduction and in chapter 1. "Canon" comes from the Greek word *kanon* meaning a rod of fixed length used for measuring. In the fourth century C.E., Christians began to speak of canon in the sense of a list of Christian writings that could be read in worship. Before that, "canon" had been used in the church in the sense of a standard of belief by which doctrine could be judged. The New Testament consists of twenty-seven books. The first extant list of books that corresponds exactly to our New Testament is found in a festal letter of Athanasius, bishop of Alexandria, written in 367 C.E. Precisely how, when, and why this list reached this form is not fully clear. Unfortunately, we have no ancient account of this process, so whatever we say is based on bits and pieces of evidence.

The Scripture of the earliest Christians was the same as Jewish Scripture. By the first century C.E., Judaism had a collection of books that it held sacred, but the collection was still somewhat fluid. Still, a large number of the books were accepted by all—the Torah (the first five books of the Bible), for example, as well as the historical books (called the "former prophets" in Jewish terminology), the prophets, and other writings such as Psalms. The process within Judaism that resulted in a final, fixed canon is as unclear as that which produced the Christian canon, but we know that it happened at about the same time.

It was natural that Christians began to write texts for a number of purposes—teaching, worship, communication between churches and individuals, and so on. Eventually, some Christian writings were judged sacred and became a "New Testament," which, when joined with what would now be called the "Old Testament," became the Christian Bible. None of the Christian writings had been written specifically to be

Scripture. By what process, then, were some writings included and others excluded from the new collection?

There is no simple answer to this question, but there are some major landmarks and principles that are generally accepted as part of the story. Our concern is with the Four Gospels, so we restrict our attention to them. The second century supplies an assortment of facts that shed some light on our topic. Papias, a bishop from the early second century, acknowledges the written Gospels of Matthew and Mark but considers oral tradition to be more reliable and valuable. From the middle of the century, we have the testimony of Justin Martyr, who says that the memoirs of the apostles are read in worship. He shows knowledge of the Synoptic Gospels but not of John. Also around the middle of the second century, Marcion rejected the Jewish Scriptures and accepted only one gospel, that of Luke, in an altered form, according to his opponents. Around 170 C.E., the Syrian Christian Tatian composed a gospel harmony (called the *Diatessaron*) that combined Matthew, Mark, Luke, and John. A variety of gospels were written in the second century and later, some of which we examined in chapter 7. Some satisfied curiosity about aspects of Jesus' birth or childhood, while others embodied a gnostic Christology and worldview. In the latter half of the second century and onward, there was a tendency to accept Matthew, Mark, Luke, and John as the authoritative Gospels. Irenaeus, bishop of Lyons, argues forcefully for the idea that there must be four and only four gospels.

The combination of these bits of evidence (and others) make the following general picture plausible. The second century saw a series of developments that led eventually to the decision to adopt Matthew, Mark, Luke, and John as the church's authoritative Gospels. Although oral tradition remained important throughout the century, there was a move to adopt written texts as reliable guides for faith. The mainline churches did not accept Gnosticism, and so gnostic gospels were considered authoritative only within gnostic groups and excluded from the developing canon of what was to become the orthodox churches. Marcion's approach was rejected as denying Christianity's Jewish roots. Tatian's harmony remained popular in Syria for some time, but it did not catch on in other churches. So the general tendency was to go beyond the one-gospel approach of Marcion and Tatian but to avoid the openness to new revelation reflected in the gnostic documents. Ultimately, the church found a middle way between one Gospel and many.

The foregoing paragraphs deal with some landmarks in canon formation, but what were the principles on which choices were made? Again, no uniform view arises from our sparse sources. In some cases, age may have played a role. The canonical gospels, Matthew, Mark, Luke, and John, are the only extant written gospels that can be traced with confidence to the first century. Some claim that a version of the *Gospel of Thomas* also dates to the first century. The fact that Matthew and Luke rewrote Mark shows that they considered Mark useful but inadequate for their purposes. Luke as much as declares Mark's inadequacy in his prologue (1:1-4). So when Luke and Matthew were written, Mark was not considered sacred Scripture, fixed and unchangeable.

The fact that two of the Gospels are attributed to apostles (Matthew and John), while the other two are thought to come from men close to apostles (Mark, depending on Peter, and Luke, depending on Paul), indicates that apostolic origin in some sense was operative. But we know of other texts attributed to apostles that did not make the cut. Particularly informative is the case of the *Gospel of Peter*, which bishop Serapion of Antioch allowed to be read in worship around 200 C.E. before he had seen it. When he read it, he decided that it was not in accord with proper Christian faith and so withdrew his permission. This shows that only those texts found to be in harmony with what was judged to be true doctrine could be accepted. Works were to be judged not just by whether they claimed apostolic origins, but also on their content.

Like Jews, Christians believed that their sacred texts were inspired by God. This can hardly be a primary criterion for inclusion in the canon in the sense that the decision whether a text is inspired is a communal one. In other words, inspiration is not something that obviously belongs to a text. The church must judge a text to have come from God.

Ultimately, the clearest criterion for inclusion in the canon is use, whether the Christians making the choice are explicitly aware of that or not. Texts to be included in the emerging canon were those that churches found useful, adequate to their faith and practice, and a proper foundation for doctrine and communal life. It would be natural that those texts popular in important church centers, such as Rome, Antioch, and Alexandria, would be prime candidates for inclusion in the canon. We do not know where our Gospels originated, but most scholars posit such prominent church centers as their probable places of composition.

The formation of the canon, particularly the choice of the Four Gospels, was a momentous development in the Christian churches.

Christian faith centers on Jesus, and in choosing these Gospels and not others, the church went a long way in defining itself. We would love to know more about just what went into these crucial choices, but the surviving evidence tells us less than we would like. There was no single, linear process that led to the canon. More evidence would probably make the picture still more complex. Many different choices made in many different situations ultimately converged in the New Testament as we know it. Recent study has revisited this problem and increased our appreciation of varieties of early Christianity and of the roads not taken by the mainstream church of the time. Noncanonical texts have shed light on choices made in Christianity's earliest years and have helped to reinvigorate discussions of the historical Jesus. Nonetheless, the choice of Matthew, Mark, Luke, and John by the early church established them as the foundation of Christianity. They will remain central in Christian faith as well as in historical study.

BIBLIOGRAPHY

Brown, Raymond E., and Raymond F. Collins. "Canonicity." *NJBC* 1034-54.

Campenhausen, Hans von. *The Formation of the Christian Bible*. Philadelphia: Fortress, 1972.

Gamble, Harry. *Books and Readers in the Early Church: A History of Early Christian Texts*. New Haven: Yale University Press, 1995.

———. "Canon: New Testament." *ABD* 1:852-61.

———. *The New Testament Canon: Its Making and Meaning*. Philadelphia: Fortress, 1985.

Metzger, Bruce M. *The Canon of the New Testament: Its Origin, Development, and Significance*. Oxford: Clarendon Press, 1987.

GLOSSARY

Androcentrism: Literally, centered on the male. A male-biased view of society, religion, and human relationships.

Angelophany: The appearance of an angel to humans.

Apocalypse: Literary genre in which a superhuman agent gives to a human seer revelation concerning the unseen world and the future.

Apocalypticism: Worldview characteristic of apocalypses.

Apologetic history: History of a people written as a means of self-definition for insiders and of favorable presentation to outsiders.

Apostle: Literally, one "sent out." In the gospels, the term is applied to the Twelve, the inner group of Jesus' disciples, but elsewhere in the New Testament it applies more broadly to important missionaries and church founders.

Aramaic: Official language of the Persian Empire; the vernacular of Palestinian Jews in Jesus' time.

Archelaus: Son of Herod the Great. Ruled Judea 4 B.C.E. to 6 C.E.

Atonement: Reconciliation with God achieved through the annulment of the consequences of sin. Christianity holds that this is attained through the passion, death, and resurrection of Jesus.

B.C.E.: "Before the Common Era"; same period often referred to as B.C. ("Before Christ").

Baptism: Symbolic washing used by John the Baptist to signify repentance in the face of impending judgment. It becomes the ritual of incorporation into the church.

Beatitude: Short blessing formula, praising someone and specifying their reward.

Beelzebul: Another name for Satan.

Booths (Tabernacles; Sukkoth): Yearly feast celebrating the fruit harvest.

C.E.: "Common Era"; same period often referred to as A.D., "Anno Domini," meaning after Christ's birth.

Caesarea Philippi: Town northeast of the Sea of Galilee where Peter's confession is said to have taken place (Mark 8:27-29 and parallels).

Caiaphas: High priest during Jesus' career.

Canaan: Ancient name of the land of Israel.

Canon: List of authoritative books; books that belong to the Bible.

Canonical: Belonging to the canon.

Capernaum: Town on the northwest shore of the Sea of Galilee; Jesus' base of operations in the area.

Centurion: Commander of 100 men in the Roman army.

Chief priests: Leading priests in Jerusalem; priests belonging to the prominent priestly families.

Christ: Greek for "messiah."

Christology: Ways in which Christians evaluated Jesus, expressed in terms of titles, functions, and assessments of his relation to God.

Church: Christian community. The word in Greek is *ekklesia*. In the Greek Bible it designates the assembly of Israel.

Composition criticism: Study of how the evangelists arranged the material in their gospels.

Covenant: Agreement between two parties; the agreement between God and Israel in which Israel is God's people, pledged to obey God's will expressed in Torah, and God is faithful to and acts on behalf of Israel.

Cynic philosophers: Wandering street preachers who challenged society's pursuit of status, wealth, and power and advocated a simple, austere, even ascetic lifestyle.

Dead Sea Scrolls: An ancient collection of texts discovered beginning in 1947 in caves near the Dead Sea.

Dedication (Hanukkah): Feast celebrating the end of a persecution of the Jews in the second century B.C.E. and the recapturing and rededication of the Jerusalem temple.

Diachronic criticism: Analysis of how a text evolved over time, including its use of sources, stages of composition, and sequence of revisions.

Dispora: Collective term for Jews living outside the land of Israel.

Docetism: Belief that Jesus only seemed to be human.

Dualism: Way of looking at the world that sees things in terms of opposites, such as light and darkness, truth and falsehood.

Ecclesiology: Study of or beliefs about the church.

Elder: Prominent citizen, head of a family.

Elijah: Ancient Israelite prophet who did not die but was taken up in a fiery chariot. Malachi 4:5-6 says that he will return to preach repentance before God comes in judgment. Early Christian tradition identified John the Baptist as Elijah returned.

Enlightenment: Movement with roots in the Renaissance that flowered particularly in the eighteenth century and that has had a profound effect on human thought since then. It privileges reason over doctrine.

Eschatology: Study of or a set of beliefs about the future, particularly concerning such things as the end of the world as we know it, and postmortem rewards and punishments (characteristic of apocalyptic eschatology).

Eschaton: The end of the world as presently constituted. It could mean the end of the world, or simply its reconstitution according to God's will.

Essenes: One of the three or four groups Josephus lists as important in Second Temple Judaism. Probably the people whose community is reflected in the Dead Sea Scrolls.

Evangelist: Gospel writer.

Exegesis: Analysis whose purpose is to discover the original meaning of a text.

Exodus: Event when God liberated Israel from Egypt and split the Red Sea.

Exorcism: Casting out a demon from a person.

Feminist criticism: A wide range of types of analysis that disclose the androcentrism and patriarchalism in biblical texts; efforts to recapture the importance of women in the biblical world and to reread texts so as to empower women in the present. Such analysis is also concerned for liberationist readings more broadly.

Form criticism: Analysis of the small units used by early Christians to transmit tradition, especially of the units that went into the formation of the Gospels, and of how they were changed and adapted over time to fit different circumstances.

Galilee: Area to the north of Judea and Samaria; location of Jesus' home town of Nazareth and of his base of operations in Capernaum.

Genre: Kind of literature, such as gospel, letter, and apocalypse.

Gentiles: Non-Jews.

Gnosticism: Diverse movement prominent in the second century in which salvation comes through knowledge (Greek: *gnosis*). It often has a negative view of this material world and sees escape from it as the goal of those who possess the divine spark.

Gospel: Either the good news about Jesus Christ, or the literary genre that told of Jesus' career.

Hebrew: Ancient language of Israel; language of most of the Jewish Bible.

Hellenism: Culture that developed in the areas conquered by Alexander the Great between 333 and 323 B.C.E.; a mixture of Greek and local cultures.

Hermeneutics: Study of the principles and methodologies of interpretation.

Herod Antipas: Son of Herod the Great. Ruled Galilee and Perea during Jesus' career.

Herod the Great: Roman-appointed King of the Jews when Jesus was born. Ruled 40 B.C.E. to 4 B.C.E.

Historical criticism: Analysis of the Bible from an historical perspective. Includes investigation of what "actually happened," but also of texts as witnesses to particular points of view in their own times. It studies texts especially for the authors' meaning and for how they would have been read by their original readers.

Holy: That which belongs to God.

Impure: That which cannot come into God's presence and be part of rituals directed toward God.

Incarnation: God becoming human in Jesus.

Irony: Situation created when the readers know more than the characters (dramatic irony), when words are made to carry a sense different from their usual sense, when characters speak the truth unwittingly, when there is incongruity between expected and actual result or discontinuity between words and action in drama.

Israel: God's chosen people, descended from Abraham, loyal to Torah, seen by Christians as those through whom God prepared the world for the coming of Jesus as Messiah.

Jerusalem: Capital of Judea and home to God's temple.

John the Baptist: Eschatological prophet whom Christians believed God sent as Jesus' forerunner.

Josephus: Jewish historian (ca. 37–100 C.E.) whose works supply much of our knowledge of Jewish affairs in first-century C.E. Jewish Palestine.

Judea: Region surrounding Jerusalem.

Kingdom of God: A central feature of Jesus' preaching. Its precise referent is debated, but it has to do with God's reign.

Kosher: Adjective or noun designating food pure for Jews.

L: Designation for material unique to Luke's gospel.

Land of Israel: The land that the Bible presents as given to Israel by God. It is often referred to as Palestine.

Law: See *Torah*.

Levites: Israel's lower clergy, who performed a variety of functions in the temple.

Liberationist readings: Readings of the Bible whose purpose is to liberate from oppressive structures.

Literary criticism: Analysis that is especially concerned with a text's literary features. A broad term encompassing a number of methodologies.

M: Designation of material unique to Matthew's Gospel.

Malachi: Postexilic prophet who prophesied the coming of Elijah to prepare the people for God's coming in judgment.

Manna: Miraculous food God gave the Israelites in the desert.

Messiah: Hebrew or Aramaic for "anointed," most commonly applying to kings and priests in the Bible. A figure who appears at the end of times as God's agent either to bring in God's kingdom or to rule in it or both. Its Greek form is "christ."

Messianic secret: Feature of Mark's Gospel in which Jesus tries to keep his messiahship secret.

Mishnah: A rabbinic collection of mainly legal rulings and beliefs, dating to around the early third century.

Moses: Ancient Israelite leader who led the people out of Egypt at the exodus, and mediated between Israel and God at Sinai.

Nain: Small town in Galilee in which, according to John 2, Jesus attended a wedding feast and turned water into wine.

Narrative criticism: A form of literary criticism that pays special attention to the narrative features of the Gospels. Different methods rely on different modern theories of narrative.

Oracle: Divine pronouncement.

Palestine: Term for the area including Judea, Samaria, and Galilee, used first by the Greek historian Herodotus.

Parable: Short story told by Jesus meant to challenge one's view of the world.

Parenesis: Exhortation, advice, practical instruction.

Parousia: Second coming of Jesus.

Passion: Jesus' suffering and death.

Passover (Pesach): Yearly feast in the spring celebrating Israel's exodus from Egypt; combined with the feast of Unleavened Bread; celebrated at the time of the barley harvest.

Patriarchy: Social and political system in which males dominate.

Pentateuch: First five books of the Bible; the Torah.

Pericope: Small unit of tradition.

Pharisees: One of the major Jewish groups in Jewish Palestine in the late Second Temple period. They had their own interpretation of Torah and stressed purity, tithing, and Sabbath observance. A political interest group, perhaps composed mainly of retainers.

Pontius Pilate: Roman prefect of Judea, 26–36 C.E.

Postmodern criticism: A broad term that refuses to privilege any particular way of reading the text.

Praetorium: Headquarters of the Roman prefect. The Gospels say that Jesus was brought to Pilate at the praetorium in Jerusalem.

Prefect: Chief Roman administrator. Title applied to the Roman administrators during the time of Jesus.

Priest: One entitled to perform sacrificial rituals in Jerusalem. All belonged to the tribe of Levi.

Pronouncement story: A short story enshrining a saying or sayings of Jesus.

Prophet: One inspired to convey God's word directly.

Proverb: Short saying or maxim embodying wisdom.

Pure: That which can come into God's presence and can be part of rituals directed toward God.

Purity rules: Rules guarding the boundaries between sacred and profane, and between pure and impure.

Q: Hypothetical source used by Luke and Matthew, consisting mostly of sayings of Jesus.

Qumran: Ruins of a settlement near the northwest shore of the Dead Sea, associated with the collection of scrolls found in nearby caves. Many think that this was the headquarters of those who collected the scrolls, perhaps the Essenes.

Rabbi: Jewish teacher of Torah.

Reader-response criticism: An approach that concentrates on the effect of a text on readers.

Redaction criticism: Analysis of how the evangelists used and edited their sources.

Resurrection: Rising from death into life in a new and glorified form. This is not the same as resuscitation, which is raising a person into normal physical life, as Jesus does for Lazarus in John 11, for example.

Retainer: One, such as a scribe, whose function was to serve the ruling class.

Sabbath (Shabbat): The seventh day of the Jewish week, which must be kept holy to the Lord through such practices as refraining from work.

Sacrifice: Something offered to God, often an animal which is killed and whose blood is poured at the foot of the altar and which is partly or completely burned on the altar as a gift to God. The blood of some sacrifices is used to purify persons and objects.

Sadducees: Group centered in Jerusalem and consisting of the high priest's allies. Perhaps composed of both priests and prominent laypersons.

Samaria: Name of both the region between Judea and Galilee inhabited by the Samaritans and of their capital city.

Samaritans: Inhabitants of the area between Judea and Galilee, whose capital city was Samaria and who revered Moses, kept Torah, and thought themselves to be the rightful descendants of the northern kingdom of Israel. Southern (Judahite) traditions consider them descendants of Gentiles whom the Assyrians transplanted.

Sanhedrin: Advisory body to the high priest in Jerusalem.

Satan: Name of the leader of the demons, God's enemy and tempter of humans.

Scribes: Those whose profession was to read and write.

Second Temple Judaism: Judaism between the rebuilding of the temple in 520–515 B.C.E. and its destruction by the Romans in 70 C.E.

Septuagint: Ancient Greek translation of the Jewish Scriptures.

Social-science criticism: Analysis using methods from sociology or anthropology.

Son of God: Title applied to Jesus. Its Jewish applications include heavenly beings such as angels, kings, righteous members of Israel, and Israel itself.

Son of Man: Phrase applied to Jesus that probably originates in Dan 7, where it indicates a heavenly figure who receives power and glory from God.

Soteriology: Teaching about salvation and how to attain it.

Source criticism: Determination of the sources of a given text.

Synagogue: Can refer either a group of Jews gathered together for worship and Torah study or to the building used for that purpose.

Synchronic criticism: Criticism that takes a text as a whole in its present form, instead of looking at the process through which it developed.

Synoptic Gospels: Matthew, Mark, and Luke; so-called because they are so similar to one another that they can be viewed side-by-side.

Synoptic Problem: The question of how to explain the similarities and differences between Matthew, Mark, and Luke.

Tatian: Second-century Christian who composed a harmonization of the Four Gospels.

Temple: Site of the sacrificial worship of God in Jerusalem. Symbolic center of Judaism throughout the world.

Textual criticism: Analysis of manuscripts to determine the most original form, as well as to classify and characterize them.

Theodicy: Defense of God's justice and fairness.

Theology: Study of or beliefs about God.

Theophany: An appearance of God to humans.

Torah: Hebrew word meaning "instruction." It can be an individual instruction, for example, of a priest, but more commonly it means the first five books of the Bible. It is often translated "Law," but it incorporates more than legal regulations. It also includes the story of the creation, of Israel's election by God, the exodus, the making of the covenant between God and Israel at Sinai, the desert wanderings, and so on. The term is later expanded to include rabbinic tradition.

Two-source theory: Hypothesis that Matthew and Luke used two main written sources—Mark and Q.

Weeks (Pentecost; Shavuot): Annual feast celebrating the wheat harvest and the giving of the Torah.

Zion: Hill in Jerusalem on which temple is located. The term can be applied to Jerusalem.

INDEX